John Timbs

Anecdote lives of William Hogarth, Sir Joshua Reynolds,

Thomas Gainsborough, Henry Fuseli, Sir Thomas Lawrence, and J.M.W. Turner

John Timbs

Anecdote lives of William Hogarth, Sir Joshua Reynolds,
Thomas Gainsborough, Henry Fuseli, Sir Thomas Lawrence, and J.M.W. Turner

ISBN/EAN: 9783337732790

Printed in Europe, USA, Canada, Australia, Japan

Cover: Foto ©ninafisch / pixelio.de

More available books at **www.hansebooks.com**

ANECDOTE LIVES

OF

WILLIAM HOGARTH,
SIR JOSHUA REYNOLDS, THOMAS GAINSBOROUGH,
HENRY FUSELI, SIR THOMAS LAWRENCE,
AND J. M. W. TURNER.

By JOHN TIMBS, F.S.A.

AUTHOR OF "CURIOSITIES OF LONDON," "THINGS NOT GENERALLY KNOWN," ETC.

Hogarth's House at Chiswick.—P. 74.

LONDON:
RICHARD BENTLEY, NEW BURLINGTON STREET.
1872.

PREFACE.

The successful sale of a large edition of the First Series of the ANECDOTE BIOGRAPHY attests the public approbation of the general design of the Work;—to narrate, *by way of Anecdote*, the Lives of some of the most distinguished Persons of the last and present centuries.

It need scarcely be repeated that a leading feature of the plan is to present the reader with these Anecdotic Illustrations *in the order of time*, and not *en melée*, the scheme, if so it can be called, of the majority of anecdote-books. By such sequence, the points of character in the lives of the individuals are most attractively illustrated; whilst the higher aim of Biography,—to discriminate as well as amuse,—is invariably kept in view throughout the chain of incidents.

The former Series comprises the Anecdote Biography of LORD CHATHAM and EDMUND BURKE. The volume now submitted to the reader is devoted to the Lives of the SIX GREATEST PAINTERS OF THE ENGLISH SCHOOL, ranging almost throughout its entire history; and the personal characteristics as well as the works of these great Artists will be found to yield a feast of rich variety of circumstance and interest.*

First, we have HOGARTH, "whose patrons were the million," and the moral of whose pictures is pointed by an unerring hand. In manners he was as opposite to the blandness of Sir Joshua Reynolds as the east side is to the west of Leicester-square. Of REYNOLDS, how many delightful traits are written in letters of gold!—how the bachelor Painter loved children, and how he preferred their artless graces to the accomplishments of the high-born beauties and noble

---

* The work contains upwards of 500 Anecdotes, several of them derived from original communications, and sources but little resorted to.

forms that made up his gay bevy of sitters!—and how the first President gathered round his hospitable board troops of friends, the wealth of whose genius yielded the highest intellectual feast he could enjoy!

To REYNOLDS succeeds GAINSBOROUGH, whose academy was the woods and fields of Suffolk, and its rustic population; and who retained his lovely power of painting natural beauty amid the artificial gaiety of Bath, and the still more artificial life of the metropolis in Pall Mall. To GAINSBOROUGH succeeds FUSELI, the classic illustrator of Shakspeare and Milton, and whose pleasantry and piquant humour gave many a charm to this artist's social circle.

To FUSELI succeeds the courtly SIR THOMAS LAWRENCE, the painter of many imperial and royal crowned heads, and the flower of our aristocracy. To his rare artistic skill he united gentleness and amiability of character; and, like the bachelor REYNOLDS, the unmarried LAWRENCE delighted in painting lovely children. To this accomplished President succeeds the uncourtly J. M. W. TURNER,—the finest painter of the finest scenes in the world, by land and sea. Though rough in his nature, and penurious in his rule of life, he hoarded for excellent purpose, and bequeathed to his country the priceless treasures of his long and brilliant artistic career.

With such wealth of materials, the Editor has neither felt inclination nor opportunity for verbose narrative; and his labour lay in the opposite direction—that of selection and condensation. Throughout the work will be found an abundant store of Characteristics and Personal Traits of the Painters, Stories of their Works, and Opinions of Art-critics; so as to assist the reader in forming an estimate of the Progress of the Art during the last century and a half; and it is hoped, through these manifold uses and attractions, to bespeak for the present volume as favourable a reception as that bestowed upon its predecessor.

LONDON, *Oct.* 1, 1860.

CONTENTS.

WILLIAM HOGARTH.

	PAGE
BIRTH-PLACE AND PARENTAGE OF HOGARTH	1
HOGARTH'S EARLY EDUCATION.—HE BECOMES A SILVER-PLATE ENGRAVER	3
"LITTLE HOGARTH"	4
HOGARTH'S ENGRAVED SILVER-PLATE	5
UNIQUE PRINT FROM AN ENGRAVING BY HOGARTH	5
JOE MILLER'S BENEFIT TICKET	6
PRINT OF "THE RAPE OF THE LOCK"	7
HOGARTH PUBLISHES HIS FIRST PLATE	8
HOGARTH'S SHOP-CARD	9
HOGARTH COMMENCES SATIRE	9
HOGARTH SATIRISES THE STAGE	10
"PRINTS FOR HUDIBRAS"	11
HOGARTH AND THE UPHOLSTERER	13
HOGARTH'S MARRIAGE	14
HOGARTH'S HOUSE IN LEICESTER-SQUARE	15
HOGARTH'S FIRST PAINTING	16
HOGARTH, KENT THE ARCHITECT, AND THE POET POPE	17
HOGARTH'S SOUTHWARK FAIR	18
JOURNEY INTO KENT	19
PORTRAITS OF SARAH MALCOLM, MISS BLANDY, AND ELIZABETH CANNING	20
DEATH OF SIR JAMES THORNHILL	22
MIDNIGHT MODERN CONVERSATION	23
ORATOR HENLEY	24
A COFFEE-ROOM SCENE	25
"THE HARLOT'S PROGRESS"	25
THE RAKE'S PROGRESS	28
HOGARTH PAINTS THE STAIRCASE OF ST. BARTHOLOMEW'S HOSPITAL	30
HOGARTH AN ANATOMICAL DRAUGHTSMAN	31
"THE STROLLING ACTRESSES"	31
THE BEGGARS' OPERA	32
"THE FOUR TIMES OF THE DAY"	33
HOGARTH EMBELLISHES VAUXHALL GARDENS	35
ROSAMOND'S POND	37

CONTENTS.

	PAGE
THE ENRAGED MUSICIAN.—THE DISTRESSED POET	38
THE MARRIAGE À LA MODE PICTURES	39
SALE OF THE MARRIAGE À LA MODE PICTURES	42
"MARRIAGE À LA MODE," AND "THE CLANDESTINE MARRIAGE"	43
A HAPPY MARRIAGE	44
HOGARTH'S BENEFACTIONS TO THE FOUNDLING HOSPITAL	44
"THE MARCH TO FINCHLEY"	48
PORTRAIT OF LORD LOVAT	50
HOGARTH FIRST SEES DR. JOHNSON	51
"INDUSTRY AND IDLENESS"	52
THE GATE OF CALAIS, AND THE ROAST BEEF OF OLD ENGLAND	54
PAUL BEFORE FELIX	56
"THE ANALYSIS OF BEAUTY"	57
HOGARTH'S "LADY'S LAST STAKE"	58
HOGARTH'S OPINION OF HIS ART	59
THE ELECTION PICTURES	59
"SIGISMUNDA"	61
HOGARTH AND HORACE WALPOLE	63
HOGARTH AND WILKES	64
PORTRAIT OF FIELDING	65
"CREDULITY, SUPERSTITION, AND FANATICISM"	66
PORTRAIT OF WILKES	66
HOGARTH'S QUARREL WITH WILKES AND CHURCHILL	67
"FINIS; OR THE TAIL-PIECE"	70
DEATH OF HOGARTH	71
TOMB OF HOGARTH	73
HOGARTH'S HOUSE, AT CHISWICK	74
MRS. HOGARTH	76
HOGARTH'S MAUL-STICK	77
COLLECTIONS OF HOGARTH'S WORKS	77

CHARACTERISTICS, RETROSPECTIVE OPINIONS, AND PERSONAL TRAITS.

HOGARTH'S EARLY PORTRAITS	78
HOGARTH'S CONCEIT	81
POETICAL TRIBUTES TO HOGARTH	82
HOGARTH PAINTED BY HIMSELF	83
CARICATURES ON HOGARTH	83
HOGARTH AND BISHOP HOADLEY	84
COPYRIGHT IN PRINTS	85
HOGARTH'S PALETTE	86
HOGARTH'S "ORATORIO"	87
THE MISER AND SIR ISAAC SHEARD	87
WALL-PAINTINGS IN FENCHURCH STREET	87
HOGARTH PAINTS "GOLDSMITH'S HOSTESS"	89

CONTENTS.

	PAGE
GENIUS OF HOGARTH	89
HISTORICAL VALUE OF HOGARTH'S WORKS	91
HOGARTH'S PRINTS.	93

SIR JOSHUA REYNOLDS, P.R.A.

BIRTH-PLACE OF SIR JOSHUA REYNOLDS.	95
BAPTISM OF REYNOLDS	97
REYNOLDS'S SCHOOL	97
REYNOLDS PAINTS HIS FIRST PORTRAIT.	99
REYNOLDS IS ARTICLED TO HUDSON THE PAINTER	100
REYNOLDS'S DESCRIPTION OF POPE	101
REYNOLDS VISITS ITALY	102
REYNOLDS SETTLES IN LONDON	104
REYNOLDS REMOVES TO LEICESTER-SQUARE	104
PORTRAITS OF KITTY FISHER.	105
PORTRAIT OF STERNE	106
PORTRAITS OF GARRICK.	106
COPIES AND ORIGINALS.	107
CHARACTER IN PORTRAITS	107
REYNOLDS AND ROMNEY	107
FRIENDSHIP OF REYNOLDS AND DR. JOHNSON	108
PAINTING ON SUNDAYS.	110
REYNOLDS'S CLUB.	110
ORIGIN OF THE ROYAL ACADEMY	111
THE FIRST ROYAL ACADEMY DINNER	112
THE ROYAL ACADEMY AT SOMERSET HOUSE	112
SIR JOSHUA ELECTED MAYOR OF PLYMPTON	113
"THE STRAWBERRY GIRL"	114
COUNT UGOLINO	115
REYNOLDS REBUKED BY GOLDSMITH	116
GOLDSMITH'S EPITAPH ON REYNOLDS	116
REYNOLDS AND BARRY.	117
MR. HONE, R.A. SATIRIZES SIR JOSHUA	117
DESIGNS FOR THE OXFORD WINDOW	118
REYNOLDS'S PORTRAIT OF SHERIDAN	118
LORD HOLLAND'S PORTRAIT	119
GEORGE III. AND SIR JOSHUA REYNOLDS	119
PORTRAITS OF GIBBON AND GOLDSMITH	120
PORTRAIT OF ADMIRAL KEPPEL	120
THE LADIES WALDEGRAVE	120
"MUSCIPULA"	121
"THE TRAGIC MUSE"	121
REYNOLDS'S CARRIAGE	122
HORACE WALPOLE AND SIR JOSHUA REYNOLDS	123
"THE INFANT HERCULES"	124

CONTENTS.

	PAGE
REYNOLDS'S DISCOURSES, AND MALONE	126
PORTRAIT OF LORD HEATHFIELD	127
ROBIN GOODFELLOW, OR PUCK	128
SIR JOSHUA RETIRES FROM THE ROYAL ACADEMY	129
REYNOLDS'S KINDNESS	130
SIR JOSHUA AND HIS PET BIRD	130
"RALPH'S EXHIBITION."	131
REYNOLDS'S DECLINING SIGHT	131
DEATH OF SIR JOSHUA REYNOLDS	132
FUNERAL OF SIR JOSHUA REYNOLDS	134
SIR JOSHUA'S WILL	135
REYNOLDS'S THRONE-CHAIR	136
SIR JOSHUA'S PALETTE	137
SALES OF REYNOLDS'S PORTRAITS	137
SALES OF REYNOLDS'S PICTURES	138

CHARACTERISTICS, RETROSPECTIVE OPINIONS, AND PERSONAL TRAITS.

REYNOLDS'S FIRST LESSON IN ART	140
HUDSON, SIR JOSHUA'S MASTER	140
REYNOLDS'S EARLY PORTRAITS	142
PORTRAIT OF LORD BUTE	143
REYNOLDS'S PRICES AND SITTERS	143
SIR JOSHUA'S SNUFF	144
HOGARTH AND REYNOLDS	145
REYNOLDS'S MODELS	146
REYNOLDS'S LIBERALITY TO OZIAS HUMPHREY	146
REYNOLDS'S DINNERS	147
SIR JOSHUA'S DEAFNESS	148
REYNOLDS'S PARSIMONY	149
REYNOLDS'S EXPERIMENTAL COLOURS	149
REMBRANDT AND REYNOLDS	150
PAINTING FOR POSTERITY	151
SIR JOSHUA'S LAST SURVIVING SITTER	151
REYNOLDS'S LANDSCAPES	152
REYNOLDS'S VILLA AT RICHMOND	152
PRINTS FROM REYNOLDS'S PICTURES	153
LAWRENCE'S TRIBUTE TO REYNOLDS	153

THOMAS GAINSBOROUGH, R.A.

BIRTHPLACE AND PARENTAGE OF GAINSBOROUGH	156
GAINSBOROUGH COMES TO LONDON	157
GAINSBOROUGH'S MARRIAGE	158

	PAGE
DETECTIVE PORTRAITS	158
GAINSBOROUGH AND GARRICK	159
GAINSBOROUGH A MUSICIAN	159
"THE PAINTER'S EYE"	160
GAINSBOROUGH AND HIS FRIEND THICKNESSE	160
GAINSBOROUGH AND HOUBRAKEN'S HEADS	161
ADVANTAGE OF A HANDSOME SITTER	162
GAINSBOROUGH AND THE CARRIER	162
GAINSBOROUGH'S MODELLING	163
RETURN OF GAINSBOROUGH TO LONDON.—SCHOMBERG HOUSE, PALL MALL	163
PAINTINGS BY GAINSBOROUGH IN SCHOMBERG HOUSE	164
GAINSBOROUGH AND REYNOLDS	165
"THE BLUE BOY"	166
SEVERE CRITICISM	166
"GIRL AND PIGS"	167
MRS SIDDONS' NOSE	167
GAINSBOROUGH'S WOODMAN, SHEPHERD BOY, COTTAGE DOOR, AND COTTAGE GIRL	167
GAINSBOROUGH'S SENSITIVENESS	168
GAINSBOROUGH'S GENEROSITY	169
DEATH OF GAINSBOROUGH	169

CHARACTERISTICS, RETROSPECTIVE OPINIONS, AND PERSONAL TRAITS.

CHARACTER OF GAINSBOROUGH, BY REYNOLDS	172
PORTRAITS BY GAINSBOROUGH	173
DRAWINGS AND SKETCHES	175
GAINSBOROUGH'S SEA-PIECES	176
GAINSBOROUGH'S LANDSCAPES	176
GAINSBOROUGH AND LEE	177

HENRY FUSELI, R.A.

BIRTH AND PARENTAGE OF FUSELI	179
FUSELI AN ENTOMOLOGIST	180
FUSELI COMES TO ENGLAND	181
FUSELI STUDIES ART.—HIS FIRST PICTURE	181
VOLTAIRE CARICATURED	182
FUSELI AND DR. ARMSTRONG	182
FUSELI IN ROME	183
FUSELI SETTLES IN LONDON	184
FUSELI AND COWPER'S "HOMER"	184
RICHARDSON'S NOVELS	185

	PAGE
M. DAVID AND FUSELI	185
FUSELI AND WEST	185
FUSELI'S ATTACHMENTS	186
FUSELI AND MRS. WOLLSTONECROFT	186
ILL-ASSORTED COMPANY	188
FUSELI AND DR. JOHNSON	189
"THE NIGHTMARE"	189
"THE SHAKSPEARE GALLERY"	190
"THE MILTON GALLERY"	191
MR. COUTTS'S LIBERALITY TO FUSELI	194
FUSELI AND THE BRITISH INSTITUTION	195
CANOVA AND FUSELI	196
FUSELI'S RESENTMENT OF A SLIGHT	196
LONDON SMOKE	196
FUSELI'S ART	197
FUSELI AS "KEEPER"	197
FUSELI'S DAY	198
PAINTING "THE DEVIL"	198
HARLOW'S CONCEIT EXPOSED	199
HARLOW'S PICTURE OF "THE TRIAL OF QUEEN KATHERINE"	199
FUSELI AND LORD ELDON	200
FUSELI'S LAST PICTURE	201
DEATH OF FUSELI	201
FUNERAL OF FUSELI	202

CHARACTERISTICS, RETROSPECTIVE OPINIONS, AND PERSONAL TRAITS.

FUSELI AND THE ELGIN MARBLES	203
FUSELI.—SKETCHED BY HAYDON	204
FUSELI AND PICTURE-HANGING	206
FUSELI'S SENSIBILITY	206
FUSELI'S RELIGIOUS FEELINGS	208
FUSELI AND YOUNG LAWRENCE	209
FUSELI'S WIT AND HUMOUR	209
CHARACTER OF FUSELI AS AN ARTIST	212
POETICAL TRIBUTES	214
LESLIE'S ACCOUNT OF FUSELI'S PICTURES	214
THE HERONS IN RAPHAEL'S CARTOON	216
CHARACTER OF FUSELI BY LAVATER	216
MICHAEL ANGELO.—BY FUSELI	217
RAPHAEL.—BY FUSELI	218
FUSELI'S ERUDITION	219
SALVATOR ROSA.—BY FUSELI	219
FUSELI AND BRITISH ARTISTS	220
ALDERMAN BOYDELL	221

	PAGE
PRESENTATION OF A CUP TO FUSELI	222
FUSELI AND LAWRENCE	224
"SOMETHING NEW"	225
CONSTABLE AND FUSELI	226
WORKS OF FUSELI	226

SIR THOMAS LAWRENCE, P.R.A.

	PAGE
BIRTH AND PARENTAGE OF LAWRENCE	228
LAWRENCE'S FIRST PORTRAIT	228
YOUNG LAWRENCE SENT TO SCHOOL	229
LAWRENCE'S EARLY DRAWINGS	229
LAWRENCE'S RECITATIONS	230
YOUNG LAWRENCE IN BATH	232
LAWRENCE AND THE STAGE	232
LAWRENCE RECEIVES THE SOCIETY OF ARTS PRIZE	233
LAWRENCE'S EARLIEST OIL-PAINTINGS	234
LAWRENCE SETTLES IN LONDON.—INTRODUCTION TO REYNOLDS	234
HISTORICAL PIECE FROM HOMER	236
LAWRENCE'S EARLY PORTRAITS	236
LAWRENCE ELECTED A.R.A.	236
DEATH OF SIR JOSHUA REYNOLDS	237
"SERJEANT-PAINTER TO THE KING"	237
LAWRENCE IN OLD BOND STREET.—ELECTED R.A.	237
FAILURE OF A PORTRAIT	238
THE TWO SATANS	239
DEATH OF LAWRENCE'S PARENTS	241
PORTRAITS OF JOHN KEMBLE	242
VERSES BY LAWRENCE	242
LAWRENCE SUPPOSED IN LOVE	244
PORTRAIT OF CURRAN	245
BUST OF MR. W. LOCK	245
LAWRENCE AND THE PRINCESS OF WALES	246
LAWRENCE AND HARLOW	247
PORTRAIT OF THE PERSIAN AMBASSADOR	249
NAPOLEON THE FIRST	250
REMOVAL TO RUSSELL-SQUARE	250
PORTRAITS OF THE EMPEROR OF RUSSIA, THE KING OF PRUSSIA, BLUCHER, AND PLATOFF	251
LAWRENCE AND CANOVA	251
LAWRENCE AND MRS. WOLFE	252
THE ELGIN MARBLES	252
LAWRENCE AT CLAREMONT	253
PORTRAITS OF THE ALLIED SOVEREIGNS	255
ON TURNER, BY LAWRENCE	257

CONTENTS.

	PAGE
LAWRENCE PAINTING IN ROME	258
SIR THOMAS LAWRENCE ELECTED PRESIDENT OF THE ROYAL ACADEMY	259
RECOVERY OF A MICHAEL ANGELO	260
LAWRENCE'S JUSTICE TO REYNOLDS	260
LORD BYRON AND LAWRENCE	261
SIR WALTER SCOTT AND SIR THOMAS LAWRENCE	261
SKETCH-BOOK OF LEONARDO DA VINCI	262
HONOURS TO SIR T. LAWRENCE	262
PRESENTS TO LAWRENCE	263
CAST OF THE EMPEROR NAPOLEON'S HEAD	264
LAWRENCE AND THE FREEDOM OF BRISTOL	264
LAWRENCE'S LAST YEAR	264
MISS FANNY KEMBLE	266
LAWRENCE'S DECLINING HEALTH	267
DEATH OF SIR THOMAS LAWRENCE	270
FUNERAL OF SIR THOMAS LAWRENCE	272
WILL OF SIR THOMAS LAWRENCE	274
LAWRENCE'S HOUSE	275

CHARACTERISTICS, RETROSPECTIVE OPINIONS, AND PERSONAL TRAITS.

LAWRENCE AND REYNOLDS COMPARED	276
HOWARD'S CHARACTER OF LAWRENCE	277
LAWRENCE AND ETTY	278
CAUSE OF LAWRENCE'S EMBARRASSMENT	279
PORTRAITS OF SIR THOMAS LAWRENCE	281
THE PAINTER'S DAY AND PRACTICE	282
PAINTING EYES	283
LAWRENCE'S PORTRAITS	284
CORONATION PORTRAITS	285
THE LAWRENCE DRAWINGS	285
LAWRENCE'S ENGRAVED PORTRAITS	286
KINDNESS AND GENEROSITY TO ARTISTS	288
LAWRENCE'S SENSITIVENESS	290
ON THE GENIUS OF FLAXMAN, BY LAWRENCE	291
PORTRAITS OF THE DUKE OF WELLINGTON, BY LAWRENCE	293
WORKS OF SIR THOMAS LAWRENCE IN LONDON, ETC.	297
CELEBRATED PORTRAITS	298
DEATH OF MR. LOCK, AND MR. HOPPNER, R.A.	300
CONSTABLE AND SIR THOMAS LAWRENCE	302
"MR. CALMADY'S CHILDREN"	303
PORTRAIT OF THE HON. C. W. LAMBTON	305
PORTRAIT OF THE HON. MRS. HOPE	306
COWPER AND LAWRENCE	307
LAWRENCE'S PORTRAIT OF WILBERFORCE	308

J. M. W. TURNER, R.A.

	PAGE
BIRTH-PLACE OF TURNER	309
TURNER ADMITTED A STUDENT OF THE ROYAL ACADEMY	311
TURNER'S FIRST PATRONS	312
TURNER'S EARLY STYLE	314
TURNER ELECTED R.A.	315
TURNER VISITS THE CONTINENT	315
"THE GODDESS OF DISCORD IN THE GARDEN OF THE HESPERIDES"	316
THE LIBER STUDIORUM	317
"ULYSSES DERIDING POLYPHEMUS"	318
TURNER AN AFFECTIONATE SON	318
THE OLD TEMERAIRE TOWED INTO HER LAST BERTH	319
"THE SLAVE-SHIP"	319
FAILURE OF TURNER'S VERY RECENT WORKS	321
DECLINE OF TURNER'S HEALTH	322
DEATH OF TURNER	322
FUNERAL OF TURNER	323
WILL OF MR. TURNER	324

CHARACTERISTICS, RETROSPECTIVE OPINIONS, AND PERSONAL TRAITS.

TURNER'S PRE-EMINENCE PREDICTED	326
TURNER'S THREE PERIODS	327
WHO WERE TURNER'S PATRONS?	330
TURNER'S INDUSTRY	330
TURNER'S LANDSCAPE ART	331
STUDYING NATURE	331
TURNER'S "COLOUR"—A HINT FROM ADDISON	332
PORTRAITS OF TURNER	333
TURNER ON VARNISHING DAYS	334
TURNER'S SEA-PIECES	336
TURNER'S VERSES	337
"TALKING DOWN"	341
TURNER AND WILKIE	341
TURNER AND CHANTREY	342
"THE SCOTTISH TURNER"	342
ARTISTIC PREDICTION	342
TURNER'S EARLY VIEWS OF LAMBETH PALACE	343
CHANGES OF RESIDENCE	343
SECRET OF HIS ADDRESS	344
TURNER AND THE CRITIC	344
QUID PRO QUO	344
PICTURES FROM THOMSON AND MILTON	345
TURNER'S ACCURACY	345

CONTENTS.

	PAGE
TURNER'S ORIGINALITY	346
TURNER'S COMPOSITION	346
UNDERSTANDING TURNER	347
MR. RUSKIN'S CRITICISM ON TURNER'S WORKS	347
THE TRUTH OF TURNER	348
CLAUDE AND TURNER COMPARED	350
TURNER'S YORKSHIRE DRAWINGS	352
TURNER'S TREES	352
THE FIRST OF TURNER'S PICTURES SENT TO AMERICA	353
NUMBER OF PICTURES BY TURNER, AND PRICES	354
TURNER'S BARGAINING	355
TURNER'S BOOK-PLATES	356
HIS PRESENT RANK AS A LANDSCAPE-PAINTER	356
ACCURACY IN SHIPPING	357
TURNER AND LORD DE TABLEY	360
PICTURES BY TURNER IN THE ART-TREASURES EXHIBITION AT MANCHESTER, 1857	360
APPRECIATION OF STOTHARD	362
PAINTINGS OF FIRES	362
TURNER'S RECREATIONS	363
PROFESSOR OF PERSPECTIVE	363
TURNER'S BRILLIANCY	364
VIEWS IN ENGLAND AND WALES	364
TURNER BIDDING FOR HIS OWN PICTURES	365
"VAN TROMP'S BARGE"	367
TURNER AND HIS EULOGISTS	367
TURNER'S WATER-COLOUR DRAWINGS.—SECRET OF HIS SUCCESS	368

APPENDIX.

HOGARTH'S SOUTHWARK FAIR	370
HOGARTH PAINTING "CHILDREN"	370
SIR JOSHUA'S FATHER	370
REYNOLDS'S STUDIES IN ITALY	371
SIR JOSHUA'S HOUSE IN LEICESTER-SQUARE	375
THE PLYMPTON CORPORATION AND REYNOLDS'S PORTRAIT	375
REYNOLDS AND ERSKINE.—JAMES BOSWELL	376
REYNOLDS'S PORTRAIT OF MRS. HARTLEY	376
SIR JOSHUA'S PRICES	377
SIR JOSHUA'S FISHMONGER	378
REYNOLDS'S PORTRAIT OF MISS BOWLS	378
EXHIBITION OF THE WORKS OF SIR JOSHUA REYNOLDS	379
TURNER'S BOYHOOD	380

ANECDOTE BIOGRAPHY.

WILLIAM HOGARTH.

BIRTH-PLACE AND PARENTAGE OF HOGARTH.

WILLIAM HOGARTH, "the Painting Moralist," whose prints we read like books, was, in his own words, "born in the City of London, on the 10th day of November, 1697, and baptized the 28th of the same month." He was descended from the Westmoreland family of Hogard, Hogart, or Hogarth, of Kirkby Thore. Nichols states that he wrote himself Hogart or Hogard; but his father wrote his name Hogarth; and Allan Cunningham considers the concluding *th*, in London pronunciation, to have been hardened into *t*, as common in northern names with similar terminations. Thus, in conversation, he was called Hogart,* which these lines from Swift's "Legion Club" prove:

> "How I want thee, humorous Hogart;
> Thou, I hear, a pleasant rogue art!
> Were but you and I acquainted,
> Every monster should be painted;
> You should try your graving tools
> On this odious group of fools;
> Draw the beasts as I describe them
> From their features while I gibe them.
> Draw them like, for I assure-a
> You'll need no caricatur-a;
> Draw them so that we may trace
> All the soul in every face."

---

* The tradition on the Borders is, however, that the Hogarths were a Scotch family. They were always a numerous and influential race. Burke, in his *Encyclopædia of Heraldry*, spells the name *Howgart*, or Howgarth. About a century ago, the name was very common on the Scotch side of the Border; but it is now very rare. The name seems to be pronounced Hog-arth.

The painter's father was Richard Hogarth, the youngest of three brothers, the eldest of whom succeeded his father on a small freehold, in the Vale of Bampton. Richard was educated at Archbishop Grindal's Free School of St. Bees, in Cumberland, and subsequently settled as a schoolmaster in that county. Thence he removed to London, and there obtained employment as *a corrector of the press*, or, in other words, reader at a printing-office. He married a woman, whose name or kindred is not recorded; and he next kept a school in Ship-court, on the west side of the Old Bailey, three doors from Ludgate-hill, and in the parish of St. Martin's, Ludgate. Here, it is believed, William Hogarth was born; and on the leaf of an old memorandum-book he records the *time* of his own birth and baptism; as quoted in the preceding page, and, as follows, of his two sisters:

> "Mary Hogarth was born November 10, 1699.
> Anne Hogarth, two years after in the same month.
> Taken from the Register of Great St. Bartholomew's."

It is curious to find that although Hogarth has left so many minute pictures of London localities of his own time, the place of his birth is disputed: if it be Ship-court, it may be interesting to add, that nearly a century after, at the corner of the court, No. 67, three doors from Ludgate-hill, William Hone kept shop, and there published the early caricatures of George Cruikshank.*

Hogarth's father died about 1721. He appears, (from among his great son's papers, found after the painter's death,) to have been a man of scholastic attainments. To an early edition of Littleton's Latin Dictionary and Robertson's Phrases he added about four hundred closely-written pages; and on one of the leaves was inscribed, in Hogarth's (the son's) handwriting, "The nondescript part of this dictionary was the work of Mr. Richard Hogarth." He made some attempts to get his labours printed, but in vain. He then published, in 1712, "Grammar Disputations," a sort of catechism for teaching children Latin.

The present representative of the family is, or lately was, living at Clifton, near Penrith.—(*Notes and Queries*, 1856.)

---

* The occupant of the house at the corner of Ship-court, has placed over his shop-front a notice of William Hogarth having been born in the court; but it is not stated on what authority this assertion is made.

HOGARTH'S EARLY EDUCATION.—HE BECOMES A SILVER-PLATE ENGRAVER.

It is a remarkable proof of the boy's shrewdness, that at an early age, he profited by observing what was passing immediately around him. In his Anecdotes of himself, he says: "My father's pen, like that of many other authors, did not enable him to do more than put me in a way of shifting for myself. As I had naturally a good eye, and a fondness for drawing, shows of all sorts gave me uncommon pleasure when an infant; and mimicry, common to all children, was remarkable in me. An early access to a neighbouring painter, drew my attention from play; and I was, at every possible opportunity, employed in making drawings. I picked up an acquaintance of the same turn, and soon learnt to draw the alphabet with great correctness. My exercises, when at school, were more remarkable for the ornaments which adorned them than for the exercise itself. In the former, I soon found that blockheads, with better memories, would soon surpass me: but for the latter I was particularly distinguished.

"Besides the natural turn I had for drawing, rather than learning languages, I had before my eyes the precarious situation of men of classical education. I saw the difficulties under which my father laboured,—the many inconveniences he endured, from his dependence being chiefly on his pen; and the cruel treatment he met with from booksellers and printers, particularly in the affair of a Latin Dictionary, the compiling of which had been a work of some years. It was, therefore, conformable to my own wishes that I was taken from school, and served a long apprenticeship to a silver-plate engraver." Walpole describes him as "bound to a mean engraver of arms on plate." Hogarth probably chose this occupation, as it required some skill in drawing, which he had much cultivated. His master was Mr. Ellis Gamble, an eminent silversmith, in Cranbourne-street, Leicester Fields. In this business it was not unusual to bind apprentices to the single branch of engraving arms and ciphers on metal; and in that particular branch young Hogarth was placed. Of his age at this time there is no special record; but Nichols states the circumstance to have been verified by a similar account from one of the head assay-masters at Goldsmiths' Hall, who was apprentice to a silversmith in the same street with Hogarth, and intimate with him during the greatest part of his life.* Gamble's shop bore the sign of the Golden Angel; and a shop-bill engraved by his eminent apprentice is much prized by every collector of Hogarth's works. Nichols relates that during Hogarth's apprenticeship, in a Sunday excursion to Highgate, he sketched with a pencil two persons in a tavern affray, one of whom had struck the other on the head with a quart-pot; when the blood running down the man's face, the agony of the wound distorted it into a hideous grin, which Hogarth drew with ludicrous effect, although the portraits of both antagonists were exact likenesses, and the surrounding figures were caricatured with equal fidelity.

On a later occasion he strolled, with Hayman the painter, into a cellar, where two women were quarrelling in their cups. One of them filled her mouth with brandy, and spirted it dexterously in the eyes of her antagonist. "See! see!" said Hogarth, taking out his tablets and sketching her,—"look at the brimstone's mouth." This virago figures in *Modern Midnight Conversation.*

"LITTLE HOGARTH."

Nichols records that, about this time, Hogarth was very poor. "Being one day distressed to raise so trifling a sum as twenty shillings, in order to be revenged of his landlady, who strove to compel him to payment, he drew her as ugly as possible, and in that single portrait gave marks of the dawn of superior genius." Nichols, however, doubts this story, since it was never related by Hogarth, who was always fond of contrasting the necessities of his youth with the affluence of his maturer age. He has been heard to say of himself: "I remember the time when I have gone moping into the city with scarce a shilling in my pocket; but as soon as I had received ten guineas there for a plate, I have returned home, put on my sword, and sallied out again, with all the confidence of a man who had ten thousand pounds in his pocket." "Let me add," says Nichols, "that my first authority may be to the full as good as my second."

J. T. Smith relates, in *Nollekens and his Times,* that his father once asked Barry, the painter, if he had ever seen Hogarth. "Yes, once," he replied. "I was walking with Joe Nollekens through Cranbourne-alley, when he exclaimed,

---

* Biographical Anecdotes of William Hogarth. Second Edition. Printed by and for J. Nichols, 1782.

'There, there's Hogarth.' 'What!' said I, 'that little man in the sky-blue coat?' Off I ran, and though I lost sight of him only for a moment or two, when I turned the corner into Castle-street, he was patting one of two quarrelling boys on the back, and looking stedfastly at the expression in the coward's face, he cried, 'D——n him! if I would take it of him; at him again!'"

HOGARTH'S ENGRAVED SILVER-PLATE.

Panton Betew, the silversmith, and dealer in works of art, in Old Compton-street, Soho, was intimate with Hogarth, and frequently purchased pieces of plate with armorial bearings engraved upon them by Hogarth, which he cleared out for the next possessor, but, unfortunately, without rubbing off a single impression. This was not the case with Morison, a silversmith of Cheapside: he took twenty-five impressions off a large silver dish, engraved by Hogarth, which impressions he not only numbered, as they were taken off, but attested each with his own signature. "Should," says J. T. Smith, in relating the above, "this page meet the eye of any branches of the good old-fashioned families, which have carefully preserved the plate of Oliver their uncle, or Deborah their aunt, I sincerely implore them, should the armorial bearings be the productions of the early part of the last century, to cause a few impressions to be taken from them; for I am inclined to believe it very possible that some curious specimens of Hogarth's drawing genius may yet in that way be rescued from future furnaces." Some beautiful specimens of Hogarth's metal engraving and chasing are in existence. At Strawberry Hill, before the Sale in 1842, was a magnificent silver-gilt Plateau, with medallions of George I., the Royal Arms, figures of Britannia and Justice, and a view of the City of London, and allegorical devices, exquisitely engraved by Hogarth. (*See Catalogue*, eleventh day's sale, lot 120.)

UNIQUE PRINT FROM AN ENGRAVING BY HOGARTH.

In a pleasant little book, entitled *A Pinch of Snuff*, published in 1840, it is related that "Some time since a gentleman sent his snuff-box to a working jeweller for repair, the embossed frame which surrounded the lid having become loose; the box was of silver, plain shaped, but ornamented on the top with a group of figures, somewhat after the manner of Watteau, engraved upon the plate. Upon removing the border, it was found necessary to take the upper part of the box entirely to pieces; and while minutely inspecting the landscape and figures, the jeweller perceived, at the edge of the plate, which had been concealed by its frame, the name of William Hogarth." Upon the suggestion of a collector of works of art, some twenty impressions were taken on India paper, and the plate restored to its original destination; but so soldered and riveted to the exterior embossing as to prevent the possibility of its ever again being submitted to the printing-press. The twenty copies were then sold, for five pounds, to Mr. W——, a great Hogarthian collector, who selected the best impression, and threw the remaining nineteen into the fire, exclaiming, "Now, I have in my possession a unique work of my idol's. No man can boast that he has a copy of this *fête champetre* but myself, and I would not part with it for fifty pounds." His feelings, however, were less enviable than those of the person who had enabled him to possess this treasure; for he handed over the five pounds to the working-silversmith, whose gratitude was equal to his surprise at such a God-send.

JOE MILLER'S BENEFIT TICKET.

Joe Miller, of Jest-book fame, was also a comedian of some repute, who played upon the boards of Drury-lane Theatre, from 1715 to 1738. In the former year, Joe took his first sole benefit, when he selected Congreve's play of the *Old Bachelor*, in which Miller performed Sir Joseph Whittol, his best hit that season. Now, "a sole benefit" led the way either to the Fleet or Fortune. These were the stakes Joe had to play for on the 25th of April, 1717; but the odds were dead in his favour. The very cards he had provided to play the game were charmed—genius had traced every line of them: the designer was no less a person than William Hogarth.

"The scene is in the third act of the *Old Bachelor*, where Noll, the companion and bully of Sir Joseph, gets a severe kicking from Sharper. "The original of the print," say Nichols and Steevens, "is extremely scarce; and there is no doubt of its being from a design by Hogarth, probably executed by the same hand who etched 'Modern Military Punishments,' though it is in somewhat of a better style." An impression has been sold for eight guineas, &c.

Samuel Ireland has engraved Miller's Ticket in his *Graphic Illustrations*, but, upon the authority of Richardson, the printseller, in the Strand, he condemns this Ticket as one of the forgeries by Rowell, "who, being a needy man, probably held it as a matter of little importance, provided it procured him the means of supplying the wants of craving hunger, penury, and sorrow." Yet, we agree with Mr. W. H. Wills, the author of the ingenious Biography, prefixed to the *Family Joe Miller*, 1848, that Nichols's and Steevens's opinion as to the genuineness of this print is admissible, notwithstanding Ireland's denunciation of it. At this date, Hogarth was not out of his apprenticeship, but he was an early boon companion of Joe Miller, at the Bull's Head, in Clare Market, and "the Shepherd and his Flock" Club. Mr. Wills asks: "Were this a spurious pasteboard, why did Jane Ireland re-engrave it; and why is her etching kept in the British Museum print-room, side by side with the original?" Lastly, it was precisely this kind of jobs—shop-cards, bill-heads, &c.—that Hogarth lived by as soon as he had served out his apprenticeship. Nevertheless, Nichols, in his *Anecdotes*, latest edition, 1833, "in a Catalogue of the Tickets said to have been engraved by Hogarth, commences with Spiller, the player's, a proof of which, before the writing, was sold, in 1832, for 12*l*. 15*s*.: for the original print, in the Royal Collection, Ireland was offered 20*l*. "This," says Nichols, "is immeasurably superior to all the other Tickets both in design and execution. *It makes one suspect all the rest to be not by Hogarth.*" In Nichols's *Anecdotes*, edit. 1783, the earliest print named is of the date 1720, three years subsequent to that of Miller's Ticket.

PRINT OF "THE RAPE OF THE LOCK."

One of Hogarth's earliest works, executed about 1717, (in his apprenticeship,) was a small oval illustration of Pope's *Rape of the Lock*. It is thus described by Ireland:

Though slight, and not intended to be impressed on paper, the air of the figures is easy, and the faces, especially of Sir Plume and the heroine of the story, extremely characteristic. It is said to have been engraven on the lid of a snuff-box, "probably for Lord Petre, who is here represented as holding the lock of hair in his hand. Sir Plume— the round-faced and insignificant Sir Plume,

> Of amber snuff-box justly vain,
> And the nice conduct of a clouded cane,"—

for Sir George Brown; he was angry that the Poet should make him talk nothing but nonsense; and, in truth, (as Warburton adds,) one could not well blame him.

As this little story was intended to be viewed on gold, the figures in the copy are not reversed, but left as they were originally engraven on the box ; from which, it is believed, there are only three impressions extant ; one of which was sold by Greenwood, at Mr. Gulston's sale, February 7, 1786, for thirty-three pounds !

HOGARTH PUBLISHES HIS FIRST PLATE.

In 1718, (according to Ireland,) Hogarth ceased to be an apprentice, being twenty-one years old ; and according to Walpole, he entered into the Academy in St. Martin's-lane, (Sir James Thornhill's,) and studied drawing from the life, in which he never attained to great excellence. It was the character, the passions, the soul, that his genius was given him to copy. In colouring he proved no great a master : his force lay in expression, not in tints and chiaro scuro.

"The instant I became master of my own time (Hogarth tells us,) I determined to qualify myself for engraving on copper." In this he readily got employment by engraving arms, crests, ciphers, shop-bills, &c.

He thus describes the hardships he had to endure in business: "The tribe of booksellers remained as my father had left them, when he died, (about 1721,) which was of an illness occasioned partly by the treatment he met with from this set of people, and partly by disappointment from great men's promises ; so that I doubly felt this usage, which put me upon publishing on my own account. But here, again, I had to encounter a monopoly of printsellers, equally mean and obstructive to the ingenious ; for the first plate I published, called the *Taste of the Town*, in which the reigning follies were lashed, had no sooner begun to take a run, than I found copies of it in the print-shops, vending at half-price, while the original prints were returned to me again ; and I was thus obliged to sell the plate for whatever these pirates pleased to give me, as there was no place of sale but at their shops.

"Owing to this and other circumstances, by engraving, until I was near thirty, I could do little more than maintain myself ; but even then I was a punctual paymaster."

Hogarth now engraved much for the booksellers : among his illustrations are thirteen folio prints for Mortraye's Travels, 1723 ; seven smaller prints for the Golden Ass of Apuleius, 1724 ; fifteen head-pieces for Beaver's Military Punishments of the Ancients ; and five frontispieces for the translation of

Cassandra, five vols. 1725. He likewise designed and engraved two cuts for Perseus and Andromeda, 1730; and two for Milton (date uncertain). Walpole says: "No symptoms of genius dawned in those early plates;" and there is, certainly, but little of that spirit which distinguished Hogarth's after works.

HOGARTH'S SHOP-CARD.

This design consists of ornamental framework, in the centre of which is inscribed, "W. Hogarth, Engraver;" beneath which, in a lozenge, surrounded with foliage and scroll-work, is the date, "April ye 29, 1720." In the upper centre of the frame are two flying children, with a festoon of fruit and flowers on each side, and a head and console at each angle of the frame; which, at the base, is flanked with a female figure looking up to one of the children—Design or Invention, the companion figure, on the opposite side being that of an old man writing—or History: of this card there is a modern copy. An impression of the original shop-card, (of the date, 1720, when Hogarth is supposed to have begun business,) has been sold for 25*l*.!

HOGARTH COMMENCES SATIRE.

Before his apprenticeship expired, Hogarth had gone far beyond drawing and engraving shields, crests, supporters, coronets, and cyphers; for his sketch of the Highgate brawl, though rough, was a satiric sitting in a new and happy style of art. "I soon found," he observes, "this (engraving) business in every respect too limited." Sir James Thornhill had already acquired Court favour, if not wealth, by painting our palaces and public buildings, and his fame had a powerful effect upon the fortunes of young Hogarth in more phases than one. He says: "The paintings in St. Paul's and Greenwich Hospital, which were at that time going on, ran in my head, and I determined that silver-plate engraving should be followed no longer than necessity obliged me to it. Engraving on copper was at twenty years of age my utmost ambition."

He tells us, also, that he saw little probability of acquiring the full command of the graver, sufficiently to distinguish himself in that walk; "nor was I," he adds, "at twenty years of age, (in 1717,) much disposed to enter upon as barren and unprofitable a study as that of merely making fine lines. I thought it still more unlikely, that by pursuing the common method, and copying *old* drawings, I could ever attain the power of making *new* designs, which was my first and greatest ambition. I therefore, endeavoured to habituate myself to the exercise of a sort of technical memory; and by repeating in my own mind, the parts of which objects were composed, I could by degrees combine and put them down with my pencil."

Though averse, as he himself expresses it, to *coldly copying on the spot* any objects that struck him, it was usual with him, when he saw a singular character, either in the street or elsewhere, to pencil the leading features and prominent markings upon his nail, and when he came home, to copy the sketch on paper, and afterwards introduce it into a print. Several of these sketches have been preserved, and in them may be traced the first thoughts of many of the characters which Hogarth afterwards introduced into his works.

"My pleasures and my studies," says Hogarth, "thus going hand in hand, the most striking objects that presented themselves, either comic or tragic, made the strongest impression on my mind; but had I not sedulously practised what I had thus acquired, I should very soon have lost the power of performing it."

HOGARTH SATIRISES THE STAGE.

It was the degeneracy of the Stage in 1723 which thus early exercised the satirical talents of Hogarth, then a young man. Immediately after the appearance of the pantomime of *Dr. Faustus* at Lincoln's Inn Fields, he published his plate of *Masquerades and Operas*, with the gate of Burlington House in the background, as a lampoon upon the bad taste of the age in every branch of art. On one side Satan is represented as dragging a multitude of people through a gateway to the masquerade and opera, while Heidegger is looking down upon them from a window with an air of satisfaction. A large signboard above has a representation of Cuzzoni on the stage, to whom the Earl of Peterborough is offering 8,000*l*. On the opposite side of the picture a crowd rushes into a theatre to witness the pantomime; and over this gateway appears the sign of Dr. Faustus with a dragon and a windmill. In front of the picture a barrow-woman is wheeling away as "waste paper for shops," the dramatic works of Shakspeare, Ben Jonson, Dryden, Congreve, and Otway.

In 1725, Hogarth published another caricature—"A just View of the British Stage," more especially levelled at the pantomimes at Drury-lane and Lincoln's Inn Fields, and suggesting a plan for combining in one piece, *Dr. Faustus* and *Jack Sheppard* with Scaramouch, Jack Hall's escape from Newgate, &c. Wilkes is dangling the effigy of Punch in exultation, exclaiming, "Poor Rich, I pity thee." Cibber holding up *Harlequin Jack Sheppard* invokes the Muses, and Booth is "letting down Hall." The Ghost of Ben Jonson rises from a trapdoor, and shows his contempt for the new-fangled contrivances of the stage in a manner that cannot be misunderstood.

In 1727, Hogarth published a large *Masquerade Ticket*, bitterly satirical upon the immoral tendency of masquerades, as well as their manager, Heidegger. Hogarth had previously immortalized the face of this person, when enraged at a masquerade by a person wearing a masque as ugly as himself —indeed, a cast from his own face—

> With a hundred deep wrinkles impress'd on thy front,
> Like a map with a great many rivers upon 't.

"PRINTS FOR HUDIBRAS."

In 1726, when Hogarth readily got employment as an engraver of "frontispieces to books," he invented and engraved the set of Twelve large Prints for Hudibras, of which Walpole, in his usual strain of depreciation, says : "This was the first of his (Hogarth's) works that marked him as a man above the common; yet in what made him then noticed, it surprises me to find so little humour in an undertaking so congenial to his talents." But Hogarth lamented to his friends that he had parted with these plates without having had an opportunity to improve them. They were purchased by Mr. Philip Overton,* at the Golden Buck, near St. Dunstan's Church, in Fleet-street; thence passed to his successor, Mr. Sayer; and next to Laurie and Whittle. Hogarth's success in these prints lies rather in his departure from the poet, when, by skilful additions, he awakens a similar train of thought and humour, and thus increases the graphic glow of his author. The work was published by subscription ;

---

* Brother to Henry Overton, the well-known publisher of ordinary prints, who lived over against St. Sepulchre's Church, and sold many of Hogarth's early pieces coarsely copied, as was subsequently done by Dicey in Bow-churchyard.

Allan Ramsay, who was a bookseller as well as a poet, subscribed for thirty copies; and the plates were dedicated by the artist "to William Ward, of Great Houghton, Northamptonshire, and Mary Ramsay of Edinburgh." A friendly intercourse sprung up between Ramsay and Hogarth: they possessed a kindred humour, and a few lines were addressed to the painter, by the poet, whose son, Ramsay, the portrait-painter, joined in the feud of his fraternity against Hogarth.

To these twelve designs were added five, and the seventeen were engraved by Hogarth of smaller size, with Butler's head, copied from White's mezzotinto of Jean Baptist Monnoyer. In 1744, twelve of those designs were engraved for Dr. Zachary Grey's edition of *Hudibras*, but not until some of their glaring indecencies had been removed by "the ingenious Mr. Wood, painter, of Bloomsbury-square," as acknowledged by Dr. Grey, in his Preface. They are engraved by J. Mynde; but are poor and spiritless, with the exception of Butler's head, by Vertue.* Subsequently, many of these Plates were copied, with violent alterations by Ross, for Dr. Nash's edition of *Hudibras*, 1795. Altogether, Hogarth cannot be considered to have done much in illustration of the graphic form and humour of Butler's poems, which were "too elusive and quicksilvery" for the engraver's hand to catch. Voltaire said that *Hudibras* unites the wit of Don Quixote with that of the Satyre Menippée—a combination beyond the reach of our painting satirist's art.

With respect to the Paintings said to have been the work of Hogarth, the evidence is doubtful. At the sale of John Ireland's collection in 1810, "Twelve pictures of Hudibras" were bought for 52 guineas by Mr. Twining; and these pictures Ireland states in his Will, to be as certainly painted by Hogarth as the *Marriage à la Mode* pictures were.

Baker, in his *History of Northamptonshire*, states there to have been in the mansion of W. Sandbridge, Esq. at East Haddon, twelve humorous sketches, said to be by Hogarth, illustrative of *Hudibras*.

Mr. W. Davies, (Cadell and Davies), the publishers in the

---

* Lowndes, in his *Bibliographical Manual*, says of these plates: "Copies in fine condition are in considerable request. The cuts are beautifully expressed, and Hogarth is much indebted to the designer of them; but who he was does not appear." This is a strange mistake, since each of the plates is inscribed, "W. Hogarth inv^t." The error is corrected, as above, by a warm admirer of Hogarth, in a communication to *Notes and Queries*, First Series, No. 52.

Strand, had, in 1816, twelve small scenes in *Hudibras*, by Lepipre, a man under whom Hogarth is said to have studied; and the subjects so familiar to all as executed by Hogarth from *Hudibras*, are so similar to these twelve pictures, that Mr. Davies considered undoubtedly Hogarth had copied them. This opinion invalidates his claim to originality, which his admirers need not be very anxious, in this case, to prove.

The late John Britton possessed a series of twelve designs on panel, illustrative of *Hudibras*, which he bought at Southgate's, in Fleet-street, as painted by Hogarth; but Sir Thomas Lawrence pronounced them to be by Vandergucht. Failing to establish the authenticity of these paintings, however, Mr. Britton, in his *Autobiography*, Part 2, describes them as in drawing, colouring, and expression, to "surpass the well-known illustrations by Hogarth." Of one of Vandergucht's paintings, as a specimen, Mr. Britton caused a small lithograph to be executed in 1842.

HOGARTH AND THE UPHOLSTERER.

For some time after Hogarth began to paint, he was little known except as an engraver—a mere etcher of copper—a remarkable instance of which occurred in the year 1727. It appears that one Morris, an upholsterer, engaged Hogarth to make a design for tapestry—the subject, the Element of the Earth. The task was performed, when Morris, having discovered that he had commissioned an engraver instead of a painter, refused to pay for the work, and was sued for the price —20*l*. for workmanship, and 10*l*. for materials. At the trial before the Lord Chief Justice Eyre, Morris stated that he was informed by Hogarth that he was skilled in painting, and could execute the design of the Element of the Earth in a workmanlike manner. On hearing, however, afterwards that he was an engraver and not a painter, Morris became uneasy, and sent a servant to tell Mr. Hogarth, who replied that it was certainly a bold undertaking for him, but if Mr. Morris did not like it when it was finished, he should not be asked to pay for it. The work was completed and sent home, when Morris's tapestry-workers, mostly foreigners, and some of the finest hands in Europe, condemned the design, and insisted that it was impossible to execute tapestry from it. Accordingly, the verdict was given in Morris's favour, and Hogarth lost his labour and had to pay the entire expense of the trial.

HOGARTH'S MARRIAGE.

We have seen how Hogarth's attention was first drawn to painting by Thornhill's works at Greenwich Hospital and St. Paul's Cathedral; and how the young painter frequented the great man's academy in Peter's-court. To what their previous intimacy amounted is not known; but, in 1729, Hogarth, then in his thirty-second year, married Jane, the only daughter of Sir James Thornhill, aged twenty. The match was without the consent of the parents, and we can imagine the couple stealing away across the fields to the little church of Paddington, then a village of some 300 houses, with its green and rural churchyard. The marriage register contains the following entry: "William Hogarth, Esq., and Jane Thornhill, of St. Paul's, Covent Garden, married March 23d, 1729." Hogarth is called an eminent designer and engraver; and his father-in-law, serjeant painter and history painter to the King. Thornhill had now acquired wealth and honours, had been knighted, and sat in parliament for his native town, Weymouth. He was much offended at his daughter's unequal match, and kept his heart and his purse-strings close. He could not foresee his unwelcome son-in-law's future eminence: indeed, he was as yet acknowledged by few even as a painter. Sir James' wrath lasted for two years; but the entreaties of his wife, the submissiveness of his daughter, and above all, the rising reputation of Hogarth, prevailed, and Thornhill forgave the young painter.

During the interval, Hogarth designed and etched the first portion of "The Harlot's Progress," so much to the gratification of Lady Thornhill, that she advised her daughter to place it in her father's way. "Accordingly, one morning, Mrs. Hogarth conveyed it secretly into his dining-room. When he rose, he inquired whence it came, and by whom it was brought? When he was told, he cried out, 'Very well, very well! The man who can make works like this can maintain a wife without a portion.' He designed this remark as an excuse for keeping his purse-strings close; but soon after became both reconciled and generous to the young people."

Hogarth now set to work in the hope of being able to maintain his wife in such fashion as became her. He laid aside his satiric designs, and commenced portrait-painter; and Walpole tells us that the young artist's facility in catching a likeness, and his method of painting conversation pieces, drew him a prodigious business for some time. Hogarth's own account of this start in life is as follows: "I married, (he says,) and commenced painter of small conversation-pieces, from twelve to fifteen inches high. This, having novelty, succeeded for a few years. But though it gave somewhat more scope for the fancy, it was still but a less kind of drudgery; and as I could not bring myself to act like some of my brethren, and make it a sort of manufactory to be carried on by the help of backgrounds and drapery painters, it was not sufficiently profitable to pay the expenses my family required. I therefore turned my thoughts to a still more novel mode, to painting and engraving modern moral subjects, a field not broken up in any country or any age."

About this time Hogarth painted a very spirited representation of "Folly:" the subject was composed of twelve figures: six males, and a like number of females; the landscape gorgeous.

HOGARTH'S HOUSE IN LEICESTER-SQUARE.

It may be interesting to take a glance at the Leicester Fields of Hogarth's time. Mr. J. T. Smith had, in the year 1825, a conversation with a gentleman named Packer, then in his eighty-seventh year, and who remembered Leicester Fields long before the accession of George III. He said, it was a dirty place, where ragged boys assembled to play at *chuck.* In the King's Mews adjoining was a cistern where the horses were watered, behind which was a horse-pond, in which pickpockets, when caught, were ducked. In 1677, when Leicester House, on the north side, stood almost alone, there were rows of elm-trees in the court before it, extending nearly half the width of the present square. It was not inclosed until sixty years later; for, in the *Country Journal, or Craftsman,* of April 16, 1737, we read, "Leicester Fields is going to be fitted up in a very elegant manner: a new wall and rails to be erected all round, and a basin in the middle, after the manner of Lincoln's Inn Fields." Some years after, the streets were so thinly built in the neighbourhood, that when the heads of the Scottish rebels of 1745 were placed on Temple Bar, a man stood in Leicester Fields with a telescope, to give persons a sight of them for a halfpenny a-piece.

It appears by the rate-books of St. Martin's parish, that Hogarth came to live there in 1733, on the east side of the square, in what is now the northern half of the Sabloniere

Hotel. The house was distinguished in the painter's time by the sign of "The Golden Head," cut by Hogarth himself from pieces of cork glued and painted together. "I well remember," says Smith, "that it was placed over the street-door, which bore the name of Hogarth on a brass plate." The house, with its sign, is shown in a good contemporary engraving of the Square by Parr. It is related that Hogarth usually took his evening walk within the inclosure, in a scarlet roquelaire and cocked hat.

HOGARTH'S FIRST PAINTING.

The first piece in which Hogarth distinguished himself as a painter, is said by Nichols to have been a representation of Wanstead Assembly. The figures in it, we are told, were drawn from the life, and without a touch of burlesque. The faces are said to have been extremely like, and the colouring somewhat better than in some of Hogarth's more finished pictures. There seems to be a reference to it in "A Poetical Epistle to Mr. Hogarth, an eminent History and Conversation Painter, written in June, 1730, and published by the author, Mr. Mitchell, in 1731," &c.: in it are these lines:

> Savage families obey your hand;
> Assemblies rise at your command.

Wanstead was a neighbourhood of some note in the last century, when the tenants of its numerous villas supported the public assemblies then in fashion, although but six miles from the metropolis itself.

The *Wanstead Assembly* was painted for Lord Castlemaine, and at once brought Hogarth into notice. It was exhibited at the British Gallery in 1814, and was then the property of William Long Wellesley, Esq., of Wanstead House; and at the sale of the effects in 1822, it was bought in by the family.

Among Hogarth's early but penurious patrons was Mr. Bowles, at the Black Horse, in Cornhill; and Nichols had been told that he bought many a plate from Hogarth by the weight of the copper; but Nichols is certain that such a bargain was made in one instance, when the elder Mr. Bowles, of St. Paul's Churchyard, (the predecessor of the Bowles and Carver of our day,) offered, over a bottle, half-a-crown a pound for a plate which Hogarth had just then completed. His next friend of this class was Mr. Philip Overton, who, however, paid the young engraver a somewhat better price.

Walpole speaks of these early performances as not above the labours of the people who are generally employed by booksellers; but Nichols, lest the reader should apply this designation to artists employed in his time in book illustration, states that Walpole's account of Hogarth, &c. was printed off above ten years previously, (1772,) "before the names of Cipriani, Angelica, Bartolozzi, Sherwin, and Mortimer, were found at the bottom of any plates designed for the ornament of poems or dramatic pieces."

HOGARTH, KENT THE ARCHITECT, AND THE POET POPE.

William Kent, a man of moderate ability as a painter and sculptor, but of considerable influence as an architect and landscape-gardener, was the first artist who felt the touch of Hogarth's satiric hand. Originally a coach-painter, he had the good fortune to persuade some gentlemen to raise funds to enable him to go and study in Italy, where he became acquainted with the Earl of Burlington, who brought him home as his *protégé*. Kent painted as an altar-piece for St. Clement's church, in the Strand, an absurd picture of St. Cecilia, which, from its being supposed to contain portraits of the Pretender's wife and children, created much ferment in the parish. This strange picture Hogarth burlesqued in a print which raised an universal laugh. Gibson, bishop of London, on his visitation to St. Clement's, ordered the churchwardens to remove the original; it was then taken to the Crown and Anchor tavern, in the Strand, whence, after several years, it was removed to the vestry-room, over the old almshouses, in the churchyard; and when this building was taken down in 1803, the altar-picture was conveyed to the new vestry-hall in Pickett-street, where it remains to this day.

The ridicule which Hogarth had thus thrown on Kent was very acceptable to Sir James Thornhill, who was jealous of the fourfold reputation of the latter, as painter, sculptor, architect, and ornamental gardener. Hogarth carried his attack on Kent still further in satirizing his friend, Pope, who in his poem of "False Taste" severely criticised the magnificent Duke of Chandos as Timon, on his display of great wealth and little taste at Canons. To Pope was added Kent's other great patron, the Earl of Burlington, and Hogarth burlesqued the trio as follows. He represented Burlington gate in Piccadilly, with Kent on the summit flourishing his pallet and pencils over his astonished supporters Michael Angelo and Raphael. On a scaffold, somewhat lower down, stands Pope, with a tie-wig on; he is washing the front, and bespattering the Duke of Chandos, who is passing by in his coach; while Lord Burlington serves the poet as a plasterer's labourer.

This print (entitled "The Man of Taste;" containing a View of Burlington Gate; 1731,) has conferred a celebrity upon the archway, which it might not otherwise have obtained. Pope took no notice of the attack. "Either Hogarth's obscurity," says Nichols, "was his protection from the lash of Pope, or perhaps the bard was too prudent to exasperate a painter who had already given such proofs of his ability in satire." This opinion is very illogical; for, proofs of ability are inconsistent with obscurity. Pope remained silent: he either feared the painter's retaliation, or he regarded him as a vulgar caricaturist, beneath notice.

Hogarth said of Kent: "Neither England nor Italy ever produced a more contemptible dauber than the late Mr. Kent —and yet he gained the prize at Rome, in England had the first people for his patrons, and to crown the whole, was appointed painter to the King. But in this country such men meet with the greatest encouragement, and sooner work their way into noblemen's houses and palaces."

HOGARTH'S SOUTHWARK FAIR.

This great metropolitan fair, which was held on St. Margaret's Hill, on the day after Bartholomew Fair, has now been abolished for nearly a century; but a few of its humours have been preserved by the pencil of Hogarth. It was first painted by him in 1733: this picture was destroyed by fire at Mr. Johnes's seat, at Hafod, in 1807; but it has been more than once engraved. It represents several notabilities of the Fair as to attract people from all parts of the kingdom; the booth-keepers used to collect money at their stalls for prisoners in the Marshalsea. It is a rare scene of

"Startling players, fire-eaters, jugglers—
————Katterfelto, with his hair on end,
At his own wonders wondering for his bread."

Simple-faced countrymen, nimble pickpockets, and ladies with roguish eyes, are the actors who fill this stage. One of the most successful characters is that of an Amazon in a hat and feather, the sole heroine in a gang of hedge comedians beating up for an audience. The notabilities portrayed are —Signor Violante vaulting; Cadman flying down a rope— he was afterwards killed at Shrewsbury; Walker, afterwards the famous Macheath; Figg, the prize-fighter, on a blind horse; Miller, a native of Saxony, eight feet high; two jugglers in senatorial wigs, Fawkes and Neve; Cibber,* with laurelled brow; the show-cloth etched by Laguerre, &c. The wonders and drolleries of Southwark Fair are described by Pepys and Evelyn.

JOURNEY INTO KENT.

Among the records of the lively incidents of our painter's career is a queer account of a holiday jaunt of five days taken by land and water, in May, 1732. The parties were Hogarth; John Thornhill;† Scott, the landscape-painter; Tothall, a member of the Club at the Bedford Coffee-house; and Forrest. They set out at midnight from the Bedford, each with a shirt in his pocket; and their excursion extended to Gravesend, Rochester, Sheerness, and adjacent places. They had particular duties: Hogarth and Scott made the drawings; Thornhill the map; Tothall was treasurer and caterer; and Forrest wrote the journal. The tourists left the Bedford with a song, and took water to Billingsgate, exchanging compliments with the bargemen as they went down the river. At Billingsgate, Hogarth made a *caricature* of a facetious porter called the Duke of Puddledock, who entertained the party with the humours of the place. Here they took to the boat for themselves; had straw to lie upon, and went down the river at night, by turns sleeping and singing jolly choruses.

Mr. Thackeray has thus grouped the incidents of this humorous excursion: "They arrived at Gravesend at six, when they washed their faces and hands, and had their wigs powdered. Then they sallied forth for Rochester on foot, and drank by the way three pots of ale. At one o'clock they went to dinner with excellent port, and a quantity more beer, and afterwards Hogarth and Scott played at hopscotch in the town-hall. It would appear that they slept most of them in one room, and the chronicler of the party describes them all as waking at seven o'clock, and telling each other their dreams. You have rough sketches by Hogarth of the incidents of this

* Cibber acted the part of ancient Pistol, in the tragedy of *Tamerlane the Great*, in a booth in Bartholomew Fair, 1733.

† John Thornhill was a natural son of Sir James Thornhill: he survived Hogarth twenty-five years.

holiday excursion. The sturdy little painter is seen sprawling over a plank to a boat at Gravesend; the whole company are represented in one design, in a fisherman's room where they had passed the night. One gentleman in a nightcap is shaving himself; another is being shaved by the fisherman; a third, with a handkerchief over his bald pate, is taking his breakfast; and Hogarth is sketching the whole scene. They describe at night how they returned to their quarters, drank to their friends, as usual, emptied several cans of good flip, all singing merrily."

On the second night after their return, Forrest produced his journal, bound, gilt, and lettered, and read the same to the members of the Club then present at the Bedford. At the same time Tothall produced the account of the Disbursements on the journey, which amounted to 6*l.* 6*s.*

A copy of the journal was left in the hands of the Rev. Mr. Gostling, at Canterbury; and he wrote an imitation of it in Hudibrastic verse, (965 lines,) of which twenty copies were printed as a literary curiosity in 1781: it is reprinted in Nichols's third edition. In the previous year, 1781, Hogarth published a Tour of nine pages, illustrated with drawings. The frontispiece, (Mr. Somebody,) was designed by Hogarth, as emblematical of the journey, viz., that it was a short tour by land and water, backwards and forwards, without head or tail. The ninth is the tail-piece, (Mr. Nobody,) the whole being intended as a burlesque on historical writers renovating a series of insignificant events entirely uninteresting to the reader.

PORTRAITS OF SARAH MALCOLM, MISS BLANDY, AND ELIZABETH CANNING.

Hogarth appears to have had a strong *penchant* for painting the portraits of criminals, and other notorieties in infamy. Among them was Sarah Malcolm, the laundress in the Temple, who was executed opposite Mitre-court, Fleet-street, on the 17th of March, 1733, for the murder of Mrs. Elizabeth Duncan, Elizabeth Harrison, and Ann Price. Hogarth drew Malcolm's portrait when she was in the condemned cell in Newgate, on the day before her execution; and to Sir James Thornhill, who accompanied him, he observed: "I see by this woman's features that she is capable of any wickedness." Upon this, Ireland remarks: "Of his (Hogarth's) skill in physiognomy I entertain a very high opinion; but as Sarah sat for her picture after her condemnation, I suspect his observation to resemble those prophecies which are made after the completion of events they professed to foretel. She has a locked-up mouth, wide nostrils, and a penetrating eye, with a general air that indicates close observation and masculine courage; but I do not discover either depravity or cruelty; though her conduct in this, as well as some other horrible transactions, evinced an uncommon portion of both, and proved her a Lady Macbeth in low life."

When Sarah sat to Hogarth, "she had put on red to look the better." This portrait was in the Green Closet, at Strawberry Hill; a copy of it was in the possession of Alderman Boydell: it was engraved, and from the print were four copies, besides one in wood, which was engraved for the *Gentleman's Magazine.* "Thus eager were the public," says Ireland, "to possess the portait of this most atrocious woman." Walpole calls her "a washerwoman," which, doubtless, arose from his mistaking the designation of *laundress,* a woman who has the care of chambers, for a washer of clothes. It is true that her picture was admitted into the Strawberry-hill collection; but Walpole rightly estimated Sarah's notoriety, though he places her in great company, and writes, some fifteen years after, (1748):

"Projectors make little noise here; and even any one who only *has* made a noise, is forgotten as soon as out of sight! The knaves and fools of to-day are too numerous to leave room to talk of yesterday. The pains that people, who have a mind to be named, are forced to take to be very particular, would convince you how difficult it is to make a lasting impression on such a town as this. * * * * Lord Bolingbroke, Sarah Malcolm, and old Marlborough, are never mentioned by their elderly folks to their grandchildren, who had never heard of them."—*Letters,* vol. ii. p. 104.

Another portrait of this class is that of *Miss Blandy,* who was executed at Oxford in 1762, for poisoning her father. The drawing, which is in every way worthy of Hogarth's pencil, was in the collection of the Duke of Buckingham at Stowe: it is in Indian-ink wash. She is represented in her prison cell, sitting at a round table, her *left* hand resting on a sheet of paper, and holding a pen, as if in the act of writing, although her countenance is turned towards the spectator: Nichols asks: " Was she left-handed ? "

Hogarth next painted *Elizabeth Canning,* whose fabricated story of being seized under Bedlam wall, partly stripped, and carried to Enfield Wash, and there shut up in a room, and kept upon bread and water, for many months turned the heads of the town, and produced a shoal of pamphlets, prints, and caricatures. Canning confessed the imposture, and was tried, and condemned to transportation: Hogarth painted her while she was in prison, and the portrait is in the Mulgrave collection.

DEATH OF SIR JAMES THORNHILL.

In 1734, Hogarth lost his father-in-law, Sir James Thornhill, whom he designated in the obituary of the *Gentleman's Magazine*—"the greatest history-painter this Kingdom ever produced: witness his elaborate works in Greenwich Hospital, the cupola of St. Paul's, the altar-pieces of All Souls' College in Oxford, and the church in Weymouth, where he was born. He was not only by patents appointed history-painter to their late and present majesties, but sergeant-painter, by which he was to paint all the royal palaces, coaches, barges, and the royal navy. This late patent he surrendered in favour of his only son John. He left no other issue but one daughter, now the wife of Mr. William Hogarth, admired for his curious miniature conversation pieces."

Thornhill was generous with his pencil: he painted the Court of Aldermen, at the Guildhall, London, with allegorical figures of Prudence, Justice, Temperance, and Fortitude; in return for which the Corporation presented the artist with a gold cup, value 225*l*. 7*s*.

Sir James designed for the Chelsea China-factory; and Walpole had, at Strawberry Hill, a dozen plates by Thornhill, which he purchased at Mrs. Hogarth's sale, in Leicester-square. Panton Betew, the silversmith of Hogarth's time, and a dealer in works of art, related the following as the cause of the breaking up of the Chelsea china works, in a conversation with Nollekens:—"Ay! that was a curious failure, the cunning rogues produced very white and delicate ware, but then they had their clay from China; which when the Chinese found out, they would not let the captains have any more clay for ballast, and the consequence was, that the whole concern failed." Nollekens once asked Panton Betew, if he knew where the Chelsea china factory stood? To which Betew replied, "Upon the site of Lord Dartery's house, just beyond the bridge."

Thornhill lived in a large house behind No. 104, St. Martin's-lane: he painted the staircase with subjects of allegory; the pictures long remained upon the walls, in excellent condition, as they have never been cleaned. In this house subsequently lived the junior Van Nost, the sculptor, who took the famous mask of Garrick from his face. After Van Nost, Frank Hayman lived in this house; and then Sir Joshua Reynolds, previous to his knighthood, and before he went to live in the house now No. 5, on the north side of Great Newport-street, whence he removed to Leicester-fields.

Upon the site of the present Friends', or Quakers' meeting-house, in St. Peter's-court, stood the first studio of Roubilliac, the sculptor; there, amongst other works, he executed his famous statue of Handel, for Vauxhall Gardens. The studio was, upon Roubilliac leaving it, fitted up as a subscription drawing academy, Mr. Michael Moser being appointed keeper. Hogarth was much against this establishment, though he presented to it several casts, and other articles, which had been the property of his father-in-law, Sir James Thornhill. He declared that it was the surest way to bring artists to beggary, by rendering their education as easy as one guinea and a half and two guineas, per quarter.

MIDNIGHT MODERN CONVERSATION.

In this famous piece, painted by Hogarth in 1735, most of the figures are portraits. It is a picture of thorough jollity. Around a table are some dozen persons, talking, swearing, singing, falling, sleeping, smoking, swilling, and huzzaing "like mad." The president of the orgy is a priest, whom, Sir Hawkins says, is Orator Henley; but Mrs. Piozzi asserts he is no other person than Parson Ford, a near relative of Dr. Johnson, and a very profligate fellow. Although his companions are falling about him, he sits, pipe in hand, using a corkscrew as a tobacco-stopper.* The figure leaning over the Parson is John Harrison, a tobacconist from Bell-yard; the lawyer, Kettleby, a vociferous barrister; the man in the

* This association of the priest and the corkscrew is traced to the following anecdote related by Lord Sandwich. "I was in company where there were ten persons, and I made a wager privately and won it, that among them was not one prayer-book. I then offered to lay another wager, that among the ten persons there were half-a-score of corkscrews—it was accepted; the better received his instructions, pretended to break his corkscrew, and requested any gentleman to lend him one, when each priest pulled a corkscrew from his pocket. A dispute was got up as to some point in the Liturgy, when a prayer-book was asked for, and not one of the priests had one."

nightcap, old Chandler, a bookbinder from Shire-lane. The jolly party have emptied twenty-three flasks, and the twenty-fourth is being decanted. Even the timepiece is infected with the fume of the liquor, for the hour and minute hands do not agree.

This picture was presented by Hogarth to Mr. Rich, of Covent-garden theatre; his widow left it to her nephew, General Wilford, who gave it to the grand-daughter of Rich, who bequeathed it to William Wightman, Esq., of Hampstead. In the Egremont collection at Petworth, is a copy of this picture; another (says Ireland) was found in an inn in Gloucestershire, and passed into the hands of J. Calverley, Esq., of Leeds; a sketch was sold at John Ireland's sale, in 1810, for 6*l*.; and in 1817, this picture, or another sketch, was in the hands of Mr. Gwennap, and thence passed into Lord Northwick's collection at Cheltenham, dispersed in 1859.

The print was very popular: in the British Museum is an impression of the plate in its first state, printed with red ink; it was copied by Kirkhall and Ripenhausen. There is a very large copy, 2 ft. 11 in. wide by $22\frac{1}{2}$ inches high, published by John Bowles, at the Black Horse, Cornhill: on each side of the title are numerous verses. The bon-vivant Duke of Norfolk possessed a copy, which, in 1816, was sold to Molteno, of Pall Mall.

The clever heads in the *Midnight Conversation*, were engraved in two small plates by Ripenhausen, and published, with a French description, in 1786; and a French copy was engraved by Creite. Indeed, the fame of print and picture seems to have been co-extensive with the love of drink. It is considered in France and Germany the best of all Hogarth's single works.

It will be seen by reference to a future page, that one of the wall-paintings discovered in the Elephant, in Fenchurch-street, in 1826, is said to have been Hogarth's first idea of the above picture, but differs from the print.

ORATOR HENLEY.

We are easily led, (says Mr. Wright,) to doubt the morality of a schemer like Henley, and the reports of his contemporaries seem to rank it rather low. Hogarth introduced him in his *Midnight Conversation;* and in another picture, performing the rites of baptism, but evidently more attentive to the beauty of the mother than to the operation he is performing on the child. Another rough sketch by Hogarth represents in burlesque the interior of the Oratory in Clare Market during service. The Orator's fame, however, was so great, that several engravings were made of him, holding forth from his pulpit, enriched with velvet and gold.—(*England under the House of Hanover*, vol. i. p. 107.)

A COFFEE-ROOM SCENE.

A good and characteristic conversation piece by Hogarth, was sold by auction in June, 1856. It was from Mr. Barwell Coles's collection, and is a true piece, with four life-size figures, over a bowl of bunch. The scene is evidently in Old Slaughter's Coffee-house, St. Martin's-lane; the persons represented are Dr. Mounsey, Slaughter himself, and it is said, Hogarth. The heads are well painted, and the whole picture is full of character.

"THE HARLOT'S PROGRESS."

Hogarth commenced painting this series of six pictures in 1731, and published the plates engraved from them in 1734. They were the first great work in which his genius became conspicuously known. "This," says Cunningham, " is no burlesque production nor jesting matter—it exhibits, in the midst of humour and satire, a moral pathos which saddens the heart." The boldness and originality of the conception of the satiric story, and the literal force with which the fashionable follies and corruptions of the age are shown up in these pictures, extended as their effect was by engraving, administered many a severe reproof to the actors in those scenes of profligacy with which the London life of the period abounded. Hitherto, painters had invested their moralities with the grace of classic fable and what may be termed the varnish of allegory. Hogarth disdained such affectations, and in their place gave us portraits of the vicious and the vile in the several stages of their infamy. The chief agents are portraits of notorieties of the day. The debauchee, in the first scene of the series, is Colonel Charteris, whom Pope had already "damned to everlasting fame," and who is here, to use Cunningham's words, "pilloried to everlasting infamy." Kate Hackabout, the frail heroine, was committed to Bridewell in 1730: her brother was hung at Tyburn. The procuress, Mother Needham, be-patched and sanctified looking, was sent out of the world in undergoing the sentence of being pilloried in Park-lane, when she was so roughly handled by the mob that she survived but a few days.

Then, with what characteristic accuracy are the accessories of the pictures chosen: in the second plate, the sign, Pontac's head, alludes to the purveyor who kept the celebrated eating-house in Abchurch-lane; the hat-box in the third plate, is James Dalton's, a notorious street-robber; the pictures are Dr. Sacheverel and Captain Macheath—the *Beggar's Opera* being just then in full run; and in the sixth plate the parson is chaplain of the Fleet Prison, scandalous for its marriages; and the principal female, Elizabeth Adams, was executed for robbery in 1737.

Of a higher class is the Justice in the third plate, this being Sir John Gonson, who was indefatigable in hunting up thieves and profligates, and is here entering the house of the Harlot. Gonson was distinguished for the extravagance of his addresses to Grand Juries; they were composed, it is said, by Orator Henley, of the Gilt-Tub, and Sir John's voice did not escape the satire of Pope :

> " Talkers I've heard; Motteaux I knew;
> Henley himself I've heard, and Budgell too,
> The doctor's wormwood style, the hash of tongues
> A pedant makes, the storm of Gonson's lungs."

The accuracy of the likeness of Sir John Gonson had much to do with the sudden popularity of the *Harlot's Progress*. Nichols relates that at a Board of Treasury, which was held a day or two after the appearance of the third scene, a copy was shown by one of the Lords, as containing, among other excellencies, a striking likeness of Sir John Gonson. It gave universal satisfaction: from the Treasury each lord repaired to the print-shop for a copy of it; and Hogarth rose completely into fame. This anecdote was related by Christopher Tilson, one of the chief clerks in the Treasury, and at that period under-secretary of state.

The fourth Plate admirably represents a scene in Bridewell: men and women are beating hemp under the eye of a savage taskmaster, and a lad too idle to work is seen standing on tiptoe, to reach the stocks, in which his hands are fixed, while over his head is written, "Better to work than stand thus!"

In the fifth Plate, the fat and lean physicians, who are squabbling beside the expiring sinner, are also portraits: the

meagre practitioner is Dr. Misaubin, the Flemish Quack;*
his fat adversary is an English worthy of the same stamp—
either Dr. Rock or Dr. Ward: an old nostrum of the latter
is in sale to this day. The apartment is the large room in
the house of the famous Dr. Misaubin,† now No. 96,
St. Martin's-lane; and in the picture are portraits of the
Doctor and his Irish wife. This plate of Hogarth's, which
has never been understood by collectors of that artist's works,
has been explained thus: The Rake, who has accompanied
the girl to whom Dr. Misaubin had given his vicious pills, is
threatening to cane him. The Doctor's wife, who has been
cleaning a lancet after a recent operation, eyes the Rake with
a full determination to enforce her vengeance, should he offer
to put his threat into execution.

The coffin in the last Plate, is inscribed September 2, 1731.
The boy in a corner winding up his top with so much unpretending insensibility in the plate of the Harlot's Funeral (the
only thing in that assembly that is not a hypocrite,) quiets
and soothes the mind that has been disturbed at the sight
of so much depraved man and woman kind. (*C. Lamb.*)

The six pictures were sold at Hogarth's auction, in 1715,
for 14 guineas each, to Alderman Beckford, who removed
them to his seat at Fonthill; and when the mansion was

---

* Dr. Misaubin, (whose father was a celebrated preacher at the Spital-
fields French church,) brought a noted pill into England, by which he
realized a large fortune. His son was murdered when returning from
Marylebone gardens: the Doctor bequeathed his wealth to his grandson,
who dissipated it, and died in St. Martin's workhouse: he supported
himself entirely by drinking gin, and died at last for want of it.

Mr. Standley is in possession of an original drawing by Hogarth, containing portraits of Dr. Misaubin and Dr. Ward, which he has had
engraved; the plate being destroyed after twelve impressions had been
taken.—*J. T. Smith,* 1828.

† Dr. Misaubin's house in St. Martin's-lane was afterwards a colour-
shop, and the front retained to the last grooves for the shutters to slide
in; the street-door frame was of the style of Queen Anne, with a spread
eagle, foliage, and flowers curiously and deeply carved in wood over the
entrance. Mr. Powel, the colourman, who long inhabited this house,
used to say that his mother, for many years, made a pipe of wine from
the grapes which grew in the garden, which at that time was nearly
100 feet in length, before the smoke of so many surrounding buildings
checked the growth of the vines.

The house has a large and curiously painted staircase, of figures
viewing a procession, which was executed for Dr. Misaubin, about 1732,
by a French painter named Clermont, who boldly charged one thousand
guineas for his labour; but the charge being contested, he was obliged
to take five hundred guineas.

burnt in 1755, five of the pictures were consumed; the sixth was saved, and is at Charlemont House, Dublin.

Nichols, in 1833, stated: "Mr. Hall, the police magistrate, of Bow-street, has what he considers to be the first four of the original sketches of the *Harlot's Progress:* they are in a very rough, obscure, and dirty condition."

For the prints of the *Harlot's Progress* above 1,200 names were entered in Hogarth's subscription-book. It was made into a pantomime by Theophilus Cibber; and again represented on the stage, under the title of *The Jew decoyed, or a Harlot's Progress,* in a ballad opera. Fan-mounts were likewise engraved, containing miniature representations of all the six plates; and it was customary in Hogarth's family, to give these fans to the maid-servants. The Empress of Russia, who highly prized Hogarth's works, had a tea service of cups and saucers with the *Harlot's Progress* painted on them in China, about the year 1793.

THE RAKE'S PROGRESS.

This admirable series of eight scenes, painted in 1735, each complete in itself, and all telling a domestic story, followed the *Harlot's Progress.* Walpole says: "The *Rake's Progress,* though perhaps superior to the *Harlot's Progress,* had not so much success as the other—from want of novelty; nor is the print of the Arrest equal to the others." The inferiority of the latter plate was felt by Hogarth himself; he tried to improve it, but without success.

Nevertheless, the success of the *Rake's Progress* must have been great, for it was satisfactory to the artist himself. Their humour, satire, and moral pathos were instantly appreciated. Even Walpole now acknowledged Hogarth's triumph. "The curtain," he says, "was now drawn aside, and his genius stood displayed in its full lustre. From time to time he continued these works, which should be immortal if the nature of his work would allow it. Even the receipts for his subscriptions had wit in them. Many of his plates he engraved himself, and often expunged faces etched by his assistants when they had not done justice to his ideas."

In the *Rake's Progress,* a young man succeeds unexpectedly to the hoards of a sordid miser—from poverty to worldly fortune. "He deserts the woman whom he had wooed, and vowed to marry—starts on a wild career of extravagance, dissipation, and folly—is beset and swindled by speculators of all kinds, from poets to punks, including rooks, and bucks, and bullies—parades through various haunts of sin and of splendour, till 'with a fortune dissipated, a constitution ruined, his fame blighted, and his mind touched, he is left raving mad in Bedlam." Many of the actors in these scenes are believed to be portraits. The hero is probably only the impersonation of the vices satirized. Around the head of the antiquated beldam whom Rakewell marries, to support his extravagance, is a halo, which is a shaft at that spiritual school of painting, on which Hogarth looked coldly. The two sedate personages at the gaming-table, are one Manners (of the Rutland family,) to whom the Duke of Devonshire lost the great estate of Leicester Abbey; and a highwayman who sits warming his feet at the fire, waiting quietly till the winner departs, that he may, with a craped face and a cocked pistol, follow and seize the whole. "Old Manners," says Ireland, "was the only person of his time who amassed a considerable fortune by the profession of a gamester." Hogarth has shown him as miser and gamester, discounting a nobleman's note-of-hand.

The second scene is Rakewell's morning levee; with the French fencing-master, Dubois, who died in a quarrel with an Irishman of his own name and profession; next is Figg, the prize-fighter, who beat half-a-dozen Hibernians—hence the label—"A Figg for the Irish;" the teacher of music resembles Handel; the French-horn player, Bridgman; the pictures are Fighting Cocks, and the Judgment of Paris. In the third plate, the fellow with a pewter-dish, Leathercoat, was many years porter at the Rose Tavern: the decapitated Cæsars are very comical. In the sixth plate, the fire alludes to an accident which happened April 23, 1733, when White's Chocolate-house, and two adjoining houses in St. James's-street, were consumed; Sir Andrew Fountaine's fine collection of paintings was destroyed; His Majesty and the Prince of Wales were present above an hour, and encouraged the firemen and others to work at the engines, by distributing money amongst them. The eighth scene is very full: the tailor is Lord L———r, who had a passion for that business;* the maniac chained to the floor is a copy of one of Cibber's figures over the gate of Bedlam; the Rake himself is the companion figure; the man sitting by the figure inscribed "Charming Betty Careless," is William Ellis, the maniac who lost his reason through

* Just as an "exquisite" Earl of our time had; and whose taste not only gave the name to a fashion, but actually cut out his own clothes.

love for his Betty: an etching of this plate has been sold for 11*l*. 0*s*. 6*d*. Mr. Knowles, of 34, Bridge-street, Blackfriars, possesses a beautiful and most valuable drawing in Indian ink of the above Bedlam scene; it was evidently drawn by Hogarth for the purpose of transferring to the copper, but the drawing is most exquisitely finished. (*Nichols*, 1833.)

The woman, discarded in the first print, receives Rakewell in the fourth, is present at his marriage, follows him into the gaol and watches over him in Bedlam.

The original sketch in oil, of the 6th plate, was, in 1782, at Mrs. Hogarth's, in Leicester Fields; the principal character is here sitting, and not thrown upon his knees in execration, which is a very effective incident of the picture.

The eight paintings were sold in Hogarth's sale, in 1745, for twenty-two guineas each, the purchaser being Alderman Beckford, at whose sale they were purchased by Col. Fullerton for 650 guineas. In 1802, they were bought by Sir John Soane for 598*l*.; and they are now in the Picture-room of the Soanean Museum, in Lincoln's Inn Fields.

Hogarth painted the *Rake's Progress* in a temporary summer residence at Isleworth. The crowd of visitors to his studio was immense. He often asked them if they knew for whom one or other of the figures in the pictures was designed, and when they guessed wrong, he set them right. It was generally believed that the heads were chiefly portraits of low characters on town.

HOGARTH PAINTS THE STAIRCASE OF ST. BARTHOLOMEW'S HOSPITAL.

Before Hogarth had done anything of much consequence in his walk "between the sublime and grotesque," he writes: "I entertained some hopes of succeeding in what the puffers in books call *the great style of History Painting;* so that without having had a stroke of this *grand* business before, I quitted small portraits and familiar conversations, and with a smile at my own temerity, commenced history painter, and on the great staircase of St. Bartholomew's Hospital, painted two Scripture stories, the *Pool of Bethesda,* and *the Good Samaritan,* with figures seven feet high." These paintings Hogarth presented to the Charity, in acknowledgment of which he was elected a Life Governor of the Hospital. The inscription records: "The historical Paintings of this staircase were painted and given by Mr. William Hogarth, and the ornamental painting at his expense, A.D. 1736." Hogarth soon left this new path, in which Walpole deals harshly with his failure: "the genius that had entered so feelingly into the calamities and crimes of familiar life, deserted him in a walk that called for dignity and grace. The burlesque turn of his mind mixed itself with the most serious subjects. In the Pool of Bethesda, a servant of a rich ulcerated lady beats back a poor man that sought the same celestial remedy." This, though justly thought, Walpole condemns as too ludicrous; but it is rather satirical. The conception of both these works is their chief merit.

Hogarth paid his friend Lambert for painting the landscape of the Good Samaritan, and afterwards cleaned the whole at his own expense.

Two fine drawings for the Bethesda painting exist. One is in black and white chalk, drawn from the life, of the principal female figure in the Pool; upon which S. Ireland notes: "this figure was drawn at St. Martin's-lane, and is said to have represented Nell Robinson, a celebrated courtezan:" it was given in 1794 by Mr. Cotton to Ireland, and is now in the Royal collection. The second drawing is in chalk, very fine, probably the study for the beggar in the Pool; it passed into Mr. John Sheepshanks's collection.

HOGARTH AN ANATOMICAL DRAUGHTSMAN.

It is not generally known that in early life Hogarth attempted to paint morbid anatomy: it was at the suggestion of Dr. Cæsar Hawkins who directed his attention to it as a field of labour not occupied; Hogarth at that time being a beginner the Doctor patronized him; and two pictures painted by Hogarth for him (of diseased viscera) were bequeathed with other pictures by the widow of the doctor, to the Royal College of Surgeons, where they are still preserved.

"THE STROLLING ACTRESSES."

This picture is one of the most imaginative and amusing of Hogarth's works. It is a huge barn fitted up as a theatre, with a company of performers preparing for the "Devil to Pay in Heaven," a sort of burlesque of a religious mystery. The principal dramatis personæ, Jupiter, Juno, Diana, Apollo, Flora, Night, Syren, Aurora, and Cupid, are accompanied by a ghost, two eagles, two dragons, two kittens, and an aged monkey. Juno is rehearsing her part on an old wheelbarrow which serves occasionally for a triumphal car; Night, in a starry robe, is mending her stocking; the Star of Evening is a scoured tin tart-mould. A veteran, one-eyed damsel represents the Tragic Muse, and is cutting a cat's tail for blood to heighten the mimic scene. Two little devils with budding horns, are struggling for a pot of ale. In the centre of the design Diana is stripped to her chemise, and having just caught the inspiration of her part, is rehearsing, heedless of dressing; she is young, blooming, and beautiful. Flora is making her toilet before a broken looking-glass; she smooths her hair with a piece of tallow candle, and holds the dredger ready. Apollo and Cupid are trying to bring down a pair of stockings, hung out on a cloud to dry; but the wings of the God of Love fail, and he is compelled to mount by a ladder. Aurora sits on the ground; the Syren is offering Ganymede a glass of gin; and the woman who personates the Bird of Jove, is feeding her child; a royal crown holds the pap-saucepan, and the child screams at the enormous beak of the eagle. In a corner a monkey in a long cloak, a bag wig, and solitaire, is moistening the plumed helmet of Alexander the Great. Two kittens are playing with a lyre and an imperial orb; and two judges' wigs and an empty noose are in suggestive juxta-position. A mitre is filled with tragedies and farces; a hen and chickens are roosting upon a set of unemployed waves; and here are the materials for dramatic thunder. The humour, sarcasms, and absurdities in the picture are endless—even the darkest nook has a meaning; and the oddity of the *properties* is well indicated by Juno having for her share "thunderbolt, trunk, wheelbarrow, saltbox, rouge, and rolling-pin." It is, indeed, a thoroughly *behind the scenes* picture. It was sold by Francis Beckford, Esq., for 27*l*. 6*s*., which price he thought too much, and returned it to the painter, who then sold it to Mr. Wood, of Littleton, for the same price; and it remains in his possession. A print in the first state, extra fine, has been sold for 6*l*. 10*s*.

THE BEGGARS' OPERA.

The talents of Hogarth did not allow him to let pass the Newgate pastoral of the *Beggars' Opera*, the greatest theatrical success of his time.

Of this subject, Hogarth painted, at least, two copies. The

original sketch in oil, represents Lucy and Polly interceding with their fathers to save Capt. Macheath: Walker as Macheath; Miss Fenton (afterwards Duchess of Bolton) as Polly; Hippisley as Peachem; Hall as Lockit: on one side, in a box, are Sir Thomas Robinson, very tall and lean, and Sir Robert Fagg, the famous horse-racer. This sketch was given by Hogarth to Horace Walpole, and remained in the Strawberry-hill collection, until the sale in 1842, when it was sold for 55 guineas. Walpole had another picture by Hogarth, of Macheath going to execution. Of this subject, Hogarth painted at least two copies for Rich, of Covent Garden Theatre. It was engraved by Blake, in 1790, with a key-plate of the personages.

Hogarth caricatured the *Beggars' Opera* in a print representing the actors with the heads of animals, and Apollo and the Muses fast asleep under the stage. In another caricature, Parnassus was turned into a bear-garden; Pegasus was drawing a dust-cart, and the Muses were employed in sifting cinders:

> Parnassus now like a bear-garden appears,
> And Apollo there plays on his crowd to the bears:
> Poor Pegasus draws an old dust-cart along,
> And the Muses sift cinders, and hum an old song.
> With a fa, la, &c.

"THE FOUR TIMES OF THE DAY."

In these four prints, Hogarth, says Ireland, "treads poetic ground." It would have been more sensible to say, they present so many scenes of the London street life of the period; just as George Cruikshank and John Leech, in our day, illustrate the humour of their period.

Of *Morning* the scene is Covent-garden of about a century and a quarter ago. The sun is newly risen, and there is snow on the house-tops; a prim old maiden lady is walking to church, with a half-starved and shivering footboy bearing her prayer-book. She is extraordinarily sour; for she sees, as if she saw them not, two fuddled beaux from Tom King's coffee-house caressing two frail women. A young fruit-girl is warming her hands at the embers of a night-fire on the pavement; while her companion, a beggar-woman, in vain solicits charity from the sour old maiden on her way to church: this is the portrait of a lady, who, it is said, was so incensed at the satire, that she struck Hogarth out of her will; she was at first pleased with the strong likeness, till some good-natured friend explained it in a way injurious to the fortune of the artist. At the door of Tom King's coffee-house* there is a drunken row, in which swords and cudgels are the weapons. There is snow on the ground, and icicles hang from the eaves; but, to suit the season, there is a liquor-shop open; and Dr. Rock is commending to a mar-velling audience the miracles wrought by his medicine, which his sign-post shows, he dispenses by letters patent.

Noon is laid, according to Ireland, at the door of a French chapel in Hog-lane, (afterwards Castle-street,) Seven Dials, a part of the town then peopled by French refugees, or their descendants. The congregation are coming out of the chapel; foremost are an affected Frenchwoman, her foppish husband, and a spoiled child; two withered beldames saluting is very ludicrous. St. Giles's clock-dial points to half-past eleven; but at this early hour there was as much good eating as now at six in the evening; and twenty pewter measures on the wall attest the rate of drinking. A servant-girl, bringing a pie from a baker's, is stopped to be kissed by a blackamoor; but the best portion of the picture is a poor boy who in resting a baked pudding on the head of a post, has broken the dish, and let out the contents; he gapes with misery, his eyes run over with tears, and he scratches his head most ludicrously; while a half-famished child is devouring some of the smoking pieces of pudding.

Evening is on the banks of the New River, near Sadler's Wells, and includes the sign of Sir Hugh Myddleton's Head. A husband and wife are walking out to take the air; *he* is in suspicious position with the head and horns of a neighbouring cow; *she* is fatigued, portly and proud, and spiteful: there are other pedestrians. A proof of this plate, before the artist's name, or any inscription, and prior to the introduc-tion of the girl, (only three known,) was sold in 1825 for 50*l*.

Night, the fourth scene, is laid near Charing-cross, on Res-toration Day, (May 29,) when the streets were dressed with

---

* *Tom King's Coffee-house* was a common shed immediately beneath the portico of St. Paul's church, Covent Garden: and was "well-known to all gentlemen to whom beds are unknown." Fielding says: "What rake is ignorant of King's Coffee-house?" Tom's widow, Mrs. Moll King, continued landlady, and was often fined for keeping a disorderly house. At length she retired from business—and the pillory—to Hampstead, where she lived on her ill-earned gains, paid for a pew in church, was charitable at appointed seasons, and died in peace in 1747.

oak-boughs, especially the signs, and the hats of mirthful spirits. A Freemason, staggering from the tavern, assisted by a waiter, has been set down for Sir Thomas de Veel, a magistrate; a Xantippe showers upon him from her chamber window, an inodorous favour. There is a bonfire, through which the Salisbury Flying Coach, in attempting to pass, is overset and broken—said by Ireland to be a burlesque upon a right honourable peer, who was accustomed to drive three or four of his maid-servants into a deep water, and there leave them in the coach to shift for themselves.

A finished sketch, said to be Hogarth's first thought for *Morning*, was sold in Yates's sale in 1827, to Mr. Tayleure for 21*l*. The picture was purchased by Sir William Heathcote for 20 guineas; and *Night* for 27*l*. 6*s*. *Noon* was sold for 38*l*. 17*s*., and *Evening* for 39*l*. 18*s*., to the Duke of Ancaster, and are now possessed by Lord Gwydir: the four were exhibited at the British Gallery in 1814.

HOGARTH EMBELLISHES VAUXHALL GARDENS.

In 1728, Spring Garden, as Vauxhall was then called, was leased to Jonathan Tyers, to whose taste and spirit this old London resort owed much of its celebrity subsequent to the time of Addison and Sir Roger de Coverley. Tyers reopened the Gardens in 1732, with a grand *Ridotto al Fresco;* he next set up an organ in the orchestra, and in the grounds, in 1738, Roubilliac's statue of Handel, which is now in the committee-room of the Sacred Harmonic Society, at Exeter Hall.

Hogarth was now rich enough to take summer lodgings at Lambeth-terrace; the house in which he resided is still shown, and a vine pointed out which the painter planted. While living there, he became acquainted with Tyers, of Vauxhall Gardens; and for the season of 1739, Hogarth designed the silver ticket of admission: the obverse bore the number, name of the holder, and date; and the reverse a figure of Euterpe. Hogarth next suggested to Tyers the embellishment of the Gardens with paintings; the principal objects in them having previously consisted of whimsical proofs of skill in mechanics, and model pictures, and arbours covered and paved with tiles. For the pavilions which Tyers had built, Hogarth drew the four parts of the Day, which Hayman copied; Hogarth also painted for the vestibule portraits of Henry the Eighth and Anne Boleyn. The print bears the lines by Allan Ramsay,

"Here struts old pious Harry," &c.

A proof has been sold for 13*l*. 2*s*. 6*d*. The portraits were said to be Frederick Prince of Wales and Lady Vane. For this assistance, which seems to have been gratuitous, Tyers presented Hogarth with a *Gold Ticket*, or perpetual admission: it bears on its obverse "Hogarth," and beneath it, "*In perpetuam beneficii memoriam;*" on the reverse are two figures, surrounded with the motto, "*Virtus voluptas felices una.*" This Ticket, (for the admission of six persons, or "one coach,") was last used for admission in 1836: it is now in the possession of Mr. Frederick Gye, who purchased it for 20*l*. After Hogarth's decease, the Ticket, or Medallion, remained in the hands of his widow, who bequeathed it to Mrs. Mary Lewis, who left it to Mr. R. F. Hart, chief clerk of the Duchy of Cornwall Office, and second Clerk of the Kitchen to George III. It next became the property of Captain Tuck, of Lambeth. The design has been engraved; and the original copper-plate, with 30 impressions, was bought by Evans, at Wilkinson's sale, in 1826, for 13*s*. only.

Such is the generally received version of Hogarth's introduction to Tyers; but Mr. J. Phillips, the nephew-in-law of Mr. Hart, tells the anecdote as related to him by Mrs. Lewis, as follows: On passing the tavern one morning, which was then kept by Jonathan Tyers, and open, together with the Gardens, as a place of recreation daily, Hogarth saw Tyers, and observing that he looked particularly melancholy, said: "How now, master Tyers, why so sad this morning?" "Sad times, master Hogarth, and my reflexions were on a subject not likely to brighten a man's countenance," said Tyers; "I was thinking, do you know, which would be likely to prove the easiest death—hanging or drowning." "Oh," replied Hogarth, "is it come to that?" "Very nearly, I assure you," said Tyers. "Then," replied Hogarth, "the remedy you think of applying is not likely to mend the matter—don't hang or drown to-day. I have a thought that may save the necessity of either, and will communicate it to you to-morrow morning: call at my house in Leicester-fields." The interview took place, and the result was the embellishment of the Gardens by Hogarth, who associated himself with Hayman in the work.

These paintings were chiefly in the sweeps of pavilions, or supper-boxes, in the Gardens; they had little of Hogarth's genius; and they were rarely seen by the company, for want of sufficient light. Many of the pictures perished; but such as remained were disposed of at the sale of the moveable property in the Gardens, in October, 1841.

Twenty-four pictures by Hogarth and Hayman produced but small sums: they had mostly been upon the premises since 1742; the canvass was nailed to boards, and much obscured by dirt. By Hogarth: Drunken Man, 4*l*. 4*s*.; a Woman pulling out an Old Man's grey hairs, 3*l*. 3*s*.; Jobson and Nell in the *Devil to Pay*, 4*l*. 4*s*.; the Happy Family, 3*l*. 15*s*.; Children at Play, 4*l*. 11*s*. 6*d*. By Hayman: Children Bird's-nesting, 5*l*. 10*s*.; Minstrels, 3*l*.; the Enraged Husband, 4*l*. 4*s*.; the Bridal Day, 6*l*. 6*s*.; Blindman's Buff, 3*l*. 8*s*.; Prince Henry and Falstaff, 7*l*.; Scene from the Rake's Progress, 9*l*. 15*s*.; Merry-making, 1*l*. 12*s*.; the Jealous Husband, 4*l*.; Card-party, 6*l*.; Children's Party, 4*l*. 15*s*.; Battledore and Shuttlecock, 1*l*. 10*s*.; the Doctor, 4*l*. 14*s*. 6*d*.; Cherry-bob, 2*l*. 15*s*.; the Storming of Seringapatam, 8*l*. 10*s*; Neptune and Britannia, 8*l*. 10*s*.; Four busts of Simpson, the celebrated Master of the Ceremonies, were sold for 10*s*.; and a bust of his royal shipmate, William IV., 19*s*.*

ROSAMOND'S POND.

This noted London haunt was a sheet of water in the south-west corner of St. James's Park,† "long consecrated to disastrous love and elegiac poetry." The earliest notice to be found of it is in an Exchequer payment in 1612: the pond was filled up in 1770. We find it mentioned as a notorious place of intrigue in the love comedies of Otway, Congreve, Farquhar, Southerne, Colley Cibber, and by Addison and Pope:

> This the Beau-monde shall from the Mall survey
> * * * * * *
> This the fleet lover shall for Venus take,
> And send up vows from Rosamanda's Lake.
> *Rape of the Lock.*

It was painted by Hogarth, about the year 1740, and the picture is now in Mr. Willett's collection. It was engraved for this gentleman about five-and-twenty years since, when only

---

* See a minute description of Vauxhall Gardens in *Curiosities of London*, pp. 745—748. The property remained in Tyers's family until 1828. The site is now built upon: a School of Art was founded upon a portion of the ground in June, 1860; the Prince of Wales laying the first stone of the edifice, and this being His Royal Highness's first act of the kind.

† Another pond in the Green Park, nearly opposite Coventry House, bore the name of Rosamond down to 1840, when it was filled up.

one hundred impressions were taken, but not one of them was published. Hogarth also painted a smaller view of Rosamond's Pond, of a cabinet size, likewise in the collection of Mr. Willett, with the receipt for 1*l.* 7*s.* (the sum charged by the painter), in the handwriting of Mrs. Hogarth. These views are in part followed by George Cruikshank, in one of his Illustrations to Ainsworth's tale of the *Miser's Daughter,* in No. 1. of *Ainsworth's Magazine,* 1842.

THE ENRAGED MUSICIAN—THE DISTRESSED POET.

The design of the first scene, which it deafens one to look at, has been variously explained. The hero of the print has been set down for Cervetto; but according to others, Dr. Arne. John Ireland attributes it to John Festin, who was an eminent player of the German flute and hautboy, and was a fashionable teacher of music. Mr. Dallaway says, Signor Castracci was intended. Ireland relates that to each of his pupils, Festin dedicated an hour a-day. "At nine o'clock, one morning, (said he,) I waited upon my Lord Spencer, but his Lordship being out of town, from him I went to Mr. V———n, now Lord V———n; it was so early that he was not arisen. I went into his chamber, and opening a window, sat down on the window-seat. Before the rails was a fellow playing upon the hautboy. A man with a barrowful of onions offered the piper an onion if he would play him a tune; that ended, he offered a second for a second tune; the same for a third, and was going on; but this was too much—I could not bear it—it angered my very soul. 'Zounds,' said I, 'stop here! This fellow is ridiculing my profession—he is playing on the hautboy for onions!'"

Upon this story Hogarth has wrought out his design, in the year 1741: the original sketch was in chiaroscuro, and was sold at S. Ireland's sale in 1801, for four guineas: thence it passed into the collection of Mr. Hall Chambers, of Southampton. Among the performers of the discord in the street, are a dustman, shouting "Dust, ho! dust, ho!" the fishmonger crying, "Flounders!" a milkmaid, "Milk above! Milk below!" a female ballad-singer chanting the doleful story of "the Lady's Fall;" the singer's child and a neighbouring parrot screaming a chorus; a little French drummer remorselessly beating a ruba-dub-dub, singing all the time; two cats squalling in the gutter-tiles; a doghowling most dismally; while an urchin-sweep, all black save his teeth and the whites of his eyes, from the top of a chimney-pot, proclaims that his job is done. Then we have a crowd of instrumentalists: a postman with his horn, a strolling hautboy player, a dustman with his bell, a paviour with his rammer, a knife-grinder grinding a butcher's cleaver; and "John Long, Pewterer," (over the door,) with the clink of twenty hammers, striking metal, accompanies the medley of out-door discords.

This picture was engraved with great success; and a copy of the plate, with that of "the Distressed Poet,"—both *first states*, in Baker's sale, 1825, produced nine guineas.

The original of "the Distressed Poet" has been set down as Theobald, the editor of Shakspeare's Plays; and the inveterate assailant of Pope. The painting was given by Hogarth to Mrs. Draper the celebrated midwife, and sold at her death for five guineas to Mr. Ward, at whose sale it was purchased by the first Lord Grosvenor for fourteen guineas; it is now in the Grosvenor Gallery. The scene of it was the house of Mr. Huggins, in St. Martin's-lane, although, by an error of the engraver, in reversing, the church of St. Martin appears on the right-hand instead of the left. Nichols says: "the musician was undoubtedly Castrucci; the wretched hautboy player was at that time well known about the streets."

THE MARRIAGE À LA MODE PICTURES.

This series of six pictures, for invention, composition, drawing, colouring, and character, are the most important and highly wrought of Hogarth's satiric comedies. Mr. Thackeray has thus emphatically and powerfully told their impressive story of domestic misery.

The care and method with which the moral grounds of these pictures are laid is as remarkable as the wit and skill of the observing and dexterous artist. He has to describe the negotiation for a marriage pending between the daughter of a rich citizen Alderman and young Lord Viscount Squanderfield, the dissipated son of a gouty old Earl. Pride and pomposity appear in every accessory surrounding the Earl. He sits in gold lace and velvet—as how should such an Earl wear anything but velvet and gold lace? His coronet is everywhere—on his footstool on which reposes one gouty toe turned out; on the sconces and looking-glasses; on the dogs; on his lordship's very crutches; on his great chair of state, and the great baldaquin behind him; under which he sits pointing majestically to his pedigree, which shows that his race is sprung from the loins of William the Conqueror, and confronting the old Alderman from the City, who has mounted his sword for the occasion, and wears his Alderman's chain, and has brought a bag-full of money, mortgage-deeds, and thousand pound notes, for the arrangement of the transaction pending between them. Whilst the steward (a methodist, therefore a hypocrite and cheat, for Hogarth scorned a papist and a dissenter,) is negotiating between the old couple, their children sit together, united but apart. My lord is admiring his countenance in the glass, while his bride is twiddling her marriage-ring on her pocket-handkerchief; and listening with rueful countenance to Counsellor Silvertongue, who has been drawing the settlements. The girl is pretty, but the painter, with a curious watchfulness, has taken care to give her a likeness to her father, as in the young Viscount's face you see a resemblance to the Earl, his noble sire. The sense of the coronet pervades the picture, as it is supposed to do the mind of its wearer. The pictures round the room are sly hints indicating the situation of the parties about to marry. A martyr is led to the fire; Andromeda is offered to sacrifice; Judith is going to slay Holofernes. Here is the ancestor of the house, (in the picture it is the Earl himself as a young man,) with a comet over his head, indicating that the career of the family is to be brilliant and brief.

In the second picture, the old Lord must be dead, for Madam has now the Countess's coronet over her bed and the toilet-glass, and sits listening to that dangerous Counsellor Silvertongue, whose portrait now actually hangs up in her room; whilst the Counsellor takes his ease on the sofa by her side, evidently the familiar of the house, and the confidant of the mistress. My lord takes his pleasure elsewhere than at home, whither he returns jaded and tipsy from the Rose, to find his wife yawning in her drawing-room, her whist-party over, and the daylight streaming in; or he amuses himself with the very worst company abroad, whilst his wife sits at home listening to foreign singers, or wastes her money at auctions, or worse still, seeks amusements at masquerades. The dismal end is known. My lord draws upon the Counsellor, who kills him, and is apprehended while endeavouring to escape. My lady goes back per force to the Alderman in the City, and faints upon reading Counsellor Silvertongue's dying speech at Tyburn, where the Counsellor has been executed for sending his lordship out of the world.

The six pictures are—1. The Marriage Contract. 2. Shortly after Marriage. 3. The Visit to the Quack Doctor. 4. The Countess's Dressing-room. 5. The Duel and the Death of the Earl. 6. The Death of the Countess.*

These pictures were exhibited gratis to the public by Hogarth, in Cock's auction-rooms, now Robins's, in the Piazza, Covent Garden.

* In this Plate occurs a curious instance of Hogarth's attention to most minute traits of character: where, as a further instance of the avarice and miserable penury of the Alderman, who is stripping his dying daughter of her trinkets, a close observer will perceive, that the servant-lad is clothed in one of his master's old coats, which has been shortened, and that the cloth cut off is turned, and made into new cuffs; this is more plainly seen in the picture, by the contrast of the colour of them with the faded hue of the coat.

In 1841, Messrs. Smith, the eminent print-sellers, of Lisle-street, had the good fortune to discover in the country a duplicate set of the *Marriage à la Mode* pictures, which appear to have escaped the researches of all the writers on Hogarth's works. They are evidently the finished sketches from which he afterwards painted the pictures in the National Gallery, which are more highly wrought. The backgrounds of these pictures are very much subdued, which gives a greater importance to the figures. They are now in the collection of the late H. R. Willett, Esq., of Merly House, Dorsetshire. They are painted in an exceedingly free and sketchy manner; and are considered to have been most probably painted at the same time as the four pictures of *The Election*, now in the Soanean Museum, the execution of which they very much resemble. There is a considerable number of variations between these and the National Gallery pictures; and such differences throw much light upon the painter's technical execution, which is somewhat disputed. "Although in some respects (says a critic) rather sketchily handled, they are not painted feebly; and if they cannot be called highly finished, these productions are worthy to rank as cabinet pictures."

Dr. Waagen says of these masterly works:—"These six pictures are in my opinion the most ingenious and most successful of his series. These pictures are well known by the engravings, and the witty descriptions of Lichtenberg. The old and new history of the lofty but hollow genealogical tree, with the dirty but well filled money-bag, with its consequences, is here represented with a most extraordinary profusion of invention, observation, humour, and dramatic power. But what surprised me is the eminent merit of these works as paintings, since Hogarth's own countryman, Horace Walpole, said he had but little merit as a painter. All the most delicate heads of his humour are here marked with consummate skill and freedom, and every other part executed with the same decision, and for the most part with ease. Though the colouring on the whole, and the pictures, as they are almost wholly painted in dead colours, with hardly any glazing, have more the look of distemper than of oil-paintings, the colouring of the flesh is often powerful; and the others, very broken, are disposed with so much refined feeling for harmonious effect, that in colouring they stand in a far higher rank than numerous productions of the most modern English School, with all glaring, inharmonious colours.

Only the fifth picture, the Death of the Husband, has lost its chiaro-obscuro by turning dark. For these six pictures Hogarth received only the miserable pittance of 110*l*."

SALE OF THE MARRIAGE À LA MODE PICTURES.

In 1750, Hogarth advertised for sale these six noble pictures by a strange plan, the result of which is thus related by Mr. Lane, who unexpectedly became the public purchaser of them.

The sale was to take place by a kind of auction, where each bidder was to write on a ticket the sum he was disposed to give, with his name subscribed to it. These papers were to be received by Hogarth for the space of one month, on the last day of which, at twelve o'clock, the highest bidder was to be the purchaser. The public, however, disliked the plan, and kept aloof: indeed, there seemed a combination against Hogarth. Mr. Lane relates that on June 6, 1750, which was to decide the fate of this capital work, when he arrived at the Golden Head, in Leicester-square, instead of finding the study full of noble and great personages—as at the sale of the *Harlot's Progress*,—he only found Hogarth, and his friend, Dr. Parsons, Secretary to the Royal Society. Hogarth had put on his best wig, strutted away one hour, fumed away two more, and in revenge muttered : "No picture-dealer shall be allowed to bid." Mr. Lane had bid 110*l*.; no one had arrived; and ten minutes before twelve, Mr. Lane told Hogarth he would make the pounds guineas. The clock struck, and Hogarth wished Lane joy of his purchase. Dr. Parsons was very much disturbed, and attributed the failure of the sale to the early hour, when Lane offered the painter till three o'clock, to find a better bidder. This was accepted, when Parsons proposed to make it public, which Lane forbade. "At one o'clock," Hogarth said : " I shall trespass no longer on your generosity; you are the proprietor, and if you are pleased with the purchase, I am abundantly so with the purchaser." Thus were sold these admirable pictures, in frames worth four guineas each ; yet no one felt them to be worth more than 90*l*. 6*s*. In less than half a century, (in 1797,) Colonel Cawthorne, who inherited the pictures from Lane, sold them to Mr. Angerstein for 1,381*l*.

Five years previously, on Jan. 25, 1745, Hogarth had offered for sale the six paintings of the *Harlot's Progress*, the eight paintings of the *Rake's Progress*, the *Four Times of the Day*, and the *Strolling Actresses*, on condition that on the day of the sale, every bidder, previously entered, should be the purchaser, if none other appeared within five minutes, and each bidding to be in gold. But, from some cause, the scheme failed ; and the painter obtained only 427*l*. 7*s*. for his nineteen pictures ! "More," says Cunningham, "has been since given, over and over again, for a single painting, than Hogarth obtained for all his paintings put together !"

The strangeness of the plan had much to do with the failure of the sale ; and, as if to make assurance doubly sure of this result, the painter's card of admission to his sale was a piece of satire and spleen, entitled "The Battle of the Pictures."

"MARRIAGE À LA MODE," AND "THE CLANDESTINE MARRIAGE."

The publication of the prints of Marriage à la Mode suggested the novel of *the Marriage Act*, a novel by D. Shebbeare ; and of the *Clandestine Marriage*, the joint production of Garrick and the elder Colman. In the Prologue to this excellent comedy, Garrick thus expressed his regard for his friend :

> Poets and painters, who from nature draw
> Their best and richest stores, have made this law :
> That each should neighbourly assist his brother,
> And steal with decency from one another.
> To night your matchless Hogarth gives the thought,
> Which from his canvas to the stage is brought.
> And who so fit to warm the poet's mind,
> As he who pictured morals and mankind ?
> But not the same their characters and scenes ;
> Both labour for one end, by different means :
> Each, as it suits him, takes a separate road,
> Their own great object, *Marriage à la Mode!*
> Where titles deign with cits to have and hold,
> And change rich blood for more substantial gold !
> And honour'd trade from interest turns aside
> To hazard happiness for titled pride.
> The painter dead, yet still he charms the eye ;
> While England lives his fame can never die :
> But he, "who struts his hour upon the stage,"
> Can scarce extend his fame for half an age ;
> Nor pen nor pencil can the actor save,
> The art, and artist, share one common grave.*

---

* This idea, (says Nichols), originally occurred in Colley Cibber's *Apology*. From thence it was transplanted by Lloyd into his celebrated

A HAPPY MARRIAGE.

Soon after the appearance of the *Marriage à la Mode*, Hogarth projected, by way of counterpart, a *Happy Marriage*, in six plates; but he does not seem to have designed more than the first scene. The time supposed was immediately after the return from church. The scene lay in the hall of an old country mansion: on one side were seated the married couple, and behind them a group of their young friends of both sexes were breaking bride-cake over the heads of the happy pair. In front the father of the bride was drinking with a seeming roar of exultation, to the future happiness of her and her husband. By the father's side was a table covered with refreshments; under the screen of the hall were rustic musicians in grotesque attitudes, together with servants, tenants, &c. Through the arch by which the room was entered, the eye was led along a passage into a kitchen: before the dripping-pan stood a well-fed parson, in his gown and cassock, with his watch in hand, giving directions to a cook, arranged in white, and basting a haunch of venison. This luxurious episode was the most laboured portion of the design: the bride was unsuccessful. Nichols says: "The painter found himself out of his element in the parlour, and therefore, hastened in quest of ease and amusement to the kitchen fire. Yet, Hogarth had succeeded so well in the refined beauty of the bride, at least, in his own opinion, that he carried the canvas in triumph to Garrick, who condemned it as showing the painter's ignorance of the graceful, and so the scheme of the series of pictures was given up; the single sketch, in part completed, was given to Mrs. Garrick."

HOGARTH'S BENEFACTIONS TO THE FOUNDLING HOSPITAL.

That Tenterden Steeple was the cause of Goodwin Sands does not appear a whit more strange than that in the Foundling Hospital originated the Royal Academy of Arts. Yet such was the case. The Hospital was established by Royal Charter, granted in 1739, to Thomas Coram, (master of a trading vessel,) "for the reception, maintenance, and edu-

poem entitled the *Actor*. Lying thus in the way of Garrick, he took it up for the prologue—already quoted. Lastly, Mr. Sheridan, in his beautiful Monody, condescended to borrow it, only because it spared him the labour of unlocking the richer storehouse of his own imagination.

cation, of exposed and deserted young children." The Governors first opened a house in Hatton Garden, in 1740-1 : here the establishment remained until 1754, when it was removed to the present Hospital, built by Jacobson, in Guilford-street facing Lamb's Conduit-street. The expenses of the institution were then more than five times the amount of the income. The Governors next applied to Parliament, who voted them 10,000*l*. One of the earliest "Governors and Guardians" who assisted Coram in his good work, was Hogarth, who joined with other eminent artists of the day in ornamenting several of the apartments of the new Hospital, which must otherwise, for want of funds, have remained without decoration. Hogarth, by the charter for incorporating the Hospital, appears as one of its constituent members : nor did he hold this appointment to be merely nominal, for we find him subscribing his money, and attending the Courts or General Meetings at the Hospital. The charter authorised the Governors to appoint persons to ask for alms on behalf of the Charity, and to receive subscriptions : and the first artistical work of Hogarth in aid of this object was to prepare a "head piece" to a Power of Attorney drawn up for the purpose.

The principal figure in the design is that of Captain Coram with the charter under his arm. Before him a Beadle carries an infant, whose mother having dropped a dagger, with which she might have been momentarily tempted to destroy her child, kneels at the feet of Coram, who looks benevolently upon her, as if to assure her that her offspring will be nursed and protected. On the dexter side of the print is a newborn infant, left close to a stream of water, which runs under the arch of a bridge. Near a gate, on a gentle eminence, a woman leaves another child; and in the distance is a village with a church. In the opposite corner are three boys coming out of a door with the King's arms over it, carrying emblems of their future employment; one poises a plummet, a second holds a trowel, and a third bears a card for combing wool. The next group wearing sailors' jackets and trousers, is headed by a lad elevating a mathematical instrument; in the next group is a lad bearing a rake, in the uniform of the school. And in the foreground are three little girls, carrying a spinning-wheel, a sampler, and broom, indicative of female industry. In the distance is the sea, with ships in the offing, &c.

Such was Hogarth's first composition, the copper-plate of which is in possession of the Hospital. In May, 1740, a few weeks after the first opening of the Charity, Hogarth presented the Governors with a full-length portrait which he had painted of Coram. This fine portrait was beautifully engraved by M'Ardell: "a brilliant proof of this head, (says J. T. Smith,) in its finest possible condition, in my humble opinion surpasses anything in mezzotinto now extant." Sir Joshua Reynolds said that M'Ardell's prints would immortalize him, and that they would perpetuate his (Sir Joshua's) pictures when their colours should be faded and forgotten.

Hogarth says of this work: "The portrait which I painted with most pleasure, and in which I particularly wished to excel, was that of Captain Coram for the Foundling Hospital; and," (he adds in allusion to his detractors as a portrait-painter,) "if I am so wretched an artist as my enemies assert, it is somewhat strange that this, which was one of the first I painted the size of life, should stand the test of twenty years' competition, and be generally thought the best portrait in the place, notwithstanding the first painters in the kingdom exerted all their talents to vie with it." *

In 1741, when the Governors opened their house in Hatton Garden, near the Charity School, Hogarth painted an emblematic shield, which was put up over the doorway: this sign has not been preserved, but it is thought to have been of similar character, if not actually the same, as the Arms of the Hospital presented to the Governors, by the Authorities of the Heralds' College, in 1747, and stated to have been designed by Hogarth: it is technically described as follows:

"Party per fesse, Azure and Vert," a young child lying naked, and exposed, extending its right hand proper. In chief a Crescent Argent between two Mullets of six points Or; and for a Crest on a Wreath of the Colours, a Lamb Argent, holding in its mouth a Sprig of Thyme proper, supported on the dexter side by a terminal figure of a Woman full of Nipples proper, with a Mantle Vert, the term Argent being the emblem of Liberty, represented by Britannia holding in her right hand upon a staff proper, a Cap Argent, and habited in a Vert Azure, girt with belt Or, the under garment Gules." Motto, "Help."

The idea of embellishing the walls of the new Hospital originated with Hogarth, associated with Ryebrack the sculptor, Zincke the enameller, and Jacobson the architect, as a Committee, to meet annually on the 5th of November. Among the painters who presented pictures were Hayman, Wills,

* The rival portraits here alluded to, are George the Second, Patron of the Foundation, by Shackleton; Lord Dartmouth, one of the Vice-Presidents, by Mr. Reynolds (afterwards Sir Joshua); Taylor White, Treasurer of the Hospital, in crayons, by Cotes; Mr. Milner and Mr. Jacobson, by Hudson; Dr. Mead, by Ramsay; Mr. Emmerson, by Highmore; and Francis l'anquier, by Wilson.

Highmore, Hudson, Ramsay, Lambert, Wilson, Pyne, &c. The Committee meetings grew into an annual dinner at the Hospital, at which the leading artists and patrons of the arts were usually present. Meanwhile the donations in paintings provided an attractive exhibition : a visit to the Foundling became a fashionable morning lounge in the reign of George II.; and the pictures to this day represent the state of British art previously to the epoch when George III. first countenanced the historical talent of West; and the *éclat* thus excited in favour of the Arts suggested the annual exhibition of the united Artists, which was the precursor of the Royal Academy.

Hogarth was not only the principal contributor, but the leader of his brother artists in all that related to the embellishment of the Hospital. On May 1st, 1750, the subscription for his picture of *The March to Finchley* being closed, and 1,843 chances subscribed for, Hogarth gave the remaining 167 chances to the Hospital, and the fortunate number for the picture being among these tickets, the prize picture was delivered to the Governors, and to this day hangs in the Committee-room. It is related in the *Gentleman's Magazine*, that "*a Lady* was the possessor of the fortunate number, and intended to present it to the Foundling Hospital; but that some person having suggested that a door would be opened to scandal, were any of her sex to make such a present, it was given to Hogarth, on the condition that it should be presented in his own name."

Hogarth next presented his picture of *Moses before Pharaoh's Daughter*, which he painted for the Hospital, according to a conjoint agreement between Hayman, Highmore, Wills, and himself, that they should each fill up one of the compartments of the court-room with pictures uniform in size, and of appropriate subjects from Scripture. The Hospital thus received from Hogarth a picture in each of the styles of painting which he had attempted.

It is singular that Hogarth, who, throughout his life, had uniformly opposed the establishment of a Public Academy of Arts, should, by encouraging and concentrating at the Foundling Hospital an exhibition of the works of British artists, have himself promoted the consummation of the object which he had all along deprecated.

Charles Lamb has remarked that Hogarth seemed to take particular delight in children; and that this characteristic was not the mere ideality of a painter, but emanated from his generous heart, is proved by the following circumstance. It was the practice of the Hospital to nurse the *infant* children of the establishment in the country; and in or about 1760, the Governors, at the request of Hogarth, sent several of the poor infants to Chiswick, where the painter resided, he engaging, along with Mrs. Hogarth, to see them properly taken care of; and the annexed is a copy of his bill for the maintenance and clothing of two of these children, who were returned to the Hospital by Mrs. Hogarth, at her husband's death in 1764:

FOUNDLING HOSPITAL.

Paid by Mr. Wm. Hogarth for the nursing of Susan Wyndham and Mary Woolaston from the 30th October, 1760, to the 1st of October, 1762, twelve pounds—and for their shoes and stockings six shillings and sixpence.

Total 12*l*. 6*s*. 6*d*.

Rec^d the contents pr Wm Hogarth.

Hogarth was associated with John Wilkes in the same work of benevolence at the Foundling Hospital, and frequently met him at the same board as Governors; but after the quarrel between them, they ceased to attend in their places, "as if each was afraid of meeting the other, even within the walls of Charity herself."

"THE MARCH TO FINCHLEY."

This celebrated picture hangs in the Committee-room of the Foundling Hospital. In the composition, Hogarth supposes the approach of Prince Charles, in the fatal 'Forty-five, to summon the heroes of London to the field; and the character of the contest is expressed in the central group of the composition, where a handsome young grenadier stands, in ludicrous indecision, between his Catholic and Protestant doxies.

The scene is laid at Tottenham Court turnpike; the King's Head, Adam and Eve, and turnpike-house, in full view; beyond which are discovered parties of the Guards, with baggage, &c., marching towards Highgate—and a beautiful prospect of the country; the sky finely painted. The picture, considered together, affords a view of a military march; but the rear, in its confusion, is the humorous foreground. Very minute accounts of this painting were written by Mr. Justice Welsh, the intimate friend and companion of Hogarth; and by Mr. Bonnell Thornton, the well-known Essayist. These are much too long for quotation; but we may notice that a baggage-waggon, with its load of women, babies, knapsacks, and camp-kettles—accompanied by disorderly soldiers, their wives, children, and sweethearts—occupy the middle way. The episodal groupes are very effective. Among the characters is the gentleman encouraging the boxers: this is Lord Albemarle Bertie. A little looker-on, with clenched fists, is Jockey James, a frequent attendant on boxing-matches. The pieman, grenadier, chimney-sweep, and fifer, are said to be portraits: the latter was noticed by the Duke of Cumberland, and was promoted to a pair of colours.

The painting was disposed of by a lottery, as already described. It was engraved in 1750 by Luke Sullivan: a finished print, in 1825, was sold for 36*l.* 15*s.*

This print of English soldiery is oddly dedicated to the King of Prussia. Before publication it was inscribed to George II., and the print was taken to St. James's Palace, for royal approbation. But the King expected a much more heroic scene, and could not appreciate the painter's humour. His first question addressed to the lord in waiting was— "Pray, who is this Hogarth?" "A painter, your majesty." "I hate *bainting and boetry!* Neither the one nor the other ever did any good! Does the fellow mean to laugh at my Guards?" "The picture, an' please your majesty, must undoubtedly be considered as a burlesque!" "What! a *bainter* burlesque a soldier? He deserves to be picketed for his insolence! Take his trumpery out of my sight." The print was returned to the artist, who, mortified at such a reception of what he justly considered his principal work, immediately altered the inscription, inserting, instead of the King of England, the *King of Prussia, an encourager of the arts and sciences!*

It was then objected that an English print should be inscribed to a foreign potentate, when Hogarth replied, "We'll soon remedy that," and directed the printer to take off a few impressions, covering the dedication with fan-paper. John Ireland received three of these impressions without the dedication, from Mrs. Lewis, who, at the time of their being taken, and until Mrs. Hogarth's death, lived with her in Leicester-square.

A description of the original picture was published soon after it was granted: it opened with this sly shaft at the old masters:—

"As you desire my sentiments on Mr. *Hogarth's* Picture, I shall begin with pointing out what is most defective. Its first and greatest Fault then is its being too new, and having too great a resemblance to the Objects it represents; if this appears a Paradox, you ought to take particular care of confessing it. This Picture has got too much of that Lustre, of that despicable Freshness which we discover in Nature, and which is never seen in the Cabinets of the Curious. Time has not yet obscured it with that venerable Smoak, that sacred cloud, which will one day conceal it from the profane eyes of the Vulgar, that its beauties may only be seen by those who are initiated into the Mysteries of Art. These are its most remarkable faults, and I am now going to give you an idea of the subject, &c. * * * Mr. Hogarth, who lets no opportunity escape him of observing the Pictorial Scenes which numerous Assemblies frequently furnish, has not failed to represent them on the Spot where he has drawn the scene of his Picture. The Painter is remarkable for a particular sagacity in seizing a thousand little circumstances which escape the observation of the greatest part of the Spectators; and it is a Collection of a Number of these Circumstances which has composed, enriched, and diversified his work. The scene is placed," &c.

A visit to the Foundling Hospital will enable the reader to compare the picture as it now is, with this criticism upon its merits when it was fresh from the master's easel. Time has dealt gently with this fine work, for Hogarth painted with a safer medium than that used by his immediate successors, but he still is quietly engaged in the process of "smoking," which the critic has anticipated, and the painter himself, in one of his well-known subjects, symbolised.

PORTRAIT OF LORD LOVAT.

This Rebel Lord of 1745 was painted by Hogarth, who also engraved some small prints of Lovat's trial. He was a man of parts, but of infamous character. He had the folly, at the age of eighty, to enter into the Rebellion, upon a promise from the Pretender, that he would make him Duke of Fraser. He was taken in Scotland, and brought to London to be tried. Hogarth met Lovat at St. Alban's, where he rested two or three days: here Hogarth certainly drew his portrait. "I took this likeness," said he, "when Simon Fraser was relating on his fingers the numbers of the rebel forces—such a chieftain had so many men, &c. He received me with much cordiality—embraced me when I entered, and kissed me, though he was under the hands of the barber. The muscles of his neck appeared of unusual strength—more so than I had ever seen."

In 1827, Mr. Horatio Rodd had on sale a portrait of Lord Lovat, 30 in. by 25, which was brought from Dr. Webster, a physician, of St. Alban's, who attended Lovat while he rested there. Mr. Rodd states, in his Catalogue : "The short stay of Lord Lovat at St. Alban's, allowed the artist but scanty opportunity of providing the materials for a complete picture; hence some carpenter was employed on the instant to glue together some deal-board, and plane one side, which is evident from the back being in the usual rough state in which the plank leaves the saw-pit. The painting, from the thinness of the priming ground, bears evident proof of the haste with which the portrait was accomplished. In the upper corner are satirical heraldic insignia, allusive to the artist's idea of his future destiny." This picture is engraved in Hone's *Table Book*, vol. i. p. 238. It should here be stated that Nichols says : "Hogarth met Lord Lovat at *Barnet*," not St. Alban's.

Hogarth etched Lovat's portrait in aquafortis. When the plate was finished, a print-seller offered its weight in gold for it. The second impressions are marked, *Price One Shilling*. The impressions could not be taken off fast enough to meet the demand, though the rolling-press was at work all night for a week together: it produced at the rate of about twelve pounds per day for several weeks.

HOGARTH FIRST SEES DR. JOHNSON.

Johnson was a frequent visitor at the house of Richardson, the novelist, in Salisbury-court,* Fleet-street, whither, one day, came Hogarth, soon after the execution of Dr. Cameron, for having taken arms for the house of Stuart, in 1745-6; and being a warm partisan of George the Second, he observed to Richardson, that certainly there must have been some very unfavourable circumstances lately discovered in this particular case, which had induced the King to approve of an execution for rebellion so long after the time when it was committed, as this had the appearance of putting a man to death in cold blood, and was very unlike his Majesty's usual clemency. While he was talking, he perceived a person standing at a window in the room, shaking his head, and rolling himself

* In Salisbury-court (now square,) Richardson wrote his *Pamela*, and printed his own novels; his printing-office being at the top of the court, now No. 76, Fleet-street. Goldsmith was once Richardson's "reader." Richardson was visited here by Hogarth, Dr. Johnson, Dr. Young; Secker, Archbishop of Canterbury; and Mrs. Barbauld, when a playful child. *Curiosities of London*, p. 306.

about in a very ridiculous manner. He concluded that he was an idiot, whom his relations had put under the care of Mr. Richardson, as a very good man. To his great surprise, however, this figure stalked forward, to where he and Mr. Richardson were sitting, and all at once took up the argument, bursting out into an invective against George the Second, as one who, upon all occasions, was unrelenting and barbarous : mentioning many instances ; particularly that when an officer of high rank had been acquitted by a court-martial, George the Second had with his own hand struck his name off the list. In short, he displayed such a power of eloquence, that Hogarth looked at him with astonishment, and actually imagined that this idiot had been at the moment inspired. Neither Hogarth nor Johnson were made known to each other at this interview.

"INDUSTRY AND IDLENESS."

In 1747, Hogarth gave to the world his twelve Plates alternating the results of Industry and Idleness, exemplified in the lives of two City Apprentices. He had been an apprentice himself, and knew from experience how hard it is to climb the ladder of life. Hogarth's own account of these prints is as follows :—

Industry and Idleness, exemplified in the conduct of two fellow-prentices ; where the one boy taking good courses, and pursuing those points for which he was put apprentice, becomes a valuable man and ornament to his country; whilst the other, giving way to idleness, naturally falls into poverty, and most commonly ends fatally, as is expressed in the last print. As these prints were intended more for use than ornament, they were done in a way that might bring them within the purchase of those whom they might most concern; and lest any part should be mistaken, a description of each print is engraved thereon * * * * * These twelve prints were calculated for the instruction of young people, and everything addressed to them is fully described in words as well as figures ; yet to foreigners a translation of the mottoes, the intention of the story, and some little description of each print may be necessary. To this may be added a slight account of our customs, as boys being usually bound for seven years, &c. Suppose the whole story was made into a kind of tale, describing in episode the nature of a night-cellar, a marrow-bone concert, a Lord Mayor's show, &c. These prints I have found sell much more rapidly at Christmas than at any other season.*

The hint for this series of prints, (says Nichols,) was evidently taken from the old comedy of *Eastward Hoe*, by Jonson,

---

* In 1851, the Christmas pantomime at Drury-lane Theatre was *Harlequin Hogarth ; or the Two London 'Prentices.*

Chapman, and Marston, reprinted in Dodsley's collection of Old Plays.

Walpole considers that these plates have more merit in their intention than their execution; but he allows that the scenes of Bedlam and the gaming-house are inimitable representations of our serious follies, or unavoidable woes; the concern shown by the Lord Mayor, when the companion of his childhood is brought before him as a criminal, is a touching picture, and big with humane admonition and reflection.

Hogarth's clever suggestion that the story of the two Apprentices should be wrought into a tale, does not appear to have been worked out; but in the following year appeared an explanation of the Moral of these Prints, sold for one shilling, at Addison's Head, in Fleet-street, and described in the titlepage as "a more proper present to be given to the Chamber of London, at the binding and enrolling an apprentice, than any other book whatever."

There are several portraits in these Plates. In Plate 1 is a figure of Philip in the Tub, a well-known beggar and cripple, who was a constant epithalamist at weddings in London. In Plate 8, the scene is Fishmongers' Hall, and the clergyman over his soup is Mr. Platell, curate of Barnet. In Plate 11 is Tiddy Doll, the well-known vendor of gingerbread. All the passages of Scripture applicable to the different scenes were selected for Hogarth by his friend, the Rev. Arnold King.

9. A scene in the Blood Bowl-house, in Chick-lane, West Smithfield, a notorious haunt of thieves and prostitutes: it was subsequently "the Red Lion tavern," and looked over the open Fleet-ditch: it remained true to Hogarth's picture until 1844, when it was demolished, in forming the new Victoria-street. Nichols, however, tells us that "Blood Bowlhouse, where seldom passed a month without the commission of a murder," was in Blood Bowl-alley, down by the fishmonger's, near Water-lane, Fleet-street.

5. Cuckolds' Point, on the Rotherhithe bank of the Thames. "That's what you'll come to, my friend," says a waterman to the Idle Apprentice, pointing at the same time to a pirate hanging in chains near Executiondock. The reply of the Idle Apprentice is—he holds two of his fingers to his forehead by way of horns—" Cuckolds' Point, you ——."

12. The City Procession on Lord Mayor's Day entering Cheapside— the seats erected on the occasion and the canopied balcony at Saddlers' Hall, hung with tapestry, containing Frederick Prince of Wales, and his Princess, as spectators of the same. The state coach is the predecessor of the present civic coach.

In the Collection at Strawberry Hill were the studies with the pen, and worked with India-ink, for these Prints, which in many instances differ from them.

Some very appropriate use has been made of the *Industry*

and Idleness plates. Thus, in the Chamberlain's Office, at the Guildhall of London, in the very room where City apprentices sign their indentures, suggestively hangs a set of fine impressions of Hogarth's speaking plates. Their good seed has been extended to schools. Mr. John Adams, the schoolmaster, of Edmonton, had a set of these prints framed and hung up in the school-room; and once a month, after reading a lecture upon their examples of vice and virtue, Adams rewarded those boys who had conducted themselves well, and caned those who had behaved ill.

THE GATE OF CALAIS, AND THE ROAST BEEF OF OLD ENGLAND.

Soon after the peace of Aix-la-Chapelle, Hogarth paid a visit to France: his impressions on landing he tells in his own natural way. "The first time an Englishman goes from Dover to Calais, he must be struck with the different face of things at so little a distance. A farcical pomp of war, pompous parade of religion, and much bustle with very little business. To sum up all, poverty, slavery, and innate insolence, covered with an affectation of politeness, give you even here a true picture of the manners of the whole nation; nor are the priests less opposite to those of Dover, than the two shores. The friars are dirty, sleek, and solemn; the soldiery are lean, ragged, and tawdry; and as to the fish-women, their faces are absolute leather.

"As I was sauntering about, and observing them near the gate, which it seems was built by the English, when the place was in our possession, I remarked some appearance of the arms of England on the front. By this and idle curiosity, I was prompted to make a sketch of it, which being observed, I was taken into custody; but not attempting to conceal any of my sketches or memorandums, which were found to be merely those of a painter for his private use, without any relation to fortification, it was not thought necessary to send me back to Paris.[*] I was only closely confined to my own lodgings till the wind changed for England."

Walpole thus chronicles this incident in a letter to Sir Horace Mann, dated Dec. 15, 1748: "Hogarth has run a great risk since the Peace; he went to France, and was so imprudent as to be taking a sketch of the drawbridge at Calais. He was seized and carried to the governor, where he was forced to prove his vocation by producing several *caricatures* of the French, particularly a scene of the shore, with an im-

---

[*] It has been said that Hogarth never went further into France than Calais; this proves he had reached Paris.—*J. Ireland.*

mense piece of beef landing for the Lion d'Argent, the English inn at Calais, and several hungry friars following it. They were much diverted with his drawings, and dismissed him." This is not quite correct; for, when the wind suited, he was put on board in a manner calculated to embitter his feelings. Two guards accompanied him, and after having insolently twirled him round and round like a top, on the deck, told him he might proceed on his voyage without further molestation. He arrived at Dover deeply incensed; he then proceeded to the house of his friend, Mr. Gostling, at Canterbury, where he slept that night.

From the evidence of Hayman, the painter, and Cheere, the sculptor, who accompanied Hogarth to France, his conduct, while there, was very indiscreet. He was dissatisfied with all he saw; was clamorously rude in the streets. A tattered bag, or a pair of silk stockings with holes in them, drew from him a torrent of imprudent observation: he was advised to be more cautious, but he laughed at such admonition, and treated the offerer of it as unworthy of residence in a free country.

Hogarth had no sooner reached home than he set about avenging the affront which had been offered to him,—by a design which he called "The Roast Beef of Old England." Walpole observes that in this piece, though it has great merit, "the caricatura is carried to excess;" it is certainly not one of his happiest productions. The gate of Calais is the background. A lean French cook appears staggering under the weight of a vast piece of roast beef, while two soldiers bear off a great kettle of soup maigre, the painter in these two dishes characterising the two countries. A well-fed monk looks longingly at the beef; and a melancholy and miserable Highlander browsing on a bit of bread and an onion is intended for one of the many that fled from England after the Rebellion of 1745. Hogarth is seated, sketching the scene, and a Frenchman arrests him by laying his hand on his shoulder; the likeness is good, and was afterwards copied for watch-papers. Pine, the engraver, sat for the fat friar, and received from that circumstance the name of "Friar Pine," which he retained till his death.* He desired to sit, "certainly not with a view to being turned into derision;" and being much laughed at and annoyed, he strove to prevail on

* John Pine, who published in 1739 "The Tapestry Hangings of the House of Lords," which, nearly a century after, were destroyed by fire.

Hogarth to give his ghostly father another face, but in vain. Soon after the picture was finished, it fell down by accident, and a nail ran through the cross on the top of the gate. Hogarth could not mend it with the same colour; and to conceal the blemish, he introduced a starved crow looking down on the roast beef.

The original picture was exhibited at Spring Gardens in 1761; and at the British Gallery in 1814: it is now in the possession of the Earl of Charlemont. It was engraved by C. Morley, in 1749. A copy of the print was likewise engraved at the top of a cantata entitled *The Roast Beef of Old England*, opening with this Recitative:

> 'Twas at the gates of Calais, Hogarth tells,
> Where sad Despair and Famine always dwells,
> A meagre Frenchman, Madam Grandsire's cook,
> As home he steer'd his carcase, that way took,
> Bending beneath the weight of fam'd Sir Loin,
> On whom he often wish'd in vain to dine.
> Good Father Dominick by chance came by,
> With rosy gills, round paunch, and greedy eye;
> Who, when he first beheld the greasy load,
> His benediction on it he bestow'd;
> And while the solid fat his finger press'd,
> He licked his chaps, and thus the Knight address'd, &c.

The figure of the half-starved French sentinel, (says Nichols,) has since been copied at the top of more than one of the printed advertisements for recruits, where it is opposed to the representation of a well-fed British soldier. Thus, the genius of Hogarth still militates in the cause of his country.

At Mr. Woodburn's, in St. Martin's-lane, was exhibited, about 1817, a valuable picture, said to have been painted by Hogarth, whilst he was in France. The subject is the gate of Amiens, with a Mountebank exposing to the people assembled the figure of Christ. Among the spectators is a soldier of the Swiss Guard, who is resting his hand on the shoulder of a simple-looking countryman; and other figures. The whole is painted with spirit and humour; but Nichols thinks it is not by Hogarth, but a French painter, Cappel. The picture was sold at Mr. Yates's sale, in 1817, for 30*l*. 9*s*.: it has been engraved, and there is a proof in Mr. Sheepshanks's collection.

PAUL BEFORE FELIX.

On the northern wall of the New Hall of Lincoln's Inn, above the paneling of the dais, hangs the picture of Paul before Felix, painted for the Society in 1750, and removed from the Old Hall, where it occupied a similar position. The origin of the Painting is as follows. By the Will of Lord Wyndham, Lord High Chancellor of Ireland, the sum of 200*l*. was bequeathed to the Society of Lincoln's Inn, to be expended in adorning the Chapel, or Hall, as the Benchers should think fit. At the recommendation of Lord Mansfield, Hogarth was engaged to paint the picture, which was at first designed for the Chapel. Its position was properly changed to the Hall.

The text of the picture is—"As he reasoned of righteousness, temperance, and judgment to come, Felix trembled." Mrs. Jameson has well-described this work as curiously characteristic, not of the scene or of the chief personage, but of the painter. St. Paul, loaded with chains, and his accuser Tertullus, stand in front; and Felix, with his wife Drusilla, is seated on a raised tribunal in the background; near Felix is the high-priest, Ananias. The composition is good, the heads are full of vivid expression—wrath, terror, doubt, attention; but the conception of character most ignoble and common-place. Mr. Peter Dupont, a merchant, had, in 1782, a drawing of this Picture, which he purchased for twenty guineas. It was engraved by Hogarth; and secondly, by Luke Sullivan. In the previous year, Hogarth had engraved a burlesque upon this serious scene: it is grotesque and full of broad humour; but in most offensive taste.

"THE ANALYSIS OF BEAUTY."

When Hogarth painted his own Portrait, in 1749, he etched upon the palette a winding-line, with this inscription —"Line of Beauty and Grace." This remained unexplained until 1753, when Hogarth published his short quarto tract, *The Analysis of Beauty, written with a view of fixing the fluctuating Ideas of Taste*, showing by various examples, that a curve is the line of beauty, and that round swelling figures are most pleasing to the eye. The author received in this work much assistance from his friends. Dr. Hoadly carried on the work to about a third part, and then declined it on account of ill health. Hogarth's neighbour, Mr. Ralph, the architectural critic, then wrote about a sheet, but failing to agree with the author, proceeded no further. Dr. Morell then finished the work; the Rev. Mr. Towneley correcting the Preface. The family of Hogarth rejoiced when the last sheet of the *Analysis* was printed off, for they had been sorely troubled by the frequent disputes in its progress.

Walpole observes: "This book had many sensible hints and observations," but it did not convince every reader. As Hogarth treated his contemporaries with scorn, "Many wretched burlesque prints came out to ridicule his system. There was a bitter answer to it in one of the two Prints that he gave to illustrate his hypothesis. In the Ball, (Wanstead Assembly,) had he confined himself to such outlines as compose awkwardness and deformity, he would have proved half his assertion; but he has added two samples of grace in a young lord and lady, who are strikingly stiff and affected. They are a Bath beau and a country beauty." Bishop Warburton congratulated Hogarth on giving, in this work, his "original masterly thoughts" on the great principles of his profession; and in showing up "the worthless crew professing vertù and connoisseurship; to whom all that grovel in the splendid poverty of wealth and taste are the miserable bubbles." Benjamin West, the cautious President of the Royal Academy, told John Thomas Smith, when a lad: the *Analysis* "is a work of the highest value to every one studying the Art; Hogarth was a strutting, consequential little man, and made himself many enemies by that book; but now that most of them are dead, it is examined by disinterested readers, unbiassed by personal animosities, and will be more and more read and studied, and understood." Hogarth's conclusion in this work is, however, unsound; though his arguments are amusing and ingenious.

HOGARTH'S "LADY'S LAST STAKE."

This painting represents a young woman of distinction in the peril of deep play with a gay and youthful man of fashion and intrigue: the lady has been unsuccessful, and lost (like Francis I.) all except honour, which the moral artist insinuates, is in danger. Of the origin of the picture, Mrs. Piozzi relates, that when she was a girl of sixteen, about the year 1756, she was an inmate of the house of her uncle, Cotton; that Hogarth paid a visit there, and in the course of the evening, turned to her, then Miss Salusbury, and said, "he hoped she would never waste her hours nor hazard her repose in the pursuit of gaming;" he then made a sketch of her, and informed her she should hear more from him on that point at a future time. Soon after the painter produced and showed her "The Lady's Last Stake;" "in which," said he, "Miss Salusbury, the lady is a likeness of yourself, because I wanted a pretty subject, and wished to give a lesson of wisdom to one who is, I trust, capable of understanding its force." The portrait was considered a good likeness; but when Mrs. Piozzi related the above anecdote, the picture had been sixty years painted; so that age, worldly cares, and much intellectual exertion, had committed their usual ravages on what had assuredly been a very fine countenance, indicating, as all who knew her must recollect, a lofty, liberal mind, and brilliant genius.

This celebrated picture hangs in a bed-chamber of Charlemont House, Dublin. Hogarth promised Lord Charlemont to write a description of his plates, which he said, the public had ignorantly misunderstood; and it was his intention to have given a breakfast-lecture upon them at Charlemont House.

Lord Charlemont, who possessed a fine collection of Hogarth's prints, remarkably good impressions, selected by the painter himself, consented to "The Lady's Last Stake" being engraved, for which purpose the painter had the picture a year, and even went so far as almost to finish the plate, which, as he told Lord Charlemont, he broke into pieces, upon finding, that after many trials, he could not bring the woman's head to answer his idea, or to resemble the picture.

In July, 1787, Mrs. Hogarth requested of Lord Charlemont, that if he should permit any one to engrave the picture, "he would give the preference to a young gentleman who lodged in her house, as by such preference she should be greatly benefited." To this his Lordship consented.

HOGARTH'S OPINION OF HIS ART.

Bishop Sandford relates that Hogarth was one day drawing in a room, where many of his friends were assembled, and among them was the Bishop's mother. She was then a very young woman. As she stood by Hogarth, she expressed a wish to learn to draw caricature. "Alas! young lady," said Hogarth, "it is not a faculty to be envied. Take my advice and never draw caricature: by the long practice of it I have lost the enjoyment of beauty. I never see a face, but distorted; I never have the satisfaction to behold the human face divine." We may suppose that such language from Hogarth would come with great effect: his manner was very earnest, and the confession is well deserving of remembrance.

THE ELECTION PICTURES.

These celebrated pictures, painted between 1755 and 1758, are among Hogarth's best productions, and present an admirable display of the great Painter's keen satire, and his talents for delineating character: they are painted with great breadth and agreeable freshness of tone.*

The Election of a Member of Parliament, "madman's holiday" in England, is here depicted in four scenes: the *Entertainment*, the *Canvassing for Voters*, the *Polling*, and the *Chairing*.

The first scene is laid at an inn, where the Court candidate, Mr. Thomas Potter, is seated at a dinner of electors—barbers, cobblers, and counsellors, rustic wits and politicians and partisans. The parson holding his perriwig is Dr. Cosserat. The woman playing on the violin is Fiddling Nan, of Oxford; the bludgeon man, having gin poured on his head, is an Oxford bruiser, Teague Carter. The person making a representation of a fan round his head is Sir John Parnell, nephew of the poet: this portrait was introduced at his own request: "my face (he said) is well known in Ireland, and will help the sale of the engraving." The *Canvassing* is in the street of the borough, where the candidates and their partisans are busy at corruption; there is a fierce attack on the Crown public-house; and Punch has declared himself a candidate for fun and frolic. Among the insignia is the British Lion—so popular in the present day—swallowing the Lily of France, which the imperial swallow has gulped long ago. The *Polling*, the third scene, shows how the lame and the blind, the dying and even the dead, were carried to the hustings in the olden elections. Among the portraits is that of Dr. Shebbeare, who had been pilloried by Lord Mansfield for a libel on the King. A sick voter, borne in a blanket, is a satire on Dr. Barrowby bringing a dying patient in his chariot, to the Westminster hustings, to vote for Sir George Vandeput; the poor fellow voted, and expired. The nobleman with the riband is "the old Duke of Newcastle." In this plate, a goose flying over his head is said to be designed for a parody on Le Brun's engraving of the battle of the Granicus, in which an eagle is represented hovering over the head of Alexander the Great. The concluding scene is the Chairing of the Member, Bubb Dodington, afterwards Lord Melcombe; the fray of the losing side has already begun; the member's wig rises from his head with fear; one of the living props of the chair has been struck down by a thrasher's flail; and the accessories of confusion thicken.

The carriage of Britannia is overturning, while the coachman and footman are cheating at cards on the box; regardless of a last dying speech, with a ready gibbet and empty noose—held up for sale.

---

* Walpole calls Zoffani "the Dutch Hogarth," and Bunbury "the second Hogarth." With less justice the term "Hogarthian" has been applied to some of Haydon's pictures; and the editor of his *Autobiography*, Mr. Tom Taylor, maintains that the wonderstruck farmer in Haydon's *Punch* is equal to anything by Hogarth. In composition, arrangement of the figures, the telling of the story, and minuteness, accuracy, and character of detail, Haydon's design will not bear comparison with the masterly productions of Hogarth; since whose time it has become too much the practice to designate as "Hogarthian" many unworthy pictures.

In 1759, appeared "A Practical Description" of these pictures, in four Cantos, written under Mr. Hogarth's sanction and inspiration." The public were so impatient for this set of prints, that Hogarth had several disagreements with his tardy coadjutors in producing them.

Garrick gave Hogarth for these four paintings some 200*l*.: they remained in the possession of his widow, after whose death, in 1823, they were purchased at the Garrick sale for 1732*l*. 10*s*. When the hammer fell, Mr. Christie said: "I am the returning officer on this occasion, and declare Sir John Soane duly elected to become the possessor of these pictures." They are now in the Soanean Museum.

The above are not the only scenes from an Election which Hogarth painted; for in 1747, he designed and engraved a Stage-coach, with an Election Procession in the inn-yard: the principal figure being a man whipping an infant child, in allusion to the Hon. John Child Tylney, a candidate in an Essex county election: the infant carries a horn-book and rattle, and the whipper exclaims, "What, you little *Child*, must you be a member?" These Election humours, as well as the Stage-coach, belong to an almost bygone age.

The engraving of these pictures was very successful. In the first, the *Entertainment*, Hogarth experimentally finished the engraving without taking a proof to ascertain how he was succeeding: he had nearly spoiled the plate, and despairingly exclaimed, "I am ruined." He soon, however, repaired the damage, and with such good fortune that the print in question is one of the clearest and cleverest of all his productions. At Baker's sale, in 1825, the *Entertainment* print, before any inscription, sold for 31*l*. 10*s*.

"SIGISMUNDA."

When, in 1758, Sir Thomas Sebright purchased for 400*l*. a *Sigismunda* imputed to Correggio,—loud was the ire of Hogarth at this reverence for the great Italian master. Walpole maintains that Hogarth had seen few good Italian pictures, and hence he persuaded himself that the praises bestowed on these glorious works were nothing but the effects of ignorance. He talked this language till he believed it; and he went so far as to aver that age did not mellow the colours and improve pictures, but only made them grow black and worse. He went further, and resolved to rival the ancients, and chose for the test the celebrated *Sigismunda*, said to be painted by Correggio, probably by Furini,* but no matter by whom. It is impossible to see the picture or read Dryden's inimitable tale, and not feel that the same soul animated both. After many essays, Hogarth produced his *Sigismunda*, but with "none of the sober grief, no dignity of suppressed anguish, no involuntary tear, no settled meditation on the fate she meant to meet, no amorous warmth termed holy by despair; in short, all is wanting that should have been there, all is there that such a story should have banished from a mind capable of conceiving real complicated woe; woe so sternly felt, and yet so tenderly." Walpole's criticism is very severe: he describes Hogarth's *Sigismunda* as no more like Sigismunda than he to Hercules: he compares her to a maudlin fallen virago, her eyes red with rage and usquebaugh, and her fingers bloodied with just having torn out her lover's heart. The latter is untrue. It was said that the picture resembled Mrs. Hogarth, who was a very handsome woman; to which circumstance Wilkes maliciously alludes in his vile attack on her husband. "If (says Wilkes,) the *Sigismunda* had a resemblance of anything ever seen on earth, or had the least pretence to either meaning or expression, it was what he had seen, or perhaps made, in real life— his own wife in an agony of passion; but of what passion no connoisseur could guess." Both Wilkes and Walpole knew that Mrs. Hogarth had sat for Sigismunda; and after her husband's death, Horace strove to heal the poor widow's heart by sending her a copy of his *Anecdotes*, but she took no notice of the present.

The *Sigismunda*, we learn from Hogarth's own memorandum-book, was painted by him for Sir Richard Grosvenor, who was as dissatisfied with it as Walpole himself. Hogarth had agreed that Sir Richard might refuse the picture if he should not be thoroughly satisfied with it; and the painter asked 400*l*. for his work; to which Sir Richard Grosvenor replied: "I understand that you have a commission from Mr. Hoare for a picture. If he should have taken a fancy to the *Sigismunda*, I have no sort of objection to your letting him have it; for I really think the performance so striking and inimitable, that the constantly having it before one's eyes

---

* The *Sigismunda*, now at the Duke of Newcastle's, at Clumber (really by Furini,) was Sir Luke Schaub's; Lady Schaub is immortalised in the long story of Gray.—*Cunningham; note to Walpole.*

would be too often occasioning melancholy ideas to arise in one's mind, which a curtain's being drawn before it would not diminish the least."

This refusal, and the ridicule of the artists of the day, deeply affected Hogarth. He sought relief in writing a versified epistle to a friend on this picture, and consoles himself as follows:

> "When other connoisseurs may arise,
> Honest as ours, and full as wise,
> To pay my works their due arrears,
> When I've been dead a hundred years."

Hogarth, who now felt age and infirmities coming upon him, enjoined his wife not to sell *Sigismunda* for less than 500*l*. This injunction was obeyed; and the picture was not sold till after the death of Mrs. Hogarth, when it was bought by Alderman Boydell for 50 guineas. It formed one of the prizes in the Shakspeare Gallery; was sold in 1807 by Christie, for 400 guineas. It was engraved in 1792.

The subject was parodied in a vulgar print entitled "A harlot blubbering over a bullock's heart; by William Hogart."

Sigismunda was announced for engraving by Hogarth, but the print was never published, and the subscriptions were returned: in the account-book of the painter, a strong line is passed through the subscribers' names, and opposite each is written "Returned," except one name, which has "Refused." Hogarth's several subscription-books for his prints contain the autographs of many distinguished persons.

HOGARTH AND HORACE WALPOLE.

Walpole writes to George Montagu, Esq., May 5, 1761: "The true frantic Œstus resides at present with Mr. Hogarth; I went t'other morning to see a portrait he is painting of Mr. Fox. Hogarth told me he had promised, if Mr. Fox would sit as he liked, to make as good a picture as Vandyke or Rubens could. I was silent. 'Why now,' said he, 'you think this very vain, but why should not one speak the truth?' This *truth* was uttered in the face of his own *Sigismunda*. . . . . She has her father's picture in a bracelet on her arm, and her fingers are bloody with the heart, as if she had just bought a sheep's pluck in St. James's-market. As I was going, Hogarth put on a very grave face, and said, 'Mr. Walpole, I want to speak to you.' I sat down, and said I was ready to receive his commands. For shortness, I will make this wonderful dialogue by initial letters.

H. I am told you are going to entertain the town with something in our way.

W. Very soon, Mr. Hogarth.

H. I wish you would let me have it to correct; I should be very sorry to have you expose yourself to censure; we painters must know more of these things than other people.

W. Do you think nobody understands painting but painters?

H. Oh! so far from it, there's Reynolds, who certainly has genius; why, but t'other day he offered a hundred pounds for a picture that I would not hang in my cellar; indeed, to say truth, I have generally found that persons who had studied painting least were the best judges of it; but what I particularly wished to say to you was about Sir James Thornhill (you know he married Sir James's daughter); I would not have you say anything against him; there was a book published some time ago, abusing him, and it gave great offence. He was the first that attempted *history* in England, and I assure you, some Germans have said that he was a very great painter.

W. My work will go no lower than the year one thousand seven hundred, and I really have not considered whether Sir J. Thornhill will come within my plan or not; if he does, I fear you and I shall not agree upon his merits.

H. I wish you would let me correct it; besides, I am writing something of the kind myself; I should be sorry we should clash.

W. I believe it is not much known what my work is, very few persons have seen it.

H. Why, it is a critical history of painting, is not it?

W. No, it is an antiquarian history of it in England; I bought Mr. Vertue's MSS., and, I believe, the work will not give much offence; besides, if it does, I cannot help it; when I publish anything I give it to the world to think of it as they please.

H. Oh! if it is an antiquarian work, we shall not clash; mine is a critical work; I don't know whether I shall ever publish it. It is rather an apology for painters. I think it is owing to the good sense of the English that they have not painted better.

W. My dear Mr. Hogarth, I must take my leave of you, you now grow too wild.

And I left him. If I had stayed, there remained nothing but for him to bite me. I give you my honour this conversation is literal, and, perhaps, as long as you have known Englishmen and painters, you never met with anything so distracted. I had consecrated a line to his genius (I mean, for wit) in my Preface; I shall not erase it; but I hope nobody will ask me if he is not mad. Adieu!

HOGARTH AND WILKES.

It appears that in this intimacy the demagogue took or affected to take great pains to dissuade the painter from political satire. Wilkes, in 1755, was the especial friend of Hogarth—actively kind towards him, admired and praised his genius, and even when they quarrelled (in 1762) their quarrel was political, not personal; and, as Wilkes said, "for several years they had lived on terms of friendship and intimacy." Hogarth, in 1762, as he admitted, to "stop a gap in his income," determined to turn his pencil to political uses; and the King's serjeant-painter resolved to attack those who were considered hostile to the King—Chatham and Temple. Wilkes, in a private and friendly letter, pointed out the folly of giving up "to party what was meant for mankind"—of dipping his pencil "in the dirt of faction"—warned him of the certain consequences, and told him that "he never would take notice of reflections on himself; but when his friends were attacked, he found himself wounded in the most sensible part, and would, as well as he could, revenge their cause." Hogarth persevered, published his caricature, and Wilkes his comment and criticism. Even, after this, Hogarth acknowledged that Wilkes had been his "friend and flatterer," was a good-tempered fellow, but now "Pitt-bitten—Pitt-mad."—*Notes and Queries*, 2d S. No. 81.

PORTRAIT OF FIELDING.

Fielding, the novelist, went to the grave without ever having sat for his portrait; but Hogarth painted him from recollection.

Arthur Murphy relates that after Hogarth had tried to bring out a likeness of Fielding "from images existing in his own fancy," and had failed, a lady, with a pair of scissors, cut a profile, which gave the distances and proportions of his face sufficiently to restore Hogarth's lost ideas of Fielding: "he caught at this outline with pleasure, and worked, with all the attachment of friendship, till he had finished the portrait," which is prefixed to the great novelist's works. Nichols, nevertheless, was assured that Hogarth began and finished the head in the presence of his wife and another lady, and that he had no assistance but from his own tenacious memory. To this sketch the engraver did such justice, that Hogarth declared he did not know his own drawing from a proof of the plate before the ornaments were added.

The story is likewise told as follows. Hogarth and Garrick, sitting together after dinner, Hogarth was lamenting there was no portrait of Fielding, when Garrick said, "I think I can make his face."—"Pray, try, my dear Davy," said the other. Garrick then made the attempt, and so well did he succeed, that Hogarth immediately caught the likeness, and exclaimed with exultation, "Now I have him. Keep still, my dear Davy." To work he went with pen and ink, and the likeness was finished by their mutual recollections. This sketch has been engraved from the original drawing, and is preserved in the illustrated copy of Lysons's *Environs*, vol. ii. p. 544, in the King's Library, British Museum.

"CREDULITY, SUPERSTITION, AND FANATICISM."

In this remarkable work—*the Medley*, designed and engraved by Hogarth, and published in 1762, his object is to literally represent the strange effects resulting from low conceptions of sacred things; and of the idolatrous tendency of pictures in churches, and prints in religious books. He has pictured a fierce preacher and a startled congregation: in his right hand he shakes a god, reserving in the other a devil: one hearer has sprung to his feet; a second has his hair standing on end; a third has fallen into a swoon; a fourth hugs an image; a fifth is fainting with extacy; and a sixth, a woman overcome by the tempter, is dropping the image of her patron saint from her bosom. A Turk, smoking, looks in at the window, and seems chuckling at superstition which surpasses his own. Among the follies satirized are Mrs. Veale's ghost, Julius Cæsar's apparition, and the shade of Sir George Villiers; Whitefield's Journal placed upon King James's Demonology; Mrs. Tofts and her Rabbits; the Cocklane Ghost and the Tedworth Drummer. Every inscription is the work of a writing-engraver. Hogarth published a similar print—*Enthusiasm Delineated*, which Walpole considered "for useful and deep satire, was the most sublime of all Hogarth's works;" but Ireland thinks these words more applicable to *the Medley*.

PORTRAIT OF WILKES.

In 1763, Hogarth drew from the life, and "etched in aquafortis" the notorious John Wilkes, and the print was published as "a direct contrast to the print of Simon Lord Lovat." The original drawing of Wilkes was thrown by Hogarth into the fire, but was snatched out of it by a lady, and passed into the hands of S. Ireland. Wilkes good-humouredly said of this portrait, that he was every day growing more like it.

Writing to his friend Churchill, he says: "I take it for granted you have seen Hogarth's print against me. Was ever anything so contemptible? I think he is fairly *felo de se*—I think not to let him off in that manner, although I might safely leave him to your notes.* He has broken into my pale of private life, and set that example of illiberality which I wished—of that kind of attack which is ungenerous in the first instance, but justice in the return." Nichols was told by a copper-plate printer that nearly 4000 copies of this caricature were worked off on its first publication.

HOGARTH'S QUARREL WITH WILKES AND CHURCHILL.

Hogarth was smarting under the attacks upon his *Sigismunda*, which were but a revival of the spleen that appeared at the time of *the Analysis*, when he got into a violent quarrel with Wilkes and Churchill, which embittered the few remaining days of the great artist's life.

In his anger, Hogarth repaired to Westminster Hall, when Wilkes was the second time brought thither from the Tower; and in Wilkes's own words, "Skulking behind in the Court of Common Pleas," Hogarth was seen in the corner of the Court, pencil and sketch-book in hand, fixing that famous caricature, from which, as long as caricature shall last, Wilkes will squint upon all posterity. Nor was it his first pictorial offence: the caricaturing had begun some little time before, greatly to the grief both of Wilkes and Churchill; for Hogarth was on friendly terms with both; and, indeed, had within the past two years drank "divine milk-punch" with them and Sir Francis Dashwood, in the neighbourhood of Medmenham Abbey. Disregarding their earnest remonstrance, he assailed Pitt and Temple at the close of the preceding year in his first print of the *Times*.† The *North Briton* retaliated in an attack on "The King's Sergeant-Painter, William Hogarth." It was sharp and malicious; and Wilkes, hearing that Hogarth contemplated a rejoinder, requested him not to meddle with *moral* subjects—and as the same request suited Churchill, it was made in both their names. Precious advice to Hogarth!

---

* Referring to the edition of his works which Churchill, in his Will, desired that Wilkes should publish, with remarks and explanations.

† The *Times*, Plate 2, was engraved soon after Plate 1, but withheld from the public till after Mrs. Hogarth's death, when the Plate was published by Messrs. Boydell, in 1790.

A coarse woodcut portrait of Hogarth headed this paper, the motto of which was—

> Its proper power to hurt each creature feels,
> Bulls aim their horns, and asses lift their heels.

The caricature—the bodily and mental image of John Wilkes—appeared; he is seated in the civic chair—this patron saint of purity and liberty—a mark for perpetual laughter and loathing. It stung Churchill—Wilkes's toad-eater—past the power of silence.

As a rejoinder, in July, 1763, Churchill put the North Briton into verse in the *Epistle to William Hogarth*. It struck Hogarth where he was weakest, in that subjection to vanity which his friends confessed in him. But it spread his genius. Amid its savage ferocity against the man, it was remarkable for a noble tribute to the artist. It predicted the duration of his works to the most distant age; and the great painter's power to curse and bless it rated as that of "a little god below." But it was of terrible severity: the passage beginning "Hogarth, I take thee, candour, at thy word," is literally appalling. All who knew the contending parties stood aghast. "Pray let me know," wrote Garrick, then visiting at Chatsworth, to Colman, "how the town speaks of our friend Churchill's *Epistle*. It is the most bloody performance that has been published in my time. I am very desirious to know the opinion of people, for I am really much, very much hurt at it. His description of his age and infirmities is surely too shocking and barbarous. Is Hogarth really ill, or does he meditate revenge? Every article of news about these matters will be most agreeable to me. Pray write me a heap of stuff, for I cannot be easy till I know all about Churchill and Hogarth." And, of course, the lively actor sends his "loves" both to Churchill and Hogarth. "Send me Churchill's poem on Hogarth," writes old money-loving Lord Bath, from Spa; "but if it be long, it will cost a large sum in postage."

With his rejoinder, such as it was, Hogarth lost little time. "Having an old plate by me," he says, "with some parts readily sunk as a background, I began to consider how I could turn so much work laid aside to some account—and so patched up a print of Master Churchill in the character of a bear;" and he issued for a shilling, before the month was out, "The Bruiser, C. Churchill, (once the Rev.) in the character of a Russian Hercules, regaling himself after having killed the monster Caricatura, that so sorely galled his virtuous friend, the heaven-born Wilkes." It was a bear, in torn clerical bands, and with paws in ruffles; a pot of porter that has just visited his jaws hugged on his right, and a knotted club of *Lies* and *North Britons* clutched on his left; to which, in a later edition of the same print, was added a scaffolding caricature of Pitt, Temple, and Wilkes.

In a second edition, Hogarth added on a label a group representing himself as a bear-master, forcing the bear, Churchill, and the monkey, Wilkes, to dance under the infliction of a severe castigation: the monkey holds a *North Briton* in his hand.

Churchill, meanwhile, wrote to Wilkes, and told him that Hogarth, having violated the sanctities of private life in this caricature, he meant to pay it back with an *Elegy*, supposing him dead; but that a lady at his elbow was dissuading him with the flattery that Hogarth was already killed.

In his poem of *Independence*, published in the last week of September, 1764, Churchill contemptuously considers the painter already in his grave: these are his words of savage exultation:

> "Hogarth would draw him, envy must allow,
> E'en to the life, were Hogarth living now."

This Walpole and others also affirmed; and Colman boldly avouched in print that the *Epistle* had snapped the last cord of poor Hogarth's heart-strings. Churchill had such faith in the terrors of his own verse, that his vanity was pleased when he heard the death of Hogarth was imputed to his satire. But Churchill himself died within nine days of the painter! Thus the assailed and the assailant passed away; and thus "was prevented the reconciliation which would surely, sooner or later, have vindicated their common genius, the hearty English feeling which they shared, and their common cordial hatred of the falsehood and pretences of the world." (*Edinburgh Review*, No. 163.)

Stacie, the landlord of the Bedford, in Covent Garden, told J. T. Smith that Churchill's quarrel with Hogarth began at a shilling rubber club, held in the parlour of the Bedford;*

---

* Woodward the comedian, who mostly resided at the Bedford Arms, was intimate with Stacie, and gave him his portrait with a mask in his hand, one of the early pictures of Sir Joshua Reynolds. Stacie related to Smith that he was allowed to play an excellent game at whist. One

when Hogarth used very insulting language towards Churchill, who resented it in the *Epistle.*

On the whole, this quarrel showed more venom than wit. "Never," says Walpole, "did two angry men of their abilities throw mud with less dexterity."

Wilkes bore Hogarth's caricature bravely. He said truly, in allusion to his own portrait, that he did not make himself, and cared little about the beauty of the case that contained his soul. He wrote to Earl Temple : "Mr. Hogarth is said to be dying of a broken heart. It grieves me much. He says that he believes I wrote that paper (the *North Briton*), but he forgives me, for he must own I am a thorough good-humoured fellow, only *Pitt-bitten.*"

"FINIS; OR THE TAIL-PIECE."

This strange print, engraved in 1764, the year in which Hogarth died, is stated by Nichols and others to have originated as follows ; though the title of the print may, probably, have suggested the story. "My next undertaking," said Hogarth, one evening, at his own table, "shall be the end of all things." "If that is the case," said one of the artist's friends, "your business will soon be finished, for there will be an end of the painter." "There will so," replied Hogarth, sighing heavily, "and the sooner my work is done the better." Accordingly, he began the next day, and worked at the picture without intermission until he had finished it : the story runs —that *he never again took up his palette.*

The design of the Tail-piece is to group such objects as denote *the end of time,* and to ridicule the gross absurdities to be seen in some of the serious works of the old masters. Hogarth named it *the Bathos, or manner of sinking in sublime paintings,* and inscribed the Plate to the dealers in dark pictures. On the left is a ruined tower, with a decayed dial-plate ; at its base is a tombstone sculptured with a skull ; and leaning upon part of the shaft of a column is Time breathing out "Finis;" his scythe and hour-glass are broken ; in one hand he holds a parchment scroll bearing his Will, in which he bequeathes all to Chaos ; the Fates, Clotho, Lachesis and Atropos executors. Beneath the Will lies a shoemaker's last, entwined with a cobbler's end. To the left are an empty ragged purse, a commission of bankruptcy against poor Dame Nature, and a play-book

---

morning, about two o clock, one of his waiters awoke him, to tell him that a nobleman had knocked him up, and had desired him to call his master to play a rubber with him for one hundred guineas. Stacie got up, dressed himself, won the money, and was in bed and asleep, all within an hour.

opened at the last page. In the foreground are a broken bow, a broken crown, and a worn out scrubbing-brush. On the right hand, opposite the tower, are a withered tree, an unroofed cottage, and a falling inn-sign of the World's End, on the globe bursting into flames. At the foot of the sign-post is the artist's own print of the *Times*, set on fire by an inch of candle. Near this are a cracked bell, a broken bottle, a worn-out broom, the stock of a musket, a rope's-end, a whip without its lash, a mutilated Ionic capital, and a painter's broken palette. In the distance are a man gibbeted in chains, and a ship foundering at sea; and in the firmament the moon is darkened by the death of Phœbus, who, with his lifeless coursers, lies extended on a cloud, his chariot wheels broken, and his light put out.

" So far, so good," exclaimed Hogarth; " nothing remains but this," taking his pencil in a sort of prophetic fury, and dashing off the painter's broken palette. " Finis," cried he; " the deed is done—*all is over!* "

On this print, the following epigram, ascribed to Churchill, appeared in the *Muse's Mirror*:

> All must old Hogarth's gratitude declare
> Since he has named old Chaos for his heir:
> And while his works hang round the Anarch's throne,
> The connoisseur will take them for his own.

DEATH OF HOGARTH.

The last years of the painter's life appear to have been partly employed in retouching his plates, with the assistance of several engravers, whom he took with him to his house at Chiswick, which had hitherto long been his residence during the summer. "The change of scene," says Cunningham, " the free fresh air, and exercise on horseback, had for a while a favourable influence on Hogarth's health; but he complained that he was no longer able to think with the readiness, and work with the elasticity of spirit, of his earlier years." Nevertheless, the powers of his humour did not forsake him. In one of his memorandum-books, he remarks: " I can safely assert that I have invariably endeavoured to make those about me tolerably happy; and my greatest enemy cannot say I ever did an intentional injury; though, without ostentation, I could produce many instances of men that have been essentially benefited by me. What may follow, God knows." This was written well-nigh the close of his life, and seems entitled to the respect of a rigid self-examination. In the venomous attack which helped to bring his days to an end, Wilkes appears to have had the principal share in embittering the parting cup. Of him Hogarth wrote: "One, till now rather my friend and flatterer, attacked me in so infamous and malign a style, that he himself, when pushed even by his best friends, was driven to so poor an excuse as to say he was drunk when he wrote it. Being at that time very weak, and in a kind of slow fever, it could not but seize on a feeling mind." Nevertheless, Churchill's virulence must not be forgotten in the base account.

Such was the state of the painter's health when, on October 25, 1764, he left Chiswick for his house in Leicester Fields: he was very weak, yet exceedingly cheerful: he was in that distressing state which is so frequent at the close of the life of a man of genius: nature was silently giving way; "his understanding continued clear, he had full possession of his mental faculties, but wanted the vigour to exert them." Next day, he replied to an agreeable letter which he had received from Dr. Franklin: it was but roughly written. Finding himself exhausted, he retired to bed: he had lain but a short time, when he was seized with a vomiting, and, starting up, rang the bell with such violence that he broke it in pieces. Mary Lewis,* his affectionate relative, who lived in the house, came and supported him in her arms, till, after two hours' suffering, he expired, from a suffusion of blood among the arteries of the heart. This is Allan Cunningham's account of Hogarth's last moments: it differs from that by Faulkner, who says that Hogarth, on retiring to bed on the night of the day on which he came from Chiswick, "was suddenly taken ill, and expired in the space of two hours." †

Walpole, in a letter to Lord Hertford, thus records the painter's end: "Hogarth is dead, and Mrs. Spence, who lived with the Duchess of Newcastle."—This is characteristic of the cynic of Strawberry Hill.

* Mary Lewis, who died in the year 1808, and is buried in Hogarth's vault at Chiswick, was the daughter of David Lewis, harper to George II. Her brother, John Lewis, married into the Clithero family, at Brentford, and is introduced, playing the flute, in one of the Marriage à la Mode pictures. Mary Lewis was the niece of Mrs. Hogarth, passed all her life in Hogarth's family, and acted as his confidential shopwoman in the publication and sale of the Prints. Hogarth painted her portrait, and signed his name on the back of the canvas. Mary Lewis died a spinster; as did also Hogarth's sister, Anne.

† History of Chiswick, p. 448.

TOMB OF HOGARTH.

Hogarth was buried in an unostentatious manner in the south side of the churchyard at Chiswick; and some time after, a costly sculptured tomb was erected over the spot, and the expense defrayed by a subscription among his friends, at the instance of Garrick. The design consists of an altar-tomb, upon which is an attic, surmounted by a votive urn. On the north side of the tomb, in bas-relief, are a laurel wreath, rest-stick, a palette, pencils, a book inscribed *Analysis of Beauty;* a mask, a portfolio decorated with oak-leaves and acorns: beneath are inscribed the following lines by Garrick:

> "Farewell, great painter of mankind!
> Who reach'd the noblest point of art;
> Whose *pictured morals* charm the mind,
> And, through the eye, correct the heart.
> If *genius* fire thee, reader, stay;
> If *nature* touch thee, drop a tear;
> If neither move thee, turn away!
> For HOGARTH's honour'd dust lies here."

These lines have been condemned as conventional: another, and a higher hand, that of Dr. Johnson, supplied the following epitaph, more to the purpose, but still unequal:

> "The hand of him here torpid lies
> That drew the essential forms of grace;
> Here closed in death the attentive eye
> That saw the manners in the face."

On the east side of the tomb is inscribed: " Here lieth the body of William Hogarth, esq., who died October 26th, 1764, aged 67 years. Mrs. Jane Hogarth, wife of William Hogarth, esq. Obiit 13th November, 1789, Ætat 80 years."

On the south side are the names and deaths of Hogarth's sister, Anne, aged 70; Mary Lewis, spinster, aged 88; and on the west side, Mrs. Hogarth's mother, Dame Judith Thornhill, aged 84 years.

"Time will obliterate these inscriptions, and even the pyramid must crumble into dust, but Hogarth's fame is engraven on tablets which shall have longer duration than monumental marble."

Arms:—On the tomb—az. a sun in splendour for Hogarth, impaling arg. a chevron gules between, three blackbirds for Thornhill; there is also the coat for Thornhill, imp. per fesse az. and erm. a pale counter-charged, three lions arg.

Faulkner stated in 1845: "The tomb is still kept up by voluntary subscriptions of some of the worthy inhabitants of this parish, who take an interest in preserving this funereal memorial of the 'great painter of mankind.'" However, in 1851, the tomb was "gradually assuming a position which the first high wind may determine, and the monument be lost to us for ever." A mason confirmed this statement; the mischief having arisen from the sinking of the earth, incidental to churchyards. This was told to Mr. John Phillips, a descendant of the Hogarth family, who, in 1832, paid a mason 11*l*. 14*s*. for extensive repairs done to the tomb. Through his uncle, Mr. Hart, many family portraits and other matters came into his (Phillips's) possession. The tomb was not, however, fully repaired until 1856, and then at the sole expense of Mr. Hogarth, of Aberdeen. The restoration was made in exact accordance with the original design. To secure the monument it was necessary to open the grave, when the plates were found on the other coffins, but not on Hogarth's coffin, which was much smaller than the rest. The painter's plate is thought to have been removed upon a former opening of the grave, about the year 1836. The few persons who witnessed the opening of the grave in 1856 saw the large coffin of Lady Thornhill; the still larger coffin of Hogarth's widow; and the "little" coffin of the great painter of mankind. One who was present assured the writer that he also saw "the torpid hand" of the painter of *Marriage à la Mode*, and the *Harlot's Progress*.

While the above repairs were in progress, a great part of the garden-wall in the rear of Hogarth's house was blown down by the violence of the wind.—(*H. T. Riley; Notes and Queries, ut ante.*)

HOGARTH'S HOUSE, AT CHISWICK.

The great Painter long possessed a house at Chiswick, where he occasionally resided during the last twenty years of his life. It stood in the lane leading from Chiswick to the Horticultural Society's Gardens: on the piers of the principal entrance was inscribed in capitals, "Hogarth's House." Faulkner has roughly engraved the garden-front of the house, which has a projecting or bay window in the centre of the first-floor: he has also represented Hogarth's "workshop," at the western end of the premises. Mr. H. Riley, who visited the place in 1854, could not find in the house itself any memorials of the great artist; but another Correspondent of *Notes and Queries*, who spent a day or two in the house, in 1820, remembers a wainscoted room on the ground-floor, and faint traces of pen or pencil sketches on some of the panels. About twenty years later, Allan Cunningham described the buildings in the neighbourhood to have "choked up the garden, and destroyed the secluded beauty of Hogarth's cottage. The garden, well stored with walnut, mulberry, and apple trees, contained a small study, with a headstone placed over a favourite bulfinch, on which the artist had etched a bird's head and written an epitaph. The cottage contained many snug rooms, and was but yesterday the residence of a man of learning and genius—Mr. Cary, the translator of Dante." *

Mr. Riley † writes: "on the lawn, in front of the house, there was (and is still, I think,) a very ancient mulberry-treee, which in Hogarth's time was struck by lightning, it is said; and the iron braces or girdles, by which it is held together, were made by his direction. In one corner of the garden there were two neat little tombs, with slabs inserted in the wall, in memory of two favourite dogs. On one of these was inscribed: "Alas! poor Dick!" with the date 1764. On the other slab was inscribed: "Life to the last enjoyed, here lies Pompey, 1790"—an evident adaptation of Churchill's epitaph at Dover. Mrs. Hogarth died in 1789; but the remembrance of the feud between Hogarth and Churchill seems by this not to have died away with the survivor of the Household!

"Over the stable, a very limited abode for some two or three horses, a room was pointed out, which I was informed, had for many years been the artist's studio. From the comparatively large dimensions of the window, (which, as seen from the outside, appears to have replaced a smaller one,) I have little doubt that such is the fact. As the stairs are narrow, his paintings, I presume, would be put down through this window, for transmission, in his carriage, to town."

Mr. afterwards Sir Richard Phillips, who was educated at Chiswick, well remembered the widow of Hogarth: and some fifty years after, Sir Richard wrote of his school-days, whilst listening to the bells of Chiswick Church:

* Lives of British Artists, vol. i. p. 175.
† Notes and Queries, 2d S. No. 47. 1856.

My scattered and once-loved schoolmates, their characters, and their various fortunes, passed in rapid review before me;—my schoolmaster, his wife, and all the gentry, and heads of families, whose orderly attendance at Divine service on Sundays, while those well-remembered bells were "chiming for church," (but now departed and mouldering in the adjoining graves,) were rapidly presented to my recollection. With what pomp and form they used to enter and depart from their house of God! I saw with the mind's eye, the Widow Hogarth, and her maiden relative, Richardson, walking up the aisle, draped in their silken sacks, their raised head-dresses, their black calashes, their lace ruffles, and their high-crook'd canes, preceded by their aged servant, Samuel; who, after he had wheeled his mistress to church in her Bath-chair, carried the prayer-books up the aisle, and opened and shut the pew. There, too, was the portly Dr. Griffiths, of the *Monthly Review*, with his literary wife, in her neat and elevated wire-winged cap. And ofttimes the vivacious and angelic Duchess of Devonshire, whose bloom had not then suffered from the canker-worm of pecuniary distress, created by the luxury of charity! Nor could I forget the humble distinction of the aged sexton, Mortefee, whose skill in psalmody enabled him to lead that wretched group of singers whom Hogarth so happily portrayed. * * * Yes, simple and happy villagers, I remember scores of you!"—*A Morning's Walk from London to Kew,* p. 214.

MRS. HOGARTH.

Hogarth, after a long and active life, left a very inconsiderable sum to his widow, with whom, as Jane Thornhill, he must have received a large portion.

By her husband's Will, Mrs. Hogarth received the sole property of his numerous plates, and the copyright was secured to her for twenty years, by Act of Parliament. There were seventy-two plates, the sale of the impressions from which produced a respectable annual income. But she outlived the period of her right; and before this, through the fluctuation of public taste, the sale of the prints had so diminished as to reduce Mrs. Hogarth to the border of want.

The King interposed with the Royal Academy, and obtained for her an annuity of 40*l.*, which she lived but two years to enjoy: Walpole says that, after her death, Mr. Steevens was allowed to ransack her house in Leicester Fields for obsolete and unfinished plates, to be completed and published.

Hogarth's sister Anne followed him to the grave in 1771; and his wife, who loved him living, and honoured him dead, was laid beside him in 1789.

At length, the stock at the Golden Head was sold; and in the "Catalogue of the Pictures and Prints, the property of the late Mrs. Hogarth, deceased, sold by Mr. Greenwood, the

Golden Head, Leicester-square, Saturday, April 24, 1790," were the following Pictures by Hogarth:

LOT.
41. Two Portraits of Ann and Mary Hogarth.
42. A daughter of Mr. Rich, the comedian, finely coloured.
43. The original portrait of Sir James Thornhill.
44. The heads of six servants of the Hogarth family.
45. His own portrait—a head.
46. A ditto—a whole length painting.
47. A ditto, Kit-Kat, with the favourite dog, exceedingly fine.
48. Two portraits of Lady Thornhill and Mrs. Hogarth.
49. The first sketch of the Rake's Progress.
50. A ditto of the altar of Bristol Church.
51. The Shrimp Girl—a sketch.
52. Sigismunda.
53. An historical sketch, by Sir James Thornhill.
54. Two sketches of Lady Pembroke and Mr. John Thornhill.
55. Three old Pictures.
56. The bust of Sir Isaac Newton, terra cotta.
57. Ditto of Mr. Hogarth, by Roubilliac.
58. Ditto of the favourite Dog, and cast of Mr. Hogarth's hand.

HOGARTH'S MAUL-STICK.

The maul-stick of the great painter, some years after his death, fell into the hands of Sir George Beaumont, who determined to keep it till a painter should appear who was worthy to receive it. Sir George kept the maul-stick until he saw the *Village Politicians* of Wilkie, and then presented it to that great artist.

COLLECTIONS OF HOGARTH'S WORKS.

A Rev. Mr. Gilpin, writing near the time of Hogarth, represents him as ignorant of composition! This shows how little the painter was then understood. There have been occasional exhibitions of collections of his works: Cook, the engraver, re-engraved Hogarth's pictures, and exhibited the prints in the Haymarket early in the present century; but Mr. Leslie doubts whether Hogarth's entire excellence was fully felt by the public until his works were collected in 1814, and exhibited at the Gallery of the British Institution.

CHARACTERISTICS, RETROSPECTIVE OPINIONS, AND PERSONAL TRAITS.

HOGARTH'S EARLY PORTRAITS.

THE success of our painter in the Wanstead Assembly led him to commence painting portraits; "the most ill-suited employment," says Walpole, "imaginable to a man whose turn certainly was not flattery, nor his talent adapted to look on vanity without a sneer. Yet his facility in catching a likeness, and the method he chose of painting families and conversation in small, then a novelty, drew him prodigious business for some time. It did not last, either from his applying to the real bent of his disposition, or from his customers apprehending that a satirist was too formidable a confessor for the devotees of self-love." Nichols adds, "There are still many family pictures by Mr. Hogarth existing, in the style of serious conversation-pieces. He was not, however, lucky in all his resemblances, and has sometimes failed where a crowd of other artists have succeeded. Nichols instances the whole length of Garrick sitting at a table, with his wife behind him taking the pen out of his hand; in which he has missed the character of Garrick's countenance while undisturbed by passion; but was more lucky in seizing his features when aggravated by terror, as in the tent-scene of King Richard III. It appears that Garrick was dissatisfied with the former portrait, or that some dispute arose between him and the painter, who then struck his pencil across the face, and damaged it. The picture was unpaid for at the time of Hogarth's death; when his widow sent it home to Garrick, without any demand."

Among the painter's early portraits was a whole-length of Mr. Western, painted for Mr. Cole's gallery at Milton, near Cambridge. Mr. Western is seated in his fellow-commoner's habit, and square cap with gold tassel, in his chamber at Clare Hall, with a cat sitting near him, as Nichols says, "agreeable to his humour, to show the situation," by his fireside. Mr. Cole relates that when he sat to Hogarth for this portrait, the custom of giving vails to servants was not discontinued. On his taking leave of the painter, and his servant opening the door, Mr. Cole offered him a gratuity, which the man politely refused, adding, it would be as much as the loss of his place, were he to accept the money, and his master know it.*

It was Hogarth's custom to sketch on the spot any remarkable face, of which he wished to preserve the remembrance; and a friend informed Nichols, that being with Hogarth at the Bedford coffee-house, he observed him drawing with a pencil *on his nail*, which proved to be a sketch of the features of a person at a small distance, in the coffee-room. At another time, he drew his friend Ben Read, sound asleep—with pen and ink, without sitting down—a curious and clever likeness, and still existing.

His sitters already included different ranks. One day, a nobleman, by no means remarkable for his personal beauty, and deformed in figure, sat to Hogarth, and the portrait proved a correct likeness, without the least attention to compliment or flattery. His lordship was disgusted at this counterpart of himself; and the painter frequently applied for payment, but without success. He then wrote to the peer as follows: "Mr. Hogarth's dutiful respects to Lord ———; finding that he does not mean to have the picture which was drawn for him, is informed again of Mr. H.'s necessity for the money; if, therefore, his lordship does not send for it in three days, it will be disposed of, with the addition of a tail, and some other little appendages, to Mr. Hare, the famous wild-beast man; Mr. H. having given that gentleman a conditional promise of it for an exhibition-picture, on his lordship's refusal." This intimation had the desired effect: the picture was sent home, and committed to the flames.

It was likewise Hogarth's practice to introduce striking resemblances of well-known characters of his time. Thus, almost all of the personages who attend the levee, in the series of the *Rake's Progress*, are undoubted portraits; and certain notabilities figure in the *Southwark Fair* and *Modern Midnight Conversation*, and the *Rake's Progress*.

At length, an opportunity occurred for bringing out Hogarth's force in portrait-painting with still greater effect. In 1729, Bambridge, warden of the Fleet Prison, and Huggins,

* Nor is it likely such a thing would happen again—Sir Joshua Reynolds gave his servant 6*l.* annually of wages, and offered him 100*l.* a year for the *door!*—*Cunningham.*

his predecessor, were accused before the House of Commons of breaches of trust, extortions, and cruelties, and sent to Newgate. "The scene," says Walpole, "is a Committee of the Commons; on the table are the instruments of torture. A prisoner in rags, half-starved, appears before them; the poor man has a good countenance that adds to the interest. On the other hand is the inhuman jailer. It is the very figure which Salvator Rosa would have drawn for Iago in the moment of detection. Villany, fear, and conscience, are mixed in yellow and livid upon his countenance, his lips are contracted by tremor, his face advances as eager to lie, his legs step back as thinking to make his escape, one hand is thrust forward into his bosom, the fingers of the other are catching uncertainly at his button-hole. If this was a portrait, it was the most striking that ever was drawn—if it was not, it is still finer." Cunningham adds: "The face was that of Bambridge—the rest was the imagination of the artist." The Committee, according to Nichols, are all portraits. The picture was painted in 1729, for Sir Archibald Grant, of Monymusk, Bart. It became the property of the son of Huggins, after whose death it passed into the collection of the Earl of Carlisle. The frame is surmounted with a bust of Sir Francis Page, one of the judges, with a halter round his neck, emblematic of his character for severity.*

A sketch in oil of Bambridge was given by Hogarth to Walpole, and added to the Strawberry-hill collection.

Hogarth painted as a companion picture to the above a scene from the *Beggars' Opera*, with a bust of Gay on its frame, which picture also became the property of Mr. Huggins.

Strangely enough, Thornhill and Hogarth afterwards jointly painted for Huggins's son an allegorical ceiling, at his house, Headley Park, Hants.

* Savage, in a "Character" of great power, has gibbeted Sir Francis Page to public detestation. Nor was Savage less severe in his prose. On the trial of this unfortunate poet, for the murder of James Sinclair in 1727, Judge Page, who was then on the bench, treated him with his usual insolence and severity; and when he had summed up the evidence, endeavoured to exasperate the jury, as Savage used to relate, with this eloquent harangue: "Gentlemen of the jury, you are to consider that Mr. Savage is a very great man, a much greater man than you or I, Gentlemen of the Jury; that he wears very fine clothes, much finer clothes than you or I, Gentlemen of the Jury; that he has abundance of money in his pocket, much more money than you or I, Gentlemen of the

HOGARTH'S CONCEIT.

Garrick himself was not more ductile to flattery than the painting moralist of Leicester Fields. An eminent surgeon of his time, Mr. Belchior, F.R.S., relates the following incident, which serves to show how much more easy it is to detect ill-placed or hyperbolical adulation respecting others than when applied to ourselves. Hogarth, being at dinner with Cheselden, the great surgeon, and some other company, was told that Mr. John Freke, surgeon, of St. Bartholomew's Hospital, a few evenings before, at Dick's Coffee-house,* had asserted that Dr. Maurice Greene was as eminent in musical composition as Handel. "That fellow Freke," said Hogarth, "is always shooting his bolt absurdly, one way or another. Handel is a giant in music; Greene only a light Florimel kind of composer." "Ay," said Hogarth's informant, "but at the same time Mr. Freke declared you were as good a portrait-painter as Vandyck." "*There* he was right," replied Hogarth, "and so, by G—, I am, give me my time, and let me choose my subject." Often he would thump the table and snap his fingers, and say, "Historical painters be hanged; here's the man that will paint against any of them for a hundred pounds. Correggio's *Sigismunda!* Look at Bill Hogarth's *Sigismunda;* look at my altar-piece at St. Mary Redcliffe, Bristol; look at my *Paul before Felix*, and see whether I'm not as good as the best of them."

Jury; but, Gentlemen of the Jury, is it not a very hard case, Gentlemen of the Jury, that Mr. Savage should therefore kill you or me, Gentlemen of the Jury?"

Pope also, *Horace*, B. II. Sect. I, has the following line :

"Hard words or hanging, if your judge be Page."

And Fielding, in *Tom Jones*, makes Partridge say, after premising that Judge Page was a very brave man, and a man of great wit : "It is indeed charming sport to hear trials on life and death."

* Dick's Coffee-house, now a tavern, 8, Fleet-street, near Temple-bar, has been in existence 180 years. Here Isaac Bickerstaff, the *Tatler*, led the deputation of "Twaddlers" from Shire-lane, across Fleet-street. When Cowper lived in the Temple, he used to breakfast at Dick's, or Richard's, as it was then called; and it was a great resort of the Templars in the good old theatrical times, when the love of the drama manifested itself in strong partisanship.

POETICAL TRIBUTES TO HOGARTH.

While Hogarth was engaged as a portrait-painter, he was not without public and poetic recognition. A certain Mr. Robinson, of Kendal, published in 1738 a series of lines in his praise appended with other poems to his play "The Intriguing Milliners." They begin as follows:

> "Ingenious Hogarth all the Town
> Britain's Apelles justly own,
> To see his portraits all repair,
> For they excel the fairest fair;
> Whate'er is beauteous there you meet,
> No flaw to pall, there all's compleat;
> He plays the God with all he draws!
> Each picture meets with just applause,
> His curious strokes with Nature strive,
> They soften into flesh, they live:
> So artfully they cheat the eye,
> You speak and wait for a reply."

Such rhymes, though not poetry, are proofs of the artist's popularity, and in the course of the lines we read—

> "For Hogarth, wheresoe'er he call,
> Is well received and thank'd by all."

We have already quoted, at page 1, Swift's distinguishing Hogarth in his "Description of the Legion Club."

Somerville, the poet of the *Chase*, dedicated his mock heroic of "Hobbinol, or Rural Games," to Hogarth, as "the greatest master in the burlesque way." Yet Fielding, in his Preface to *Joseph Andrews*, says: "he who should call the ingenious Hogarth a burlesque painter would, in my opinion, do him very little honour; for sure it is much easier, much less the subject of admiration, to paint a man with a nose, or any other feature, of a preposterous size, or to expose him in some absurd or monstrous attitude, than to express the affections of men on canvas. It hath been thought a vast commendation of a painter to say his figures seem to breathe; but surely it is a much greater and nobler applause that they appear to think."

Vinney Bourne, the classical usher of Westminster school, and the elegant Latin poet, addressed some gratulatory lines "Ad Gulielmum Hogarth." *

---

* Hogarth painted a portrait of a celebrated Westminster, Bishop Hooper, whose future success Dr. Busby foretold to "this boy—the

HOGARTH PAINTED BY HIMSELF.

Hogarth's portraits of himself are very clever, and excellently like. In one, (says Cunningham,) he is accompanied by a bull-dog of the true English breed; and in another he is seated in his study, with his pencil ready and his eye fixed and intent on a figure which he is sketching on the canvas. He has a short, good-humoured face, full of health, observation, and sagacity. He treated his own physiognomy as he treated his friends',—seized the character strongly, and left grace and elegance to those who were unable to cope with mind and spirit. On the palette, which belongs to the first-named of these two portraits, there is drawn a waving line with the words "Line of Beauty and Grace,"—the hieroglyphic of which no one could at first divine the meaning.

Hogarth thus describes his own original style, upon which his fame rests: "The reasons which induced me to adopt this mode of designing were, that I thought both writers and painters had, in the historical style, totally overlooked that intermediate species of subjects which may be placed between the sublime and grotesque."

CARICATURES ON HOGARTH.

Mr. Thomas Wright, F.S.A., in his ingenious work, *England under the House of Hanover*, thus clearly sketches the flood of caricature drawn upon Hogarth by his quarrel with Wilkes and Churchill.

"They hold him up now as the pensioned dauber of the unpopular Lord Bute, and the calumniator of the friends of liberty. In one, entitled 'the Beautifyer, a touch upon the Times,' Hogarth is represented upon a huge platform, daubing an immense *boot*, (the constant emblem of the obnoxious minister,) while, in his awkwardness, he bespatters Pitt and Temple, who happen to be below. This is a parody on Hogarth's own satire on Pope. Beneath the scaffold is a tub full of Auditors, Monitors, &c., labelled The Charm: Beautifying Wash. A print, entitled 'The Bruiser Triumphant,' represents Hogarth as an ass, painting the Bruiser, while Wilkes comes behind, and places horns on his head,—an allusion to some

least favoured in features of any in the school." Hogarth was not the portrait-painter most likely to improve these features. The picture hangs in the Hall of the School.

scandalous intimations in the *North Briton*. Churchill, in the garb of a parson, is writing Hogarth's life. A number of other attributes and allusions fill the picture.

"A caricature entitled 'Tit for Tat,' represents Hogarth painting Wilkes, with the unfortunate picture of Sigismunda in the distance. Another 'Tit for Tat, Invt. et del. by G. O'Garth, according to act or order is not material,' represents the painter partly clad in Scotch garb, with the line of beauty on his palette, glorifying a boot surmounted by a thistle. The painter is saying to himself 'Anything for money: I'll gild this Scotch sign, and make it look glorious; and I'll daub the other sign, and efface its beauty, and make it as black as a Jack Boot.' On another easel is a portrait of Wilkes, 'Defaced by order of O'Garth,' and in the foreground 'a smutch-pot to sully the best and most exalted characters.' In another print, 'Pug, the snarling cur,' is being severely chastised by Wilkes and Churchill. In another he is baited by the bear and a dog; and in the background is a large panel, with the inscription, 'Panel-painting.' In one print, Hogarth is represented going for his pension of 300*l*. a year, and carrying as his vouchers the prints of 'The Times' and Wilkes. 'I can paint an angel black, and the devil white, just as it suits me.' 'An Answer to the print of John Wilkes, Esq.' represents Hogarth with his colour-pot, inscribed 'Colour to blacken fair characters;' he is treading on the cap of liberty with his cloven foot, and an inscription says '300*l*. per annum for distorting features.'

"Several other prints, equally bitter against him, besides a number of caricatures against the Government, under the fictitious names of O'Garth, Hoggart, Hog-ass, &c., must have assisted in irritating the persecuted painter.

"Hogarth left an engraving of 'The Times,' plate II., in which Wilkes was represented in the pillory, by the side of 'Miss Fanny;' but it was not given to the world till many years after his death."

HOGARTH AND BISHOP HOADLEY.

Upon pulling down the palace of the Bishop of Winchester, at Chelsea, at the upper end of Cheyne Walk, (near the present Pier Hotel,) a singular discovery was made. In a small room of the north front, were found, on the plaster of the walls, nine life-size figures, three men and six women, drawn in outline, with black chalk, in a bold and spirited style. Of these figures correct copies have been published. They display much of the manner of Hogarth, who often visited Bishop Hoadley at this palace; and it is supposed that these figures apply to some incident in the Bishop's family, or to some scene in a play. His lordship's partiality for the drama is well known; and his son, Dr. Hoadley, the physician, who resided at Chelsea, just beyond Cremorne House, wrote the admirable comedy of the *Suspicious Husband*.

Hogarth was admitted to the Doctor's private theatricals. Upon one occasion he performed with Garrick, and his entertainer, a burlesque on that scene in *Julius Cæsar* where the ghost appears to Brutus. Hogarth personated the spectre; and to heighten the absurdity of the scene his speech of two lines was written upon an illuminated paper lantern, that he might read them when he came upon the stage. This piece of humour has been perverted by some of the narrators of anecdotes of Hogarth into a proof of Hogarth's unretentive memory!

Hogarth painted for this performance a scene of a suttling booth, with the Duke of Cumberland's head as a sign: he likewise embellished the play-bill with characteristic designs.

It has been said that Bishop Hoadley wrote some of the verses appended to Hogarth's prints; but the evidence is doubtful.

COPYRIGHT IN PRINTS.

No sooner had Hogarth begun to reap fame and profit by engraving his works than needy artists and worthless printsellers began to prey upon him. Indeed, *before* the prints of the *Rake's Progress* were published, they were pirated by Boitard, and that with skill. Hogarth complained of such dishonesty; and to protect painters generally in future, and to make their works property, like other productions of human art, he obtained from Parliament, in 1735, an Act for recognising a legal copyright in designs and engravings, and restraining copies of such works from being made without the consent of the owners. Unfortunately, the Act was loosely and vaguely drawn; so that when resorted to in the case of Jeffreys, the printseller, it was the opinion of Lord Hardwicke, before whom the action was tried, that no person claiming an assignment from the original inventor of the paintings or designs copied could receive any benefit from it.

Nevertheless, Hogarth, in commemoration of the passing of this Bill for the encouragement of designing and engraving, executed a small print with emblematic devices, and a laudatory inscription. On the top of the plate Hogarth etched a royal crown, shedding rays on mitres and coronets, on the Great Seal, the Speaker's hat, and other symbols of the "Collective Wisdom."

This plate he afterwards made to serve for a receipt for subscriptions to Hogarth's *Election Entertainment*, and a few other prints.

J. T. Smith states, as a curious fact, that of the print of the Cockpit, by Hogarth, as well as those of the gates of Calais, and Southwark Fair, he had never seen, read, or heard of an etching, nor of any impression whatever with a variation from the state in which they were published. "This," continues Smith, "is the more extraordinary, as they are all highly-finished plates, and the artist must have required many proofs of them in their progress before he could have been satisfied with their effect; particularly in that of Southwark Fair, which, in my opinion, is not only the deepest studied as to composition and light and shade, but the most elaborately finished, and perhaps the most innocently entertaining of all his works. For great as Hogarth was in his display of every variety of character, I should never think of exhibiting a portfolio of his prints to the youthful inquirer; nor can I agree that the man who was so accustomed to visit, so fond of delineating, and who gave up so much of his time to the vices of the most abandoned classes, was in truth 'a moral teacher of mankind.' My father knew Hogarth well, and I have often heard him declare, that he (Hogarth) revelled in the company of the drunken and profligate;—Churchill, Wilkes, Hayman, &c. were among his constant companions. Dr. John Hoadley,* though in my opinion it reflected no credit on him, delighted in his company; but he did not approve of all the prints produced by him, particularly that of the first state of 'Enthusiasm Displayed,' which, had Mr. Garrick or Dr. Johnson ever seen, they could never for a moment have entertained their high esteem of so irreligious a character."

At Strawberry Hill, before the sale in 1842, were 365 prints and drawings, engraved by and after Hogarth, all first impressions, and some original drawings; and stated by Walpole, in his *Anecdotes of Painting*, to be the most complete and perfect collection of Hogarth's Prints.

HOGARTH'S PALETTE.

The palette used by Hogarth is still preserved in the Royal Academy; it is of very peculiar form, shaped something like an heraldic escutcheon, with a long handle, and a ring at the end for the thumb to pass through.

* Who was Dr. *John* Hoadley? Does Mr. Smith refer to Dr. Benjamin Hoadley, Bishop of Winchester?

HOGARTH'S "ORATORIO."

In 1835, the Rev. Bishop Luscombe,* showed to a correspondent of *Notes and Queries*, at Paris, the original picture of "the Oratorio," a subject well known from Hogarth's etching. Mr. Luscombe had bought it at a broker's shop in the Rue St. Denis: on examination, he found the frame to be English, but as he only gave thirty francs for the picture, he purchased it without supposing it to be more than a copy. Sir William Knighton, on seeing it, told Mr. Luscombe that Hogarth's original had belonged to the Dukes of Richmond, and had been in their residence at Paris until the first Revolution, since which time it had not been heard of; and Sir William had no doubt that Mr. Luscombe had been so fortunate as to obtain it.

THE MISER AND SIR ISAAC SHEARD.

At Rusper, in Sussex, lived Sir Isaac Sheard, so proverbial for his penurious habits, that Hogarth introduced him into a picture which he painted, as a miser trying a mastiff for robbing his kitchen. This circumstance coming to the ears of Sheard's son, a high-spirited young man, he called at the painter's to see the picture, and being informed by the servant that the figure was considered to be like Sir Isaac Sheard, he cut the painting to pieces with his sword.

WALL-PAINTINGS IN FENCHURCH STREET.

In the year 1826, was taken down the old *Elephant* public-house, in Fenchurch-street, whereat Hogarth is said to have lodged for some time, when young. The house had been built before the great Fire of London, and narrowly escaped its ravages. Previous to the demolition of the premises, there were removed from the wall of the tap-room, three pictures which Hogarth is said to have painted while a lodger there: one represented a group of the Hudson's Bay Company's porters going to dinner, they at that time frequenting the house; the background was Fenchurch-street, as it appeared nearly a century and a half ago, with the old Magpie and

---

* The Rev. Bishop Luscombe was, for many years, chaplain to the British Embassy at Paris. His christian name was Bishop, which often led to the error of episcopal rank being attributed to him, in his being referred to as Bishop Luscombe.

Punch-bowl public-house in the distance. The second painting was set down as Hogarth's first idea for his *Modern Midnight Conversation*, differing from the print in an incident too broad in its humour for the graver: there were one or two figures less in the print, but Orator Henley and the other principal characters occupy the same situation in both performances. The third picture was Harlequin and Pierrot seeming to be laughing at one of the figures in the second picture. There was also on a wall of the first-floor of *the Elephant* a picture of Harlow Bush Fair, covered over with paint.

The circumstances under which these pictures were painted were in 1829, thus related by the landlady of the public-house, in whose family the business had been for more than a century, and for whom the house was rebuilt in 1826. It appears that it had been customary for the parochial authorities to hold certain entertainments at *the Elephant*, (she stated,) the celebration of which, however, was, from some cause, removed to *Henry the Eighth's Head*, opposite. This transfer being mentioned to Hogarth, on his return home one night, when the feast was being held at the opposite house, the painter was much irritated, more especially as he had not been invited, as formerly. He, therefore, went over to the *Henry's Head*, where some altercation took place between the authorities and the painter, who left, threatening to stick them all up on the walls of the tap-room of *the Elephant*. This he proposed to the landlord: the picture of jollity and feasting was painted, with the clock at past four in the morning, and it was so profitable an attraction that the landlord of *the Elephant* wiped out a debt of Hogarth's, as a remuneration; so that, although the house lost the parish dinner party, it gained by persons coming to see the authorities *stuck up on the walls*. Subsequently, was painted as a companion picture, the Hudson's Bay Company's porters; and the two other pictures are said to have been produced under similar circumstances.

Before the house was taken down, the pictures were removed from the walls at no small risk and trouble by Mr. Lyon, of Walworth, and Mr. H. E. Hall, of Leicestershire; and they were subsequently sold at the gallery of Mr. Penny, in Pall Mall.

The Elephant public-house has been engraved; and at the foot of the print, the information as to Hogarth having executed these paintings is rested upon the evidence of "Mrs.

Hibbert, who has kept the house between thirty and forty years, and received her information relating to Mr. Hogarth from persons at that time well acquainted with him."

Although the evidence is thus circumstantial, Hogarth's biographers do not record his abode in Fenchurch-street; and the particulars of the interval between his apprenticeship and his marriage are few and far between.

HOGARTH PAINTS "GOLDSMITH'S HOSTESS."

The only memorial said to be left of Goldsmith's friendly intercourse with Hogarth, is a portrait in oil, known by the name of "Goldsmith's Hostess," and exhibited in London some years since, as the work of Hogarth's pencil. Still, the evidence is but putative. Mr. Forster says: "it involves no great stretch of fancy to suppose it painted in the Islington lodgings, at some crisis of domestic pressure: Newbery's accounts reveal to us how often it was needful to mitigate Mrs. Flemming's impatience, to moderate her wrath, and, when money was not immediately at hand, to minister to her vanities. It is but to imagine a visit from Hogarth at such a time. Though the copyrights of his prints were a source of certain and not inconsiderable income, his money at command was scanty; and it would better suit his generous good humour, as well as better serve his friend, to bring his easel in his coach some day, and enthrone Mrs. Flemming by the side of it. So the portrait was painted; and much laughter there was in its progress, I do not doubt, at the very different sort of sitters and subjects, whose coronet-coaches were crowding the west side of Leicester-square."

GENIUS OF HOGARTH.

J. T. Smith has ably vindicated the genius of Hogarth, in a sort of appendix to his *Nollekens and his Times.* "I believe," (says Smith,) "that in no instance has the name of a painter been so freely used as that of Hogarth. His reputation has become public property, and is considered fair game; since, a picture exhibiting a large white wig, a three-cornered Macheath hat, an old apothecary's capeless coat with immense basket buttons on the sleeves and flap-pockets, rolled-up stockings and square-toed buckle shoes,—has been, without hesitation, ascribed to Hogarth's pencil, which, if examined, would very soon be proved the contrary. Mercier, Van

Hawkin, Highmore, Pugh, or that drunken pothouse painter Hamskirk, (originally a singer at Sadler's Wells,) are artists now rarely mentioned; though several of their performances have been elevated by second-rate picture-dealers and brokers in old panels, as the works of Hogarth; and even a head from a picture from Rosalba has been engraved and published as the genuine production of Hogarth.

"For myself, I am decidedly of opinion, that several of the copies of Prize-fighting and Playhouse benefit-tickets, published in Samuel Ireland's *Graphic Illustrations of Hogarth*, are from plates neither designed nor etched by him. They are destitute of wit or talent, both of which Hogarth possessed, in a supereminent degree, even in his youthful days, when he engraved ornaments and coats-of-arms for his master Gamble; and for his wit, where can we find any prints to equal most of the plates for the small set of Hudibras, which were some of his earliest productions? They are full of character, well drawn, spiritedly etched, and most of them possess admirable effect; and I must say, as a supporter of the honour of Hogarth as an artist, that until Mr. Samuel Ireland raked up many of the wretched things which he caused to be copied for a publication unquestionably with a view to raise money,—no collectors admitted the originals into their portfolios as the works of Hogarth.

"I am credibly informed that there is even at this moment (1828) an artist who finds it rather a successful occupation to make spirited drawings from Hogarth's prints, which he most *ingeniously* deviates from by the omission of some figure or other object, or insertion of an additional one, in order to give his drawing the appearance of a first thought, upon which Hogarth is supposed to have made some alteration in his plate as an improvement. These drawings are discoloured, put into old black frames, and then, after passing through several hands, are finally sold, accompanied by a very long story, to those over-cunning collectors, destitute of sufficient knowledge to enable them to detect the forgery.

"Having ventured in a former page to mention my own opinion as to Hogarth's want of morality, I must not, even for a moment, allow the reader to suppose that I am in any degree wanting in my respect for his powerful talents as an artist. His easy and perfectly natural mode of grouping, his sweetness and harmony of colouring, his excellent pencilling and general brilliancy of effect, must be perceived and felt by every one possessing a single spark of taste, when viewing that inestimable series of pictures entitled the *Marriage à la Mode*, in our National Gallery.

"The prints by this artist, in freedom of etching and vigour of tooling, display his powers to the highest advantage. The plates of *Southwark Fair* and the *Cockpit* are unrivalled in this or any other country. The former displays most conspicuously the four classes of composition in art; namely, the diverging, the S-like or line of beauty, (see pp. 57–58 *ante*,) the festoon, and the triangle or pyramidal."

Mr. Leslie considered there to be many hints of French fashions in Hogarth's works. He says: "The bridegroom in the first picture of *Marriage à la Mode* is evidently dressed on the model of a Paris beau; the boy beating a drum in the *Enraged Musician* has been metamorphosed, as far as dress could do it, into a little Frenchman; the two gallants in the boxes in the *Laughing Audience* are as French as possible, while the pit is filled with plain English folk, who are not too fine to take an interest in the performance; and in *Taste in High Life*, the antiquated beau, dressed in the extreme of the Parisian fashion, has succeeded in making himself look very like a monkey."

Fuseli made a false estimate of Hogarth's genius when, in his Lecture, he said: "The characteristic discrimination and humourous exuberance which we admire in Hogarth, but which, like the fleeting passion of a day, every hour contributes something to obliterate, will soon be unintelligible by time, or degenerate into caricature: the chronicle of scandal, and the history-book of the vulgar."

When Reynolds was blamed for his slight mention of Hogarth in his Letters and Discourses, a distinguished member of the Royal Academy remarked publicly—that Sir Joshua might as well be censured for not naming Fielding and Richardson, as Hogarth was *no painter !*

Charles Lamb's *Essay on Hogarth* (says Leslie) is the best written; though it is much to be regretted that, in praising Hogarth, he thought fit to disparage Reynolds.

HISTORICAL VALUE OF HOGARTH'S WORKS.

To the student of History, these admirable works must be invaluable, as they give us the most complete and truthful pictures of the manners, and even the thoughts, of the past century. We look, and see pass before us the England of a hundred years ago—the peer in his drawing-room, the lady of fashion in her apartment, foreign singers surrounding her, and the chamber filled with gew-gaws in the mode of that day; the church with its quaint florid architecture and singing congregation; the parson with his great wig, and the beadle with his cane: all these are represented before us, and we are sure of the truth of the portrait. We see how the Lord Mayor dines in State; how the prodigal drinks and sports at the bagnio; how the poor girl beats hemp in Bridewell; how the thief divides his booty and drinks his punch at the nightcellar, and how he finishes his career at the gibbet. We may depend upon the perfect accuracy of these strange and varied portraits of the by-gone generation: we see one of Walpole's members of Parliament chaired after his election, and the lieges celebrating the event, and drinking confusion to the Pretender; we see the grenadiers and train bands of the City marching out to meet the enemy; and have before us, with sword and firelock, and white Hanoverian horse embroidered on the cap, the very figure of the men who ran away with Johnny Cope, and who conquered at Culloden. The Yorkshire waggon rolls into the inn-yard; the country parson, in his jack-boots, and his bands and short cassock, comes trotting into town, and we fancy it is Parson Adams with his sermons in his pocket. The Salisbury Fly sets forth from the old Angel—you see the passengers entering the great heavy vehicle, up the wooden steps, their hats tied down with their handkerchiefs over their faces, and under their arms, sword, hanger, and case-bottle; the landlady,—apoplectic with the liquors in her own bar—is tugging at the bell; the hunchbacked postilion—he may have ridden the leaders to Humphrey Clinker,—is begging a gratuity; the miser is grumbling at the bill; Jack of the Centurion lies on the top of the clumsy vehicle, with a soldier by his side—it may be Smollett's Jack Hatchway—it has a likeness to Lismahago. You see the suburban fair and the strolling company of actors; the pretty milkmaid singing under the window of the enraged French musician. You see noblemen and blacklegs bawling and betting in the Cockpit; you see Garrick as he was arrayed in *King Richard*; *Macheath* and *Polly* in the dresses which they wore when they charmed our ancestors, and when noblemen in blue ribbons sat on the stage and listened to their delightful music. You see the ragged French soldiery, in their white coats and cockades, at Calais Gate.* You see the judges on the bench; the audience laughing in the pit; the student in the Oxford theatre; the citizen on his country walk; you see Broughton, the boxer, Sarah Malcolm the murderess, Simon Lovat the traitor; John Wilkes the demagogue, staring at you with that squint which has become historical, and that face which, ugly as it was, he said he could make as captivating to woman as the countenance of the handsomest beau in town. All these sights and people are with you. After looking in the *Rake's Progress* at Hogarth's picture of St. James's Palace-gates, you may people the street, but little altered within these hundred years, with the gilded carriages and thronging chairmen that bore the courtiers, your ancestors, to Queen Caroline's drawing-room more than a hundred years ago.—*Mr. Thackeray's Lectures on the English Humourists of the Eighteenth Century.*

HOGARTH'S PRINTS.

How much of the moral effect of Hogarth's works is due to their being engraved, and the prints sold at prices *available by all classes*, must be evident to every one who has bestowed any thought upon the subject. If we refer to the list of "Prints published by Mr. Hogarth; Genuine Impressions of which are to be had at Mrs. Hogarth's House in Leicester Fields, 1781," we shall find the prices as low as One Shilling, and rarely to exceed One Guinea. Here are a few:

	£	s.	d.
Harlot's Progress, 6 prints	1	1	0
Rake's Progress, 8 prints	2	2	0
Marriage à la Mode, 6 prints	1	11	6
Four Times of the Day, 4 prints	1	0	0
Before and After, 2 prints	3	5	0
Midnight Conversation	0	5	0
Enraged Musician	0	3	0
Southwark Fair	0	5	0
Garrick in King Richard III.	0	7	6

---

* Mr. Leslie, when at Calais, in November, 1855, noted as an object of interest to him "the old gate, painted by Hogarth. (See pp. 54—56 of the present volume.) The draw-bridge, with its chains depending from the projecting beams, is exactly like that in the picture; but the portcullis is gone, and the gate much altered. Whatever remains there may have been of the English arms upon it in Hogarth's time are now wholly removed."—*Autobiography*, p. 232.

	£	s.	d.
Calais; or, the Roast Beef of Old England, &c.	0	5	0
Paul before Felix	0	7	6
March to Finchley	0	10	6
Strolling Actresses dressing in a Barn	0	5	0
An Election, 4 prints	2	2	0
Idleness and Industry, 12 prints	0	12	0
Lord Lovat *.	0	1	0
Sleeping Congregation	0	1	0
Columbus breaking the Egg	0	1	0
Beer-street and Gin-lane, 2 prints	0	1	0
Four Stages of Cruelty, 4 prints	0	6	0

Sufficient margin was left for framing, but glass was comparatively dear; in this respect we have the advantage.

Mr. Leslie has thus admirably illustrated the above views. "Had there been no such art as engraving, there would have been no such patronage as Boydell's, which gave birth to some of the greatest works of the British School; and to this same art of engraving it is scarcely too much to say that we owe the very existence of Hogarth. His patrons were the million. The great people were told by Walpole that he was no painter; and Walpole being one of themselves, they believed him. But for engraving, therefore, Hogarth must have confined himself to portraits, on which he might have starved, for he was never popular as a portrait-painter. But when the prints of the *Harlot's Progress* appeared, 1,200 copies were immediately subscribed for. This was the beginning of the patronage produced for painting by engraving."—*Autobiography*, p. 214.

* Hogarth made the drawing for his print of Lord Lovat the night before he took leave of Major Gardner, under whose escort he was travelling to the Tower, and to whom Lord Lovat presented the original sketch. A Correspondent of *Notes and Queries*, No. 288, who has seen the drawing, states that Hogarth made it August 14, 1746; the execution of Lord Lovat took place in the following April.

SIR JOSHUA REYNOLDS, P.R.A.

BIRTH-PLACE OF SIR JOSHUA REYNOLDS.

JOSHUA REYNOLDS, "the founder of the British School of Painting," was born at Plympton, an ancient town of Devonshire, in a fertile valley, about five miles from Plymouth, and contiguous to the high road leading from Exeter. Here "the lover of the picturesque will find much to please him in the surrounding scenery; and he whose delight it is to linger in the haunts of genius, will stop to contemplate the humble and unassuming residence of the schoolmaster, where Joshua Reynolds first saw the light; and while standing under the arcades of the old Grammar School, will picture to himself the youthful artist, sitting apart from his schoolfellows, regardless of their sports, and seeking pleasure in his own favourite pursuit, with the *Jesuit's Perspective* in his hand, busily engaged in applying its rules to the delineation of the building." *

Joshua was born on the 16th of July, 1723, and was the seventh of either ten or eleven children, five of whom, it is said, died in their infancy. His father, grandfather, and two uncles, were all in Holy Orders. His father, the Rev. Samuel Reynolds, is described in the baptismal register of Plympton, as "clerk and schoolmaster": he was a Fellow of Balliol College, Oxford; and there is in existence a letter from Young, the author of the *Night Thoughts*, addressed to Mr. Samuel Reynolds, Fellow of Balliol College. Northcote, and most of Sir Joshua's biographers, have erroneously described the Rev. Samuel Reynolds as the Incumbent of Plympton.†
He was master of the Grammar School of the town: "although

---

* Sir Joshua Reynolds and his works. By William Cotton, M.A. Edited by John Burnet, F.R.S. 1856.

† A portrait of the Rev. Samuel Reynolds, painted by Sir Joshua, which belonged to the late Dean of Cashel, is in the Cottonian Library, at Plymouth.

(says Cotton) possessed of a high character for learning, he appears to have been ill fitted for the office of a schoolmaster, and before his death it is said that the number of his scholars was literally reduced to one." The mother of Sir Joshua was Theophila, daughter of the Rev. Mr. Potter, near Torrington, in the north of Devon. Samuel Reynolds had a Parson-Adams-like absence of mind; and it is said that in performing a journey on horseback, one of his boots dropped off by the way, without being missed by the wearer. Of his humour it is related that, in allusion to his wife's name, *Theophila*, he made the following rhyme:

> When I say The
> Thou must make tea—
> When I say Offey
> Thou must make coffee.

The house in which Reynolds was born at Plympton was visited by Haydon and Wilkie in 1809, when they saw in the chamber* reputed as the birth-room, an early attempt at a portrait drawn with a finger dipped in ink, showing an air of Reynolds's later works. This and other sketches, Mr. Cotton tells us, have been obliterated by the unsparing hand of some renovator. At the period of Haydon's and Wilkie's visit, the house was occupied by Haydon's schoolmaster. From "the Shrine of Reynolds," as it is called, Wilkie went to the Hall of Guild, where he saw, he says, a very fine portrait of Sir Joshua himself; and portraits of two naval officers, painted before he went to Italy, which for composition were as fine as he ever did afterwards. From the Hall he went to the house of an old lady, who showed him a very early picture by Reynolds, which, in spite of want of spirit, and experience of touch, had much in it which promised future excellence. At the residence of Mrs. Mayo, he likewise saw the portrait of an old man, which, though a little faded, was very finely painted: such was her reverence for it, that she would not allow a servant to clean it with either brush or towel, but caused the dust to be blown off with a pair of bellows; nevertheless, adds Wilkie, the best schemes are sometimes frustrated: a giddy housemaid one day drove the bellows-pipe through the canvas.

---

* Mr. Cotton has engraved this room, the window of which commands a view of the Grammar School.

BAPTISM OF REYNOLDS.

The father of Reynolds is said to have given him the Scripture name of Joshua, in the hope that such a singular or at least uncommon name, might at some future period of his life lead a patron with a similar prefix to give him a fortune. Malone received this story from Dr. Percy, Bishop of Dromore; but Northcote has completely refuted it. He says: "I know from undoubted authority, having seen it in Sir Joshua's own handwriting, that he had an uncle, whose name was Joshua, and dwelt at Exeter, and who was his godfather, but not being present at the baptism, was represented by a Mr. Aldwin." This statement has been fully confirmed.

A strange mistake was, however, made in the baptismal entry; and the *Joshua* of all the rest of the world (Cunningham aptly says,) is a *Joseph* at Plympton. In the register is:

"1723. Joseph, son of Samuel Reynolds, clerk, baptized July the 30th."

On another page is the following memorandum:

"In the entry of Baptisms for the year 1723, the person by mistake named *Joseph*, son of Samuel Reynolds, clerk, baptized July 30, was *Joshua* Reynolds, the celebrated painter, who died Feb. 23, 1792."

The above was copied by the Incumbent of Plympton, from the register, and communicated to *Notes and Queries*, in 1853, by a correspondent, who asks: "Was Sir Joshua by mistake *baptized Joseph?* or was the mistake made after baptism, in *registering the name?*"

REYNOLDS'S SCHOOL.

The young Joshua entered early the Grammar School at Plympton. Beneath the school-room is an open arcade or cloister, forming a playground for the scholars in wet weather. This cloister was the subject of one of Reynolds's juvenile performances with the pencil, which excited the astonishment of his father. Northcote relates: "Young Reynolds had accidentally read the *Jesuits' Perspective*, when he was not more than eight years old, a proof of his capacity and active curiosity. He attempted to apply the rules of that treatise in a drawing which he made of his father's school, a building well suited to his purpose, as it stood on pillars. On showing it to his father, who was merely a man of letters, he exclaimed, 'How this exemplifies what the author of the

Perspective asserts in his Preface, that by observing the rules laid down in this book, a man may do wonders; for this is wonderful.'"

This drawing is carefully preserved by the Palmer family; and Mr. Robert Palmer has also in his possession three nicely executed pen-and-ink sketches: one a perspective drawing on the back of a Latin exercise, "*De labore*," on which his father, the schoolmaster, has written, "*This is drawn by Joshua in school, out of pure idleness.*" How little (says Mr. Cotton,) did he guess to what such idleness would tend!

Another of the above drawings is the interior of a book-room, or library, apparently copied from a small engraving, with all the minuteness and delicacy of Callot, or Della Bella; the third is a drawing of a fish, also done with a pen, and inscribed, apparently by his father, " Copied from nature."

Sir Joshua related to Malone that the *Perspective* happened to be in the parlour-window in the house of his father. He made himself at eight years old so completely master of this book that he never had occasion to study any other work on the subject, and the knowledge of perspective then acquired served him ever after. Reynolds also told Malone that his first essays in drawing were copying some light drawings made by two of his sisters, who had a turn for art; he afterwards eagerly copied such prints as he met with among his father's books: particularly those which were given in the translation of Plutarch's Lives, published by Dryden. But his principal fund of initiation was Jacob Catt's Book of Emblems, which his great grandmother, by the father's side, a Dutchwoman, had brought with her from Holland.*

The father seems to have strangely neglected the education of his son. It is true that the boy, like Hogarth before him, was inspired by Richardson's *Treatise on Painting*, to make private drawings rather than public exercises in school. Northcote, Reynolds's pupil and biographer, reluctantly admits his master's deficiency in classical attainments. "The mass of general knowledge by which he was distinguished," says Northcote, "was the result of much studious application in his riper years."

* In Devonshire Reynolds saw the pictures which first fixed his attention; these were portraits by William Gandy, of Exeter, who thus became Reynolds's first instructor. Gandy's father was a pupil of Vandyke.

REYNOLDS PAINTS HIS FIRST PORTRAIT.

This was painted when he could not have been more than twelve years old. It was the portrait of the Rev. Thomas Smart, in whose family the tradition is that in 1735, young Joshua coloured the likeness in a boat-house at Cremyll beach under Mount Edgcumbe, on canvas which was part of a boat-sail, and with the common paint used by shipwrights. Mr. Smart was tutor in the family of Richard Edgcumbe, Esq., who afterwards became the first Lord Edgcumbe, the "Dick Edgcumbe" of Walpole's correspondence; and young Reynolds seems to have been passing the holidays at Mount Edgcumbe with one of his sons. The portrait is said to have been painted from a drawing "taken in church, and on the artist's thumb-nail:" Hogarth was wont to sketch in a similar manner. The picture was for many years at Mount Edgcumbe, but was afterwards sent to Plympton, and hung up in one of the rooms belonging to the Corporation, of which Mr. Smart was a member. It was subsequently returned to Mount Edgcumbe, and given by the present Earl to Mr. Boger, of Wolsdon, the descendant and representative of Mr. Smart, by whom these circumstances were related to Mr. Cotton. This portrait has been accurately engraved by S. W. Reynolds. Mr. Boger has also a small portrait or panel of the daughter of Mr. Smart, which is supposed to have been painted by Reynolds.

At the above time, Mr. Edgcumbe was one of the patrons of the Borough of Plympton, which accounts for the acquaintance between the boys. Young Richard Edgcumbe had also a good deal of taste for drawing, and some of his paintings are still at Mount Edgcumbe. He became one of Walpole's constant Christmas and Easter guests at Strawberry Hill; and Reynolds, who painted the tutor on sail-cloth, in 1735, in his boyhood, likewise painted young Edgcumbe for Walpole, when he had reached the zenith of his fame, in a charming picture with Selwyn and Gilly Williams. Walpole describes this picture as by far one of the best things Reynolds had executed: it is engraved in Cunningham's edition of Walpole's Letters; the original picture, a little larger than cabinet size, was bought by the Right Hon. Henry Labouchere, (now Lord Taunton,) at the Strawberry Hill Sale, in 1842.

There is also at Mount Edgcumbe a portrait of Richard

Lord Edgcumbe, painted by Sir Joshua when he was an untaught boy at Plympton, and before he went to London.

According to Eastlake, the earliest portrait Reynolds painted of himself was one in the possession of his niece, Miss Gwatkin, of Princess-square, Plymouth; it is a fine Vandyke-like picture, and in good preservation.—*Cotton.*

REYNOLDS IS ARTICLED TO HUDSON THE PAINTER.

Joshua's father hesitated for some time whether to make him an apothecary or a painter. Seeing his son's propensity for painting, by the advice of Mr. Cranch, a neighbour and friend of the family, he sent the youth to London, to be placed under Hudson, then the most celebrated portrait painter of the day. Joshua consented, from his having seen a print from one of Hudson's paintings, which much delighted him. His father preferred for him the practice of physic; and the painter, in after-life, observed to Northcote, if medicine had been his career in life, he should have felt the same determination to become the most eminent physician, as he then felt to be the first painter, of his age and country. He believed, in short, that genius is but another name for extensive capacity, and that incessant and well-directed labour is the inspiration which creates all works of taste and talent.

Joshua was now drawing near to seventeen, and his father writing to Mr. Cutcliffe, attorney, of Bideford, says that—"Joshua has a very great genius for drawing, and lately on his own head, has begun even painting, so that Mr. Warmel, who is both a painter and a player, having lately seen but his first performance, said if he had his hands full of business, he would rather take Joshua for nothing than another with fifty pounds. Mr. Cranch told me, as to the latter, he could put me in a way. Mr. Hudson (who is Mr. Richardson's son-in-law) used to be down at Bideford;" Mr. Reynolds then asks Mr. Cutcliffe's judgment and advice, adding that "what Joshua has principally employed himself in has been perspective, of which, perhaps, there is not much in face-painting. His pictures strike off wonderfully, if they be looked on with a due regard to the point of sight, and the point of distance."

Joshua reached London on October 13, 1740. We learn from his father's letter, that Hudson was to receive the sum of 120*l.*, as a premium with his pupil, one half to be paid by his father, and the remainder, it is presumed, young Reynolds engaged to pay when he was in a position to earn money for himself. Of Joshua's progress we gather from a letter of his father, dated Jan. 1, 1741: "Just now I had a letter from Joshua, wherein he tells me, 'on Thursday next, Sir Robert Walpole sits for his picture: Master says he has a great longing to draw his picture, because so many have drawn it and none like.' Joshua writ me some time ago that many had drawn Judge Willes's picture, but that by his master was most approved of."

Instead of studying from the best models, Hudson caused his pupil to waste his time in making careful copies from the drawings of Guercino; these he executed with much skill, so that it was difficult to distinguish them from the originals.

Of young Reynolds's further progress we have the following evidence from his father:—

April 20, 1742.

Joshua goes on very well, which I must always acquaint you with. Dr. Huxham, who saw a Laocoon, a drawing of his, said that *he who drew that would be the first hand in England*. Mr. Tucker, a painter, in Plymouth, who saw that and three or four more, admired them exceedingly, as I had it from Mr. Cranch; yet when he saw some later drawings of Joshua's, in his second year (of his apprenticeship), he still saw an improvement.

Although Reynolds in his letters expressed much satisfaction at the arrangement with Hudson, in two or three years their connexion was terminated by some slight misunderstanding. It appears that Hudson became jealous of his superior ability, from his painting the head of a female servant in a taste so superior to the painters of the day, that his master involuntarily predicted his future success. Malone, however, states that Reynolds remained three years at Plympton, after he had parted from Hudson. He paid a second visit to London, during which he lived in St. Martin's-lane, nearly opposite to May's-buildings.

REYNOLDS'S DESCRIPTION OF POPE.

Reynolds once saw Pope, about the year 1740, at an auction of books or pictures. He remembers that there was a lane formed to let him pass freely through the assemblage, and he proceeded along, bowing to those who were on each side. He was, according to Joshua's account, about four feet six inches high; very humpbacked and deformed; he wore a black coat; and, according to the fashion of the time, had on a little sword. Reynolds adds that he had a large and very fine eye, and a long, handsome nose; his mouth had those peculiar marks which are always found in the mouths of crooked persons; and the muscles which run across the cheek were so strongly marked as to appear like small cords. Roubilliac, the statuary, who made a bust of Pope from life, observed that his countenance was that of a person who had been much afflicted with headache; and he should have known the fact from the contracted appearance of the skin between his eyebrows, though he had not otherwise been apprised of it.

Reynolds was a great admirer of Pope. He purchased a fan, which the poet presented to Martha Blount, and on which he had painted with his own hand, the story of Cephalus and Procris, with the motto, "Aura, veni." "See," said Sir Joshua, throwing this fan to his pupils, "see the painting of Pope: this must always be the case when the work is taken up from idleness, and is laid aside when it ceases to amuse; it is like the work of one who paints only for amusement. Those who are resolved to excel must go to their work, willing or unwilling, morning, noon, or night; they will find it to be no play, but very hard labour." The fan was afterwards stolen out of Sir Joshua's studio.

REYNOLDS VISITS ITALY.

During his residence at Plymouth Dock, Reynolds became acquainted with the third Lord Edgcumbe, and also with Captain (afterwards Viscount) Keppel. This led to the young painter visiting Italy. He accompanied Capt. Keppel, who had been appointed to the command of a squadron in the Mediterranean. They sailed on May 11, 1749, touching at Lisbon, Cadiz, Gibraltar, and Minorca; and landed at Port Mahon, on August 23. Here Reynolds received much kindness from the Governor, General Blakeney. He was detained here nearly two months by a severe accident: being out riding, his horse rushed with him down a precipice, his face was severely cut, and his lip so much bruised that he was compelled to have it cut away. A slight deformity marked his mouth ever after. His deafness, (says Cunningham,) was imputed by some to the same misfortune; but that affliction dated from a dangerous illness in Rome. During his detention in Minorca, Reynolds painted portraits of all the officers in the garrison, and as he lived, free of expense, at the Governor's table, the painter added considerably to his travelling fund. On his recovery, he proceeded to Leghorn, and thence to Rome.

In this Metropolis of Art, Reynolds chiefly occupied himself in studying the works of Raphael and Michael Angelo, and in acquiring that knowledge of chiaro-oscuro and effect, which he was soon to display in his own paintings. Caricature, strange to say, employed him; for while at Rome, he painted a sort of parody on the School of Athens. The picture, (says Cotton,) still exists: it contains about thirty likenesses of English students, travellers, and connoisseurs; and among others, that of Mr. Henry Straffan, in Ireland, in whose family the picture still remains. Reynolds also painted two other caricatures while in Rome; and in after life he was heard by Northcote to say that, although it was universally allowed that he executed subjects of this kind with much humour and spirit, he held it absolutely necessary to abandon the practice, since it must corrupt his taste as a portrait-painter. Of his technical studies in Rome he has left a minute account, which is chiefly valuable to the student in painting.

Reynolds had for his companion at Rome John Astley, who had been his fellow-pupil in the school of Hudson. Astley was then poor and proud, and strove to conceal his embarrassments. One summer day, when the sun was hot, and he and Reynolds, and a few others, were on a country excursion, there was a general call to cast off coats. Astley obeyed reluctantly—and for this reason: he had made the back of his waistcoat out of one of his own landscapes, and when he stripped, he displayed a foaming waterfall, much to his own confusion, and the mirth of his companions.

From Rome, Reynolds went to Bologna and Genoa; hence to Parma and Florence, and Venice, and then home. His stay in Venice was very short, which is the more remarkable, since the Venetian school influenced his professional character far more powerfully than all the other schools of art put together. While at Venice, in compliment to the English residents there, the manager of the opera one night ordered the band to play an English ballad tune, which brought tears into Reynolds's eyes. On his way home over Mont Cenis, he met Hudson and Roubilliac hastening to Rome. At Paris he found Chambers the architect: here he painted the portrait of Mrs. Chambers, daughter of Wilton, the sculptor, who was very beautiful.

REYNOLDS SETTLES IN LONDON.

In October, 1752, Reynolds returned to England, and after visiting Devonshire for a few weeks, at the solicitation of Lord Edgcumbe, the painter established himself in London, hiring a large house, No. 5, on the north side of Newport-street, Long Acre, then inhabited partly by gentry. He had to surmount such opposition as genius is commonly doomed to meet with : the boldness and freedom of his conceptions, and the brilliancy of his colouring, were innovations upon the old style of portrait manufacture which raised a swarm of objectors. Hudson, Reynolds's former master, vowed that he did not paint so well as when he left England ; and another portrait-maker, who had studied under Kneller, said, "Ah ! Reynolds, this will never answer. Why, you don't paint in the least like Sir Godfrey." This and other sharp treatment, in which the names of Lely and Kneller were frequently bandied, begat in Reynolds a dislike of those two popular painters, which he retained through life.

Reynolds was now abundantly employed, and soon gained celebrity. He painted the second Duke of Devonshire, and thus increased his fame. He next painted Commodore Keppel —a noble, whole-length portrait: he is represented just escaped from shipwreck, walking on the sea-beach in a storm, his hair dishevelled, and everything indicative of a high wind. The likeness is perfect ; and in this picture Reynolds was the first English painter who ventured to enliven the backgrounds of his portraits by momentary action and expression.

REYNOLDS REMOVES TO LEICESTER SQUARE.

Early in the year 1760, Reynolds once more removed his residence to the house No. 47, on the west side of Leicester Square.* It appears from his pocket-book † for this year, that the house was purchased on the 3d of July, for we find the following entry, "house bought," and on the 11th of September, "paid the remainder of the purchase-money, 1,000*l*." We learn from Farington, that he gave 1,650*l*. for a lease of forty-seven years, and laid out 1,500*l*. more in the

* Called Leicester Fields until the year 1714, when it began to be called Leicester *Square*.—*A Journey through England,* 1724.

† Mr. Cotton's access to Sir Joshua's pocket-books for many years, has enabled him to give many interesting data in his work.

erection of a gallery and painting-room. The house was subsequently the residence of the Earl of Inchiquin, who married Miss Palmer, Sir Joshua's favourite niece, to whom he left the bulk of his large fortune, estimated at 80,000*l.* He was created Marquis of Thomond, and died in 1808. After the death of his widow, the Marchioness of Thomond, in 1821, her pictures, containing a larger number of Reynolds's works than had been before offered, were sold at Christie's; and there was a second sale of drawings, sketch-books, oil sketches, and unfinished pictures, by Sir Joshua. Three previous sales of his pictures by ancient masters, his own subjects and unclaimed portraits, and drawings and prints—in 1794, 1796, and 1798, produced nearly 17,000*l.*

Allan Cunningham tells us that

> Sir Joshua's study was octagonal, some 20 feet long, 16 broad, and about 15 feet high. The window was small and square, and the sill 9 feet from the floor. His sitter's chair moved on castors, and stood above the floor a foot and a-half. He held his palettes by handles, and the sticks of his brushes were 18 inches long. He wrought standing, and with great celerity; he rose early, breakfasted at 9, entered his study at 10, examined designs, or touched unfinished portraits till 11 brought a sitter, painted till 4, then dressed, and gave the evening to company.

After the death of the Marchioness of Thomond, the house in Leicester-square was let to the Western Literary and Scientific Institution, and during their occupation some premises in the rear of the house, in Spur-street, were taken down, and a Theatre built for the Society, from the designs of Mr. George Godwin, the architect. The house is now let to Messrs. Puttick and Simpson, the book-auctioneers.

PORTRAITS OF KITTY FISHER.

The beauty of this celebrated courtezan has been preserved on canvas by Reynolds, who painted her portrait several times. Her name occurs three times in his pocket-book for 1759;* and on the end leaf is: "Miss Fisher's portrait is for Sir Charles Bingham."

There is a pleasing portrait of Kitty, by Reynolds, at Petworth: she has her arms crossed, and is apparently rumina-

---

* In the same year Reynolds painted the celebrated beauty. Miss Gunning, (Duchess of Hamilton,) to look at whom the noble mob in the Queen's drawing-room clambered on tables and chairs.

ting on a letter which lies before her. and on the open fold of which is written: "My dear Kitty Fisher, June 9, 1782."

Another portrait of Kitty Fisher as Cleopatra dissolving the Pearl, is in the collection of the Earl of Morley, at Saltram. Some one wrote under it:—

> "To her fam'd character how just thy right!
> Thy mind as wanton, and thy form as bright."

Kitty Fisher, we are told, spent in nine months 12,000*l*.: she lived in 1779, in Carrington-street, May Fair.

She appears to have been a favourite model of Sir Joshua's. A half-length, with doves, was sold in 1845 for 190 guineas, and sent to America. A repetition of this picture is in the collection of H. A. Munro, Esq.; and at Lansdowne House, there is a portrait supposed to be of the same person, a half-length with a bird. At the British Institution, in 1841, a portrait of Kitty Fisher was also exhibited by Lord Crewe. She was called a "*huckaback*" beauty through the exquisite pictures of her from the pencil of Reynolds.

PORTRAIT OF STERNE.

In the same year (1761,) that Reynolds exhibited the large equestrian portrait of Lord Ligonier, now in the National Gallery, he also exhibited the half-length of Sterne, seated, and leaning on his hand. This portrait was painted for the Earl of Ossory, and afterwards came into the possession of Lord Holland, on whose death, in 1840, it was purchased for 500 guineas, by the Marquis of Lansdowne. "This," says Mrs. Jameson, "is the most astonishing head for truth of character I ever beheld; I do not except Titian; the character, to be sure, is different: the subtle evanescent expression of satire round the lips, the shrewd significance in the eye, the earnest contemplative attitude,—all convey the strongest impression of the man, of his peculiar genius, and peculiar humour."

PORTRAITS OF GARRICK.

Garrick related to Reynolds that he once sat to Gainsborough, whose talents he did not admire, and whom he puzzled by altering the expression of his face. Every time the artist turned his back, the actor changed his countenance, till the former in a passion dashed his pencils on the floor, and cried, "I believe I am painting from the devil rather than a man!"

Garrick often sat to Reynolds for different portraits; and on one of these occasions complained wofully of the unceasing sarcasms of Foote. "Never mind him," replied the shrewd painter, "he only shows his sense of his own inferiority: it is ever the least in talent who becomes malignant and abusive."

COPIES AND ORIGINALS.

In 1763, the eminent portrait-painter, the Chevalier Vanloo, being in England, boasted to Reynolds of his accurate knowledge and experience in the works of the great masters: saying, he could never be deceived or imposed upon by a copy. Reynolds then showed him the head of an old woman, which he had himself copied from a picture by Rembrandt, asking his opinion of it, and was highly amused when Vanloo pronounced it to be *an undoubted original*.

Reynolds himself was very nearly deceived in the following instance, thus related by him in a letter to Mr. C. Smith, a nephew of Mr. Caleb Whiteford: "I saw the other day, at Mr. Bromel's, a picture of a child with a dog, which, after pretty close examination, *I thought was my own painting;* but it was a copy, it appears, made by you many years ago."

Sir Joshua said of Gainsborough, that he could copy Vandyke so exquisitely, that, at a little distance, *he could not distinguish the copy from the original.—Abridged from Cotton's Sir Joshua Reynolds and his Works.*

CHARACTER IN PORTRAITS.

Of mere likeness in portraiture, says Cotton, Reynolds thought very little, and used to say that he could instruct any boy that chance might throw in his way, to paint a likeness in half-a-year; but to give an impressive and just expression and character to a picture, or to paint it like Velasquez, was quite another thing.—"What we are all," he said, "attempting to do with great labour, he does at once."

REYNOLDS AND ROMNEY.

It may be said of Reynolds that he could not bear a rival near his throne. He had a great antipathy to Romney, who commenced his career in London by painting heads for four guineas. In 1763, he obtained the prize of the Society of Arts for his picture of the Death of Wolfe; but through the influence of Reynolds, the decision was reversed in favour of a picture by Mortimer. Romney received a present of twenty-five guineas. This circumstance is said to have made Romney and Reynolds ever after enemies.

Romney became the acknowledged rival of the President in portraits. Northcote says: "Certain it is that Sir Joshua was not much employed in portraits after Romney grew in fashion." Lord Thurlow is also reported to have said: "Reynolds and Romney divide the town: I am of the Romney fashion." These were *factions of form and colour*—the former being that of Romney.* Reynolds grew jealous of him, and spoke of him as "the man in Cavendish-square," where he lived in the house No. 32, afterwards Sir Martin Archer Shee's. Northcote represents Garrick as saying of Cumberland, the dramatist, "He hates you, Sir Joshua, because you do not admire the painter whom he considers a second Correggio." "Who is that?" said Reynolds. "Why, his Correggio," answered Garrick, "is Romney, the painter."

FRIENDSHIP OF REYNOLDS AND DR. JOHNSON.

Few men in the world have more highly appreciated the value of friendship, especially in exerting an important influence upon his mind, than Reynolds. From the friendship of Burke and Johnson he learnt much to supply the deficiencies of his early education. Although Johnson was profoundly ignorant of art, Reynolds derived much from him: "he qualified my mind," he says, "to think justly. The observations he made on poetry, on life, and on everything about us, I applied to our art, with what success others must judge." This mode of adapting the knowledge possessed by others to our own requirements is one of the greatest benefits which men derive from intercourse with each other.

To no one, perhaps, was Reynolds more indebted than to his countryman, the Rev. Zachariah Mudge, Vicar of St. Andrew's, Plymouth,—a man, (says Dr. Johnson,) "equally eminent for his virtues and abilities, at once beloved as a

* The secret was this. Romney had painted Lord Chancellor Thurlow, a whole-length, and a handsomer man than he had appeared in the half-length of Reynolds. Romney avoided all indication of the suppressed temper that was so apt to explode in violent paroxysms, and thus rendered his picture more acceptable to the original. But he missed what Reynolds alone could give—that extraordinary sapience which made Charles Fox say, "No man could be so wise as Lord Thurlow looked."—*Leslie's Handbook*, p. 301.

companion and reverenced as a pastor." Northcote had also heard Sir Joshua declare that the elder Mr. Mudge was, in his opinion, the wisest man he had ever met with in his life.

How Reynolds acquired the friendship of Johnson is related by Boswell. The artist, some time in the year 1754, was visiting in Devonshire, and chanced to open the Life of Savage. He began to read, and it seized his attention so strongly, that he was not able to lay down the book till he had finished it. He was solicitous to know an author, one of whose books had thus enchanted him; and by accident or design he met with him as follows:

> When Dr. Johnson lived in Castle-street, Cavendish-square, he went frequently to visit two ladies, who lived opposite to him, Miss Cotterells, daughters of Admiral Cotterell. Reynolds used also to visit them, and thus they met.—*Boswell, ed. Croker.*

Dr. Johnson's regard for Reynolds was thus expressed in an affectionate letter to him, after his serious illness, in 1763: "If I should lose you, (wrote Johnson,) I should lose almost the only man I can call a friend."

Sir Joshua painted a portrait of Dr. Johnson, with his arms raised and his hands bent: this picture was, in 1770, in the possession of Miss Lucy Foster, at Lichfield, where Johnson having seen it, wrote to Reynolds as follows:

Ashbourne, July 17, 1771.

Dear Sir,

When I came to Lichfield, I found that my portrait had been much visited and admired. Every man has a lurking wish to appear considerable in his native place, and I was pleased with the dignity conferred, by such a testimony of your regard.

Be pleased, therefore, to accept the thanks of,

Sir,

Your most obliged and humble Servant,

SAM. JOHNSON.

Compliments to Miss Reynolds.

This picture is now the property of the Duke of Sutherland, and is at Stafford House.

Dr. Johnson sat to Reynolds, also, in 1775: the picture shows him holding a manuscript near his face, and pondering as he reads. The near-sighted "Cham of literature" reproved the painter in these words—"It is not friendly to hand down to posterity the imperfections of any man." Mr. Thrale interposed and said—"You will not be known to posterity for your defects, though Sir Joshua should do his worst." The artist was right—he gave individuality and character to the head.

Reynolds and Johnson differed in their opinions as to the effects of wine. One evening, at the Crown and Anchor Tavern, in the Strand, a favourite supper-house with Johnson, Sir Joshua Reynolds was maintaining the advantages of wine in assisting conversation, and referring particularly to himself, Johnson observed, "I have heard none of those drunken—nay, drunken is a coarse word—none of those *vinous flights.*"

"I know no man," said Johnson, "who has passed through life with more observation than Reynolds." And he had so exalted an opinion of Sir Joshua's benevolence, that he once said to him, with a smile, "Reynolds, you hate no person living, but I like a *good hater.*"

Sir Joshua relates this interesting trait in Johnson's nature. When the Doctor had been rough to any person in company, he took the first opportunity of reconciliation by drinking to him; if, however, the other had not grace to accept this reconciliation, then it gave him no more concern.

Dr. Johnson appointed Sir Joshua one of his executors, and bequeathed him his great French Dictionary of Moreri, and his own corrected folio copy of his English Dictionary.

PAINTING ON SUNDAYS.

Sir Joshua used to say: "he will never make a painter, who looks for the Sunday with pleasure as an idle day;" and his pocket journals afford indisputable proofs that it was his habit to receive sitters on Sundays as well as on other days. This was naturally enough displeasing to Dr. Johnson, and we are told by Boswell that he (Johnson) made three requests of Sir Joshua, a short time before his death: one was to forgive him 30*l.* which he had borrowed of him; another was that Sir Joshua would carefully read the Scriptures; and lastly, that he would abstain from using his pencil on the Sabbath day; to all of these requests Sir Joshua gave a willing assent—and kept his word.

REYNOLDS'S CLUB.

Sir Joshua was by nature a "clubable" man. In 1763, he founded, with Johnson, "the Club," as it was then called, at the Turk's Head, in Gerard-street, Soho. It did not receive the name of *the Literary Club* till many years later; but that Reynolds was its Romulus, and this the year of its foundation, is unquestionable. After numerous changes of location, the Club settled at the Thatched-house Tavern, in St. James's-street, where its meetings are held to this day. Here is the portrait of Reynolds with spectacles on, similar to the one in the Royal Collection : this picture was presented by Sir Joshua, as the founder of the Club.

Sir Joshua was also a member of the *Dilettanti Society*, at the Thatched-house Tavern ; and he painted for the club-room three capital pictures :—

1. A group in the manner of Paul Veronese, containing the portraits of the Duke of Leeds, Lord Dundas, Constantine Lord Mulgrave, Lord Seaforth, the Hon. C. Greville, Charles Crowle, Esq., and Sir Joseph Banks. 2. A group in the manner of the same master, containing portraits of Sir William Hamilton, Sir Watkin W. Wynne, Richard Thomson, Esq., Sir John Taylor, Payne Galway, Esq., John Smythe, Esq., and Spencer S. Stanhope, Esq. 3. Head of Sir Joshua, by himself, dressed in a loose robe, and in his own hair. The earlier portraits are by Hudson, Sir Joshua's master.

Sir Joshua acknowledged that he had Paul Veronese in view when he painted the pictures for the Dilettanti, particularly that next the door.

ORIGIN OF THE ROYAL ACADEMY.

Haydon, in his Journal, July 20, 1836, records :

"Went to the British Museum, and found two interesting pamphlets connected with the Royal Academy, by which it appears decidedly that the Directors who were expelled from the chartered body of artists became Academicians, and that not being able to carry their exclusive intentions in the constituent body, they resorted to the scheme of an Academy of forty, securing a majority of their own way of thinking that they might enact their exclusive laws. This is indisputable from Strong's pamphlet, 1775, and another in the Museum, 1771, entitled 'Considerations of the Behaviour of the Academicians who were expelled the Chartered Body of 1760—69.'

"Reynolds promised the chartered body, of which he was member, not to exhibit with the expelled directors; but finding the King protecting them, he broke his word, did exhibit, and was expelled the incorporated body. This is not known, nor did I know it till to-day. Tickled by a knighthood, he joined the Directors, and this was the origin of the Royal Academy—founded in intrigue, based on injustice, treachery, and meanness.

"Reynolds was properly, and very severely, punished after, but the art has suffered ever since."

Such is Haydon's opinion ; but Sir Martin Archer Shee, in his evidence before Parliament, states that the artists who have been represented as guilty of the "basest intrigue" in forming the Royal Academy, were Sir Joshua Reynolds, the greatest portrait-painter that ever lived in any country, and one of the most respectable men that ever graced the annals of society; Benjamin West, the greatest historical painter since the days of Caracci; the greatest architect of the day, Sir W. Chambers; Paul Sandby, the greatest landscape-painter in water-colours of his day; and several others.

Reynolds, who had been mainly instrumental in forming the Academy, was unanimously elected president. It is recorded that Dr. Johnson was so much delighted with his friend's elevation, that he broke through a rule of total abstinence in respect to wine, which he had maintained for several years, and drank bumpers on the occasion.

To the first Exhibition Sir Joshua contributed with others two pictures: 1. The Duchess of Manchester and her Son, as Diana disarming Cupid. 2. Lady Blake as Juno receiving the Cestus from Venus. In the Exhibition Catalogue, purchased by Mr. Sheepshanks, at the Strawberry Hill Sale, Horace Walpole had remarked, that, in the former of these pictures, *the attitude is bad;* and in the latter, *very bad.*

THE FIRST ROYAL ACADEMY DINNER.

On the 23d of April, St. George's Day, 1771, the first Annual Dinner of the Royal Academicians was held in the great exhibition room, in old Somerset House, the walls of which were covered with Works of Art about to be exhibited. Sir Joshua Reynolds, who was the first to suggest this elegant festival, presided in his official character. Dr. Johnson and Goldsmith, of course, were present, as Professors of the Academy; and besides the Academicians, there was a large assembly of the most distinguished men of the day as guests.

THE ROYAL ACADEMY AT SOMERSET HOUSE.

Upon the rebuilding of Somerset House, the Royal Academicians received apartments in the western wing, and here the first Exhibition was opened, May, 1780. Sir Joshua Reynolds painted the centre of the Library ceiling with "The Theory of Painting"—a majestic female sitting on a cloud, and holding compasses, and a label inscribed "Theory is the knowledge of what is truly nature." When the Academy removed to the National Gallery in 1838, Sir Joshua's painting, and those of the other Academicians, were removed from the ceiling of Somerset House, with great care, and transferred to that of the new council-room in Trafalgar-square : here also are one of Reynolds's palettes, and his diploma picture, a whole-length portrait of George III.

The Lords of the Treasury paid Reynolds thirty guineas for this painting, as appears by the existence of the receipt in the handwriting of Sir William Chambers, and signed by Sir Joshua.

SIR JOSHUA ELECTED MAYOR OF PLYMPTON.

In 1773, Reynolds paid a visit to Plympton, and was elected Mayor of the town ; when he testified his gratification at the circumstance by presenting his portrait to the Corporation, who placed it in the Town-hall. Reynolds wears his academical dress, as Doctor of Laws. Cotton was informed that it was slightly painted, and sent off in such a hurry, that the colours being scarcely dry, the picture received some damage from the dust and dirt, which penetrated into the case.

When Sir Joshua had finished his portrait for the Townhall, he wrote to Sir William Elford, requesting him to get it hung in a good situation, which Sir William attended to by hanging it between two old pictures ; and in his reply to Reynolds he said the bad pictures on each side acted as a foil, and set it off to great advantage. Sir Joshua was highly diverted, as these very pictures were two early ones of his own painting.

Sir William Elford's estimate of the merits of these pictures was, however, very erroneous. The first was the portrait of Captain Ourry, painted by Sir Joshua for the Corporation of Plympton, for which he only received four guineas, including the frame! He is attended by a black boy, thought to be extremely well painted ; and this picture and its companion, Captain Edgecumbe, which Wilkie saw, in 1809, in the mayoralty-room, adjoining the Guildhall, he declared to be for composition as fine as anything Sir Joshua ever did afterwards.

Sir Joshua commemorated the fact of his having been Mayor of Plympton in a Latin inscription, which he inserted on the back of his own portrait, painted for the Grand Duke's Gallery at Florence, in these words :

I

"Nec non oppidi natalis, dicti Plympton, Comitatu Devon præfectus, Justiciarius, morumque censor."

After the disfranchisement of the borough of Plympton, the above portrait of Reynolds was sold by the Corporation. Haydon says: "It was offered to the National Gallery, and ignorantly refused:" it was purchased by the Earl of Egremont for 150*l.*, and is now at his seat, Silverton, near Exeter. There are several copies of this picture at Plympton. Sir Joshua painted a similar portrait of himself, which he gave to his pupil Northcote: it was sold in 1816, for 56*l.* 14*s.*

Soon after Sir Joshua's election, it happened that he was walking with a party of friends in Hampton Court gardens, when they suddenly and unexpectedly met the King, accompanied by some of the Royal Family; and as His Majesty saw Reynolds, it was impossible to withdraw. The King called Sir Joshua to him, and in conversation said he was informed of the office he was soon to be invested with, that of Mayor of his native town. Sir Joshua assured His Majesty of the truth of the statement, saying that it was an honour which gave him more pleasure than any other he had ever received in his life,—but, recollecting himself, he immediately added, "except that which your Majesty was graciously pleased to confer upon me," alluding to his knighthood.

"THE STRAWBERRY GIRL."

It was Reynolds's opinion that no man ever produced more than half a dozen original works in his whole life-time; and when he painted "The Strawberry Girl," he said, "This is one of *my* originals." This picture was painted in 1773 for the Earl of Carysfort. It was for many years in the collection of Mr. Rogers, that nonagenarian bard, who was in full manhood when Reynolds was still in health and activity; and who lived with and outlived three generations of poets and artists. After Mr. Rogers's death, in 1855, "The Strawberry Girl" was sold; and as an instance of the extraordinary rise in the value of really standard productions of the English school, this work, for which the Earl of Carysfort paid 50 guineas, was, in 1856, acquired by the Marquis of Hertford for 2205*l.*, or forty-two times the original price.

"Reynolds depicted, (says Dr. Waagen,) the youthful bloom and artless manner of children with admirable effect. This it is that makes his celebrated Strawberry Girl so attractive.

With her hands simply folded, a basket on her arm, she stands in her white frock, and looks full at the spectator with her fine large eyes. The admirable impasto, the bright golden tone, clear as Rembrandt, and the dark landscape background, have a striking effect." Sir Joshua looked upon this as one of his best pictures.

COUNT UGOLINO.

In 1773, Reynolds painted *Count Ugolino and his Children in the Dungeon*, as described by Dante in the 33rd Canto of the Inferno, against which Walpole wrote, in his catalogue of the Exhibition, "most admirable." This picture, (says Cotton,) was bought by the Duke of Dorset for 400 guineas, and is now at Knowle. It is generally supposed that the head of Count Ugolino was painted from White, the paviour; but Walpole says it was a study from an old beggarman, who had so fine a head that Sir Joshua chose him for the father, in his picture from Dante. Miss Gwatkin and Northcote corroborate this origin. Northcote says, the head was painted previous to the year 1771, and finished on a half-length canvas, in point of expression exactly as it now stands —but without any intention on the part of Sir Joshua of making it the subject of an historical composition. Being exposed to view in the picture-gallery, with the painter's other works, it caught the eye of Goldsmith, who immediately exclaimed that it was the precise countenance and expression of Count Ugolino, as described by Dante.*

Another portrait or study, (continues Cotton,) from the head of the same old beggar, was exhibited by Sir Joshua in the following year, as a Captain of Banditti, which Walpole remarked was *painted in the style of Salvator Rosa;* and that there were in the same Exhibition, several pictures by different artists, from Reynolds's beggar-man.

This picture is said to have affected Captain Cooke's Omiah so much, that he imagined it a scene of real distress, and ran to support the expiring child.

The *Banished Lord*, in the National Gallery, and Dionysius, the Areopagite, in the possession of Mr. Bentley, were likewise painted from the same model; and it seems very probable that White the paviour, and the old beggar-man, were identical.

* By others, Burke is said to have suggested the picture to Sir Joshua.

REYNOLDS REBUKED BY GOLDSMITH.

When the anti-infidel, Dr. Beattie, used to harangue the "ale-house in Gerard-street," against the Voltaire and Hume philosophy, great was the vexation of Goldsmith at the adhesion of Reynolds to the Scotch professor. This was the only grave difference that had ever been between them; and it is honourable to the poet that it should have arisen on that incident in the painter's life which has somewhat tarnished his fame. Reynolds accompanied Beattie to Oxford; partook with him in an honorary degree of civil law; and on his return painted his fellow doctor in Oxonian robes, with the *Essay on Truth* under his arm, and at his side the angel of Truth overpowering and chasing away the demons of Infidelity, Sophistry, and Falsehood; the last represented by the plump and broad-backed figure of Hume, the first by the lean and piercing face of Voltaire. "It is unworthy of you," said Goldsmith to Sir Joshua, and his 'fine rebuke will outlast the silly picture,' "to debase so high a genius as Voltaire before so mean a writer as Beattie. Beattie and his book will be forgotten in ten years, while Voltaire's fame will last for ever. Take care it does not perpetuate this picture, to the shame of such a man as you." Reynolds persisted, notwithstanding the protest; but was incapable of any poor resentment of it. He produced the same year, at Goldsmith's suggestion, his painting of *Ugolino.—Forster's Life of Goldsmith*, pp. 666-7.

GOLDSMITH'S EPITAPH ON REYNOLDS.

In these last lines, on which Goldsmith is said to have been engaged when his fatal illness seized him, was the gratitude of a life. They will help to keep Reynolds immortal:

>Here Reynolds is laid, and, to tell you my mind,
>He has not left a wiser or better behind.
>His pencil was striking, resistless, and grand;
>His manners were gentle, complying, and bland;
>Still born to improve us in every part,
>His pencil our faces, his manners our heart.
>To coxcombs averse, yet most civilly steering,
>When they judged without skill, he was still hard of hearing:
>When they talked of their Raphaels, Correggios, and stuff,
>He shifted his trumpet, and only took snuff.
>By flattery unspoiled * * *   *The Retaliation.*

It is not unpleasing to think that Goldsmith's hand should have been tracing that unfinished line, when illness struck the pen from it for ever.

REYNOLDS AND BARRY.

Sir Joshua, supreme head as he was of the Royal Academy, was doomed to vexations; but his sagacious spirit and tranquil temper brought him off triumphant. Barry differed with Reynolds in everything but his admiration of Michael Angelo. Barry had become Professor of Painting, but having neglected to deliver the stipulated lectures, Reynolds, in performance of his duty as President, inquired if they were composed. Barry, a consequential little man, rose on tiptoe, and clenching his fist, exclaimed, "If I had only in composing my lectures to produce such poor mistaken stuff as your Discourses, I should have my work done, and ready to read." To reply suited neither the dignity nor the caution of Reynolds, and his fiery opponent very properly received a large share of public censure for his offensive conduct.

MR. HONE, R.A. SATIRIZES SIR JOSHUA.

In 1775, Reynolds's pre-eminence drew upon him the envy of Nathaniel Hone, a miniature-painter, who, about this time, commenced oil-painting on a large scale. He did not succeed, and finding that Reynolds monopolised the chief patronage, Hone sent to the Exhibition a picture which he termed *The Conjuror displaying his whole art of Optical Deception*, intended as a satire upon Sir Joshua's method of composing his pictures. It was rejected with becoming scorn by the Academicians, as a malicious attack upon their President. Hone then determined to have his own Exhibition, and *the Conjuror* was shown in a great room nearly opposite New Slaughter's Coffee-house, in St. Martin's-lane. There was introduced some indelicacy in the centre of the picture, in allusion to a slanderous report concerning Angelica Kauffman. This intention Hone denied: he, however, made out but a discreditable case; Nollekens refused to join him against Reynolds, adding: "you're always running your rigs against Sir Joshua; and you may say what you please, but I have never had any opinion of you ever since you painted that picture of *the Conjuror*, as you called it. I don't wonder they turned it out of the Academy. And pray, what business had you to bring Angelica into it? You know it was your intention to ridicule her, whatever you, or your printed papers, or your affidavits may say: however, you may depend upon it, *she* won't forget it, if Sir Joshua does."

DESIGNS FOR THE OXFORD WINDOW.

In 1779, Sir Joshua sent to the Exhibition his picture of *the Nativity*, designed for the window of New College chapel, Oxford; and emblematical figures of Faith, Hope, and Charity. The grand piece of *the Nativity* was immediately purchased by the Duke of Rutland for 1,200 guineas, the Duke saying it was a larger price than was ever paid before for a picture painted in England. It was, unfortunately, destroyed by fire at Belvoir Castle, in 1816: it was engraved by Earlom. Two of the emblematical figures were subsequently purchased by the Earl of Normanton, at Lady Thomond's sale: *Charity* was bought for Lord Normanton for 1,575*l.*; *Justice* for 1,155*l.* The easel of Sir Joshua was also sold on this occasion.

As a proof of the rapid increase in the value of Sir Joshua's works, Mr. Cotton states that the seven allegorical figures, and other compartments of the Oxford window, which (it is said) had been offered to a nobleman for 300*l.*, were sold, after Reynolds's death, for upwards of 12,000*l.*

Walpole says: "Jarvis's Window, from Sir Joshua's *Nativity*, is glorious. The room being darkened and the sun shining through the transparencies, realised the illumination that is supposed to be diffused from the glory, and has a magic effect." But, at Oxford, Walpole states that the effect was just the reverse of the glorious appearance it made in the dark chambers in Pall Mall.

Again, he says of this window: "the old and the new are mismatched as an orange and a lemon, and destroy each other; nor is there room enough to retire back, and see half of the new; and Sir Joshua's washy 'Virtues' make the 'Nativity' a dark spot from the darkness of the Shepherds, which happened, as I knew it would, from most of Jarvis's colours not being transparent."

REYNOLDS'S PORTRAIT OF SHERIDAN.

This fine portrait was engraved, in 1791, by John Hall, who was then living at No. 83, in Berwick-street, Soho. Raimbach, Hall's pupil, relates that Sheridan came twice or thrice during the engraving; "and," says Raimbach, "my memory dwells with pleasure to this hour on the recollection of his having said a few kindly and encouraging words to me when a boy, drawing at the time in the study. I was, however, most struck with what seemed to me, in such a man, an undue and unbecoming anxiety about his good looks in the portrait to be executed. The efflorescence in his face had been indicated by Sir Joshua in the picture, not, it may be presumed, *à bon gré* on the part of Sheridan, and it was strongly evident that he deprecated its transfer to the print. I need scarcely observe that Hall set his mind at ease on that point."

LORD HOLLAND'S PORTRAIT.

The unfinished appearance of some of Reynolds's pictures, when they were sent home, caused occasional disappointment. It is said that Lord Holland, when he received his portrait, could not help remarking that it had been hastily executed; and making some demur about the price, asked Reynolds how long he had been painting it, when the offended artist replied, "All my life, my Lord."—*Northcote's M.S. in the Plymouth Library.*

GEORGE III. AND SIR JOSHUA REYNOLDS.

On one of Sir Joshua Reynolds's friends observing to Dr. Johnson that it was extraordinary the King should have taken so little notice of him, having on all occasions employed Ramsay, West, &c. in preference to Sir Joshua, he said he thought it a matter of little consequence; "His Majesty's neglect could never do him any prejudice; but it would reflect *eternal disgrace* on the King not to have employed Sir Joshua Reynolds."

In 1779, the King and Queen honoured Reynolds by sitting for their portraits, at His Majesty's particular request, for the Council of the Royal Academy. The King, who was an early riser, sat at ten in the morning. The entry in Reynolds's pocket-book is: "Friday, May 21, at 10, the King." The Queen's name does not occur until December. These, Mr. Cotton believes, were the only portraits of their Majesties painted by Reynolds: he was never the Court-painter, nor were his pictures much admired by George III., who, being near-sighted, and consequently obliged to look close at them, said they appeared to be rough and unfinished.

PORTRAITS OF GIBBON AND GOLDSMITH.

In 1779, Sir Joshua painted Gibbon's portrait, which hung over the chimney-piece in his house at Lausanne. M. Rogers says, in this wonderful portrait, while the oddness and vulgarity of the features are refined away, the likeness is perfectly preserved.

Cotton states that Miss Reynolds remarked Sir Joshua never gave a more striking proof of his excellence in portrait-painting than in giving dignity to Dr. Goldsmith's countenance, and at the same time preserving a strong likeness. To this treatment all Reynolds's sitters were subjected, so that even the most deficient in grace came off his easel ladies and gentlemen.

PORTRAIT OF ADMIRAL KEPPEL.

This picture was presented to Mr. Burke by Admiral Keppel himself, at his trial at Portsmouth, in February, 1779. Of his full and honourable acquittal, Sir Joshua, in a letter to the Admiral, says: "The illuminations were universal, I believe, with the exception of a single house. Lord North and Lord Bute had their windows broken. The Admiralty gates were unhinged: to-night, I hear, Sir Hugh (Palliser) is to be burnt in effigy before your door. I have taken the liberty to lend *your picture* to an engraver, to make a print from it."

Sir Joshua painted Keppel's portrait, *con amore*, several times.

THE LADIES WALDEGRAVE.

Of this celebrated work Walpole wrote, in 1780: "Sir Joshua has begun a charming picture of my three fair nieces, the Waldegraves, and very like. They are embroidering and winding silk; I rather wished to have them drawn like the Graces adorning a bust of the Duchess as Magna Mater; but my ideas are not adopted."

This very fine picture is still at Strawberry Hill. It is lucky that Sir Joshua did not adopt Walpole's idea, or we should have had something as still and formal as the Blessington picture, by the same hand, of the three daughters of Sir William Montgomery, as "The Graces decorating a terminal figure of Hymen," now in the National Gallery. "Sir Joshua gets avaricious in his old age," Walpole remarked to Pinkerton. "My picture of the young ladies Waldegrave is doubtless very fine and graceful, but it cost me 800 guineas."

"MUSCIPULA."

Count d'Adhemar was the original purchaser of Sir Joshua's *Muscipula* (the Girl with the Mousetrap). Reynolds, who fancied that he was bargaining for a different and less important picture, told him that the price was fifty guineas; and on discovering the mistake, allowed him to have *Muscipula* for that sum. Fox had been anxious to possess *Muscipula* when it was first painted, and he bought it at the ambassador's sale for (I believe) fifty guineas. It is now at St. Anne's Hill. It would fetch, in the present day, a thousand guineas.—*Rogers.*

"THE TRAGIC MUSE."

In 1784, about sixteen months after Sir Joshua's paralytic attack, he sent to the Exhibition his noble picture of Mrs. Siddons, as "The Tragic Muse," which Lawrence, in 1823, pronounced to be a work of the highest epic character, and indisputably the finest female portrait in the world. It was valued by Sir Joshua at 1,000 guineas, but was sold to Mr. Smith, M.P. for Norwich, for the sum of 700*l.*, and subsequently purchased by Lord Grosvenor for 1,760*l.*, in whose Gallery it remains. In the Dulwich Gallery is a duplicate of this celebrated picture; for this Sir Joshua received 800 guineas, although it is allowed to be very inferior to the other. The Dulwich picture was purchased of Reynolds by M. De Calonne: at the sale of his collection in 1795, it was purchased, together with the Spanish Flower-girl of Murillo, by Mr. Noel Desenfans, and bequeathed by his heir, Sir. F. Bourgeois, to Dulwich College.

When Mrs. Siddons sat for this portrait, she was in her twenty-eighth year, "in the prime of her glorious beauty, and in the full blaze of her popularity."

It is said that Sir Joshua took a hint from the Isaiah of Michael Angelo, as the basis of his figure of Mrs. Siddons; but Phillips states that Mrs. Siddons told him it was the production of pure accident. Sir Joshua had begun the head and figure in a different way, and while he was preparing some colour, she changed her position to look at a picture hanging on the wall of the room. When he again looked at her, and saw the action she had assumed, he requested her not to move; "and thus arose the beautiful and expressive figure we now see in the picture." Mrs. Siddons's own version of the story is, however, as follows:

> When I attended for the first sitting, after more gratifying encomiums than I can now repeat, he (Sir Joshua,) took my hand, saying: "ascend your undisputed throne, and graciously bestow upon me some good idea of the Tragic Muse." I walked up the steps, and instantly seated myself in the attitude in which the Tragic Muse now appears.

Sir Joshua has painted his name in the gold border of the drapery, as some of the old masters painted theirs on the garment of the Madonna. When Mrs. Siddons, stooping down to examine what she supposed to be a piece of classic embroidery, noticed it, the painter replied, "I could not lose the honour this opportunity afforded me of going down to posterity on the hem of your garment."

This picture has Reynolds's peculiarity—that, however loaded and enriched in every part of the work, the head is kept smooth and thinly painted. Mrs. Siddons, looking at the picture when unfinished, begged Sir Joshua not to touch the head any more; and, having promised her, he refrained, notwithstanding the richness and depth of the fearless glazings would seem to demand a corresponding force in the head.

REYNOLDS'S CARRIAGE.

When Sir Joshua started his coach, he employed Catton to paint the panels with figures of the Four Seasons; the wheels were also carved and gilt; indeed, it was a state or full-dress carriage. His sister complained that it was too showy— "What?" said the painter, "would you have one like an apothecary's carriage?" This has been mentioned as an instance of vanity and ostentation; it has been likewise said that Reynolds's coachman made money by showing the carriage, which may have been done without his master's knowledge. There was nothing remarkable in having the carriage ornamentally painted; for coach-painting was then a higher profession than at present, and Sir Joshua was perhaps anxious to show his friend Catton's skill and proficiency in the art. Nor did Reynolds keep his carriage merely for ostentation, but for use: he frequently devoted it to the comfort and convenience of his friends, and Boswell relates that a party having been invited to dine at Twickenham, Sir Joshua lent his carriage, and went himself on horseback.

Catton was a native of Norwich, and a distinguished coach painter: at the Academy in St. Martin's-lane, he learned to draw the human figure, and at the foundation of the Royal Academy, he was appointed one of its members. In 1784, he served as Master of the Painter Stainers' Company, when Reynolds dined in their Hall on St. Luke's Day, taking with him Boswell. Sir Joshua was a member of the Company, to which he was presented in 1784. Peter Cunningham significantly remarks, "No Royal Academician of the present day would ever dream of becoming a member;" but it is gratifying to record that in 1860, the Painter Stainers' Company gave in their Hall in Little Trinity-lane, an exhibition of works of Decorative Art, thus reviving the object of the ancient guild; and the exhibition is to be continued annually. Catton is believed by some to have painted the allegorical subjects on the panels of the present City state-coach, which was built in 1757; by others, the panels are said to have been repainted by Dance.

HORACE WALPOLE AND SIR JOSHUA REYNOLDS.

Walpole had several tiffs with Reynolds. Thus, he writes, in 1785, to the Countess of Ossory: "I am not quite in charity with Sir Joshua: he desired to come and see my marvellous Henry VII.; when he saw it, he said, 'It is in the old hard Flemish manner.' For hard, it is so bold, that it is one of the greatest reasons for doubting its antiquity; and for Flemish, there is nothing Flemish in it, except a *chiareoscuro*, as masterly as Rubens's; but it is not surprising that Sir Joshua should dislike colouring that has lasted so long!"

Upon another occasion, however, we find Walpole yielding, when he says of "Prior's picture, an uncommonly fine head," "I do not pretend to dispute Sir Joshua's skill, as he must know better than I do, the pencilling of different masters. At first sight, I merely supposed the Prior was painted by old Dahl, but I dare say Sir Joshua is in the right."

Walpole is very severe upon Sir Joshua's Last Discourse to the Academy, which "will rather do hurt than good on his disciples, and make them neglect all kind of finishing. Nor is he judicious in quoting Vandyke, who at least specified silks, satins, velvets. Sir Joshua's draperies represent clothes, never their materials. Yet more: Vandyke and Sir Godfrey Kneller excelled all painters in hands; Sir Joshua's are seldom even tolerably drawn. I saw t'other day one of, if not the best of, his works, the portrait of Lord Richard Cavendish. Little is distinguished but the head and hand; yet the latter, though nearest to the spectator, is abominably bad: so are those of my three nieces; and though the effect of the whole is charming, the details are slovenly, the faces only red and white; and his journeyman, as if to distinguish himself, has finished the lock and key of the table like a Dutch flower-painter."—*Letter to Mason*, 1783.

In 1786, Walpole writes to Lady Ossory: "Sir Joshua has bought a profile of Oliver Cromwell, which he thinks the finest miniature by Cooper he ever saw. But all his own geese are swans, as the swans of others are geese. It is most clearly a copy, and not a very good one; the outline very hard, the hair and armour very flat and tame." Sir Joshua left this miniature to Richard Burke, from whom it descended through the Crewes, to its present possessor, Richard Monckton Milnes, Esq. M.P. "It is a poor copy," says Cunningham,— and not by Cooper—of the profile Devonshire miniature."

In 1787, Horace again writes to Lady Ossory: "I called at Sir Joshua's, while he was at Ampthill, and saw his Hercules for Russia. I did not at all admire it: the principal babe put me in mind of what I read so often, but have not seen, *the monstrous craws*. Master Hercules's knees are as large as, I presume, the late Lady Guilford's. *Blind* Tiresias is *staring* with horror at the terrible spectacle. If Sir Joshua is satisfied with his own departed picture, it is more than the possessors or posterity will be. I think he ought to be paid in annuities only for so long as his pictures last: one should not grudge him the first-fruits."

Again: "Sir Joshua Reynolds is a great painter; but, unfortunately, his colours seldom stand longer than crayons."

"THE INFANT HERCULES."

In 1786, Sir Joshua seemed more bewitched than ever with his palette and pencils, and was painting from morning till night. He now began a picture for Catherine, Empress of Russia, who desired he would paint her an historical one— the subject to be left to his own choice. He selected the

Infant Hercules strangling the Serpents in the Cradle: from West's Translation of Pindar—the first Nemæan Ode, which Cowley has thus beautifully imitated:—

> The big-limb'd babe in his huge cradle lay,
> Too weighty to be rock'd by nurse's hands,
>   Wrapp'd in purple swaddling bands:
> When lo! by jealous Juno's fierce commands,
>   Two dreadful serpents came,
> Rolling and hissing loud into the room:
> To the bold babe they trace their hidden way:
> Forth from their flaming eyes dread lightning went;
> Their gaping mouths did forked tongues like thunderbolts present.
>   *   *   *   *
>   The mighty infant seem'd well pleas'd
>   At his gay gilded foes:
> And as their spotted necks up to the cradle rose,
> With his young warlike hands on both he seized:
>   In vain they raged, in vain they hiss'd,
>   In vain their armed tails they twist,
>   And angry circles cast about;
> Black blood, and fiery breath, and poisonous soul, he squeezes out.

Cotton relates that Sir Joshua, who was always thinking of his Art, was one day walking with Dr. Lawrence, near Beaconsfield, where they met a beautiful little peasant-boy. Reynolds, after looking earnestly at the child, exclaimed, "I must go home and deepen the colouring of my 'Infant Hercules.'" *

The picture was exhibited in 1788; and in the following year, it was sent to St. Petersburg, with two sets of Sir Joshua's *Discourses*, one in French, the other in English. Next year, the Russian ambassador, Count Woronzow, presented Reynolds with a gold box, having the Empress' portrait on the lid, set with large diamonds. His executors afterwards received 1,500*l.* as the price of the picture.

"The Infant Hercules," which was remarkable for its rich effect of colour and forcible *chiaro-oscuro*, was the principal of Sir Joshua's historical pieces, and met with universal applause, from the critics of the day. Even the eccentric Barry approved of it: he said—"The prophetical agitation of Tiresias and Juno enveloped with clouds, hanging over the scene, like a black pestilence, can never be too much admired, and are, indeed, truly sublime." The effect of the tone and colour

---

* It is likewise related that the child was entirely painted from the infant of a cottager living at Beaconsfield.—See *Anecdote Biography: Edmund Burke.*

cannot be better expressed than by a painter of the day, who said that "it looked as if it had been boiled in brandy."

It is likewise related that Mr. Cribb sat to Sir Joshua for the *Infant Hercules*. He is the son of Sir Joshua's frame-maker, Mr. Cribb, of Holborn. Reynolds presented the father with an excellent drawing of himself in crayon, which the son has now in his possession.

REYNOLDS'S DISCOURSES, AND MALONE.

The intimacy of Sir Joshua with Edmund Malone appears to have ripened into a cordial attachment. They often met at the houses of mutual friends, and sometimes took short country excursions together. Both were, as Malone has minutely recorded, of similar stature and weight, and although of considerable difference in age, each fond of testing his physical vigour as a pedestrian. At a later period, the painter occasionally took Malone's opinion on minor points connected with the composition of his Discourses; and he did the same, probably, with Johnson and Burke. Hence the ungenerous rumour found circulation, that he was indebted for much of their matter as well as manner to Burke.* Sir James Prior found the following short note in Malone's correspondence, in proof that the President did not always ask even Burke for those smaller critical offices which friends are free to exact from and render to each other:

December 15th, 1786.

My dear Sir,—I wish you could just run your eye over my Discourse, if you are not too much busied in what you have made your own employment. I could wish that you would do more than merely look at it; that you would examine it with a critical eye, in regard to grammatical correctness, the propriety of expression, and the truth of the observations.

Yours, &c. J. REYNOLDS.

Northcote, the pupil of Reynolds, who lived some years in his house, thus fully answers the scandalous fiction in his *Memoirs*:

"At the period when it was expected that he should have composed them (the Lectures), I have heard him walking at intervals in his room till one or two o'clock in the morning; and I have on the following day, at an early hour, seen the papers on the subject of his art, which had been written the

---

* See in disproof of this opinion—"Did Edmund Burke write Sir Joshua Reynolds's 'Lectures'?" *Anecdote Biography.*

preceding night. *I have had the rude manuscript from himself, in his own handwriting*, in order to make a fair copy from it for him to read in public. I have seen the manuscript also, after it had been revised by Dr. Johnson, who has sometimes altered it to a wrong meaning, from his total ignorance of the subject and of art; *but never, to my knowledge, saw the marks of Burke's pen in any of the manuscripts.*"

Elsewhere, Northcote contradictorily says: "I can't help thinking that Burke had a hand in the Discourses—that he gave some of the fine graceful turns."

Mr. Cotton must, however, be considered to have set the question at rest; and in his circumstantial work, to which we have so often referred, he has engraved *fac similes* of a portion of the third Discourse, in Sir Joshua's own handwriting, *word for word*, as in the printed copy.

Haydon also demolished the argument, both positively and inferentially; as well as by a letter communicated to him by a then (1844) living niece of Sir Joshua's.

Lastly, Mr. F. T. Colby, of Exeter College, Oxford, states that the original MSS., in Sir Joshua's own handwriting, are still preserved at Great Torrington, Devon, where Sir Joshua's nephew, and Mr. Colby's maternal grandfather, the Rev. John Palmer, resided.—(*Notes and Queries*, No. 320.) *Anecdote Biography: Edmund Burke.*

Haydon relates that the reading of these *Discourses* settled his walk in life. Accidentally turning over his father's apprentice's collection of books, he hit upon *Reynolds's Discourses*. He read one: it placed so much reliance on honest industry; it expressed so strong a conviction that all men were equal, and that application made the difference, that he fired up at once. He took them all home, and read them through before breakfast the next morning. The thing was done. He felt his destiny fixed. The spark which had for years lain struggling to blaze, now burst out for ever. And, on the evening before he started to try his fortune in the metropolis, Haydon notes: "I thought only of London, Sir Joshua, Drawing, Dissections and High Art."

PORTRAIT OF LORD HEATHFIELD.

In 1788, Reynolds sent to the Exhibition, eighteen pictures, the greatest number he ever sent, including his fine portrait of Lord Heathfield, now in the National Gallery; of which Haydon affirmed, he would rather be the painter than of Vandyke's Gevartius. "There is more (he said) of what is understood by the word *genius* in it, than in the other; and it is astonishing how its breadth and tone comes upon you as you enter the room—it affected me like the explosion of a bomb."

This picture was painted for Alderman Boydell, and is one of Sir Joshua's most strikingly characteristic portraits. The intrepid veteran holds in his hand the Key of the fortress of Gibraltar; the background is a view of the rock, with the smoke of artillery, in allusion to the celebrated defence of 1779-83, of which Lord Heathfield, then Lieut.-Gen. Elliot, was the hero. The French and Spanish besieging forces consisted of an army of 40,000 men, and a fleet of 47 sail of the line, besides several smaller vessels. Barry said of the introduction of the key of the fortress into the general's hand, "Imagination cannot conceive anything more ingenious and heroically characteristic."

ROBIN GOODFELLOW, OR PUCK.

This picture was painted in 1789, for Mr. Alderman Boydell's Shakspearian Gallery. Walpole depreciates it as "an ugly little imp (but with some character) sitting on a mushroom half as big as a mile-stone."

Mr. Nicholls, of the British Institution, related to Mr. Cotton that the Alderman and his grandfather were with Sir Joshua, when painting the *Death of Cardinal Beaufort*. Boydell was much taken with the portrait of a naked child, and wished it could be brought into the Shakspeare. Sir Joshua said it was painted from a little child he found sitting on his steps in Leicester-square. Nicholls's grandfather then said, "Well, Mr. Alderman, it can very easily come into the Shakspeare, if Sir Joshua will kindly place him upon a mushroom, give him fawn's ears, and make a Puck of him." Sir Joshua liked the notion, and painted the picture accordingly.

The morning of the day on which Sir Joshua's *Puck* was to be sold, Lord Farnborough and Davies the painter, breakfasted with Mr. Rogers, and went to the sale together. When the picture was put up, there was a general clapping of hands, and yet it was knocked down to Mr. Rogers for 105 guineas. As he walked home from the sale, a man carried *Puck* before him, and so well was the picture known, that more than one person, as they passed in the street, called out, "There it is!" At Mr. Rogers's sale, in 1856, it was purchased by Earl Fitzwilliam for 980 guineas. The grown-up person of the sitter for Puck was in Messrs. Christie and Manson's room, during the sale, and stood next to Lord Fitzwilliam, who is also a survivor of the sitters to Sir Joshua. The merry boy, whom Sir Joshua found upon his door-steps, was subsequently a porter at Elliot's brewery, in Pimlico.

SIR JOSHUA RETIRES FROM THE ROYAL ACADEMY.

The close of the President's life was embittered by a feud with the Royal Academy, where he had reigned paramount from its first institution. He had carried his zeal too far in behalf of Bonomi, an Italian architect, in opposition to Fuseli, in the choice of Academician; and the latter being elected by a majority of two to one, Sir Joshua quitted the chair deeply offended, and wrote a cold and courteous farewell. The Academy endeavoured to soothe him; and the King, through Sir William Chambers, conveyed the royal wish that Sir Joshua would continue President. He relented, and resumed the chair, but only to resign it, with more kindly feeling,—after an occupation of twenty-one years.

Reynolds made his last appearance in the Academy in 1790, when he addressed the students on the delivery of the medals. Mr. Rogers thus describes the scene: "I was present when Sir Joshua Reynolds delivered his last lecture at the Royal Academy. On entering the room, I found that a semicircle of chairs, immediately in front of the pulpit, was reserved for persons of distinction, being labelled, 'Mr. Burke,' 'Mr. Boswell,' &c. &c.; and I, with other young men, was forced to station myself a good way off. During the lecture a great crash was heard; and the company, fearing that the building was about to come down, rushed towards the door. Presently, however, it appeared that there was no cause for alarm, and they endeavoured to resume their places; but, in consequence of the confusion, the reserved seats were now occupied by those who could first get into them; and I, pressing forwards, secured one of them. Sir Joshua concluded the lecture by saying, with great emotion: 'And I should desire that the last words which I should pronounce in this Academy and from this place might be the name of—

Michael Angelo.' As he descended from the rostrum, Burke went up to him, took his hand, and said,—

> 'The Angel ended, and in Adam's ear
> So charming left his voice, that he awhile
> Thought him still speaking, still stood fix'd to hear.'"

When the crash was heard, Sir Joshua sat silent and unmoved in his chair; the floor, which had only sunk a little, was soon supported, the company resumed their seats, and he recommenced his discourse with perfect composure. He afterwards remarked, that, if the floor had fallen, the whole company must have been killed, and the arts in Britain, as a consequence, thrown back two hundred years.

REYNOLDS'S KINDNESS.

The great painter's goodnature, and his liking to contribute to the enjoyment of young persons, was proverbial, and there is not a better evidence of a kindly disposition. This amiable feeling is shown in the following incident.

In the year 1790, a youth named Buckingham, a scholar at Mr. King's Academy, Chapel-street, Soho, presuming upon his father's knowledge of Sir Joshua Reynolds, called in Leicester-square, and asked the *President of the Royal Academy* if he would draw him a flag for the next breaking-up of the school. Sir Joshua kindly told him if he would call on a certain day, he would see what could be done. The youth went, accompanied by a schoolfellow,* when Sir Joshua presented them with a flag, about a yard square, on which he had painted the king's coat-of-arms. This flag was accordingly borne in the breaking-up procession to the Yorkshire Stingo, in the New Road—an honour to the school, and a still greater honour to him who had painted it, and given up his valuable time to promote their holiday amusements.

SIR JOSHUA AND HIS PET BIRD.

The classic fable of the unstrung bow is frequently illustrated in the lives of great men, who, in simple recreation bordering upon child's play, often seek relief from society. Sir Joshua is related to have made a companion of a little bird which used to perch on his hand: and with this feathered favourite,

* Mr. Williamson, the artist, by whom this anecdote was related to Mr. Roffe, the engraver, in 1830. See *Mirror*, vol. xvi. p. 297.

he was often found by his visitors, pacing his room, and speaking to it as if it were endowed with intelligence beyond instinct. One summer morning, the bird which was thus fondly caressed, was tempted by an open window, to fly away; and Sir Joshua rushed forth into Leicester-square, and there for hours in vain sought the lost favourite of his spare minutes.

"RALPH'S EXHIBITION."

Malone tells us that Sir Joshua always considered the possession of the works of Titian, Vandyke, and Rembrandt, the best kind of wealth; and that instead of saving money, he laid it out faster than he got it, in purchasing the finest examples of art that could be procured. The collection of pictures, prints, and drawings, which he thus acquired, he offered, before his death, to the Royal Academy, at a sum much below their value; but the Academicians could not avail themselves of the offer. He then made a public exhibition of the collection in a room which he hired in the Haymarket; and, as he could no longer work at his profession, he employed himself in composing and arranging the catalogue. Sir Joshua gave the profits arising from this exhibition to his old servant, Ralph Kirkley: hence it was called "Ralph's Exhibition."

REYNOLDS'S DECLINING SIGHT.

In July, 1789, when Sir Joshua had nearly finished the portrait of Lady Beauchamp, (the last female portrait, according to Malone, he ever painted,) his eyesight was so affected that he found it difficult to proceed. "He laid down his pencil, sat a little while in mute consideration, and *never lifted it more*." This touching record is by Cunningham.

Miss Palmer, December 26, 1789, wrote to her cousin, describing her being called from Devonshire by the sad occurrence: Sir Joshua, before she left town, had a complaint in his eye, but it was thought of no consequence.

"Alas (writes Miss Palmer,) he very soon totally lost it, and when I returned to him, he was under the most violent apprehension that the other was going too. But thank God, these fears vanished, and although one eye is gone, he sees as well as ever with the other. However, the dread of what may happen, if he uses it much, entirely deters him from either painting, writing, or reading; for the last four months I have spent all my time in reading to him, and writing all that he wants to have done. He now amuses himself by sometimes cleaning or mending a picture, for his ruling passion still continues in force, and he enjoys his pictures as much as ever.

"His health is perfect, and his spirits good, surprisingly so, considering what a loss an eye is to him; and as it is the gutta serena which is affected, there is not the least chance of his ever recovering his sight. I expected he would have been depressed by such an event, almost to melancholy; but far from it, he enjoys company (in a quiet way), and loves a game of cards as well as ever."

Mr. Cotton has engraved from Sir Joshua's pocket-book his record of the calamity—Monday, the 13th of July—"prevented by my eye beginning to be obscured." Still, there are several subsequent entries, from which it may be inferred that Sir Joshua worked more or less upon other portraits. Miss Palmer, writing in March, 1790, speaks of his still painting occasionally; and the author of the *Testimonials* dates his entire cessation from painting in Nov. 1791; "from which period, (he says) Sir Joshua never painted more," and adds: "His last male portrait was that of Charles James Fox, and when the last touches were given to this picture, the hand of Reynolds fell to rise no more."

DEATH OF SIR JOSHUA REYNOLDS.

Sir Joshua now became much depressed in spirits, from his apprehension that a tumour, accompanied by inflammation which took place above the eye that perished, might affect the other; and it could not be dispersed. Under these infirmities, he resigned for ever the Presidency of the Royal Academy. He now grew melancholy, and sorrowfully silent. A concealed malady was sapping his life and spirits. Mr. Burke says: "His illness was long, but borne with a mild and cheerful fortitude, without the least mixture of anything irritable or querulous, agreeable to the placid and even tenor of his whole life. He had from the beginning of his malady, a distinct view of his dissolution, which he contemplated with an entire composure, that nothing but the innocence, integrity, and usefulness of his life, and an unaffected submission to the will of Providence, could bestow."

"I have been fortunate," said Reynolds, "in long good

health and constant success, and I ought not to complain. I know that all things on earth must have an end, and now I am come to mine." With these simple words of resignation, Sir Joshua expired, without any visible symptoms of pain, on the night of Thursday, February 23, 1792, in the 69th year of his age.

Next day, his body was opened by Mr. Hunter, the eminent surgeon, when his liver was found to have become præternaturally enlarged, and to have increased from about five pounds to nearly eleven pounds. Though during the whole of his illness from December to Feb. 23, he *felt* and therefore thought that his malady was mortal, he submitted to the Divine Will with perfect resignation, at the same time following the prescriptions of his physicians, though with little or no hope of their being useful. He died with very little pain.

Mr. Malone left among his papers the following touching details of the last hours of Sir Joshua.

"The dear friend so often mentioned in these papers, Sir Joshua Reynolds, died at his house in Leicester Fields, (Feb. 23, 1792,) at half-past eight o'clock. . . He had long enjoyed such constant health, looked so young, and was so active, that I thought, though he was sixty-nine years old, he was as likely to live eight or ten years longer as any of his younger friends.

"On our return from an excursion to Mr. Burke's at Beaconsfield, last September, we alighted from his coach, and while the horses baited at the half-way house, we walked five miles very smartly in a warm day without his being fatigued. About three years ago, he found some defect in his sight, whilst painting the picture of Lady Beauchamp, if I remember right, and then determined to paint no more. Soon afterwards he entirely lost the sight of his left eye. From that period he became very apprehensive of losing the other also, yet his uniform cheerfulness never forsook him till very lately.

"I cannot help thinking that we should not have lost this most amiable man for some years, had there not been want of exertion, combined with some want of skill in his physicians. In September he was much distressed by swelling and inflammation over the lost eye, owing as has since been thought, to some extravasated blood. For this Mr. Cruikshank, who was called in as surgeon, bled him with leeches, purged and blistered him repeatedly, all in vain; for the swelling and pain remained in that part till the period of death. This pain led him to fear that the other eye would soon be affected; and from this or other causes, his spirits became depressed, and his appetite daily decreased. In this state he continued in the month of November. The physicians who then attended, Sir George Baker and Dr. Warren, assured him that his remaining eye was in no danger, and that with respect to any other complaint, if he would but exert himself, take exercise, and think himself well, he would be well.

"Unfortunately, they paid little attention to his loss of appetite and depression of spirits. Even while he was gradually wasting, their constant language was—'What can we do for a man who will do nothing for himself?' At the same time, they owned they could not discern his disorder, though he was ready and willing to follow such prescriptions as they should direct. All this while, that is, during the months of November, December, and January, they made not the least *attempt* to investigate the seat or origin of his disease; nor did they call for the aid of a surgeon to examine his body minutely, and thus discover the latent mischief.

"Dr. Blagdon (Secretary of the Royal Society, who had studied physic, and practised for some time in America) *alone* uniformly declared he was confident the complaints of Sir Joshua Reynolds were not imaginary, but well founded, and that some of the principal *viscera* were affected. His conjecture proved but too correct; for on his body being opened, his liver, which ought to have weighed about five pounds, had attained the great weight of eleven pounds. It was also somewhat scirrhous. The optic nerve of the left eye was quite shrunk, and more flimsy than it ought to have been. The other, which he was so apprehensive of losing, was not affected. In his brain was found more water than is usual in men of his age."—*Sir James Prior's Life of Edmond Malone.*

In his stature, Sir Joshua Reynolds was rather under the middle size, of a florid complexion, roundish blunt features, and a lively aspect; not corpulent, though somewhat inclined to it, but extremely active; with manners uncommonly polished and agreeable. He was never married.

FUNERAL OF SIR JOSHUA REYNOLDS.

The remains of the great painter, after lying in state in the great room of the Royal Academy, at Somerset House, were interred, with great ceremony, in St. Paul's Cathedral, on March 3, 1792. The mourners included many of the most illustrious men of the land: they were conveyed in forty-two coaches, followed by forty-two empty carriages of the nobility. The coffin was deposited in a grave in the south aisle of the crypt of the cathedral, where have since been interred many of our greatest painters. Hence, if Westminster Abbey has its *Poets' Corner*, so has St. Paul's its *Painters' Corner*. Above, in the nave of the cathedral, many years after the interment, here was erected a marble statue of Reynolds, one of the finest works of Flaxman: the President wears his robes of office; in his right hand he bears his *Lectures*, and his left rests upon a pedestal surmounted with a bust of Michael Angelo. Upon the pedestal is a long inscription in Latin, from the pen of Mr. R. Payne Knight.

The ceremonial of the funeral was superintended by Mr. Burke, who at the close attempted to thank the members of the Academy for the attention shown to the remains of their late President; but the orator's feelings found vent in tears; and after several efforts, he gave up the attempt: his eloquence was mute grief—he could not utter a word.

A print, engraved by Bartolozzi, was presented to each of the gentlemen attending the funeral. The design is, a female clasping an urn; near her is a boy holding an extinguished torch in one hand, and pointing with the other to a tablet on a sarcophagus, inscribed: "Succedet Fama, vivusque per ora feretur." Beneath, on a scroll, are these words:

The Executors and Family of Sir Joshua Reynolds return thanks for the tribute of respect paid to departed Genius and Virtue, by your attendance at the funeral of that illustrious painter and most amiable man, in St. Paul's Cathedral, on Saturday, March 3, 1792.

SIR JOSHUA'S WILL.

His will, made Nov. 5, 1791, begins with this melancholy paragraph: "As it is probable that I shall soon be totally deprived of sight, and may not have an opportunity of making a formal will, I desire that the following memorandums may be considered as my last will and testament."

The principal portion of his property, which amounted upon the whole to 80,000*l.*, he bequeathed to his niece, Miss Palmer, who was shortly afterwards married to the Earl of Inchiquin, subsequently created Marquis of Thomond.

Sir Joshua bequeathed to Mr. Burke for the trouble of executorship, 2,000*l.*, and also cancelled a bond for the same amount, lent on a former occasion. Their intimacy—the extent of a generation—had been close and uninterrupted—their feelings and sentiments consonant—and in this protracted friendship they had conjointly missed many a brilliant ornament from the gay circle that was wont to assemble round Reynolds's hospitable board in Leicester-square.

Sir Joshua Reynolds, (says Burke,) was on very many accounts one of the most memorable men of his time. He was the first Englishman who added the praise of the elegant arts to the other glories of his country. In taste, in grace, in facility, in happy invention, in the richness and harmony of colouring, he was equal to the greatest inventors of the renowned ages. He possessed the theory as perfectly as the practice of his art. To be such a painter he was a profound and penetrating philosopher. His talents of every kind, powerful from nature, and not merely cultivated by letters, his social virtues in all the relations and all the habitudes of life, rendered him the centre of a very great and unparalleled variety of agreeable societies, which will be dissipated by his death. He had too much merit not to excite some jealousy, too much innocence to provoke any enmity. The loss of no man of his time can be felt with more sincere general and unmixed sorrow. Hail! and Farewell!

REYNOLDS'S THRONE-CHAIR.

This interesting relic, having fallen into the hands of Dr. Fryer, was after his death inserted in a catalogue of his household property for sale by auction, when Mr. J. T. Smith apprised Sir Thomas Lawrence of the fact. However, on the day of sale, the President of the Royal Academy had nearly lost it; as the lot was about to be knocked down for ten shillings and sixpence, just as the rescuing bidder entered the room; which enabled him, after a slight contest of biddings, to place the treasure, on that very day, by Sir Thomas's fireside in Russell-square. In the sale of the Leicester Gallery of Pictures, consisting entirely of the productions of British artists, a comparatively diminutive chair, of French character, was conspicuously advertised as the throne-chair of Sir Joshua Reynolds; but on the error being pointed out to Mr. Christie, the auctioneer, he acknowledged the error to the company, adding, that the real unostentatious chair was in the possession of the President of the Royal Academy.

The chair had some years previously been presented by Lord and Lady Inchiquin to Barry, the painter, who acknowledged the gift in the following letter:

"Mr. Barry presents his respectful compliments to Lord and Lady Inchiquin, with every acknowledgment and thanks for their inestimable favour conferred on him this morning in the gift of Sir Joshua's chair.

"Alas! this chair, that has had such a glorious career of fortune, instrumental as it has been in giving the most advantageous stability to the otherwise fleeting, perishable graces of a Lady Sarah Bunbury, or a Waldegrave, or in perpetuating the negligent, honest exterior of the author of the 'Rambler,' the 'Traveller,' and of almost every one whom the public admiration gave a currency for abilities, beauty, rank, or fashion: the very chair that is immortalised in Mrs. Siddons's 'Tragic Muse,' where it will have as much celebrity as the chair of Pindar, which for so many ages was shown in the porch at Olympia.

"This chair, then, of Sir Joshua Reynolds may rest, very well satisfied with the reputation it has gained; and although its present possessor may not be enabled to grace it with any new ornament, yet it can surely count upon finding a most affectionate, reverential conservator, whilst God shall permit it to remain under his care.

"Jan. 30, 1794.
No. 36, Castle-street, Oxford Market."

SIR JOSHUA'S PALETTE.

Mr. Cribb, of King-street, Covent Garden, possesses a palette, which belonged to Sir Joshua Reynolds. It descended to Mr. Cribb from his father, to whom it was given by the Marchioness of Thomond. It is of plain mahogany, and measures eleven inches by seven inches, and has a sort of loop handle.

SALES OF REYNOLDS'S PORTRAITS.

Mr. Cotton was present at the sale of the library and effects of Mrs. Piozzi, at Streatham Park, in May, 1816, when the following portraits, painted by Sir Joshua, for Mr. and Mrs. Thrale, were sold by Squibb, the auctioneer:

Lot.		Guineas.
56.	Lord Sandys	80
57.	Lord Lyttleton	41
58.	Mrs. Thrale and Daughter . . . . (Withdrawn)	
59.	Arthur Murphy	98
60.	Oliver Goldsmith	127

LOT.		GUINEAS.
61. Sir Joshua Reynolds		122
62. Sir William Chambers		80
63. David Garrick		175
64. Miss Owen	(Withdrawn)	
65. Mr. Baretti		82
66. Dr. Burney		20
67. Edmund Burke		240
68. Dr. Johnson		360

Lot 58 was purchased, after the sale, by Mr. S. Boddington, for 78 guineas. The portrait of Arthur Murphy is now in Sir Robert Peel's gallery. This noble picture was bought at Mr. Wright's sale, in 1845, by Sir Robert Peel, for 500 guineas. The portrait of Dr. Johnson was bought by Mr. Watson Taylor, at whose sale in 1825, it fetched 493*l.*

SALES OF REYNOLDS'S PICTURES.

At the great sale of Reynolds's works, at Christie's, in May, 1821, the spirited competition and the high prices were regarded by Haydon as the most triumphant thing for the art of this country. He compares the indifference with which a fine Teniers, a respectable Titian, and an undoubted Correggio were put up and knocked down, and carried off, with the enthusiastic eagerness when a picture of Reynolds's was offered. On the principle of seeking in each master his characteristic excellence, he avows his preference of the *Charity* to any of his larger productions. "It may take its place triumphantly," he says, "by any Correggio on earth." And next to this he thinks the *Piping Shepherd* one of the finest emanations of Reynolds's sentiment. On the 19th of May he made Mr. Phillips buy this picture for 400 guineas, who, being a new hand at buying, looked rather frightened at having given so much. "But it was worth 1000 guineas," says Haydon. "It is the completest bit of a certain expression in the world. Eyes and hands, motions and look, all seem quivering with the remembrance of some melodious tone of his flageolet. The colour and preservation are perfect. It is a thing I could dwell on for ages."

Next day, Haydon went again to Reynolds's sale, and found the 400 guineas of yesterday had made a great noise in town, and Phillips was assailed by everybody as he came in. Northcote was next to him. Phillips asked him how he liked the *Shepherd Boy.* At first he did not recollect it, and then said, "Ah! indeed, ah! yes! it was a very poor thing! I remember it." Poor Mr. Phillips whispered to Haydon, "You see people have different tastes." "It served him heartily right," says Haydon, "I was very glad of it; he does not deserve his prize." The moment these people heard Haydon was the adviser, they all began to undervalue it; and as soon as Northcote had said what he thought would make Phillips unhappy for two hours, he slunk away.

In May, 1856, five months after the death of Mr. Rogers, were sold the celebrated pictures by Reynolds, which had been collected in the poet's residence in St. James'-place. They had been removed to the great room at Christie's. The first picture put up was Lot 581, *The Mob-cap*—the principal figure in the celebrated composition of *The Infant Academy*. The biddings commenced at 250 guineas, and were finally closed by Mr. Radclyffe, for 780 guineas: purchased for Miss Burdett Coutts. Lot 591, *April Sketching*, formed the companion to the *Girl with a Kitten*, in Lord Normanton's collection, and had been purchased by Mr. Rogers at Lady Thomond's sale, for 100 guineas—350 guineas. Lot 691, *The Strawberry Girl*, the great gem of the collection, was bought for the Marquis of Hertford, at 2,100 guineas. This is a duplicate of the picture now at Bowood, the seat of the Marquis of Lansdowne, and was bought of Sir Joshua, by Lord Carysfort, for 50 guineas! Lot 695, the *Sleeping Girl*, described by Northcote as one of Reynolds's *richest performances*, sold for 150 guineas.

Lot 702, *The Study from the Window of Sir Joshua's Villa at Richmond Hill*, bought by Mr. Rogers at Lady Thomond's sale for 155 guineas,—sold for 430 guineas.

Lot 706, *Cupid and Psyche*, one of the most beautiful of Sir Joshua's fancy subjects, was bought by Mr. Radclyffe, for 400 guineas.

Lot 714, *Puck, or Robin Goodfellow*, sold to Earl Fitzwilliam, for 980 guineas.

When West was told of Rogers's purchase of Puck, he exclaimed, "Sir, that man has taste, he runs away with all the fine things."

The poet's brother, Mr. Henry Rogers, of Highbury, among other beautiful specimens of art, possessed Sir Joshua's first picture of the Girl sitting for her portrait, in Lord Palmerston's celebrated picture of the *Infant Academy;* and also the lovely picture of the *Girl sketching from Nature*.

CHARACTERISTICS, RETROSPECTIVE OPINIONS, AND PERSONAL TRAITS.

REYNOLDS'S FIRST LESSON IN ART.

Mrs. Jameson says of the important influence which Richardson's *Treatise* exercised over the mind of Sir Joshua:

"It appears to me that the boy who at eight years old was ever found with a pencil in his hand, copying prints out of books, who at the same time had mastered the *Jesuits' Perspective*, would have been a painter in any case; but the perusal of Richardson's book at the age of fifteen or sixteen, elevated and directed his boyish enthusiasm; it made him *the* painter which he afterwards became. He closed it, he says, with the conviction that Raphael was the greatest man who had ever existed. But this was nothing compared with the aspirations of a still higher kind, produced by the same striking book. It is impossible, I think, to look back upon the whole tenour of Sir Joshua's life, without a perception of the excellent moral influence its perusal left upon his mind and character. The lofty claims which Richardson set forth in behalf of painting as an art; the union of knowledge and virtue with creative genius; of high qualities with great attainments, which he requires in the artist; seem to have made an ineffaceable impression on the thoughtful, dreaming boy, and to have produced, or at least developed, that singular union of self-respect and pride in his art, with modesty and humility, which distinguished him through life. Some passages of Richardson's book would seem to have been written before Sir Joshua's time, and intended to apply to him, if we did not know to the contrary, that it was actually published some years before he was born. . . . . It is clear that Richardson's ideal of portraiture, and the qualities and aims of a portrait-painter, were ever present in Sir Joshua's mind throughout the whole of his career."

HUDSON, SIR JOSHUA'S MASTER.

"Thomas Hudson, the scholar and son-in-law of Mr. Richardson, enjoyed for many years the chief business of portrait-painting in London, after his master and Jervas were gone off the stage; though Vanloo first, and Liotard afterwards, for a few years, diverted the torrent of fashion from the established professor. Still, says Walpole, the country gentlemen were faithful to their compatriot, and were content with the fair-tied wigs, blue velvet coats, and white satin waistcoats which he liberally bestowed on his customers. His likenesses were good: his portraits of Handel, one of which is in the Bodleian Gallery at Oxford, exhibit much character and spirited execution; but having painted the head, Hudson's genius failed him, and he was obliged to employ another to paint the figure and drapery. He chiefly employed Vanaken, or Vanhááken, and when he died, in 1749, Hudson, it is said, was nearly driven to quit his profession; and, says Mr. Cotton, Hogarth, (whose genius was too great, and his employment too little, to require a drapery painter,) drew a caricature of his funeral attended by the painters he worked for, exhibiting every mark of grief and despair.

"Hudson lived in Great Queen-street, Lincoln's-Inn-Fields, in the house in which Hoole, the translator of Tasso, lived: it is now divided into Nos. 55 and 56. Hudson painted most of the portraits of the Dilettanti Society, which now hang in their dining-room, at the Thatched House Tavern, St. James's-street. His manner of painting was woolly, possessing little variety of attitude, and no depth of knowledge in reflected lights. All that Hudson was famous for was his collection of fine drawings by the great painters, particularly Rembrandt. Hudson's name is frequently mentioned when Sir Joshua Reynolds is spoken of, as having been his master; but Sir Joshua's mind and talent were his own, and a host of Hudsons could have rendered him but little service."—*J. T. Smith.*

Joshua, immediately after his quarrel with his master, returned to Devonshire, but remained there only a few months, when he went back to London, became reconciled to Hudson, who not only received him kindly, but even consulted him upon the pictures he had in hand; and a letter of Joshua's father states that Hudson had introduced the young painter into a club of the most famous men in their profession. This letter shows that Joshua was living in London in 1744 and 1745. He was summoned to Devonshire towards the close of 1746: his father died on Christmas-day, 1746. Soon after this, and when the family were obliged to remove from the schoolmaster's residence at Plympton, Joshua took a house in Plymouth Dock, now Devonport. Malone, however, states that Reynolds told him that when about the age of nineteen or twenty, he became very careless about his profession, and lived for near three years at Plymouth in a great deal of dissipation with but indifferent company. He much lamented the loss of these three years; however, he saw his error in time, and sat down seriously to his art about the year 1743 or 1744, painted his first portrait—Captain Hamilton, a naval officer, who married Lord Eliot's mother.

This portrait of Captain Hamilton was the first of his performances at this period, which brought Reynolds into notice.

REYNOLDS'S EARLY PORTRAITS.

Reynolds resided with his two unmarried sisters at Plymouth Dock. Here, among his early portraits, he painted the greatest man of the place, the Commissioner of the Dock-yard, Philip Vanbrugh, Esq.; and his father wrote soon after, "Joshua is painting in the Dock: he has drawn twenty already, and has ten more bespoke." Mr. Kendal, of Pelyn, M.P., informed Mr. Cotton that he had in his possession some family portraits, with Reynolds's name, and the date 1744, upon them. A portrait of Alderman Facey, in the Athenæum, at Plymouth, is said to have been painted by Reynolds. Many of the pictures he executed at this period were carelessly drawn, and frequently in common-place attitudes like those of his master, Hudson; nor do these portraits exhibit those excellencies of colouring and power of expression for which the painter was afterwards distinguished.

Nevertheless, Reynolds now produced several fine portraits, particularly one of himself as a young man, with pencils and palette in his left hand, shading the light from his eyes with the right.* There is also a beautiful portrait of Mrs. Field, the sister-in-law of the Rev. J. Reynolds, Sir Joshua's uncle, which must have been painted before he went to Italy. The carnations are of great delicacy and clearness, and the features well defined. About the same time he painted the portrait of Elizabeth Chudleigh, afterwards Duchess of Kingston, which is engraved in Walpole's Letters to Sir Horace Mann.

* This portrait, in fine preservation, is in our National Portrait Gallery.

PORTRAIT OF LORD BUTE.

This magnificent full-length portrait of the Minister, Lord Bute, is in finer condition than it was known to have been when it passed from the easel of Sir Joshua to Caen-wood House, then the princely seat of the unpopular Premier. Reynolds, in painting this portrait, stripped to the labour. He was disliked at Court, and Allan Ramsay, his then rival, was in high reputation for an excellent full-length portrait he had newly completed of the same nobleman. It was Reynolds's aim to remove the effect of Ramsay's portrait, and to place himself not only above Ramsay, but on a rank with the greatest masters; and he succeeded. Oddly enough, this picture is not to be found in any catalogue of Sir Joshua's portraits: it now belongs to Lord Wharncliffe.

Ramsay, the painter, used to say, that Lord Bute's leg was allowed to be the handsomest in England, and that whilst he was standing to him for his whole-length portrait, engraved by Ryland, his Lordship held up his robes considerably above his right knee, so that his leg should be entirely seen; in which position he remained for the space of an hour; and the forefinger of the right hand supporting the robe, is pointing down to the leg. When the Marquis of Rockingham was standing to Sir Joshua Reynolds for his whole-length portrait, engraved by Fisher, his Lordship asked the Painter if he had not given a strut to the left leg: "My Lord," replied Sir Joshua, "I wish to show a leg with Ramsay's Lord Bute."

REYNOLDS'S PRICES AND SITTERS.

Cotton states that while residing in St. Martin's-lane, Reynolds's prices were 10, 20, and 40 guineas, for the three usual sizes of Portraits, a head, half-length, and whole length; while those of Hudson, at the same time, were 12, 24, and 48 guineas. After his removal to Newport-street, his practice increased so rapidly that he engaged as an assistant Mr. Toms, an artist, whom Hogarth used to call "Reynolds's drapery-man," to forward the preparation of his pictures. About the same time he also received Thomas Beach and Hugh Barron as pupils, and raised his prices to a level with those of Hudson. Four or five years later, they both raised them to 15, 30, and 60 guineas.

Northcote tells us, on the authority of Dr. Johnson, that in 1750, the price of Reynolds for a head, was 20 guineas; and that at this time he often received six sitters in a day, and found it necessary to keep a list of the names of those who waited until vacancies occurred. He then received them in the order in which they were set down; and many portraits were sent home before the colours were dry.

Reynolds is stated to have received sitters as early as six or seven o'clock in the morning; but this is not borne out by Sir Joshua's diary, where no instance is recorded of a sitter coming earlier than nine o'clock. Yet, there was no intermission for some hours: thus in the pocket-book for 1761, we find on one day, the names of seven sitters in as many consecutive hours. According to Reynolds's pocket-book, 1766, his prices were then: whole-length, 150*l*.; half-length, 70*l*.; kit-cat, 50*l*.; head, 30*l*.

In 1780, Sir Joshua raised his price from 30 to 50 guineas for a head size, which he continued for the remainder of his life. (*Cotton*.)

SIR JOSHUA'S SNUFF.

Reynolds's snuff was Hardham's 37, of which occurs this memorandum in the painter's pocket-book for 1761: "Hardham of Fleet-street, Snuff No. 37." It was so named from the number of Hardham's shop, No. 37, on the north side of Fleet-street. He had been Garrick's *numberer* (to count the audience in the theatre); and when Hardham invented his "mixture," Garrick rendered him this service. While enacting the character of a man of fashion on the stage, David offered a pinch of his snuff to a fellow-comedian, observing that it was the most fashionable mixture of the day, and to be had *only* at Hardham's, No. 37, Fleet-street. The puff succeeded beyond Garrick's expectation, and Hardham's 37 was the favourite mixture for many years afterwards, when snuff-taking was the rage and fashion of the time.*

Reynolds took snuff so freely when he was painting, that it sometimes inconvenienced his sitters. Colonel Phillips related to Northcote, that when Sir Joshua was painting the

---

* Hardham was born at Chichester, and having made a large fortune by his snuff-trade in Fleet-street, he retired to his native city, where he died in 1772, having bequeathed a portion of his well-earned wealth to charitable institutions of Chichester.

large picture at Blenheim, of the Marlborough family, the Duchess one day ordered a servant to bring a broom and sweep up Sir Joshua's snuff from the carpet; but Reynolds, who would not suffer any interruption during his application to his art, desired him to let the snuff remain until he had finished the painting; observing that the dust raised by the broom would do more injury to his picture than the snuff could possibly do to the carpet.

Mr. Rogers tells us that at an Academy dinner, Sir Joshua's waistcoat was literally powdered with snuff.

A gentleman told Wilkie he sat to Sir Joshua, who dabbled in a quantity of snuff, laid the picture on its back, shook it about till it settled like a batter-pudding, and then painted away. This, says Cotton, was to get a surface like Rembrandt's, and in accordance with Gandy's advice to Reynolds, for a rich texture, and creamy colour: Sir Joshua often repeated observations by Gandy, and considered some of his portraits equal to those of Rembrandt.

HOGARTH AND REYNOLDS.

The "painting moralist" is scarcely mentioned by "the founder of the English School," save in the following instance.

Before Hogarth had done anything of consequence in his own walk, he entertained some hopes of succeeding in the higher branches of historical painting. "He was not," says Sir Joshua Reynolds, (*Discourses*, vol. ii. p. 163,) "blessed with the knowledge of his own deficiency, or of the bounds which were set to the extent of his own powers." "After he had invented a new species of dramatic painting, in which probably he will never be equalled, and had stored his mind with infinite materials to explain and illustrate the domestic and familiar scenes of comic life, which were generally and ought always to have been the subject of his pencil, he very imprudently, or rather presumptuously, attempted the great historical style, for which his previous habits had by no means prepared him; he was, indeed, so entirely unacquainted with the principles of this style that he was not even aware that any artificial preparation was at all necessary."

REYNOLDS'S MODELS.

The *Girl with a Muff*, at Lansdowne House, purchased at Lady Thomond's sale, in 1821, is said to be the portrait of Sir Joshua's favourite niece, Theophila Palmer. The same young lady was, probably, his model for several other pictures of a similar character, as a *Girl with a Bird*, in the collection at Knowsley; a *Girl caressing a Lamb;* and a *Girl holding a Cat in her arms*, called *Felina*. In all these pictures the female countenance is very much alike, and may be supposed to have been painted from the same model. The *Girl with a Muff* was, probably, painted in 1767 or 1768, when Miss Palmer was eleven or twelve years of age, and is mentioned in Sir Joshua's private notes.

Miss Gwatkin herself told Mr. Cotton that her mother sat to Sir Joshua for the head of Comedy in the celebrated picture of *Garrick between the muses of Tragedy and Comedy*. This picture was exhibited in Spring Gardens, in 1762, and was purchased of the Earl of Halifax for 300 guineas: after his death it was sold to Mr. Angerstein for 250 guineas, perhaps the only instance of a depreciation in the value of a fine picture by Sir Joshua Reynolds.

REYNOLDS'S LIBERALITY TO OZIAS HUMPHREY.

When, about 1768, Humphrey came to London, being a great admirer of Mr. Reynolds's pictures, he ventured to show him some of his miniatures. The great painter received him with the utmost cordiality, and requested to know from what county he came, and what his parents were. When Reynolds heard that he was from Devonshire, and that his mother was a lace-maker, he exclaimed: "Born in my county, and your mother a lace-maker!—why, Vandyke's mother was a maker of lace!" at the same time adding, that he should be welcome to copy any of his Vandykes. "Or, perhaps," he said, "you had better allow me to lend you some of mine, as they are better suited by their dress to answer your present purpose."

The generous offer was accepted with the greatest extasy, and Humphrey copied several pictures, which highly improved his natural taste for richness of colouring. He also produced in enamel one of Reynolds's finest works, his famous head of *King Lear in the Storm*, which so highly pleased Sir Joshua, that he exclaimed, "This is a beautiful copy; it is so finely painted, that you must allow me to purchase it. What is your price ? it will enable me to serve you." The artist, glowing with modesty, begged his patron to accept it. "No; that," he said, "he could not think of." "Three guineas, then, sir, is the price," replied he. "That is too little," observed the great painter; "I shall give you five; and let that be your price for such a picture;" at the same time advising him to take lodgings near him. Accordingly, in 1768, he took the house now No. 21, in King-street, Covent Garden, where he remained till 1771; during which time he fell in love with the daughter of Payne, the architect; the poor girl being compelled by her sordid father to marry another, Humphrey was so stung with disappointment, that, in 1773, he left London for Rome.

REYNOLDS'S DINNERS.

Mr. Forster, in his eloquent *Life and Adventures of Oliver Goldsmith*, has the following admirable picture of the gay festal meetings which Sir Joshua gave for many years at his house in Leicester-square.

"Well, Sir Joshua," said lawyer Dunning, on arriving at one of these parties, "and who have you got to dine with you to-day? The last time I dined in your house the company was of such a sort, that by—— I believe, all the rest of the world enjoyed peace for that afternoon." But though vehemence and disputation will at times usurp quieter enjoyments, when men of genius and strong character are assembled, the evidence that has survived of these celebrated meetings in no respects impairs their indestructible interest. They were the first great example that had been given in this country, of a social intercourse between persons of distinguished pretensions of all kinds; poets, physicians, lawyers, deans, historians, actors, temporal and spiritual peers, House of Commons men, men of science, men of letters, painters, philosophers, and lovers of the arts; meeting on a ground of hearty ease, good humour, and pleasantry, which exalts my respect for the memory of Reynolds. It was no prim fine table he set them down to. There was little order or arrangement; there was more abundance than elegance; and a happy freedom thrust conventionalism aside. Often was the dinner-board prepared for seven or eight, required to accommodate itself to fifteen or sixteen; for often on the very eve of dinner, would Sir Joshua tempt afternoon visitors with intimation that Johnson, or Garrick, or Goldsmith was to dine there. Nor was the want of seats the only difficulty. A want of knives and forks, of plates and glasses, as often succeeded. In something of the same style, too, was the attendance; the kitchen had to keep pace with the visitors; and it was easy to know the guests well acquainted with the house by their never failing to call instantly for beer, bread, or wine, that they might get them before the first course was over, and the worst confusion began. Once Sir Joshua was prevailed upon to furnish his table with dinner-glasses and decanters, and some saving of time they proved; yet as they were demolished in the course of service, he could never be persuaded to replace them. "But these trifling embarrassments," added Mr. Courtenay, describing them to Sir James Mackintosh, "only served to enhance the hilarity and singular pleasure of the entertainment." It was not the wine, dishes, and cookery, not the fish * and venison, that were talked of or recommended; those social hours, that irregular convivial talk, had matter of higher relish, and far more eagerly enjoyed. And amid all the animated bustle of his guests, the host sat perfectly composed; always attentive to what was said, never minding what was eat or drank, and leaving every one at perfect liberty to scramble for himself. Though so severe a deafness had resulted from cold caught on the Continent in early life as to compel the use of a trumpet, Reynolds profited by its use to hear or not to hear, or as he pleased to enjoy the privileges of both, and keep his own equanimity undisturbed. "He is the same all the year round," exclaimed Johnson, with honest envy. "In illness and in pain he is still the same. Sir, he is the most invulnerable man I know: the man with whom, if you should quarrel, you will find the most difficulty how to abuse." Nor was this praise obtained by preference of any, but by cordial respect to all; for in Reynolds there was as little of the sycophant as the tyrant. However high the rank of the guests invited, he waited for none. His dinners were served always precisely at five o'clock. "His was not the fashionable ill-breeding," says Mr. Courtenay, "which would wait an hour for two or three persons of title," and put the rest of the company out of humour by the invidious distinction.

SIR JOSHUA'S DEAFNESS.

Sir Martin Shee used to relate a singular fact with regard to the President's deafness, which compelled the constant use of an ear-trumpet. While at breakfast with Sir Joshua, in Leicester-square, in 1790, and during a long protracted interview which followed, the conversation was carried on in the ordinary tone, without any assistance from the acoustic tube, or any indication of imperfect hearing on the part of Sir Joshua. During the morning, however, they were not unfrequently interrupted by the entrance of a servant, with a message or some communication that required his master's attention and oral reply; and on each of such occasions the appearance of a third person was the signal for the President

* In 1859, disappeared the old fishmonger's shop, No. 8, on the north-side of Coventry-street, whence for many years Sir Joshua's table was supplied with fish. It is related that Reynolds often took an early morning walk, and a glance at the stock of fish for the day, and would then send his niece to cheapen such fish as he required for dinner.

to snatch up his trumpet, and resume a look of anxious inquiry and uncertain comprehension. Mr. Shee, the author of Sir Martin's *Life*, remarks: "I believe it is no uncommon thing for a deaf person to hear better in a *tête-à-tête* colloquy, than when surrounded by the buzz of general conversation in a large party. But in Sir Joshua's case the contrast seems to have been unusually marked and calculated to impart a peculiar significancy to Goldsmith's couplet:

> When they talked of their Raphaels, Correggios, and stuff,
> He shifted his trumpet, and only took snuff.

REYNOLDS'S PARSIMONY.

Odd stories are current of the President's meanness in small matters. Rogers used to relate that he happened to be passing by Sir Joshua's house in Leicester-square, when he saw a poor girl seated on the steps and crying bitterly. He asked what was the matter; and she replied that she was crying "because *the one shilling* which she had received from Sir Joshua for sitting to him as a model had proved to be a bad one, and he would not give her another."—Mr. Leslie discredits this story, and very properly.

REYNOLDS'S EXPERIMENTAL COLOURS.

It is to be regretted that Sir Joshua continued his experiments in colours for a long course of years, and that they infected more or less many of his finest works. He was (says Cunningham) exceedingly touchy of temper on the subject of colouring, and reproved Northcote with some sharpness for insinuating that Kneller used vermilion in his flesh-colour. "What signifies," said he, "what a man used who could not colour? you may use it if you will." He never allowed his pupils to make experiments, and on observing one of them employing some unusual compounds, exclaimed, "That boy will never do good, with his gallipots of varnish and foolish mixtures."

The secret of Sir Joshua's own preparations was carefully kept: he permitted not even the most favoured of his pupils to acquire the knowledge of his colours; he had all securely locked, and allowed no one to enter where these treasures were deposited. What was the use of all this secrecy? those who stole the mystery of his colours could not use it unless they stole his skill and talent also.

He was fond of seeking into the secrets of the old painters, and dissected some of their performances, without remorse or scruple, to ascertain their mode of laying on colour and finishing with effect. Titian he conceived to be the great master-spirit in portraiture; and no enthusiast in usury ever sought more incessantly for the secret of the philosopher's stone than did Reynolds to possess himself of the whole theory and practice of the Venetian. But this was a concealed pursuit: he disclosed his discoveries to none. "To possess," said the artist, "a real fine picture by that great master (Titian) I would sell all my gallery, I would willingly ruin myself." The capital old paintings of the Venetian School which Sir Joshua's experiments destroyed were not few, and it may be questioned if his discoveries were a compensation for their loss.

Some soot fell on a picture of Sir Joshua's drying at the fire: he took it up and said, "A fine cool tint that," and actually scumbled it beautifully into the flesh. Jackson had this anecdote from Sir George Beaumont.

The elder Reinagle remembered Sir Joshua using so much asphaltum that it dropped on the floor.

Reynolds said once, "Northcote, you don't clean my brushes well." "How can I?" replied Northcote, "they are so sticky and gummy."

REMBRANDT AND REYNOLDS.

Burnet remarks, that Rembrandt's etching of "Old Haring" has always struck him as one of the foundations of Reynolds's style in portraiture: a fine impression of this print, he observes, is more like Sir Joshua than many prints after his own pictures. Hudson had an excellent collection of Rembrandt's works, and therefore, he must have been early imbued with their merits and peculiarities.

I think (says Sir William Beechey,) Rembrandt seduced Sir Joshua, for he seems to have used something of the consistence of butter, which is a most bewitching vehicle certainly. Sir Joshua may, however, have learned this from Gandy, who said that a picture ought to have richness in its texture, as if the colours had been composed of cream or cheese, and the reverse of a hard and husky or dry manner.

PAINTING FOR POSTERITY.

Burnet tells us that when Reynolds's sister asked him the reason why we never see any of the portraits of Jervas now, he replied, "Because, my dear, they are all up in the garret." Yet, this man rode in his chariot-and-four, and received the praises of Pope in verse. Sir Godfrey Kneller would sometimes receive a sum of money and a couple of portraits by Vandyke as payment; but now a single portrait of the great founder of the Dutch school would outweigh in true value a large collection of Kneller's collected talents; yet Rembrandt died insolvent, and Sir Godfrey accumulated a large fortune. And such will be the fate of all those who paint for posterity, "and look beyond the ignorant present."

The Rev. H. Crowe, the Vicar of Buckingham, relates: "The Marquis of Drogheda was painted in early life by Sir Joshua Reynolds. His Lordship shortly after went abroad, and remained there between twenty and thirty years; during which time he ran into excesses, became bilious, and returned to Ireland with a shattered constitution. He found that the portrait and the original had faded together, and corresponded, perhaps, as well as when first painted."

SIR JOSHUA'S LAST SURVIVING SITTER.

In 1856, it was said that Lord Fitzwilliam was then the last survivor of the sitters to Sir Joshua; but another then remained in the grown-up person of the sitter for *Puck*, late a porter at Elliot's brewery, in Pimlico. *Puck* was obtained by Mr. Rogers at Boydell's Shakspeare Gallery sale, for 100 guineas,—the sum, Northcote states, Sir Joshua received for it.

Lord Melbourne remembered, when a child, sitting to Sir Joshua,* who played with him and rode him on his foot, and said: "Now, be a good boy, and sit a little longer, and you shall have another ride." Lord Melbourne died in 1848.

Sir Joshua loved his art; and though compelled to take occasional excursions into the country for the benefit of his health, he was never so happy as when painting. Such was his application, that, according to Farington, from 1753 until

* Mr. Leslie says of this portrait: "No likeness between a child and a man of 60 (an age at which I remember Lord Melbourne), was ever more striking."

Reynolds's death in 1792, a period of thirty-nine years, excepting the visits which he paid to the Continent for improvement in his art, and twice visiting his native county, he was never absent from his painting-room for more than a few days at a time.

REYNOLDS'S LANDSCAPES.

In regular landscape-painting, Sir Joshua's works are very scarce. At Port Eliot there is a long narrow view of Plymouth and the adjoining scenery, painted by Reynolds in 1748, the year before he went to Italy.

The landscape backgrounds introduced into his whole-length portraits were executed with great breadth and freedom of pencilling, rich in colour, and brilliant in effect, many of them not inferior to the works of Titian and Paul Veronese. Although Reynolds made some studies from nature, yet it is not known that he finished more than three pieces, one of which was a view from his own house, on Richmond Hill. This picture, which may be considered rather an arrangement of rich and brilliant colours, than a defined landscape, was purchased by Mr. Samuel Rogers, at the sale of Lady Thomond's pictures in 1821, for 155 guineas. At the same time was sold a woody landscape; and a bold landscape with figures, in the style of Salvator Rosa: both by Sir Joshua.

REYNOLDS'S VILLA AT RICHMOND.

The second house on the right from the Terrace on Richmond Hill is the villa which Sir William Chambers built for his friend, Sir Joshua Reynolds; but it has been much enlarged since his decease.* The situation is delightful; but it lacks the privacy which must have been so desirable for Sir Joshua. His niece, Miss Palmer, has well described this villa as "a house stuck upon the top of a hill, without a bit of garden, or ground of any sort near it, but what is as public as St. James's Park." Sir Joshua's last sojourn here extended to several days, which refutes the assertion that, although he frequently visited it, he never passed a night there. Fox observed that Sir Joshua never enjoyed Richmond, for he used to say that the *human face* was his landscape. This was a piece of pleasantry; for Reynolds must

* In one of the houses on the left of the road, Sir John Soane resided for a short time previously to his death.

SIR JOSHUA REYNOLDS. 153

have enjoyed the prospect of unequalled richness from Richmond Hill—over all the intervening flat country to the distant high grounds of Stoken Church, Maidenhead Thicket, Windsor Forest and Castle, Cooper's Hill, and St. Ann's Hill; and on the east, a fine view over London, to the Hampstead and Highgate hills.

Hudson, who resided at Twickenham, once observed to his pupil, Sir Joshua Reynolds, of his villa at Richmond, "Little did I think we should ever have had country-houses opposite each other;" to whom Sir Joshua replied: "Little did I think, when I was a young man, that I should at any time look down upon Mr. Hudson."

PRINTS FROM REYNOLDS'S PICTURES.

The earliest mezzotinto engravings which were published from Reynolds's pictures are the portraits of Lady Charlotte Fitzwilliam, with her hair curled and decorated with a feather and beads; and a half-length of Lady Ann Dawson, daughter of the Earl of Pomfret, as Diana. Both prints are dated 1745, and are by McArdell, in mezzotinto, which Reynolds considered best calculated to express a painter-like feeling, particularly in portraits; and he often was heard to declare, that the productions of McArdell would perpetuate his pictures when their colours should be faded and forgotten.

The finest and most complete collections of engravings from the works of Reynolds are those of the Marquis of Lansdowne, and the Duke of Buccleuch. The latter has been arranged by Mr. Colnaghi, in 17 vols. folio, and contains upward of 2,000 engravings. (*Cotton.*) The prints after Sir Joshua's pictures amount to about 700. (*Wornum.*)

LAWRENCE'S TRIBUTE TO REYNOLDS.

To the mutual honour of Sir Joshua Reynolds and Sir Thomas Lawrence we select the following from the address delivered by the latter President to the students of the Royal Academy, December 10, 1823, in allusion to the exhibition of Sir Joshua's pictures at the British Institution, in Pall Mall:

"With what increased splendour did that genius lately reappear amongst us! Many of us remember, when after long absence, the great Tragic Actress of our time returned for a season to the stage, to correct the forgetfulness of taste, and restore the dignity of her art: it was so with the return—the recovered glories of Sir Joshua! They who believed themselves best acquainted with his works, and entitled by their knowledge to speak of them with enthusiasm, felt how much of that knowledge they had forgotten; how inadequate to their merits was the praise they had bestowed. The prejudices, so injurious to modern art, were gone. Time seemed to have advanced the future with double speed, and presenting truth, invested her with new radiance! The few remaining competitors and scholars of this great artist saw him then with the eyes of posterity, and beheld, in their own narrow period, the sure stability of his fame.

"It is singular that the judgment, the unpretending sense and manly simplicity, so generally acknowledged to have marked the character of Sir Joshua, should have been impugned only on those opinions of Art, which seem to have been the most deliberately formed, and were enforced by him with parental zeal, as his last remembrance to this Academy. Sufficient proof of the sincerity of his admiration of Michael Angelo had previously existed in the actions of some of his finest groups having been taken from him; but we want no other evidence of its truth, than his picture of Mrs. Siddons—a work of the highest epic character, and indisputably the finest female portrait in the world.

"The link that united him to Michael Angelo was the sense of ideal greatness—the noblest of all perceptions. It is this sublimity of thought that marks the first-rate genius; this impelling fancy, which has nowhere its defined form, yet everywhere its image; and while pursuing excellence too perfect to be attained, creates new beauty that cannot be surpassed! It belongs only to the finer sagacity, which sees the essence of the beautiful or grand, divested of incongruous detail; and whose influence on the works of the great President is equally apparent in the calm, firm defender of the national Poet, as in the dying Queen of Virgil, or the grandeur of the Tragic Muse.

"To a mind so enlarged and liberal as Sir Joshua's, who decried not the value of an art that gave the world its Shakspeare, and in whose society a Garrick and a Kemble lived in grateful intercourse with Mr. Burke and Dr. Johnson, we may well imagine how gratifying were the contemplation and progress of that divine work; and allowing much to anticipate fame, we may equally believe, that part of the noble purpose was, protection of the genius he admired, to affix to passing excellence an imperishable name; extend the justice withheld by the limits of her art; and in the beauty of that unequalled countenance, fixed in the pale abstraction of some lofty vision, whose 'bodiless creations' are crowding on her view and leave in suspended action the majestic form, to verify the testimony of tradition, and, by the mental grandeur that invests her, record in resistless evidence the enchantment of her power.

"That the works, Gentlemen, of this illustrious man should have the strongest influence upon you cannot be matter of surprise: that the largest *style* of painting that perhaps is known, should captivate the scholar as it has charmed the teacher, is the most natural result that could have been produced in minds of sensibility and taste; but let it not mislead them. If they determine to make the labours of Sir Joshua their example, let them first examine by what only means their excellence was acquired.

"His early pictures bear evidence of the utmost delicacy of finishing; the most careful imitation. The sensitiveness of taste, which probably from boyhood he possessed, could never have permitted him to enter into the mean details of Denner; or content himself with the insipidity of Cornelius Jansen: but in mere finishing he was inferior to neither; and the history of the greatest masters is but one. Truth is the Key of Art, as Knowledge is of Power: within the portals you have ample range, but each apartment must be opened by it. The noblest work that perhaps was ever yet projected, the loftiest in conception, and executed with an unequalled breadth, is the ceiling of Michael Angelo: the miniatures of Julio Clovio are not more finished than his studies.

"On you, Gentlemen, who, with the Candidates of this evening, are entering on the first department of the Art, the conduct of Sir Joshua should act with treble force. Mr. Burke says of him: 'In painting portraits he appeared not to be raised upon that platform, but, to descend to it from a higher sphere!' To that sphere let his example guide you, and it will lead you to the highest: to Correggio, to Titian, to Raffaelle, to Michael Angelo! To those divine men, in whose presence, (to use his own language,) 'it is impossible to think or invent in a mean manner; and by the contemplation of whose works a state of mind is acquired, that is disposed to receive those ideas of art only which relish of grandeur or simplicity'".

THOMAS GAINSBOROUGH, R.A.

BIRTHPLACE AND PARENTAGE OF GAINSBOROUGH.

THIS eminent painter, who, with Richard Wilson, laid the foundation of our School of Landscape, was born at Sudbury, in Suffolk, in 1727,—the day or the month is not recorded. He was baptised at the Independent Meeting-house of the town, on May 14th in the same year. The house in which he was born was originally the Black Horse inn, and was one of the picturesque dwellings, with lofty gables and overhanging storeys, of the ancient town of Southburgh, as Sudbury was originally named. Here the Flemish weavers settled in the reign of Edward II., and taught the English their art. They excelled in making "sags" and crapes; and Gainsborough's father is described at different periods, as a milliner, clothier, and crape-maker: he also introduced into Sudbury the shroud trade from Coventry. He was a fine old man, and in full dress, wore a sword, and was an adroit fencer. He had a family of nine children, of whom Thomas was the youngest of five sons. The painter's mother was an accomplished woman, and excelled in flower-painting; she affectionately encouraged her son Thomas in his boyish attempts at drawing, and she lived to witness his high artistic fame.

The ancient buildings of Southburgh, doubtless, had the effect of forming young Gainsborough's taste; and he told Philip Thicknesse, his first patron, that "there was not a picturesque clump of trees, nor a single tree of any beauty, nor even hedge-row, stem, or post" in or around his native town, which was not, from his earliest years, treasured in his memory. Two of his brothers were men of mechanical genius: one, "Scheming Jack," contrived a pair of wings to fly with, a self-rocking cradle, and a singing cuckoo; and Humphry

THOMAS GAINSBOROUGH.

Gainsborough constructed a working model of a steam-engine, which he unsuspiciously showed to a stranger said to have been connected with Watt as an engineer.*

At ten years old, Thomas Gainsborough made sketches of trees, rocks, shepherds, ploughmen, and pastoral scenes, while at the Grammar School in Sudbury, then kept by his uncle; and he usually passed his holidays in rambling through the rich hanging woods, and sketching their majestic oaks and elms, winding glades, and sunny nooks. He is also said to have cut a caricature of his master upon the school-wall; and sketched a peasant who came to rob an orchard, which effort was preserved for many years, and ultimately made into a finished painting, as "Tom Pear-tree's Portrait." To obtain a holiday, he once forged the written request of his father, who muttered, "Tom will come to be hanged"; but, on learning that Tom employed the holiday in sketching, his parent, with very opposite feelings, exclaimed, "The boy will be a genius." He had little technical instruction, or graphical education. It has been truly said of him that "Nature was his teacher, and the woods of Suffolk were his Academy."

GAINSBOROUGH COMES TO LONDON.

At the age of fifteen, Gainsborough left Sudbury for the metropolis: here he resided with a silversmith, who introduced him to Gravelot, the engraver, from whom he learned etching and aqua-tint. He then obtained admission to the Academy in St. Martin's-lane; and next associated with Hayman, from whom, however, he learned little of painting, and less of morality. Within three years, he hired rooms in Hatton Garden, and began to paint landscapes, which he sold to picture-dealers; and portraits at from three to five guineas. He also modelled excellently, cows, dogs, and horses: a cast in the plaster-shops, of an old horse modelled by Gainsborough, obtained conventional reputation. This employment, however, proved so unprofitable, that Gainsborough packed up his canvas and colours, and returned to Sudbury, after four years' absence.

* There is in the British Museum a curious sun-dial with "Humphry Gainsborough" deeply cut in it; he anticipated the contrivance of fire-proof boxes, and received the Society of Arts premium of 50*l.* for a tide-mill of his invention. These pursuits occupied the leisure hours of Humphry, who was a dissenting minister at Henley-upon-Thames.

GAINSBOROUGH'S MARRIAGE.

The young painter now began to study landscape in the woods and fields of Suffolk. About this time he became acquainted with Margaret Burr, the memory of whose extraordinary beauty, (says Mr. Fulcher,*) is still preserved in Sudbury. She sat to the young artist for her portrait: she alike admired the picture and the artist, and after a short courtship they were married, the lady bringing with her hand an annuity of 200*l*. She is said to have been the natural daughter of one of our exiled princes, which she did not forget; for, many years after, when her husband was in high fame, she vindicated some little costliness in her dress, by whispering to her niece: "I have some right to this, for you know, my love, I am a prince's daughter." Mr. T. Green, of Ipswich, states her to have been a "natural daughter of the Duke of Bedford." About six months after his marriage, Gainsborough hired a house at Ipswich, at the rent of six pounds a-year.

DETECTIVE PORTRAITS.

When Gainsborough was living at Ipswich, one day seeing a country fellow with a slouched hat, looking wistfully over his garden-wall at some wind-fall pears, he caught up a piece of board, and painted him so faithfully, that, the figure being shaped out, and set upon a wall, in a gentleman's garden at Ipswich, induced many persons to speak to that *melancholy-looking man*.

One of Gainsborough's neighbours was a clergyman named Coyte,† whose garden had been robbed of a great quantity of wall-fruit, without the thief being detected. Young Gainsborough having, one summer morning, risen at an early hour, and walked into the garden to sketch an old elm, seated himself in an obscure corner, when he observed a man peeping over the garden-wall next the road, to see if the coast was clear. He made a sketch of the head of the man, and so accurate was the resemblance, that he was identified as coming from a neighbouring village, and proved to be the fellow who had robbed the parson's garden.

* Life of Thomas Gainsborough, R.A. By the late George William Fulcher, edited by his Son, 1856: a charming work, to which we are indebted for corrective details.

† Gainsborough painted one of Mr. Coyte's sons, so true to nature that the portrait was known as "Coyte alive."

GAINSBOROUGH AND GARRICK.

After his removal from Ipswich to Bath, Gainsborough's success as a portrait-painter was very great. Here he painted Garrick, as Mrs. Garrick said, "the best portrait ever painted of her Davy," which he presented to the corporation of Stratford-on-Avon, where it hangs in the Town-hall. He is leaning against a pedestal, surmounted by a bust of Shakspeare, which he encircles with one arm: the background is a favourite haunt in Garrick's retreat at Hampton.

Hazlitt wrote in the *Morning Chronicle*, of another portrait of Garrick (in the possession of General Wallis), this picture "is as interesting as a piece of biography. He looks much more like a gentleman than in Reynolds's tragi-comic representation of him. There is a considerable lightness and intelligence in the expression of the face, and a piercing vivacity about the eyes, to which the attention is immediately directed."

Gainsborough told the writer of Garrick's memoir, in the obituary of the *Gentleman's Magazine*, that he never found any portrait so difficult to hit as that of Mr. Garrick; for, when he was sketching the eyebrows, and thought he had hit upon the precise situation, and looked a second time at his sitter, he found the eyebrows lifted up to the middle of his forehead; and when he looked a third time, they were dropped, like a curtain, close over the eye,—so flexible was the countenance of the great actor.

GAINSBOROUGH A MUSICIAN.

Our painter gave all the hours of intermission in his profession to fiddles and rebecs. His musical taste was very great; and he himself thought he was *not intended by Nature for a painter, but for a musician.* Happening to see a theorbo in a picture of Vandyke's, he concluded it must be a fine instrument. He recollected to have heard of a German professor; and, ascending to his garret, found him dining on roasted apples, and smoking his pipe, with his theorbo beside him. "I am come to buy your lute—name your price, and here's your money." "I cannot sell my lute." "No, not for a guinea or two;—but you must sell it, I tell you." "My lute is worth much money—it is worth ten guineas." "Aye, that it is!—see, here's the money." So saying, he took up the instrument, laid down the price, went half-way down stairs, and returned. " I have done but half my errand; what is your lute worth, if I have not your book ? " " What book, Master Gainsborough ? " " Why, the book of airs you have composed for the lute." " Ah, sir, I can never part with my book ! " " Poh ! you can make another at any time —this is the book I mean—there's ten guineas for it—so, once more, good day." He went down a few steps, and returned again. " What use is your book to me if I don't understand it ?—and your lute, you may take it again, if you won't teach me to play on it. Come home with me, and give me the first lesson." " I will come to-morrow." " You must come now." " I must dress myself." " For what ? You are the best figure I have seen to-day." " I must shave, sir." " I honour your beard." " I must, however, put on my wig." " D—n your wig ! your cap and beard become you ! Do you think if Vandyke was to paint you, he'd let you be shaved ? " In this manner Gainsborough frittered away his musical talents ; and though possessed of ear, taste, and genius, he never had application enough to learn his notes. He scorned to take the first step—the second was of course out of his reach—the summit became unattainable.

"THE PAINTER'S EYE."

Gainsborough was very successful in repartee. He was once examined as a witness on a trial respecting the originality of a picture, when a counsel endeavoured to puzzle him by saying, " I observe you lay great stress on a *painter's eye*—what do you mean by that expression ? " " A *painter's eye*," answered Gainsborough, " is to him what a lawyer's tongue is to you."

GAINSBOROUGH AND HIS FRIEND THICKNESSE.

Although the painter's Bath friend was governor of Landguard Fort, and a man of proud pretension, Gainsborough found that money would not be unwelcome in his friend's household, and he appears to have taken a singular and delicate mode of lending his assistance. Thicknesse relates that among the instruments of music which Gainsborough loved was the viol-di-gamba, and Mrs. Thicknesse had one, made in the year 1612, on which she played with much skill and effect. He appeared one evening to be exceedingly charmed with the instrument, and said : " I love it so much, that I would willingly give an hundred guineas for it." She desired him to stay to supper: she placed the viol-di-gamba beside him; he took it up, and played in a manner so masterly, that Mrs. Thicknesse said: "You deserve an instrument on which you play so well; and I beg your acceptance of it, on the condition that you will give me my husband's picture to hang beside the one which you painted of me." The artist acquiesced: the viol-di-gamba was sent to him next morning; he stretched a canvas, took one sitting of some fifteen minutes' duration, and then laid it aside for other works. The lady was incensed, and the husband remonstrated; Gainsborough returned the viol-di-gamba, and never touched the picture more.

Such is the story of Thicknesse: the family version communicated to Allan Cunningham* by a lady, who had it from Mrs. Gainsborough herself, is somewhat different. The painter (according to this account,) put one hundred guineas privately into the hands of Mrs. Thicknesse for the viol-di-gamba; her husband, who might not be aware of what passed, expressed his wish for the portrait, and obtained what he conceived to be a promise that it should be painted. This double benefaction, however, was more than Gainsborough had contemplated: he commenced the portrait, but there it stopped; and, after a time, resenting some injurious expressions from the lips of the Governor, the artist sent him the picture, rough and unfinished, and returned also the viol-di-gamba.

Thicknesse sent back the portrait, with a note, requesting Gainsborough to take his brush, and first rub out the countenance of the truest and warmest friend he ever had; and having so done, then blot him for ever from his memory.

However, when Gainsborough removed from Bath to London, Thicknesse followed him, and affected to fear his chance in the great world. It was the old story of the spangle on the lion's tail. Thicknesse urged Lord Bateman to patronise the painter, to which the Governor had the vanity to ascribe much of Gainsborough's success—although he had already painted many noble pictures, and had exhibited them for thirteen years in succession in the Royal Academy.

GAINSBOROUGH AND HOUBRAKEN'S HEADS.

When Gainsborough became a pupil of Mr. Gravelot, under his instructions, he drew most of the ornaments which decorate the illustrious Heads admirably engraved by Houbraken.

* Lives of British Painters, vol. i. p. 343.

ADVANTAGE OF A HANDSOME SITTER.

Soon after Gainsborough came to London, he applied to Major James Johnston, of the 1st or Royal Dragoons, requesting him, as a great favour, to sit for his portrait, in order to bring himself into vogue—which he did; and he being a great favourite with the fair sex, and so handsome and fashionable at the time, the picture had the desired effect: after it had been exhibited the usual time, Gainsborough made Major Johnston a present of it, and it is now in the possession of Sir Alexander Johnston.—*Note to Walpole, by Cunningham.*

GAINSBOROUGH AND THE CARRIER.

One of the painter's acquaintances in Bath was Wiltshere, the public carrier, a kind and worthy man, who loved Gainsborough, and admired his works. In one of his landscapes, he wished to introduce a horse, and as the carrier had a very handsome one, he requested the loan of it for a day or two, and named his purpose; his generous neighbour bridled it and saddled it, and sent it as a present. The painter was not a man to be outdone in acts of generosity: he painted the waggon and horses of his friend, put his whole family and himself into it, and sent it, well-framed, to Wiltshere, with his kind respects. It is considered a very capital performance. From 1761, when Gainsborough began to exhibit his paintings at the Royal Academy, till his removal from Bath in 1774, Wiltshere was annually employed to carry his pictures to and from London :* he took great care of them, and constantly refused to accept money, saying: "No, no! I admire painting too much;" and plunged his hands in his pockets to secure them against the temptation of the offered payment. Perceiving, however, that this was not acceptable to the proud artist, the honest carrier hit upon a scheme which pleased both. "When you think," said he, "I have *carried* to the value of a little painting, I beg you will let me have one, sir; and I shall be more than paid." In this coin the painter paid Wiltshere, and overpaid him. When Allan Cunningham wrote the above, Wiltshere's son was still in possession of several of these pictures, among which was a portrait of the Parish Clerk of Bradford, very Rembrandtish.

* John Britton, in 1801, saw, in a house in the Circus, more than fifty of Gainsborough's paintings and sketches.

GAINSBOROUGH'S MODELLING.

Gainsborough modelled very rapidly, and with great fidelity. Thicknesse relates, that after returning home from a concert at Bath, where he had been charmed by Miss Linley's voice, he sent his servant for a bit of clay from the small-beer barrel, with which he modelled and then coloured Miss Linley's head, and that in a quarter of an hour, in such a manner that it seemed superior to his paintings. Mr. Leslie had in his possession, some years ago, an exquisite plaster cast of a head of Miss Linley, from a clay model by Gainsborough, probably the above. He would now and then mould the face of his friends in miniature, finding the material in the wax candles burning before him: and the models were as perfect in their resemblance as his portraits.

RETURN OF GAINSBOROUGH TO LONDON.—SCHOMBERG HOUSE, PALL MALL.

In the summer of 1774, Gainsborough returned to the metropolis, nearly thirty years having elapsed since he left the studio of Hayman. An old race of artists had passed away, and a new race had succeeded; and West, Barry, and Fuseli were following in the track already struck out by Hogarth, by Wilson, and by Reynolds.

Gainsborough was now in possession of a splendid income, high in fame. He rented at 300*l.* a-year part of Schomberg House, in Pall Mall,—another portion being occupied by John Astley, "the Beau," a portrait-painter of little merit. Before Gainsborough had been many months in London, George III. and Queen Charlotte sat to him for their portraits. Peers and commoners followed so rapidly that he could not satisfy his sitters. One disappointed gentleman inquired of the Painter's porter, in a voice loud enough to be overheard, "Has that fellow Gainsborough finished my portrait?" Ushered into the painting-room, he beheld his picture, approved of it, and desired it might be sent home at once, adding, "I may as well give you a cheque for the other fifty guineas." "Stay a minute," said Gainsborough, "it just wants a finishing stroke;" and snatching up a background brush, he dashed it across the smiling features, indignantly exclaiming, "Sir, where is my fellow now?"

In 1777, Gainsborough contributed several Portraits to the

Academy, besides a large Landscape, "in the style of Rubens," says Walpole, "and by far the finest landscape ever painted in England, and equal to the great masters."

The Painter (says Fulcher,) was now in the zenith of his fame. Eminent churchmen, lawyers, statesmen, players, dramatists, sailors, naturalists—Pennant, Howe, Sheridan, Edwin, Burke, Skinner, Hurd, were among his sitters. He had also painted Blackstone, and Clive, and Paul Whitehead; and the literary negro, Ignatius Sancho.

Schomberg House, on the south side of Pall Mall, was built about 1650, and is named after the Duke of Schomberg, who was killed at the battle of the Boyne. It was next inhabited by his son. The house was taken by the Duke of Cumberland, "the hero of Culloden," in 1760. The bas-relief of Painting over the central door was set up by Astley, the painter: of the caryatidal figures supporting the portico we do not know the artist. Astley divided the house into three; he lived in the centre himself, and Gainsborough in the western wing: he died in a second-floor chamber. Cosway, the miniature painter, succeeded Astley in the centre. Attempts were made to sack and burn the premises in the Riots of 1780. Part of the house was subsequently occupied by Bowyer, for his *Historic Gallery;* and by Dr. Graham, the quack, for his "Celestial Bed," and other impostures. Payne and Foss, the booksellers, lived here till 1850. The uniformity of this fine specimen of a ducal mansion of the seventeenth century has been spoiled by the eastern wing being taken down, and rebuilt in another style; but *Gainsborough's wing* remains.

PAINTINGS BY GAINSBOROUGH, IN SCHOMBERG HOUSE.

A tradition long existed that Gainsborough had executed some *frescoes* upon the walls of Schomberg House during his occupancy of that historic mansion. In 1857, those so-called frescoes, completely begrimed with gas fuligen, were removed from the plaster, and being lined with canvas, proved to be capital oil-paintings, representing pleasing landscapes by this great master, when in all the ease and potency of his brush. They were originally four in number; but a change having been made in the interior construction of the house, at the time of the imposition of the Window Tax, one picture was destroyed. Three remained, and two of them being lined and cleaned are interesting and unexpected reminiscences of the master. No evidence exists as to the subjects—they are presumed to be "compositia." Both represent mountainous landscapes, with water in the foreground. One of them, with a waterfall, is distinguished by a most masterly breadth of touch and knowledge of effect; the other is of a more quiet, confined, and pastoral character, with a fine golden tone, balanced by sky slightly diapered with that substance which has received the name of arbor Græcum. They are not cabinet pictures, but architectural decorations to be looked at from the distance of eight or ten feet, and were probably thrown off with ease and rapidity. Still, the harmony of tone, and the handling of the brush, show all the spirit of a true master.

GAINSBOROUGH AND REYNOLDS.

Soon after Gainsborough settled in London, Sir Joshua Reynolds thought himself bound in civility to pay him a visit. Gainsborough took not the least notice of the call for some years, but at length returned it, and solicited Reynolds to sit for his picture. Sir Joshua sat *once;* but being soon afterwards afflicted by slight paralysis, he was obliged to go to Bath. On his return to town, perfectly restored to health, he sent word to Gainsborough, who only replied that he was glad to hear he was well; and never after desired him to sit, or called upon him, or had any other intercourse with him until he was dying, when he sent and thanked him for the very handsome manner in which he had always spoken of him—a circumstance which the President has thought worth recording in his Fourteenth *Discourse.* Gainsborough was so enamoured of his art, that he had many of the pictures he was then working upon brought to his bedside to show them to Reynolds, and flattered himself that he should live to finish them. This was related by Sir Joshua to Malone.

Reynolds once observed to Northcote, after attentively looking at a picture by Gainsborough, "I cannot make out how he produces his effect;" and Gainsborough, when looking at several of Reynolds's works, in company with Sir George Beaumont, exclaimed, as he glanced from one to another, "D—n him, how various he is!"

"THE BLUE BOY."

This celebrated picture, a full-length portrait of a son of Mr. Buttall, was painted by Gainsborough in 1779, to controvert a point of art. Sir Joshua Reynolds had maintained, in one of his *Discourses*, that "the masses of light in a picture should be always of a warm mellow colour, yellow, red, or a yellowish-white; and that the blue, the grey, or the green colours, should be kept almost entirely out of these masses, and be used only to support and set off these warm colours." To refute the President's objection to *blue in the mass*, Gainsborough painted Master Buttall in a blue dress; in spite of which, says Dr. Waagen, "Gainsborough has succeeded in producing a harmonious and pleasing effect; nor can it be doubted that in the cool scale of colours, in which blue acts the chief part, there are very tender and pleasing harmonies, which Sir Joshua, with his way of seeing, could not appreciate. On the whole, too, he may be so far right that painters would certainly do well to avoid the use of pure, unbroken blue in large masses." Mr. Leslie, in his *Handbook for Young Painters*, "agrees with the opinion of Sir Thomas Lawrence, that in this picture the difficulty is rather ably combated than vanquished. Indeed, it is not even fairly combated, for Gainsborough has so mellowed and broken the blue with other tints, that it is no longer that pure blue colour Sir Joshua meant; and after all, though the picture is a very fine one, it cannot be doubted that a warmer tint for the dress would have made it still more agreeable to the eye." This fine picture is in the Grosvenor Gallery; with *a Cottage Door* and *a Coast Scene*, by Gainsborough. At Mr. Buttall's death, the *Blue Boy* was purchased by Mr. Nesbitt; thence it passed to Mr. Hoppner, the painter, who sold it to the first Earl Grosvenor. The Bishop of Ely has a finished sketch of the *Blue Boy;* and Mr. Charles Ford, of Bath, has the *original* sketch in oil—dress unfinished.

SEVERE CRITICISM.

Gainsborough painted two portraits of Mr. Bate, then editor of the *Morning Post*, and subsequently Sir Bate Dudley, Bart. In the second portrait, he is standing in a garden with his dog—a work of great beauty of design and handling. It is said that a political opponent of Dudley remarked on this picture, that "the man wanted execution, and the dog wanted hanging."

"GIRL AND PIGS."

The expression of truth and nature in this picture by Gainsborough, (remarks Northcote,) were never surpassed. Sir Joshua was struck with it, though he thought Gainsborough ought to have made the girl a beauty. Reynolds, indeed, became the purchaser of the painting at one hundred guineas, Gainsborough asking but sixty. During its exhibition, it attracted the notice of a countryman, who remarked, "They be deadly like pigs, but nobody ever saw pigs feeding together but what one on 'em had a foot in the trough."

MRS. SIDDONS' NOSE.

In 1784, Mrs. Siddons, "then in the prime of her glorious beauty, and in the full blaze of her popularity," sat to Gainsborough. The portrait is a three-quarters length: she is seated; her face appears rather more than in profile; she wears a black hat and feathers, and a blue and buff striped silk dress—in a mass resembling dark sea-water with sunshine on it. Two years before the death of Mrs. Siddons she was seen by Mrs. Jameson seated near her picture; it was like her still, at the age of seventy. Gainsborough, however, found some difficulty in delineating her features—the nose especially; after repeatedly altering its shape, he exclaimed, "Confound the nose, there's no end to it!"

This year, the Council refusing to hang a picture by Gainsborough agreeably to his wishes, he resolved never again to send any paintings to the Academy, and he kept his word. He then opened an exhibition of his own at his house in Pall Mall, but with little success.

GAINSBOROUGH'S WOODMAN, SHEPHERD BOY, COTTAGE DOOR, AND COTTAGE GIRL.

The first of these famous pictures, which won especial praise from George III., remained unsold until after Gainsborough's death, although only his portrait price, one hundred guineas, was demanded. Lord Gainsborough then became its purchaser for the sum of 500 guineas: the painting was subsequently burnt at Eaton Park. Peter Simon's print, and Mr.

Lane's copy of the sketch, show the great merit of the work. The terror of the Woodman, the fear of the dog crouching close to its master, yet unable to turn its face from the descending rain and lightning's flash,—with Gainsborough's powerful colouring, must have been truly splendid. The painter made a model of the Woodman's head from the man who stood for the picture. Northcote thought the *Shepherd's Boy in the Shower* very superior to the *Woodman*. Hazlitt says: " What a truth and beauty is there! He (the Shepherd boy) stands with his hands clasped, looking up with a mixture of timidity and resignation, eyeing a magpie chattering over his head, while the wind is rustling in the branches. It is like a vision breathed on the canvas."

The Cottage Door represents a cottage-matron, with an infant in her arms, and several older children playing around her. The close-wooded nook, and the glimpses of knolls and streams through the trees, are beautiful; and the work has uncommon breadth and mass, with richness of colouring, a sort of brown and glossy goldenness, common in the works of the artist.

The Cottage Girl, with her Dog and Pitcher, says Mr. Leslie, " is unequalled by anything in the world. I recollect it in the British Gallery, forming part of a very noble assemblage of pictures, and I could scarcely look at or think of anything else in the rooms. This inimitable work is a portrait, and not of a peasant child, but of a young lady who appears also in the picture of the girl and pigs, which Sir Joshua purchased."

GAINSBOROUGH'S SENSITIVENESS.

Sir George Beaumont used to relate that he, Sheridan, and Gainsborough, had dined together, and the latter was more than usually pleasant and witty. They agreed to have another day's enjoyment, and an early day was named when they should dine again together. They met, but a cloud had descended on the spirit of Gainsborough, and he sat silent, with a look of fixed melancholy, which no wit could dissipate. At length, he took Sheridan by the hand, led him out of the room, and said, " Now, don't laugh, but listen. I shall die soon—I know it—I feel it—I have less time to live than my looks infer, but for this I care not. What oppresses my mind is this—I have many acquaintances and few friends; and as I wish to have one worthy man to accompany me to the grave, I am desirous of bespeaking you—will you come—aye or no?" Sheridan could scarcely repress a smile as he made the required promise: the looks of Gainsborough cleared up like one of his own landscapes; throughout the rest of the evening his wit flowed, and his humour ran over, and the minutes, like those of the poet, winged their way with pleasure.—*Allan Cunningham.*

GAINSBOROUGH'S GENEROSITY.

The painter had a most feeling heart, and strong sympathy with misfortune. Thus, we find him, on being shown a letter from a fallen and forsaken woman, turning back on his way to the theatre, to send the poor supplicant a five pound note.

If he selected for painting a child from a cottage, all the inmates generally participated in the profits of the picture; and some of them frequently found in his house a permanent abode. His liberality was not confined to this alone: needy relatives and unsuccessful friends were further incumbrances on a spirit which could not deny. "Scheming Jack" was often supplied with money, and whenever he visited London, Schomberg House was his home.

Money and pictures were alike bestowed inconsiderately. Fulcher relates that he presented twenty drawings to one lady, who was so ignorant of their value that she pasted them on the wall of her dressing-room; and he gave Colonel Hamilton the *Boy at the Stile* for playing a solo on the violin.

DEATH OF GAINSBOROUGH.

In February, 1788, the trial of Warren Hastings lured Gainsborough from his easel. Sitting in Westminster Hall, with his back to an open window, he suddenly felt something inconceivably cold touch his neck. It was accompanied with stiffness and pain. On his return home, his wife and his niece saw on his neck a mark, about the size of a shilling, hard to the touch, and which, he said, still felt cold. Mrs. Gainsborough became alarmed, and called in Dr. Heberden and Mr. John Hunter. They declared it to be only a swelling in the glands, which the warm weather would remove. Little was thought of the malady, and Gainsborough went, for change of air and scene, to his cottage at Richmond. He grew worse, and returned to town; and suppuration having taken place, Mr. Hunter acknowledged the protuberance to be a cancer. "If this be a cancer," said Gainsborough to Mrs. Gibbon, who had arrived from Bath, "I am a dead man." Other medical men confirmed Mr. Hunter's opinion; and Gainsborough then, with perfect composure, proceeded to arrange his affairs.

Towards the close of July, Gainsborough rapidly became worse. He now felt there was one whom he had not treated with courtesy—it was Sir Joshua Reynolds; and to him he wrote, desiring to see him once more before he died. "If any little jealousies had subsisted between us," says Reynolds, "they were forgotten in those moments of sincerity; and he turned towards me as one who was engrossed by the same pursuits, and who deserved his good opinion by being sensible of his excellence." The two great Painters were alone in the chamber at Schomberg House: Gainsborough said he did not fear death, but regretted leaving his art, more especially as he now began to see what his deficiencies were. His words began to fail, and the last he uttered to Reynolds were: "We are all going to Heaven—and Vandyke is of the company." A few days after, on August 2, 1788, in the sixty-second year of his age, Gainsborough died.*

Other accounts state that the occasion of Gainsborough's death was a wen in the neck, which grew internally, and so large as to obstruct the passages. After death, the part was opened, the excrescence examined and replaced.

According to Gainsborough's own wish, he was buried in Kew churchyard, on the south side of the church, near the grave of his friend Joshua Kirby. On August 9, Gainsborough's remains were borne from his house in Pall Mall to Kew. His nephew, Mr. Dupont, attended as chief mourner. The pall was borne by Sir Joshua Reynolds, Sir William Chambers, West, Bartolozzi, Paul Sandby, and Mr. Cotes. Among the mourners were Linley, the musical composer; Meyer, the miniature-painter; Kirby's son-in-law, Mr. Trimmer; and, faithful to his compact, Richard Brinsley Sheridan. In the same grave are interred Gainsborough's wife and nephew. The stone has neither arms nor ornament, as the painter expressly desired; but it appears to have been neglected.

* He died in possession of 56 of his pictures and 148 drawings, which were exhibited at Schomberg House, in the year after his death, and subsequently sold. Gainsborough is said never to have put his name to any picture.

When Sir Richard Phillips visited the spot in his *Morning's Walk from London to Kew*, "Ah! friend," said he to the clerk's assistant who conducted him to the grave, "this is a hallowed spot; here lies one of Britain's favoured sons, whose genius has assisted in exalting her among the nations of the earth." "Perhaps it was so," said the man, "but we know nothing about the people buried, except to keep up their monuments, if the family pay; and perhaps, sir, you belong to the family; if so, I'll tell you how much is due." "Yes, truly, friend," said Sir Richard, "I am one of the great family bound to preserve the monument of Gainsborough; but if you take me for one of his relatives, you are mistaken." "Perhaps, sir, you may be of the family, but were not included in the will, therefore are not obligated." Sir Richard adds: "I could not now avoid looking with scorn at the fellow; but, as the spot claimed better feelings, I gave him a trifle for his trouble, and mildly told him I would not detain him.

"The monument being a plain one, and making no palpable appeal to vulgar admiration, was disregarded by these people; for it is in death as in life, if you would excite the notice of the multitude, you must in the grave have a splendid mausoleum, or in walking the streets you must wear fine clothes. It did not fall in the way of the untaught, on this otherwise polite spot, to know that they have among them the remains of *the first Painter of our National School*, in fancy pictures, and *one of the first* in the classes of landscape and portrait; a man who recommended himself as much by his superiority as by his genius; as much by the mode in which his genius was developed, as by the perfection of his works; and as much by his amiable private character as by his eminence in the chief of Fancy's Arts. Such a man was Thomas Gainsborough, before whose modest tomb I stood!"

CHARACTERISTICS, RETROSPECTIVE OPINIONS, AND PERSONAL TRAITS.

CHARACTER OF GAINSBOROUGH, BY REYNOLDS.

WHEN Gainsborough had been lain in the grave about four months, Sir Joshua, in his *Fourteenth Discourse,* drew attention to the excellencies and defects of the deceased painter, observing : " If ever this nation should produce genius sufficient to acquire to us the honourable distinction of an English School, the name of Gainsborough will be transmitted to posterity, in the history of the Art, among the very first of that rising name."

Sir Joshua then refers to the customs and habits of Gainsborough, and the causes of his excellence, the love which he had for his art.

He had a habit of continually remarking to those who happened to be about him, whatever peculiarity of countenance, whatever accidental combination of figure, or happy effects of light and shadow occurred in prospects, in the sky, in walking the streets, or in company. If in his walks he found a character that he liked, and whose attendance was to be obtained, he ordered him to his house : and from the fields he brought into his painting-room stumps of trees, weeds, and animals of various kinds, and designed them, not from memory, but immediately from the objects. He even framed a kind of model of landscapes on his table, composed of broken stones, dried herbs, and pieces of looking-glass, which he magnified and improved into rocks, trees, and water.*

Sir Joshua then refers to Gainsborough's custom of painting by night, a practice very advantageous and improving to an artist. "Another practice Gainsborough had, which is worth mentioning, as it is certainly worthy of imitation : I mean his

---

* He made (says Jackson,) little laymen for human figures, he modelled his horses and cows, and knobs of coal sat for rocks—nay, he carried this so far, that he never chose to paint anything from invention, when he could have the objects themselves. The limbs of trees, which he collected, would have made no inconsiderable wood-rick, and many an ass has been led into his painting-room.

manner of forming all the parts of his picture together, the whole going on at the same time, in the same manner as Nature creates her works. Though this method is not uncommon to those who have been regularly educated, yet probably it was suggested to him by his own natural sagacity."

Reynolds then briefly alludes to his last interview with Gainsborough, and resumes :

"When such a man as Gainsborough arrives to great fame, without the assistance of an academical education, without travelling to Italy, or any of those preparatory studies which have been so often recommended, he is produced as an instance how little such studies are necessary, since so great excellence may be acquired without them. This is an inference not warranted by the success of any individual, and I trust it will not be thought that I wish to make this use of it."

Reynolds then adverts to Gainsborough's method of handling, his habit of *scratching.*

"All these odd scratches and marks," he observes, "which, on a close examination, are so observable in Gainsborough's pictures, and which, even to experienced painters, appear rather the effect of accident than design ; this chaos, this uncouth and shapeless appearance, by a kind of magic, at a certain distance assumes form, and all the parts seem to drop into their proper places; so that we can hardly refuse acknowledging the full effect of diligence, under the appearance of chance and hasty negligence. That Gainsborough himself considered this peculiarity in his manner, and the power it possesses of exciting surprise, as a beauty in his works, I think, may be inferred from the eager desire which we know he always expressed, that his pictures, at the Exhibition, should be seen near as well as at a distance."

PORTRAITS BY GAINSBOROUGH.

Among the famous portraits of famous men, painted by Gainsborough at Bath, was the first Lord Camden, a kind friend to the artist; Cramer, the metallurgist, the gilt buttons of whose coat are rendered with appropriate truthfulness ; and the authors of *Pamela* and the *Sentimental Journey*. To Sterne's picture we may apply the words of *Tristram Shandy :* "Reynolds himself, great and graceful as he was, might have painted it." Richardson's head is a splendid performance; the parted lips and animated face seem to indicate that he must, when taken, have been discoursing on a favourite subject. Mr. Fulcher, whose Life we quote, adds: "it is said that Chatterton also sat to Gainsborough, and that the portrait of the marvellous boy, with his long flowing hair and child-like face, is a master-piece."

Upon the latter, a Bristolian correspondent of *Notes and Queries*, Second Series, No. 35, states this presumed portrait was not painted for Chatterton, but some youth in Bristol, name unknown, and that it was picked up at an old-clothes shop in the Pithay, in that city. It has been also proved to be the son of a Mr. Morris, who painted it, the name upon the back having been altered to Chatterton. Mr. Fulcher received his information from a Mr. Naylor, the possessor of the portrait: it reached down to the boy's waist: he is dressed in green, apparently a charity-coat; this is worthy of note, for Chatterton was placed at Colston's Charity School, and remained there till July 1, 1767, when he had not quite attained the age of fifteen; so that, while he was in the garb of a charity-scholar, Chatterton *may* have sat to Gainsborough.

Gainsborough painted several portraits of himself, two of which stood in his gallery at the time of his death, but with their faces modestly turned towards the wainscot. Miss Gainsborough gave one to the Royal Academy,—its members presenting her with a silver vase, designed by West, "as a token of respect to the abilities of her Father." This vase is now in the possession of the painter's great-nephew, the Rev. Gainsborough Gardiner, of Worcester.—(*Fulcher.*)

Two of his finest female portraits (whole lengths) are in the Dulwich Gallery: Mrs. Sheridan and Mrs. Tickell. Mrs. Sheridan was Maria Linley, the first wife of R. B. Sheridan. Madame D'Arblay said her beauty surpassed almost any she had ever seen, and Reynolds thought it nearly divine. Gainsborough, we have related, modelled Maria Linley, at Bath; he had often watched the wondrous grace of her light form; he had been charmed with the gentleness, the modesty, and feminine sweetness, of her who was "half-way between a woman and an angel."

All our living princes and princesses in Gainsborough's time were painted by him, the Duke of York excepted, of whom he had three pictures bespoken.

Gainsborough painted, under interesting circumstances,

Master Heathcote, a little boy four years of age, holding in one hand his black hat and feathers, and in the other a bunch of flowers. The painter chanced to be on a visit at Bath, when a destructive sickness was raging in different parts of the kingdom. The parents of Master Heathcote, having lost their other children by the epidemic, were anxious to secure a portrait of the one yet spared to them. They applied to Gainsborough, who declined, as he had visited Bath for recreation; but, on hearing the circumstances of the case, he requested Mrs. Heathcote to let him see her son. The next morning, the boy, dressed in a plain white muslin frock, with a blue sash, was taken to Gainsborough. "You have brought him simply dressed," he said; "had you paraded him in a fancy costume, I would not have painted him; now I will gladly comply with your request."

Mr. Fulcher describes Gainsborough's portrait of Dr. Schomberg as one of the finest pictures in the world: he is looking towards the spectator, and is dressed in velvet, in colour something between pink and crimson; the landscape background is admirably painted.

DRAWINGS AND SKETCHES.

Of these Gainsborough made, perhaps, more than any other artist, ancient or modern. Jackson had seen, at least, one thousand, not one of which but possessed some merit, and some in a transcendent degree. These were executed in oil and water colours, in chalks—black, white, and coloured,—in lead-pencil, sepia, bistre, and Indian ink. Many of these studies were in black and white, applied thus: a small bit of sponge, tied to a bit of stick, served as a pencil for the shadows, and a small lump of whiting, held by a pair of tea-tongs, were the instruments by which the high lights were applied,—a method of execution to which a lady applied the appropriate epithet of "mopping."

One of Gainsborough's finest drawings is a portrait of Pitt, in crayons, purchased by the Earl of Normanton at the sale of Sir Thomas Lawrence's pictures: on the portrait Sir Thomas had written the words, "unique and inestimable." These studies were executed with marvellous rapidity, Mr. Richmond has a head of young Dupont, in oil, which Thicknesse says, was painted in an hour, a work of most masterly execution, equal to anything by Vandyke.—*Fulcher.*

GAINSBOROUGH'S SEA-PIECES.

He painted but four. "He never pretended," observes Jackson, "to the correctness of rigging, &c., but I have seen some general effects of sea, sea-coast, and vessels, that have been truly masterly." He usually introduced the sea and a ship by way of background to his portraits of sailors, as in those of Admiral Vernon, Captain Augustus Hervey, and Captain Roberts, the companions of Captain Cook in his last voyage round the world. "In the Exhibition of 1781, he had," says Walpole, "two pieces of land and sea, so free and natural, that one steps back *for fear of being splashed.*"

GAINSBOROUGH'S LANDSCAPES.

Finishing was not the painter's aim; for he usually painted with a very long and very broad brush, stood very far from his canvas, and in a room with very little light. Portraits were not his forte; yet, during fifteen years, he had contributed to the Artists' Society and the Academy, about fifty portraits, and but eleven landscapes, with some drawings. "Gainsborough's landscapes," says Sir William Beechey, " stood ranged in long lines from his hall to his painting-room; and they who came to sit for their portraits, for which he was chiefly employed, rarely deigned to honour them with a look as they passed." To the Exhibition of 1780, however, Gainsborough contributed no less than five landscapes, which Walpole has characterised as charming, very spirited, &c., "one especially is worthy of any collection, and of any painter that ever existed."

The first master Gainsborough studied was Wynants, whose thistles and dock-leaves he has frequently introduced into his early pictures. The next was Ruysdael; but his colouring is less sombre, though the pencilling of the Englishman was less accurate than that of the Fleming. He has sometimes very happily seized upon the best manner of Teniers. In a view of company in St. James's Park, he even excelled Watteau.* He made Snyders his model for animals.

The late Sir William Curtis was so warm an admirer of

* The *View in the Mall of St. James's Park*, painted in 1786. Northcote says:—"It is all in motion and in a flutter like a lady's fan. Watteau is not half so airy." Most of the figures are portraits, and Gainsborough has introduced himself, sketching the gay assemblage.

Gainsborough's landscapes, that, during an illness, he had one hung in his chamber, that he might see it through the opening of his bed-curtains.

Gainsborough's earlier landscapes are imitations of the manner of Wynants; they have the same clayey and sandy grounds, and a similar arrangement of objects to that which is seen in the smaller pictures of that eminent master. He had a second manner, more original and more English, but rather heavy. His last manner may be seen in the *Market Cart* and the *Watering-place*, in the National and Vernon Galleries. The *Market Cart* was purchased at Lord Gwydir's sale, in 1828, for 1,102*l*. 10*s*. Lord Northwick possessed a duplicate of this fine picture in his gallery at Cheltenham.

GAINSBOROUGH AND LEE.

The appearance in *Blackwood's Magazine* of a critique on the Royal Academy Exhibition, 1842, the writer of which preferred Mr. Lee, R.A., to Gainsborough, drew from Mr. Ruskin the following admirable *exposé* of the critic's shortcomings in his craft. The controverted passage is: "'He (Mr. Lee,) often reminds us of Gainsborough's best manner; but he is *superior* to him always in subject, composition, and variety.'

"Shade of Gainsborough!—deep-thoughted, solemn Gainsborough—forgive us for re-writing this sentence; we do so to gibbet its perpetrator for ever, and leave him swinging in the winds of the Fool's Paradise. It is with great pain that I ever speak with severity of the works of living masters, especially when, like Mr. Lee's, they are well-intentioned, simple, free from affectation or imitation, and evidently painted with constant reference to nature. But I believe these qualities will always insure him that admiration which he deserves—that there will be many unsophisticated and honest minds always ready to follow his guidance, and answer his efforts with delight; and therefore, that I need not fear to point out in him the want of those technical qualities which are more especially the object of an artist's admiration.

"Gainsborough's power of colour (it is mentioned by Sir Joshua as his peculiar gift,) is capable of taking rank beside that of Rubens; he is the purest colourist—Sir Joshua himself not excepted—of the whole English school; with him, in fact, the *art* of painting did in great part die, and exists not now in Europe. In management and quality of single and particular tint, in the purely technical part of painting, Turner is a child to Gainsborough. Now, Mr. Lee never aims at colour: he does not make it his object in the slightest degree—the spring-green of vegetation is all that he desires; and it would be about as rational to compare his works with studied pieces of colouring, as the modulation of the Calabrian pipe to the harmony of a full orchestra. Gainsborough's hand is as light as the sweep of a cloud—as swift as the flash of a sunbeam; Lee's execution is feeble and spotty. Gainsborough's masses are as broad as the first division in heaven of light from darkness; Lee's (perhaps necessarily, considering the effects of flickering sunlight at which he aims) are as fragmentary as his leaves, and as numerous. Gainsborough's forms are grand, simple, and ideal; Lee's are small, confused, and unselected. Gainsborough never loses sight of his picture as a whole; Lee is but too apt to be shackled by its parts. In a word, Gainsborough is an immortal painter; and Lee, though on the right road, is yet in the early stage of his art; and the man who could imagine any resemblance or point of comparison between them, is not only a novice in art, but has not capacity to be ever anything more. He may be pardoned for not comprehending Turner, for long preparation and discipline are necessary before the abstract and profound philosophy of that artist can be met; but Gainsborough's excellence is based on principles of art long acknowledged, and facts of nature universally apparent."—*Notes to Preface to Modern Painters*, vol. i. second edition.

HENRY FUSELI, R.A.

BIRTH AND PARENTAGE OF FUSELI.

Henry Füessli (for such is the family name), the second son of John Caspar Füessli, was born Feb. 7, 1741, N. S., at Zurich, in Switzerland, which place had been the native place of his family for many generations. His father, John Caspar, a painter of portraits and landscapes, was also distinguished for his literary attainments. He married Elizabeth Waser, and by this marriage he had eighteen children, three of whom only reached manhood: Rodolph, who became a painter; Henry; and Caspar, well known for his able works on entomology.

Henry received his early education from his mother; and he profited much by the society of Solomon Gessner, the poet and painter, who was his godfather. Henry showed very early a predilection for drawing and for entomology; but his father designed him for the clerical profession. He discouraged the idea of his being an artist, probably from thinking that he would never excel in the mechanical part of painting; for in youth he had so great an awkwardness of hand, that when precious articles were shown to visitors, his father often said: "Take care of that boy, for he destroys or spoils whatever he touches." He always spoke of his age with reluctance. Once, when pressed about it, he peevishly exclaimed: "How should I know? I was born in February or March—it was some cursed cold month, as you may guess from my diminutive stature and crabbed disposition."

Notwithstanding sore discouragement, young Fuseli bought with his pocket-money candles, pencils, paper, &c., in order to make drawings when his parents believed him to be in bed. Some of these early sketches are still preserved; and among them is one of "Orestes pursued by the Furies," telling the story wonderfully for a boy eleven years of age.

His rapidity in making drawings and caricatures was surprising: the better to escape observation, he drew with his *left hand*, a practice which made him ambidextrous through life.

Fuseli was placed at the Caroline College, in Zurich, where he had for his friends Lavater, Usteri, Toman, Jacob, and Felix Hess, names well known in German literature. He studied hard—in fact, he was capable of any mental labour, however severe. He was enamoured with the plays of Shakspeare, and attempted to translate Macbeth into German; he read with avidity Richardson's novels, Rousseau's works, and the poetic flights of Dante aroused his feelings and afforded subjects for his daring pencil.

Lavater said: Nature designed him for a great orator.

FUSELI AN ENTOMOLOGIST.

Fuseli was an enthusiastic entomologist, and greatly assisted his brother in collecting insects for his museum. Mr. W. Raddon relates that Fuseli once chided him for apathy in the pursuit, and concluded by saying: "When I was of your age, I often went at two or three o'clock in the morning into the corn-fields and woods to collect for my brother, and many of the insects figured by him were from my drawings." Nor did this love of entomology leave the Professor in the decline of life: for when he had delivered his last lecture, and was descending from the rostrum, the first inquiry he made was, "Where is Raddon? (his brother entomologist.) Has he taken *Atropos?* (the Death's-head moth.)"

His great love of entomology induced him occasionally to introduce moths into his pictures; these he painted with great care and fidelity, and when much taken with the subject, he made them frequently incongruous. Thus, in a picture of Lycidas, from the passage in Milton,

> Under the opening eyelids of the morn,
> What time the grey-fly winds his sultry horn,

where the shepherd and the shepherdess are only ten inches in length, happening to find, in Mr. Johnson's garden at Fulham, a beautiful moth, he was so delighted with it, that, in spite of all propriety, and his better knowledge, he painted it the size of nature, hovering above the figures with expanded wings. This singular appearance attracted the notice

HENRY FUSELI.

of the celebrated Dr. Jenner, who was also skilled in entomology, and who, on being informed of the line it was intended to illustrate, said, "No, no; this is no grey-fly, but a moth, and winds no horn; it is a mute." Fuseli, who heard this remark, knew well its accuracy, and therefore said nothing.

FUSELI COMES TO ENGLAND.

In 1761, Fuseli entered into holy orders; he made some attempts to bring about a better style of preaching at Zurich; but having written a pamphlet in conjunction with Lavater, exposing the conduct of an unjust magistrate, to avoid his vengeance, Fuseli resolved to travel awhile. After visiting Germany, he came to England, partly as an agent to establish a literary communication between the latter country and his native place. In London he was introduced to Mr. Coutts, the banker; and Millar and Johnson, the publishers. He first took lodgings in Cranbourne-alley, to be near Mr. Coutts, then residing in St. Martin's-lane. He was soon much employed as a translator, by the booksellers; and among his literary acquaintance were Falconer, the poet; and Dr. Smollett, for whose *Peregrine Pickle* Fuseli made several drawings. He next became acquainted with Mr. Moser, Keeper of the Royal Academy, and Mr. Kauffman, father of Angelica, the painter. He then accepted the office of travelling tutor to Viscount Chewton, but soon threw up his charge, referring to which, in after life, he used to say, "The noble family of Waldegrave took me for a bear-leader, but they found me the bear." Fuseli, however, soon relinquished the pen for the pencil.

FUSELI STUDIES ART,—HIS FIRST PICTURE.

In 1767, the high patronage of Artists, which led to the formation of the Royal Academy, induced Fuseli to study for a painter. He obtained an introduction to Mr. (afterwards Sir Joshua) Reynolds, to whom he showed a portfolio of drawings and etchings. Reynolds was much struck with their style, grandeur, and original conception, and said to Fuseli, "were he at his age, and endowed with the ability of producing such works, if any one were to offer him an estate of one thousand pounds a-year, on condition of being anything but a painter, he would, without the least hesitation, reject the offer." With such encouragement from the greatest painter of the age, Fuseli directed nearly the whole of his attention to drawing; and on the recommendation of Reynolds, tried oil colours. His first picture was "Joseph interpreting the dreams of the Butler and Baker of Pharaoh." On showing this to Reynolds, he remarked that "he might if he would be a colourist as well as a draughtsman." This picture Mr. Knowles describes as remarkably well-coloured, and for a first attempt in oil, a surprising production.

VOLTAIRE CARICATURED.

In 1767, when Hume and Voltaire were constantly attacking Rousseau, Fuseli published anonymously a small volume in defence of his countryman, and for this work he designed the frontispiece. This represents in the foreground, Voltaire, booted and spurred, riding upon man, who is crawling upon the earth; in the back of the picture, justice and liberty are gibbeted. Rousseau is witnessing Voltaire's pranks, and by his attitude, seems to threaten disclosure. This work is now very rare; most of the impressions having been destroyed by an accidental fire at Mr. Johnson's, the publisher, in Paternoster-row.

FUSELI AND DR. ARMSTRONG.

In 1769, Fuseli, accompanied by Dr. Armstrong, (who wrote the poem on *The Art of Preserving Health*, and whom he met at Mr. Coutts's table, and had formerly known at Berlin,) left London for Italy, intending to go to Leghorn by sea. The voyage was long and tedious,—both the voyagers were of naturally irritable tempers, and they finally quarrelled about the pronunciation of an English word; Fuseli pertinaciously maintaining that "a Swiss had as great a right to judge of the correct pronunciation of English as a Scotsman;" and being driven by a gale of wind into Genoa, Fuseli and Armstrong parted in a mood far from friendly. Upon Fuseli's return to England, he was reproved by Mr. Coutts for his rudeness to the Doctor, who lay dangerously ill. The painter called upon him, when he said: "So you have come back?" Fuseli replied: "Yes; I have come home." Armstrong: "Come, you mean to London! 'the needy villain's general home;' however, (putting out his hand,) I thank you for this visit: you find me in bad plight; but I am glad to see you again." They then conversed amicably; but the Doctor did not long survive the reconciliation.

FUSELI IN ROME.

Fuseli arrived in the seat of the fine arts early in 1770, and set about studying its treasures, making the antique and Michael Angelo his masters, and forming his style upon their principles. He had, from his boyhood, admired Michael Angelo in engravings, and he adored him now in his full and undiminished majesty. It was a story which he loved to repeat, how he lay on his back, day after day, and week succeeding week, with upturned and wondering eyes, musing on the splendid ceiling of the Sistine Chapel—on the unattainable grandeur of the Florentine. He imagined that he drank, as he lay, the spirit of the sublime Michael; and that by studying in the Sistine, he had the full advantage of the mantle of inspiration suspended visibly above him. He fulfilled the injunctions of Reynolds—he ate, and drank, and slept, and waked on Michael Angelo. He examined living models, attended the school of anatomy, and used the dissecting-knife, in order to trace the origin and insertion of the outer layer of muscles of the human body. He rapidly improved, and soon acquired boldness and grandeur of drawing. His friends in England knew nothing of his progress until 1774, when he sent to the Royal Academy Exhibition, a drawing of *the Death of Cardinal Beaufort*, from Shakspeare. In 1779, he sent to the Exhibition an oil picture of a scene from *Macbeth*.

Fuseli left Rome in 1778. He was not very partial to the modern Italians, who, he said, "were lively and entertaining, but there was the slight drawback of never feeling one's life safe in their presence." He then related: "When I was one day preparing to draw from a woman selected by artists for a model, on account of her fine figure, on altering the arrangement of her dress, I saw the hilt of a dagger in her bosom, and on inquiring with astonishment what it meant, she drew it, and quaintly answered, "Contre gl' impertinenti."

Although Fuseli's talents were highly appreciated in Italy, he never obtained a diploma, or other honour, from any academy: indeed, he refused all overtures made to him on the subject; for he considered the institution of academies to be "symptoms of art in distress."

Upon his return to England, he visited his native Zurich, after an absence of sixteen years, and while there, painted some pictures, including "The Confederacy of the Founders of Helvetian Liberty," which he presented to the Senate House.

FUSELI SETTLES IN LONDON.

Fuseli, on his return from the continent, took apartments in the house of Mr. Cartwright, an artist, at No. 100, St. Martin's-lane. Among his early patrons were Lord Orford, and Mr. Lock, of Norbury Park, and his son, Mr. William Lock, jun.: and at the house of the latter he occasionally met Sir Joshua Reynolds and Dr. Moore, author of *Zeluco*.

In 1788, on his marriage with Miss Rawlins, Fuseli removed from St. Martin's-lane, to No. 72, Queen Anne-street, (now Foley-street,) where he painted most of the pictures which form his "Milton Gallery." Early in 1790, he was elected a Royal Academician, by a large majority over Mr. Bonomi, the opposing candidate proposed and warmly supported by Sir Joshua Reynolds, who, in consequence, resigned the Presidency, but was unaltered in his kindness to Fuseli during the remainder of his life. Fuseli was elected to succeed him in the Professorship of Painting, which office, conjointly with that of Keeper of the Academy, he was permitted to retain during the remainder of his life.

FUSELI AND COWPER'S "HOMER."

In 1786, when Cowper was about to publish his translation of Homer, Johnson, the publisher, sent a few lines of the manuscript to Fuseli, who, unhesitatingly, made several alterations in it. Johnson sent the MSS. to Cowper, without mentioning the name of the critic, when the poet readily adopted the alterations as improvements, and consented to Fuseli looking over the whole translation. Upon this, Hayley remarks: "It is a singular spectacle to observe a foreigner, who has raised himself to high rank in the arduous profession of a painter, correcting, and thanked for correcting, the chief poet of England, in his English version of Homer."

It is singular, that Fuseli never saw Cowper, nor did he ever write to him, or receive a letter from him; all communications being carried on either through General Cowper, the relation of the poet, or Johnson, the publisher.

RICHARDSON'S NOVELS.

Fuseli ever considered Richardson a man of great genius, and one who had a key to the human heart. He was very indignant, in the latter period of his life, with a gentleman who spoke contemptuously of *Clarissa Harlowe*. This person said in his presence, "No one now reads the works of Richardson." "Do they not?" said Fuseli, "then, by G—d they ought. If people are tired of old novels, I should be glad to know your criterion of books. If Richardson is old, Homer is obsolete. *Clarissa* to me is pathetic; I never read it without crying like a child."

M. DAVID AND FUSELI.

When, in 1802, Fuseli visited Paris, his society was much courted by the principal painters of the French school. David, whom he had known at Rome, paid him much attention, and wished to introduce him to the First Consul; this he, however, declined, as well as many other civilities, for he frequently said, "When he looked at David, he could not divest his mind of the atrocities of the French Revolution, nor separate them from the part which he had then acted, for they were stamped upon his countenance:" his face was disfigured by a hare-lip.

FUSELI AND WEST.

Fuseli was, at no time of his life, an admirer of West. At his re-election to the chair of the Royal Academy, in 1803, after a secession of twelve months, the votes for his return to the office of President were unanimous, except one, which was in favour of Mrs. Lloyd, (Miss Moser,) then an academician. Fuseli was taxed by some of the members with having given this vote, and answered, "Well, suppose I did; she is eligible to the office, and is not one old woman as good as another?"

This year, Fuseli left Queen Anne-street and removed to No. 13, Berners-street, which had been built by Sir William Chambers for his own residence. Here he remained until December 1804, when he was elected Keeper of the Royal Academy, Mr. Rigaud being his competitor.

Northcote and Opie voted against Fuseli, and being conscience-stricken, not only on account of his abilities, but from having received favours at his hands, they called upon him the day after the election to explain their motives. After having heard them, he replied in his usual sarcastic manner, "I am sorry you should have taken this trouble, because I shall lose my character in the neighbourhood. When you entered my house, the one must have been taken for a little Jew creditor, the other for a bumbailiff; so, good morning."

Northcote painted animals of the brute creation with great power. When his picture of Balaam and the Ass was exhibited at the Macklin Gallery, Northcote asked Fuseli's opinion of its merits: he instantly replied, "My friend, you are an angel at an ass, but an ass at an angel."

FUSELI'S ATTACHMENTS.

The youth, fine manly countenance, and conversational talents of Fuseli, (says Knowles,) made a deep impression upon most female hearts and minds. He was very susceptible of the passion of love, and appears to have formed many attachments. He was much enamoured of Angelica Kauffman, and thought much more of her personal charms than her professional talents. Miss Mary Moser experienced the influence of Fuseli's attentions, and she flattered herself that the feelings which she had were mutual. Miss Wollstonecroft avowed a passion for him which was not returned; and although he was thus favoured with the affections of more ladies than one, until he met with the lady whom he married, Miss Rawlins, of Bath Eaton, a curious perversity seems to have prevented any of the attachments from being mutual.

When at Zurich, in 1779, his affections were gained by the daughter of a magistrate, whom he calls in his correspondence "Nanna": she was very accomplished, and her proficiency in music is celebrated in a poem by Göethe; but her father was opulent and did not consider the connexion suitable for his daughter: the disappointment drove Fuseli almost to frenzy.

FUSELI AND MRS. WOLLSTONECROFT.

Of all Fuseli's attachments, by far the most extraordinary was his Platonic regard for Mary Wollstonecroft,* whom he met, in 1790, at the table of Johnson, the publisher, and who at the first interview conferred upon him the favour of her

* The lady, however, always asserted her right to be called Mrs. Wollstonecroft.

love. The French Revolution was at this time inculcating new notions of liberty, and Fuseli and Mary Wollstonecroft were alike smitten : the lady went so far as to assert that the new order of things had loosened all the old moral obligations, and that marriage was but an idle ceremony to be easily disposed of. Fuseli did not go so far ; but instead of repelling the lady's ridiculous advances, he imagined himself possessed with the pure spirit of Platonic love. Yet Mrs. Fuseli appears to have had little serious cause for jealousy in the mutual attachment. In her letters to Fuseli, Mary considered that "she was designed to rise superior to her earthly habitation;" and that she "always thought, with some degree of horror, of falling a sacrifice to a passion which may have a mixture of dross in it." In Fuseli, she discovered one "possessed of those noble qualities, that grandeur of soul, that quickness of comprehension, and lively sympathy, which she fancied would be essential to her happiness, if she entered into the married state." But there was a bar to her hopes in this quarter—for Fuseli was already married to the woman whom he loved.

Mary Wollstonecroft falsely reasoned with herself, and expressed to some of her intimate friends, that although Mrs. Fuseli had a right to the person of her husband, she, Mrs. Wollstonecroft, might claim, and for congeniality of sentiments and talents, hold a place in his heart ; for, "she hoped," she said, "to unite herself to his mind." Thenceforth she became an admirer of his person, dressed fashionably, and even took more elegant apartments. These advances availed but little with Fuseli : he chiefly admired her talents, and she complained of his coldness and neglect, for he allowed her letters to be some days unopened in his pocket. At length, Mrs. Wollstonecroft grew desperate, and told Mrs. Fuseli that she wished to become an inmate of her family ; "for," said she, "I have such sincere affection for your husband, that I find I cannot live without the satisfaction of seeing and conversing with him daily." Mrs. Fuseli was alarmed, and not only refused her solicitation, but instantly forbade her the house. She then resolved to give up the chase, and wrote to Fuseli, begging pardon "for having disturbed the quiet tenour of his life," and at the close of 1792, left London for France. Here she remained nearly two years and a half, and then returned to London, and renewed her attack upon Fuseli, who, however, received her coldly ; she then wrote the following strange letter to the persecuted painter :—

"When I returned from France, I visited you, Sir, but finding myself, after my late journey, in a very different situation, I vainly imagined you would have called upon me. I simply tell you what I thought, yet I write not, at present, to comment on your conduct, or expostulate. I have long ceased to expect kindness or affection from any human creature, and would fain tear from my heart its treacherous sympathies. I am alone. The injustice, without alluding to hope blasted in the bud, which I have endured, wounding my bosom, have set my thoughts adrift into an ocean of painful conjectures. I ask impatiently what—and where is truth? I have been treated brutally; but I daily labour to remember that I have still the duty of a mother to fulfil.

"I have written more than I intended,—for I only meant to request you to return my letters: I wish to have them, and it must be the same to you. Adieu!
"MARY."
"Monday Morning,—To Mr. Fuseli."

All communication then ceased between the parties until after Mrs. Wollstonecroft's marriage with Mr. Godwin, the author of *Caleb Williams*: upon which event Fuseli wrote to a friend, "You have not, perhaps, heard that the assertrix of female rights has given her hand to the *balancier* of political justice."* Fuseli saw Mrs. Godwin but seldom: she died in 1797, after having given birth to a female child (Mrs. Bysshe Shelley). Fuseli could not but feel much regret on the occasion; but as "grief does not give utterance to words," so he hardly noticed the catastrophe in the postscript of a letter to Mr. Roscoe, in these terms—"Poor Mary!"

ILL-ASSORTED COMPANY.

Shortly after Mrs. Godwin's marriage, she invited Fuseli to dinner, to meet Horne Tooke, Curran, and Grattan, and two or three other men of that stamp: he had no objection to their political opinions, but as they engrossed the whole conversation, and that chiefly on politics, he suddenly retired, and joining Mrs. Godwin in the drawing-room, petulantly said to her, "I wonder you invited me to meet such wretched company."

* Alluding to Godwin's *Treatise on Political Justice*, by which he is chiefly known as a writer.

FUSELI AND DR. JOHNSON.

Of Johnson, whom Fuseli met at Sir Joshua Reynolds's table, he said: "Johnson had, to a physiognomist, a good face, but he was singular in all his movements; he was not so uncouth in appearance as has been represented by some; he sat at table in a large bushy wig and brown coat, and behaved decently enough." On one occasion the conversation turned upon ghosts and witches, in the existence of which he believed, and his only argument was, that great and good men in all times had believed in them. Fuseli's fingers itched to be at Johnson, but he knew, if he got the better of the argument, that his celebrity was so great, it would not be credited. "You know," he said, "that I hate superstition. When I was in Switzerland, speaking with Lavater upon the appearance of the spirit after death, it was agreed between us, that if it were allowed by the Deity to visit earth, the first who died should appear to the other; my friend was the most scrupulous man in existence, with regard to his word; he is dead, and I have not seen him."

Fuseli used to say: "I always think in the language in which I write, and it is a matter of indifference to me whether it be in English, French, or Italian; I know each equally well; but if I wish to express myself with power, it must be in German." For the pleasure of reading Sepp's work on Insects, he gained late in life a competent knowledge of Dutch: indeed, he had a peculiar facility of acquiring languages. He told Mr. Knowles, that, with his knowledge of general grammar, and with his memory, six weeks of hard study was sufficient time to acquire any language with which he was previously unacquainted.

'THE NIGHTMARE.'

In 1781, Fuseli painted his most popular picture, *The Nightmare*, the drawing for which has the words, "St. Martin's-lane, 1781," written by him in the margin; it is chiefly in black chalk, and is composed without the head of the mare, which was an afterthought. The picture was sent to the Exhibition in 1782: it was sold for 20 guineas; it was engraved by Burke, and published by J. R. Smith, who acknowledged to have gained upwards of 500*l.* by the sale of the prints, though sold at a low price. Dr. Darwin thus described the subject:

> So on his *Nightmare*, through the evening fog,
> Flits the squab fiend o'er fen, and lake, and bog;
> Seeks some love-wilder'd maid with sleep oppress'd,
> Alights, and grinning, sits upon her breast—
> Such as of late amid the murky sky,
> Was marked by *Fuseli's* poetic eye;
> Whose daring tints, with *Shakspeare's* happiest grace,
> Gave to the airy phantom form and place—
> Back o'er her pillow sinks her blushing head,
> Her snow-white limbs hang helpless from the bed;
> While with quick sighs, and suffocative breath,
> Her interrupted heart-pulse swims in death.

Fuseli painted, at different times, several variations of this extraordinary picture.

Notwithstanding the apathy of the public, latterly towards his works, Fuseli (says Haydon, his pupil,) had had his day. His *Nightmare* was decidedly popular all over Europe Fuseli was paid 30*l*. for the picture, and the engraver cleared 600*l*. by the print.* His great works were from Milton. His conception of Adam and Eve for pathos, and Uriel contemplating Satan for sublimity, have never been excelled by the greatest painters of the greatest period of art either in Greece or Italy. With a fancy bordering on frenzy, as he used to say, the patience, humility, and calmness necessary for embodying great conceptions in an art, the language of which, in spite of all the sophistry about style and gusto, is undeniably grounded on a just selection and imitation of beautiful nature, angered and irritated him. His great delight was conception, not embodying his conceptions, and as soon as he rendered a conception intelligible to himself and others, by any means, he flew off to a fresh one, too impatient to endure the meditation required fully to develope it.

His *Œdipus and his Daughters* is, however, a work of far higher order. The desolate old man is seated on the ground in dread of the coming vengeance of heaven, and his daughters are clasping him wildly. "Pray, sir, what is that old man afraid of?" said some one to Fuseli, when the picture was exhibited. "Afraid, sir," exclaimed the painter, "why, afraid of going to hell!"

"THE SHAKSPEARE GALLERY."

This magnificent idea was started at the table of the nephew of Alderman Boydell. Fuseli had long imagined a temple

* The smaller sums named on the preceding page, are correct.

filled with pictures from our great dramatic poet. Boydell cut the design down to working dimensions. Reynolds, on receiving 500*l*., entered, though reluctantly, into the undertaking; but Fuseli, with his heart in the subject, made no preliminary stipulations, but prepared his palettes and began, choosing the wildest passages from the most imaginative plays. *The Tempest, the Midsummer Night's Dream, King Lear,* and *Hamlet,* suggested the best of the eight Shakspearian pictures which he painted; and of these that from *Hamlet* is the noblest. An eminent metaphysician, when he saw this picture (Hamlet's Ghost), exclaimed, "Lord preserve me!" He declared that it haunted him round the room.

The paintings which composed the Shakspeare Gallery were supplied by various hands. The design was novel, and was much praised, but its excellence was not felt by the people at large. The superiority of Fuseli in poetic composition over all his compeers was, however, appreciated by the judicious few.

"THE MILTON GALLERY."

This undertaking was meditated by Fuseli, while at Ramsgate, in 1790, and originated from a commission of Johnson to the artist to paint thirty pictures, of the sublime, the pathetic, and the playful scenes, in Milton, for Cowper's projected edition of the poet's works. This did not appear; but Fuseli transferred the progress he had made to a scheme of his own, which he thus broached to his friend Roscoe, who, in a previous letter, had made a comparison between his own pursuits and those of Fuseli, who thus writes:

"No doubt, I make the most advantageous figure on paper, I am on a road of glory; you are only crawling about from the white to the brown bed. I should not, however, be very uneasy if I could, without a total situation of change, obtain a little of that 'elbow-room' for my mind, which it seems you get by moving from a larger house to a smaller one. Notwithstanding the success of my election at the Academy, and of the pictures which I have painted for the Shakspeare Gallery, my situation continues to be extremely precarious. I have been and am contributing to make the public drop their gold into purses not my own; and though I am, and probably shall be, fully employed for some time to come, the scheme is hastening with rapidity towards its conclusion. 'There are,' says Mr. West, 'but two ways of working successfully, that is, lastingly, in this country, for an artist. The one is to paint for the King; the other, to meditate a scheme of your own.' The first he has monopolised; in the second he is not idle; witness the prints from English history, and the late advertisement of allegorical prints to be published from his designs by Bartolozzi. In imitation of *so great a man*, I am determined to lay, hatch, and crack a egg for myself too, if I can. What it shall be, I am not yet ready to tell with certainty; but the sum of it is, a series of pictures for *exhibition*, such as Boydell's and Macklin's. To obtain this, it will be necessary that I should have it in my power to work without commission, or any kind of intermediate gain, for at least three years; in which time I am *certain* of producing at least twenty pictures of different dimensions. The question is, what will enable me to live in the meantime? With less than three hundred a-year *certain*, I cannot do. My idea is to get a set of men (twenty, perhaps,—less, if possible, but not more,) to subscribe towards it. Suppose twenty pounds each annually, to be repaid either by small pictures or drawings, or the profits of the exhibition, should it succeed, of which there can be no very great doubt."

In 1797, six of Fuseli's intimate friends agreed to advance him 300*l*. per annum, until the task was completed. These generous patrons were Messrs. Coutts, Lock, Roscoe, G. Steevens, Seward and Johnson; and Mr. Coutts, in addition, presented Fuseli with 100*l*., under the injunction that his name should not appear in the transaction. Roscoe also bought pictures by the artist to a considerable amount, and induced his friends and connexions at Liverpool to make purchases.

On May 20, 1799, the rooms in Pall Mall, formerly occupied by the Royal Academy,* were opened for the exhibition of the Milton Gallery: Fuseli renting the premises at 210*l*. per annum. The exhibition consisted of forty pictures of different sizes; the following being the dimensions of some of the principal ones: *Satan starting from the touch of Ithuriel's spear*, and *Satan calling up his Legions*, each 13 feet by 12. *Satan encountering Death, Sin interposing; Adam and Eve first discovered by Satan; Satan flying up from Sin and Death in his enterprise;* and *The Vision of Noah;* each 13 feet by 10. *Death and Sin bridging the waste of Chaos*, and

* This house stood in Pall Mall, opposite Market-lane, leading to St. James's Market, at the south west end of Norris-street.

The Vision of the Lazar House, each 10 feet by 10. *The Creation of Eve, Christ on the Pinnacle of the Temple, The Fall of Satan, Adam resolved to share the Fate of Eve,* and *Eve at the Tree of Knowledge,* each 10 feet by 7.

Mr. Knowles describes the *Vision of the Lazar-house* as the *chef-d'œuvre* of the Gallery. It is a composition of seventeen figures and parts of figures, in which the painter creates both terror and pity in the spectator, by judiciously excluding most of the objects represented by the poet as suffering under bodily diseases calculated to create disgust, and confining himself chiefly to the representation of the maladies of the mind, which are so forcibly described by the passage,—

> Demoniac Phrensy, moping Melancholy,
> And moon-struck Madness.

Fuseli shone not only in the grand, the sublime, and the pathetic scenes, but also in the playful ones. Unfortunately for Fuseli, some of the newspapers of the day were so inimical to this Exhibition, that it was difficult for him to get them to insert an advertisement; and some well-timed lines which Mr. Roscoe wrote on the Milton Gallery, lay in the hands of the editor of a popular journal for some weeks before he gave them insertion.

Meanwhile, the whole of the money taken at the doors was not adequate to the payment of the rent of the premises, and the expenses incurred for advertisements and attendants. Fuseli was dismayed, and said: "I have dreamt of a golden land, and solicit in vain for the barge which is to carry me to its shore." But the consciousness of his own merit did not allow him to sink under the disappointment; he determined to try the effect of another season, and laboured diligently upon pictures to be then added to the Gallery.

Barry, who was Professor of Painting, had now rendered himself so obnoxious to the Royal Academy, that they not only dispossessed him of the chair as Professor, but expelled him the Academy. Opie then intimated an intention of offering himself as a candidate for the vacant Professorship; but on being told that Fuseli had the same intention, Opie withdrew, saying: "I would not have surrendered my pretensions to any other artist but Fuseli," who was therefore elected. "The power," says Mr. Knowles, "which he had displayed in the pictures of 'The Milton Gallery,' his learning, and well-known critical knowledge, were the causes which influenced the Academicians in their choice."

The Gallery was reopened in 1800, but did not attract the public; notwithstanding the President, Council and other members of the Royal Academy gave some *éclat* to the exhibition by publicly dining in the Gallery: the seven additional pictures were much admired; but all that Fuseli got on the occasion, to use his own words, was "mouth honour."

Fuseli closed the Exhibition on July 18, 1800, saying to a friend: "I am fed with honour, and suffered to starve, if they could starve me." The painter sometimes lounged in the Gallery to hear the remarks of the visitors. He did not brood over his failure, but bore it with good humour. One day, a coarse-looking man left his party, and coming up to him, said, "Pray, sir, what is that picture?" Fuseli answered, "It is the Bridging of Chaos; the subject from Milton." "No wonder," said he, "I did not know it, for I never read Milton; but I will." "I advise you not," said Fuseli, "for you'll find it a d—d tough job."

Fuseli's friends, feeling his embarrassment by these unsuccessful exhibitions, relieved him by becoming purchasers of some of the pictures.

Sir Thomas Lawrence, in his discourse as President of the Royal Academy, December 10, 1823, said, in reference to the *Milton Gallery*: "The many sublime designs by the great author of this, whose unapproached invention and high attainments, enforce this tribute to living genius."

MR. COUTTS'S LIBERALITY TO FUSELI.

For a period of sixty years, the opulent banker was the unchangeable friend of the painter. He once waited on his patron, and said, "I have finished the best of all my pictures—the *Lazar House*—when shall I send it home?" "My friend," said Coutts, "for me to take this picture would be a fraud upon you and upon the world. I have no place in which it could be fitly seen. Sell it to some one who has a gallery—your kind offer is sufficient for me, and makes all matters straight between us."

The apprehensions which Fuseli entertained of poverty were frequently without cause, and Coutts, on such occasions, was known to assume a serious look, and talk of scarcity of cash, and of sufficient securities. Away flew Fuseli, muttering oaths and cursing all parsimonious men; and having found a friend, returned with him breathless, saying, "There! I stop your mouth with a security." The cheque for the sum required was given, the security refused, and the grateful painter went on his way. That Fuseli respected every obligation to this stedfast friend is proved by the Countess of Guildford (Mr. Coutts's daughter) and her family attending the painter in his dying moments; and by the Duchess of St. Albans paying the last tribute of respect to Fuseli, by sending her carriage to his funeral.

FUSELI AND THE BRITISH INSTITUTION.

In 1805, (the same year in which Fuseli edited, for Mr. Johnson, Pilkington's *Dictionary of Painters*,) a number of noblemen and gentlemen, anxious for the encouragement of the fine arts in England, and especially historical painting, established the British Institution, in Pall Mall; and Fuseli was solicited to send thither some pictures for exhibition and sale. He, however, had no high opinion of the scheme; for, although, in common with other artists, he wished it to succeed—for he held that "the man who purchases one picture from a living artist, which may have some pretensions to the highest class of art, does more real service to the fine arts than he who spends thousands upon the works of the old masters"; yet he thought, to use his own words, "from the colour of the egg, it was more likely to produce an ichneumon than a sphynx," and expressed reluctance to be a contributor.

Mr. Coutts, who used every endeavour to promote the establishment and prospects of the British Institution, advised Fuseli to become an exhibitor, and to send, among other pictures, the *Lazar House;* observing, "I never intended to deprive you of this—it is yours; therefore, sell it if you can." In addition to this picture, the price of which was fixed at 300 guineas, Fuseli sent the *Nursery of Shakspeare*, for which he asked 150 guineas; and *Christ disappearing at Emmaus*, the price of the latter, 100 guineas.

The leading members of the Institution, however, hesitated to admit the admirable picture of the *Lazar House*, considering the subject too painful for the public eye; and they had three meetings before they came to the resolution of exhibiting it. This hesitation on their part, a slight degree of damage which the *Nursery of Shakspeare* sustained in its removal from the rooms, and the not finding of a purchaser for either of the pictures, made Fuseli resolve never to exhibit at the Institution again, to which resolution he pertinaciously adhered.—*Life, by Knowles.*

CANOVA AND FUSELI.

When Canova visited England in 1816, he was much struck with the paintings by Fuseli, as well as with his society. The eminent sculptor remarked, that he not only showed the brilliancy of his genius in his conversation, but that he spoke Italian with the purity of a well-educated native of Rome. And on his return to the Academy of St. Luke, at Rome, Canova sent a diploma, constituting Fuseli a member of the first class.

FUSELI'S RESENTMENT OF A SLIGHT.

One day the painter went, with Mr. Knowles, to the private view of a picture: after they had been in the room a few minutes, Fuseli pointed out a clergyman, and said, "That is Howley, the Bishop of London; he and I were very intimate. Before he became a dignitary of the Church, he used to come to my house frequently, and sit there for hours together; but for some years he seems to forget even my person." Shortly after, Lord Rivers came into the room, and accosted Fuseli in his usual familiar manner, and perhaps, not knowing that he had been acquainted with the Bishop, took an opportunity of introducing him. Fuseli immediately said, "I have seen his Lordship before now," and turned upon his heel. The Bishop, without reference to this passage, which perhaps he had not seen, told Mr. Leslie that, greatly as he admired the genius of Fuseli, he was obliged to withdraw from him on account of his ungovernable temper, which was apt to explode in downright insult on his associates.

LONDON SMOKE.

Haydon notes: "So far from the smoke of London being offensive to me, it has always been to my imagination the sublime canopy that shrouds the city of the world. Drifted by the wind, or hanging in gloomy grandeur over the vastness of our Babylon, the sight of it always filled my mind with feelings of energy such as no other spectacle could inspire."

"Be gode," said Fuseli, to me one day, "it's like the smoke of the Israelites making bricks." "It is grander," said I, "for it is the smoke of a people who would have made the Egyptians make bricks for them." "Well done, John Bull!" replied Fuseli.

FUSELI'S ART.

When Mr. Knowles, in 1808, bought Fuseli's picture of the *Night-Hag*, the painter looked earnestly at him, and said: "Young man, the picture you have purchased is one of my very best—yet no one has asked its price till now—it requires a poetic mind to feel and love such a work." It was the rarity of this poetic perception that made Fuseli's grand pieces unproductive. He even complained of the splendour in which his fancy invested them, and declared that he could not paint up to his imagination. In comparing these splendid fictions with living nature, he was struck, he often said, with the lamentable deficiencies of the latter; yet conscious that by nature he must be tried and judged, he was heard to exclaim in a fit of peevishness, "Hang Nature! she always puts me out."

FUSELI AS "KEEPER."

Mr. Leslie has left some interesting reminiscences of Fuseli, who was Keeper, when he was admitted a student in the Antique Academy. "I had been impressed," he says, "with the greatest respect for his genius, both as a painter and a writer, before I left America. The engraving from his *Hamlet and the Ghost* had scared me from the windows of a print-shop in Philadelphia, and I still contemplate that matchless spectre with something of the awe which it then inspired. I had hoped for much advantage from studying under such a master, but he said little in the Academy. He generally came into the room once in the course of every evening, and rarely without a book in his hand. He would take any vacant place among the students, and sit reading nearly the whole time he stayed with us. I believe he was right. For those students who are born with powers that will make them eminent, it is sufficient to place fine works of art before them. They do not want instruction, and those who do are not worth it.

Art may be *learnt*, but can't be *taught.* Under Fuseli's wise neglect, Wilkie, Mulready, Etty, Landseer, and Haydon distinguished themselves, and were the better for not being made all alike by teaching, if indeed that could have been done."

"Edwin Landseer, who entered the Academy very early, and was a very pretty little curly-headed boy, attracted Fuseli's attention by his talents and gentle manners. Fuseli would look round for him, and say, 'Where is my little *dog boy?*'"

FUSELI'S DAY.

Fuseli was habitually an early riser: in London, in summer, between six and seven o'clock, but in the country, between four and five. To this, and the practice of standing while he painted, he attributed the more than usually good state of health which he had enjoyed. He possessed his faculties to the last period of his life: his fancy was vivid, his memory unimpaired, and his eyesight so good that he could read the smallest print without the aid of glasses. He was a man of strict method. If the weather was fine, he usually walked an hour or two before breakfast: if otherwise, he read some classic author. At breakfast, he would read some book on entomology. After he had breakfasted, while under the hands of the hairdresser, he read Homer in Greek. At half-past ten, he went to his study, and painted till four; then dressed, and walked till the dinner hour. In the evening, if not in society, he amused himself with prints or drawings, or reading. When out of London, the middle of each day was spent either in drawing, writing, or reading.

PAINTING "THE DEVIL."

One day, when Fuseli was dining out, a gentleman of the company called to him from the other end of the room, "Mr. Fuseli, I have lately purchased a picture of yours." Mr. F. "Did you? what is the subject?" Gent. "I really don't know." Mr. F. "That's odd enough: you must be a strange fellow, to buy a picture without knowing the subject." Gent. (a little nettled) "I don't know what the devil it is." Mr. F. "Perhaps it is the *devil;* I have often painted him." Gent. "Perhaps it is." Mr. F. "Well, you have *him* now; take care that he does not one day have *you!*"

HARLOW'S CONCEIT EXPOSED.

Harlow, the pupil of Lawrence, on one occasion remarked to Knowles: "It is extraordinary that Fuseli, who is so fine a scholar, should suffer engravers to place translations under the plates taken from the classical subjects painted by him;" and remarked, "I was educated a scholar, having been at Westminster School, and therefore wish to see the subjects given in the original language;" and then imprudently instanced the print taken from the picture of the death of Œdipus. Knowles mentioned this conversation to Fuseli, on their way to Harlow's house. "He has made, I think," said Fuseli, "an unfortunate choice; for, if I recollect rightly, the Greek passage, as well as my translation of it, are scratched in under the mezzotinto. But before we part I will bring his knowledge to the test." After he had sat to Harlow (for his portrait) the usual time, he asked for a piece of chalk, and wrote, in large letters, on the wainscot, a passage from Sophocles. After having done so, he said to Harlow, "Read that;" and finding, by his hesitation, that he did not understand a letter, he resumed, "On our way hither Knowles told me you had said that I ought not to permit engravers to put translations under the prints taken from me, and that you had instanced the Œdipus; now, that is the Greek quotation whence the subject is taken, and I find you cannot read a letter of it. Let me give you this advice: you are, undoubtedly, a good portrait-painter, and I think in small pictures, such as you are painting of me, stand unrivalled; this is sufficient merit; do not then pretend to be that which you are not, and probably from your avocations never can be —a scholar."

Mr. Leslie allows Harlow's portrait of Fuseli to be the best; "but it would have required a Reynolds to do justice to the fine intelligence of his head. His keen eye, of the most transparent blue, I shall never forget."

Harlow painted the above portrait of Fuseli in 1817 for Mr. Knowles: it is on panel, cabinet size, and Fuseli gave for the picture twelve sittings of two hours each.

HARLOW'S PICTURE OF "THE TRIAL OF QUEEN KATHERINE."

Harlow, in painting this, his best and most esteemed work, owed many obligations to Fuseli for his critical remarks: for when he first saw the picture (chiefly in dead colouring,) he said: "I do not disapprove of the general arrangement of your work, and I see you will give it a powerful effect of light and shadow; but you have here a composition of more than twenty figures, or I should rather say parts of figures; because you have not shown one leg or foot, which makes it very defective. Now, if you do not know how to draw legs and feet, I will show you;" and taking up a crayon, drew two on the wainscot of the room. Harlow profited by these remarks, and changed the whole arrangement of the foreground. Fuseli then said: "So far you have done well; but now, you have not introduced a back figure, to throw the eye of the spectator into the picture;" and then pointed out by what means he might improve it in this particular. Accordingly, Harlow introduced the two boys who are taking up the cushion; that which shows the back is altogether due to Fuseli, and is certainly the best drawn figure in the picture. Fuseli afterwards attempted to get him to improve the drawing of the arms of the principal object (Mrs. Siddons), who is represented as Queen Katherine, but without much effect, particularly the left; and after having witnessed many ineffectual attempts of the painter to accomplish this, he desisted, and remarked, "It is a pity that you never attended the Antique Academy." This account of the picture is from Knowles's *Life of Fuseli*, and differs, in some respects, from the particulars related by Mr. Cribb, for whom Harlow's picture was subsequently engraved.

FUSELI AND LORD ELDON.

In 1825, Fuseli sat for a half-length portrait to Sir Thomas Lawrence, which this great artist painted admirably. At this time, the Earl of Eldon was also sitting for his likeness, and Fuseli, not recognising the countenance, asked Sir Thomas who it was? he answered, "It is the Chancellor." Fuseli took a piece of chalk, and immediately wrote on the picture:

———————Quia me vestigia terrent
Omnia te adversum spectantia, nulla retrorsum.*

This passage is from one of Horace's Epistles, first book, in which the fox declines to enter the "royal cave" of the sick lion; and the foregoing passage is thus imitated by Pope:

* From this passage is borrowed the sun-dial motto—"Vestigia nulla retrorsum."—(*See Essex-court, Temple.*)

> Because I see, by all the tracks about,
> Full many a beast goes in, but none comes out.

When Lord Eldon saw the quotation, he was much amused; and on being told that it was written by Fuseli, he laughed heartily.

FUSELI'S LAST PICTURE.

He evinced "the ruling passion strong in death;" for, just before his last illness, he had sent two pictures for the then ensuing Exhibition of the Royal Academy: the larger one, *A Scene from Comus*, finished; the smaller, *Psyche passing the Fates*, in an unfinished state, intending, as is the common practice with the Academicians, to glaze and harmonize this picture in the situation where it was to be placed. Its unfinished condition frequently occupied his thoughts during his illness, and he, but two days before his death, spoke of it with great solicitude to Sir Thomas Lawrence, wishing it either to be withdrawn, or that some painter of talent would harmonize it for him.

The last work on which his pencil was employed, and on which he painted a few days previously to his death, was a scene from Shakspeare's *King John:* in this picture, the figure of Lady Constance, in particular, is finely designed, and grief is admirably depicted in her countenance: he was painting this for James Carrick Moore, Esq., and it was nearly completed when the artist died.

DEATH OF FUSELI.

It was on Sunday, April 10, 1825, that Fuseli, being then on a visit to the Countess of Guildford, at Putney Hill, complained of illness, while walking in the pleasure-grounds. He was engaged on that day to dine in St. James's Place, with Mr. Samuel Rogers; but as his illness continued, Mrs. Fuseli prevailed upon him (with difficulty) to remain in the house, and he gave up the engagement. On the evening before, being out on the lawn with the Ladies North, and looking at the stars, which shone with great brightness, he said (possibly from the consciousness of symptoms which he considered dangerous,) "I shall soon be amongst them." On Monday, he grew much worse; his physicians, and Mr. Alexander Crichton and Dr. Holland said, they could not give any specific name to the complaint; for it appeared to them, that all the functions of nature had given way, and, in their opinion, he could not last many days. From the commencement of his illness, he seems not to have expected to recover. On Wednesday, he put his hand in that of Mr. Knowles, and said, "My friend, I am fast going to that bourne whence no traveller returns." But he neither expressed regret at his state, nor, during his illness, showed any despondency or impatience. He remained perfectly collected, and his mind apparently not impaired; but his articulation was feeble, and the last words which he addressed to his physicians, the death-gurgles being then in his throat, were in Latin; so perfect was his mind at this time, that he said to Mr. Knowles, "What can this mean? When I attempt to speak, I croak like a toad." Next morning, shortly after he had been raised in his bed, and his mouth and lips had been moistened by a feather dipped in liquid, he breathed his last, without much apparent pain, and in complete possession of his faculties.

FUNERAL OF FUSELI.

The remains were removed from Putney Hill to Somerset House, where they were placed in the room around which were arranged "the Lazar-house," "the Bridging of Chaos," and other sublime productions of Fuseli's pencil, the subjects being chiefly from Milton. The funeral, by a resolution of the Council of the Royal Academy, was a private one, but attended by the President, the Secretary, and Council; and several private friends, followed by their carriages. The body was deposited on April 25, in a small vault formed for the purpose, in the south crypt of St. Paul's Cathedral, near the remains of his friends, Sir Joshua Reynolds and Opie.

The inscription upon the coffin of Fuseli states his age at eighty-six years: he was, however, in his eighty-fifth year, having completed his eighty-fourth on Feb. 7 preceding his death.

CHARACTERISTICS, RETROSPECTIVE OPINIONS, AND PERSONAL TRAITS.

FUSELI AND THE ELGIN MARBLES.

About the Elgin Marbles, (says Haydon,) Fuseli did not behave so grandly as West and Canova and Lawrence. I was the first who took him to see these divine works. Wilkie had taken me. Tired, I went to Fuseli, set him in a blaze, and he put on his great coat directly.

Thrown off his guard by their beauty, he strode about the collection in his fierce way, saying, "the Greeks were gods—they were gods!" We went home and looked over Quintilian and Pliny, and every author who alluded to the Parthenon, and the Greek artists.

A day or two afterwards, reflecting on what he had written about the Apollo, &c. he tried to *unsay*, but it would not do. One side of the Ilissus was too short! I showed him a cast which was shorter. One arm of the Theseus was too thick. I proved it right by the different actions. His belly was too flat. I convinced him it was owing to the bowels falling in, while the bowels leaned out in the Ilissus, and then the belly protruded. This was irrefutable. I had never differed as strongly before. He saw he was wrong, and had passed life on a wrong scent. A really great soul, like Canova's, would have acknowledged it. I fear Fuseli's self-love was too strong for this. He flew into a passion, and we were never cordial after. I regretted it, as no man owed more to Fuseli than myself.

To some remark of Westmacott, in praise of the Theseus, Fuseli replied:

"The Apollo is a god, the man in the Mews[*] is a demi-god,[†] and the Theseus is a man."

[*] It is strange that Mr. Knowles does not, in his Life of Fuseli, extending to 400 pages, once mention the high service which he rendered to Art by his appreciation of the Elgin Marbles, which, however, Haydon may possibly have made the most of, in his Autobiography.

[†] A cast from the colossal figure of the Monte Cavallo, then exhibited in the King's Mews, at Charing Cross.

"You will admit," said Westmacott, "that he is a hero?"
"No," replied Fuseli, "he is only a strong man."

FUSELI—SKETCHED BY HAYDON.

When Haydon first came to London, in 1805, Mr. Prince Hoare, to whom he had a letter of introduction, told him that he had seen Fuseli, who wished him to call on him with his drawings. Accordingly, he went.

Fuseli, (says Haydon,) had a great reputation for the terrible. His sublime conception of Uriel and Satan had impressed me when a boy. I had a mysterious awe of him. Prince Hoare's apprehensions lest he might injure my taste, or hurt my morals, excited in my mind a notion that he was a sort of gifted wild beast.

My father had just the same feeling, and in a letter I received just before my calling, he concluded by these words: —"God speed you with the terrible Fuseli."

This sort of preparation made everything worse, and I was quite nervous when the day arrived. I walked away with my drawings to Wardour-street. I remember that Berners-street had a golden lion on the right corner-house, and blundered on, without knowing how or remembering why, I found myself at Fuseli's door. I deliberated a minute or two, and at last making up my mind to see the enchanter, I jerked up the knocker so nervously, that it stuck in the air. I looked at it, so much as to say "is this fear?" and then drove it down again with such a devil of a blow, that the door rang again. The maid came rushing up with astonishment. I followed her into a gallery, or show-room, enough to frighten anybody at twilight. Galvanized devils—malicious witches brewing their incantations—Satan bridging Chaos, and springing upwards, like a pyramid of fire—Lady Macbeth, Paolo and Francesca—Falstaff and Mrs. Quickly—humour, pathos, terror, blood, and murder, met me at every look. I expected the floor to give way!—I fancied Fuseli himself to be a giant. I heard his footsteps, and saw a little bony hand slide round the edge of the door, followed by a little white-headed, lion-faced man in an old flannel dressing-gown, tied round his waist with a piece of rope, and upon his head the bottom of Mrs. Fuseli's work-basket. "Well, well," thought I, "I am a match for you at any rate, if bewitching is tried;" but all apprehension vanished, on his saying in the mildest and kindest way, "Well, well, Mr. Haydon, I have heard a good deal of you from Mr. Hoare. Where are your drawings?" In a fright I gave him the wrong book, with a sketch of some men pushing a cask into a grocer's shop—Fuseli smiled and said, "By Gode, de fellow does his business at least with energy." I was gratified at his being pleased in spite of my mistake.

"You are studying anatomy? You are right. Show me some drawings. I am Keeper of de Academy, and hope to see you dere de first nights." I went away, feeling happy that my bones were whole and my breathing uninterrupted.

Fuseli took his place as Keeper in 1805, after the Christmas vacation, and I well remember on my first night of attendance, he came up to me, to the astonishment of the students, and pointing his finger at me, in a voice of thunder, said, "I know enough of you." The students took it oddly, and said, "Why, what does he know of you?" Half in a fright, I began to ask myself unconsciously if I had been guilty of murder.

Fuseli made us a speech before he went away, and thus began my academical career.

My incessant application was soon perceived by Fuseli, who coming in one day, when I was at work, and all the other students were away, walked up to me, and said in the mildest voice, "Why, when de devil *do* you dine?" and invited me to go back with him to dinner. Here I saw his sketches, the sublimity of which I deny. He had a strong Swiss accent, and a guttural energetic diction. This was not affectation in him. He swore roundly, a habit which he told me he had contracted from Dr. Armstrong. He was about five feet five inches high, had a compact little form, stood firmly at his easel, painted with his left hand, never held his palette upon his thumb, but kept it upon his stone, and being very nearsighted, and too vain to wear glasses, used to dab his beastly brush into the oil, and sweeping round the palette in the dark, take up a great lump of white, red, or blue, as it might be, and plaster it over a shoulder or face. Sometimes, in his blindness, he would put a hideous smear of Prussian blue in his flesh, and then, perhaps, discovering his mistake, take a bit of red to deaden it, then prying close in, turn round to me, and say, 'By Gode, dat's a fine purple! it's vary like Correggio, by Gode!' and then, all of a sudden, he would burst out with a quotation from Homer, Tasso, Dante, Ovid, Virgil, or perhaps the Nibelungen, and thunder round to me with '*paint* dat.' I found him the most grotesque mixture of literature, art, scepticism, infidelity, profanity, and kindness. He put me in mind of Archimago in Spenser. Weak minds he destroyed. They mistook his wit for reason, his indelicacy for breeding, his swearing for manliness, and his infidelity for strength of mind : but he was accomplished in elegant literature, and had the art of inspiring young minds with high and grand views. I told him I would never paint portraits,—but devote myself to High Art. "Keep to dat!" said Fuseli, looking fiercely at me: "I will, sir." We were more intimate from that hour.

FUSELI AND PICTURE-HANGING.

When Haydon sent his first picture to the Royal Academy, in 1807, he was so nervous as to its fate that he bored Fuseli, who, being Keeper, saw what was daily doing by the Committee ; until, at last, one morning, after a timid knock, Haydon opened the door at the usual "Come in." Fuseli turned suddenly round with his lion head, the white hair glistening as the light quivered down upon it from the top of his high window, and roared out, "Wale, is it you? For your comfort den, you are hung, be Gode, and d——d well, though not in chains yet." "Where, sir, for God's sake?" "Ah! date is a sacrate, but you are in de great room. Dey were all pleased. Northcote tried to hurt you, but dey would not listene ; he said, 'Fye, sure, I see Wilkie's hand there.' 'Come, come,' said Westall, 'dat's too bad even for you!'" "Wilkie's hand!" replied Haydon, "what malice! I would as soon let Wilkie feed me with a pap spoon as touch a picture of mine. But what petty malignity!" "Wale, wale," said Fuseli, "I told him (Northcote,) 'you are his townsman, hang him wale.' When I came back, where de deyvil do you tink he was hanging you? Be Gode, above de whole-lengts and small figures about eight inches. 'Why,' said I, 'you are sending him to haven before his time. Take him down, take him down; dat is shameful!'" And so, down Haydon was taken, and hung on the right of the entrance-door in the old Great Room at Somerset House, a situation of great honour.

FUSELI'S SENSIBILITY.

It has often been remarked, (says Mr. Knowles,) that old men do not feel so acutely the loss of relations and friends, as those who are of a less advanced age. But this was not the case with Fuseli; for, although when in his eighty-first year, his faculties were unimpaired, he still possessed a great degree of sensibility. As one friend dropped into the grave after another, he felt the loss of each, and constantly exclaimed, "It is my turn next," advising me, at the same time, as I advanced in life, to cultivate the friendship of men younger than myself, that I might not be left without friends in old age. Although when a younger man he appeared to his acquaintances to cling much to life, yet later when he spoke of death, it was without fearful forebodings. "Death," (he used to say,) "is nothing; it is the pain and feebleness of body under a lingering disease, which often precedes death, that I dread; for, at my time of life, I can look forward but to a day, and that passes quickly." The following extract of a letter to the Countess of Guildford, dated Nov. 17, 1821, shows his feelings on this subject:

"Taciti, soli, e senza compagnia.

"We jogged on, though at a swifter pace than Dante and his guides, sympathising (one at least,) with autumn's deciduous beauty, and whispering to every leaf the eye caught falling, *soon* shall I follow *thee!*

"Indeed, were it not for those I should leave behind, I would not care *if now.*"

From infancy, Fuseli possessed very impetuous passions, which required, when a boy, some degree of coercion, on the part of his parents, to control. This irritability, in one instance, nearly cost him his life. At Lyons, when a young man, he had a dispute with a person, which aroused his feelings to such a height, that in a momentary fit of passion he made use of that agility which he possessed in a considerable degree, and kicked his antagonist in the face. The man coolly drew his sword, and immediately inflicted a very severe wound upon the offending leg. Notwithstanding this violence of disposition, when his anger was aroused even to a high pitch, a kind word or look appeased him in a moment. In the several relations of husband, friend, and master, he was most affectionate and kind; but he required to be sought: if neglected, he ceased to think of the objects whom he had before loved or esteemed; and his constant expression on such occasions was—"I can live without them who can do without me."

FUSELI'S RELIGIOUS FEELINGS.

Fuseli was seldom induced to speak on religion; but as he attached himself to no particular form or sect, it would be difficult to give a precise idea of his tenets. He was deeply read in the Bible, and recollected, when in conversation, not only those passages which, for historical facts, sublimity, pathos, or poetic beauty, are impressed on most minds, but also the minor circumstances; for he could, from memory, trace the several tribes, and tell you accurately, the genealogy of any particular person. He seldom took up the Bible, which he frequently did, without shedding tears.

He had a perfect reliance on a future state of existence. "If I had not hope in this," he said, "I should hang myself, for I have lived, and still live, for nothing. I am certain I shall exist hereafter, for I feel that I have had powers given me by the Deity, which time has not allowed me to exert or even to develope. I am capable of doing ten times more than I have done."

This prevailing impression broke forth on many occasions. He had accompanied Sir Thomas Lawrence to see a collection of fine casts from the antique, which were arranged in a gallery built for the purpose by Mr. Smirke, at Battersea. In a niche at the end of the gallery was placed the colossal statue of the Farnese Hercules, and by a novel arrangement of the lamps, (the rest of the gallery being in total darkness,) a very powerful effect was given to the statue, which had been turned with its back to the spectator, and thus presented a vast mass of shadow, defined only by its grand outline and the strength of the light beyond it; the source of which was concealed by the pedestal. In the course of the evening, Mr. Fuseli was taken to see this statue, when Sir Thomas Lawrence was for a few moments disappointed by the silence of his friend; but on a servant bringing a light into the entrance-room, he perceived Fuseli excited even to tears, as he exclaimed, with deep tremulous energy: "No man shall persuade me, that these motions which I now feel are not immortal."

Fuseli was once maintaining the immortality of the soul; when a gentleman present, said, "I could make you or any man of sense disbelieve this in half an hour's conversation." Fuseli immediately answered, "That I am sure you could not, and I will take care you shall not."

Being one day pressed by his friend, the Rev. John Hewlett,

upon his belief in the resurrection of Christ, he answered : "I believe in a resurrection ; and the resurrection of Christ is as well authenticated as any other historical fact."

He more than once said to Mr. Knowles : "There are now no real Christians, for the religion of Christ died with its great Author; for where do we witness in those who bear His name the humility, self-abasement, and charity, of their Master, which qualities He not only taught, but practised."

FUSELI AND YOUNG LAWRENCE.

Mr. Knowles, in his *Life of Fuseli*, states that shortly after young Lawrence's arrival in London from Bath, Fuseli saw the future promise in the youth, and was gratified at making remarks upon his portraits for his improvement. This kind notice from a man whom Lawrence held in the highest esteem for his various acquirements, made a deep impression upon his mind : he sought an intimacy with him, which, upon more mature knowledge of the individual, ripened into the closest friendship. At the death of Mr. West, in the year 1820, Fuseli was among the most forward of the Academicians to propose that his friend Lawrence, who was then on the Continent, should fill the Presidential chair.

Such is the statement of Mr. Knowles, the intimate friend of Fuseli ; but it does not accord with an anecdote related in the *Life of Sir Thomas Lawrence*, vol. i. p. 98, where it is stated that young Lawrence called upon Fuseli, bringing with him a letter of introduction from an old friend. Fuseli, being miraculously in a good humour, received Lawrence kindly, saying, "I shall be very happy to see you whenever you are disengaged." The ingenuous youth took this literally, and called the next day. "By Gort !" cried Fuseli, as he entered the room, "you must have plenty of spare time on your hands !" The young man retired in confusion, nor did he call again.

FUSELI'S WIT AND HUMOUR.

Fuseli was discoursing one day at his friend Mr. Johnson's table, upon the power and merits of Phocion, the brave Athenian general ; when a stranger, who had apparently listened with attention to the conversation, gravely put the question, "Pray, Sir, who was Mr. Phocion ?" Fuseli immediately answered, "From your dialect, Sir, I presume you are from Yorkshire; and, if so, I wonder you do not recollect Mr. Phocion's name, as he was Member for your county in the Long Parliament!"

Calling one morning upon Mr. Johnson, Fuseli found him bargaining with an author for the copyright of a book. When the gentleman left, Mr. Johnson said, "That is Mr. Kett, and his work is to be called the *Elements of Useful Knowledge.*" "In how many volumes?" said Fuseli. "In two octavos," was the answer. "No, no, Johnson," said he, "you cannot be serious: the ocean is not to be emptied with a tea-spoon."

Discoursing with a lady upon sculpture, who was, however, too well read in the classics to be a subject of his mischievous pleasantry, he pretended to inform her of a fine bas-relief which had been received by the Royal Academy from Rome. "What is the subject?" she asked. "Hector and Andromache," said he, "dashing out against a wall the little Astyanax's brains!" "Pooh! why do you tell me such stuff?" said she. "Ay! *you* may laugh," replied Fuseli, "but it would go down with many a one. I have often said such things in company without detection."

The students were constantly amused with Fuseli's oddities. He heard a violent altercation in the studio one day, and inquired the cause. "It is only those fellows the students, sir," said one of the porters. "Fellows," exclaimed Fuseli; "I would have you to know, sir, those *fellows* may one day become Academicians." The noise increased—he opened the door and burst in upon them, exclaiming, "You are a den of wild beasts." One of the offenders, Munro by name, bowed, and said, "And Fuseli is our keeper." He retired smiling, and muttering, "The fellows are growing witty."

A student, as he passed, held up his drawing, and said confidently, "Here, sir, I finished it without using a crumb of bread." "All the worse for your drawing," replied Fuseli; "buy a twopenny loaf, and rub it out."

A person who desired to speak to the Keeper of the Academy, followed the porter so closely, that he announced himself, with "I hope I don't intrude." "You do intrude," said Fuseli, in a surly tone. "Do I?" said the visitor; "then, sir, I will come to-morrow, if you please." "No, sir," replied he, "don't come to-morrow, for then you will intrude a second time: tell me your business now."

When Blake, a painter infinitely more wild in conception that Fuseli himself, showed him one of his strange productions, he said, "Now some one has told you this is very fine." "Yes," said Blake, "the Virgin Mary appeared to me, and told me it was very fine: what can you say to that?" "Say?" exclaimed Fuseli, "why nothing—only her ladyship has not an immaculate taste."

Condemning in general terms a large historical picture, which a person at table had admired, he was asked for some specific fault: "Why," said he, "the fellow has crammed into his canvas fifteen figures, besides a horse, and, by Gort, he has given only three legs among them." "Why, where has he hidden the others?" was asked. "How should I know?" he answered, "I did not paint the picture; but I wonder how any man can talk of a painter, and praise him, who has given fifteen men and a horse only three legs."

William Roscoe, who sat in Parliament for Liverpool, was a friend of Fuseli, and on a visit in 1804, he pointed out to him the great improvements made in the town within a few years. The painter replied: "I do not wonder that you look upon these with some degree of complacency; for they may be considered as the work of your hands, and as such I view them with interest; but, methinks, I everywhere smell the blood of slaves;" alluding to the wealth derived by the Liverpool merchants from the Slave Trade, and Roscoe's efforts for its abolition.

Fuseli had a great dislike to idle talk, and unmeaning observations. After sitting silent in his own room, during the "bald disjointed chat" of some idle callers-in, who were gabbling about the weather, he suddenly exclaimed, "We had pork for dinner to-day!" "Dear! Mr. Fuseli, what an odd remark!"—"Why, it is as good as anything you have been saying for the last hour."

Fuseli spared no one—and was merciless to the miser Nollekens. Once, at a party at Mr. Coutts's, Mrs. Coutts, dressed like Morgiana, came dancing in, presenting her dagger at every breast: as she confronted Nollekens, Fuseli cried out, "Strike—strike—there's no fear: Nolly never was known to bleed."

Fuseli could not argue soundly, but illustrated everything by brilliant repartee; Horne Tooke was the only man who was an overmatch for him. He said of him: "Tooke is the greatest chatterer I ever sat down with; one cannot, in his company, put in a word edgewise."

In his temper Fuseli was irritable and violent, but appeased in an instant. In his person small, with a face of independent, unregulated fire; Leslie says: his front face had very much the character of *a lion*. Haydon heard he was handsome when young, and with women (when gratified by their attentions) no man could be more gentle.

Fuseli frequently invented the subjects of his pictures without the aid of poet or historian. On one occasion, he was much amused by the following inquiry of Lord Byron:—"I have been looking in vain, Mr. Fuseli, for some months, in the poets and historians of Italy, for the subject of your picture of Ezzelin; pray, where is it to be found?" "Only in my brain, my Lord," was the answer; "for I invented it."

One evening, Fuseli said to Bonnycastle: "Pray, Bonnycastle, what do you consider the reason that I am not popular as a painter, in a country which has produced Shakspeare and Milton?" Bonnycastle answered: "Because the public like familiar subjects, in which there may be individual beauty with fine colouring." "Is that their taste?" said Fuseli, hastily: "then, if I am not their painter, they are not my critics."

CHARACTER OF FUSELI AS AN ARTIST.

Mr. William Young Ottley, (to whom the history of Art owes so much,) wrote, a short time previously to the death of Fuseli, a judicious and elegant paper upon his character as an artist, from which we quote a few passages.

"In the highest department of painting, which not improperly may be termed poetic or epic painting, we had no artist of eminence till, in the year 1779, Mr. Fuseli, after a stay of eight years in Italy, came and settled among us. An intimate acquaintance with the learned languages, had early enabled him to fill his mind from the rich storehouses of ancient poesy; he was all energy and imagination. But in his youth, not then intending to practise painting professionally, he had not subjected himself, as an artist, to the restraints of an academic education. To curb his genius afterwards was impossible; and to this circumstance we must attribute much of that fine wildness of character which distinguishes his performances; not unmixed, it is true, with a certain amount of exaggeration of manner in the drawing and action of the figures, but which, still, no person of fancy would consent to exchange for the regulated but cold manner too often learned in schools. Had it been the intention of Mr. Fuseli to devote his pencil to the representation of subjects of real, sober history, the every-day occurrences of life, this peculiarity in his style, often amounting to extravagance, would have been inapplicable. But it has ever been his aim, especially in his larger works, to soar in the sublime regions of Poetry; and what, it may be asked, is Poetry, if entirely divested of amplification?"

Mr. Ottley then adduces certain examples to show that the greatest artists have not thought that a style of drawing strictly imitative of common nature, was well adapted to ideal subjects; and that Mr. Fuseli's style of design is of the most elevated kind, and consequently best suited to subjects of a very elevated character.

"In respect of invention, composition, *clair-obscure*, the works of Mr. Fuseli generally merit unmixed praise; and although, in the more technical parts of colouring, they have not equal pretensions, still in this also they deserve commendation; being commonly painted in that solemn tone of colouring which we admire in the works of the greatest fresco-painters, and which Sir Joshua Reynolds observes to be so well adapted to the higher kind of pictorial representation. As an inventor, he equals the greatest painters that have lived since the restoration of the art. No one was ever more fully gifted with the rare faculty of at once discovering, in the writer he is perusing, the point of the story, and the moment of time best calculated to produce a forcible effect in painting. The loftier his subject, the more easily he reaches it; and when he undertakes that at which another artist would tremble, he is the most sure of success." Mr. Ottley then refers to Fuseli's exhibition of the Milton Gallery, the subjects mostly taken from the *Paradise Lost;* and adds: "the magnificent imagery of this poem, the beautiful, the sublime, or the terrific character of the personages represented in it, and of the action described, all combined to fit it for the display of the artist's surprising genius in its fullest force; besides which, the style of Mr. Fuseli was here exactly suited to his subject. But although the series, as a whole, was one of the greatest works of painting ever produced, (certainly in its kind the most perfect) elevating the painter to the same rank as the poet, it failed, as the poem itself had originally done, to insure to its author that immediate share of public favour which was his due, and which is sure to be attendant upon successful endeavours in those inferior branches of the art which are more within the range of public capacity.

"But the fashion or opinion of the day, in matters of taste, is not always the judgment of posterity; and it cannot be too much regretted that the principal pictures of the series, at least, have not been kept together for the future advantage of our artists, and the gratification of those whose studies might hereafter qualify them to appreciate their excellence. For be it remembered, by such persons as might otherwise be too readily induced to undervalue that which they do not understand, that Sir Joshua Reynolds became, in the latter part of his life, 'clearly of opinion that a relish for the higher excellencies of the art is an acquired taste, which no man ever possessed without long cultivation, great labour, and attention.'"

POETICAL TRIBUTES.

To Mr. Fuseli some Verses were addressed by Mr. Roscoe, on his Pictures from Milton. Henry Kirke White penned an Ode "on seeing Engravings from his Designs;" and "A Vision," by a Lady, is printed with the above, in the Appendix to Knowles's *Life of Fuseli*.

LESLIE'S ACCOUNT OF FUSELI'S PICTURES.

In 1816 Mr. Leslie went to see Fuseli's Pictures at the Academy.* He received Leslie very politely, and took him into his painting-room. He was about a picture of *Perseus flying off with the Head of Medusa*. The figure of Medusa was very happily conceived, and he had contrived to hide all

---

* Fuseli's paintings at Somerset House appear to have been for several years one of the Picture Exhibitions of the metropolis: we find it in the *Picture of London*, 1806 and 1810.

the disgusting part—the stump of the neck and the blood—very judiciously. Mr. Leslie also saw here the picture of the *Lazar House*, from the Milton Gallery. He describes it as one of the most tremendous exhibitions of appalling sights he had ever beheld. The figures glare across the picture like a horrible dream. Fuseli has certainly never been equalled in the visionary, and there it is he shines as a genius: but whenever he attempts commonplace, he is contemptible.

Mr. Leslie adds: "Fuseli, I believe, has never painted from nature, and consequently, does not know what it is. His illustrations of Cowper are ridiculous in the extreme. He is a great master of light, and shadow, and colour, as far as it can be made an engine of the terrific. His paintings are very coarse, and have an uncertain kind of execution which is very fine in ghosts and witches, but very bad in ladies and gentlemen."

Elsewhere Leslie says: "With no artist of powers so great as those of Fuseli were those powers confined within so narrow a circle; but within that circle he has expressed the terror and the evanescence of the world of phantoms, with a power unequalled by any painter that ever lived. Perhaps, the finest of all his works is the *Sin and Death*; and in this he has done that which, had he not done it, we might have thought impossible—he has embodied Milton's words:

"What seemed his head, the likeness of a kingly crown had on."

"In the *Satan* of Sir Thomas Lawrence, (the worst portrait he ever painted,) all is so material as to be wholly unnatural with reference to the subject. The body and limbs of the fiend are as solid as the shaft of the spear he holds; and the helmet, sword, and shield, seem borrowed from the property-room of a theatre. In the *Sin and Death* of Fuseli there are a ponderous key (the key of the gates of Hell,) and a chain. But they are forged by no earthly smith, and are not otherwise thought of by the spectator than as parts of a terrible vision.

"Fuseli was profoundly acquainted with all in nature that could help his conceptions of the visionary. He was a perfect master of *chiaro-scuro* and of the evanescence of colour; and he possessed such a competent knowledge of the anatomical structure of the human figure, as to be able to give ideal probability to attitudes in which it was impossible he could be helped by living models. Hence, he could also give to his ghosts that general and uncertain look that belongs to shadowy beings, without the omission of the leading characteristics of form; and his breadth, to borrow an expression of his own, is never 'emptiness.' Fuseli, therefore, was as much indebted to the knowledge of nature for his power in the visionary as to his imagination; and it was in a great measure the want of such knowledge that rendered the art of Blake abortive. Everybody can laugh at the extravagance that so often disfigures the works of Fuseli. But it would require eloqence equal to his own to do justice to his finest things; and in spite of his great faults, I cannot but look on him as a great genius, a genius of whom the age in which he lived was unworthy."—*Leslie's Handbook*, p. 138.

Opie, after he came to London, soon enlarged his perceptions from seeing the works of Fuseli, the evanescent negative colour of whose best pictures he greatly admired; and the influence of Fuseli told on his later practice.

THE HERONS IN RAPHAEL'S CARTOON.

Fuseli objects to the introduction of the herons in "The Miraculous Draught of Fishes"; they were painted by Giovanni d'Udine. "But," says Leslie, "when it is remembered that these birds were and are held sacred in the East, being considered emblematic of piety, their presence is certainly not out of place, and their tameness in approaching so close to the figures is accounted for. One of them elevates its head in the act of drinking, an action noticed by Bunyan in domestic fowls as expressive of giving thanks to Heaven; and it may not, perhaps, be an over-refinement to suppose that such a thought occurred also to Raphael."

Fuseli said of the *Aurora* of Guido, that the goddess "deserves to precede Hours less clumsy."

CHARACTER OF FUSELI BY LAVATER.

This early and attached friend of Fuseli has left the following character of him—personal and mental, in which physiognomy, as might be expected, takes the lead. "The curve which describes the profile in whole is obviously one of the most remarkable: it indicates an energetic character which spurns at the idea of trammels. The forehead, by its contours and position, is more suited to the poet than the thinker. I perceive in it more force than gentleness—the fire of imagination rather than the coolness of reason. The nose seems to be the seat of an intrepid genius. The mouth promises a spirit of application and precision, and yet it costs the original the greatest effort to give the finishing touch to the smallest piece. Any one may see, without my telling it, that this character is not destitute of ambition, and that the sense of his own merit escapes him not. It may also be suspected that he is subject to impetuous emotions, but will any one say that he loves with tenderness—with warmth to excess ? Though capable of the greatest actions, to him the slightest complaisance is an effort. His imagination is ever aiming at the sublime and delighting itself with prodigies. Nature intended him for a great poet, a great painter, and a great orator—but, to borrow his own words, 'inexorable fate does not always proportion the will to our powers; it sometimes assigns a copious proportion of will to minds whose faculties are very contracted, and frequently associates with the greatest faculties a will feeble and impotent.'"

MICHAEL ANGELO.—BY FUSELI.

We have already described Fuseli's admiration of Michael Angelo—in his boyhood, and in later years, and as he lay in the Sistine Chapel studying its splendid ceiling. That he was no ignorant admirer of this great master is proved by the following tribute from his pen.

"Sublimity of conception, grandeur of form, and breadth of manner, are the elements of Michael Angelo's style. By these principles he selected or rejected the objects of imitation. As painter, as sculptor, as architect, he attempted—and, above any other man, succeeded—to unite magnificence of plan and endless variety of subordinate parts with the utmost simplicity and breadth. His line is uniformly grand; character and beauty were admitted only so far as they could be made subservient to grandeur; the child, the female, meanness, deformity, were by him indiscriminately stamped with grandeur. A beggar rose from his hand the patriarch of poverty; the hump of his dwarf is impressed with dignity; his women are moulds of generation; his infants teem with the man; his men are a race of giants. This is the "Terribil via" hinted at by Agostino Caracci, though perhaps as little understood by the Bolognese as by the blindest of his Tuscan adorers, with Vasari at their head. He is the inventor of epic painting in that sublime circle of the Sistine Chapel which exhibits the origin, progress, and final dispensation of Theocracy. He has personified motion in the groups of the Cartoon of Pisa; embodied sentiment in the monuments of St. Lorenzo; unravelled the features of meditation in the prophets and sybils of the Chapel of Sixtus; and in the Last Judgment, with every attitude that 'varies the human body, traced the master trait of every passion that sways the human heart. Though as sculptor he expresses the character of flesh more perfectly than all who came before or after him, yet he never submitted to copy an individual, Julio the Second only excepted, and in him he represented the reigning passion rather than the man. In painting, he contented himself with negative colour, and as the painter of mankind, rejected all meretricious ornament. The fabric of St. Peter, scattered into infinity of jarring parts by Bramante and his successors, he concentrated, suspended the cupola, and to the most complex, gave the air of the most simple of edifices."

RAPHAEL—BY FUSELI.

The inspiration of Michael Angelo, (says Fuseli,) was followed by the milder genius of Raphael—the father of dramatic painting—the painter of humanity: less elevated, less vigorous, but more insinuating; more pressing on our hearts; the warm master of our sympathies. What effort of human connexion—what feature of the mind, from the gentlest emotion to the most fervid burst of passion, has been left unobserved—has not received a characteristic stamp from that examiner of men? Michael Angelo came to nature—nature came to Raphael—he transmitted her features like a lucid glass—unstained, unmodified. We stand with awe before Michael Angelo, and tremble at the height to which he elevates us. We embrace Raphael and follow him wherever he leads us. Perfect human beauty he has not represented. No face of Raphael's is perfectly beautiful—no figure of his, in the abstract, possesses the proportions which could raise it to a standard of imitation: form to him was only a vehicle of character or pathos; and to those he adapted it, in a mode and with a truth that leave all attempts at emendation hopeless. His invention connects the utmost stretch of possibility with the most plausible degree of probability, in a way that equally surprises our fancy, persuades our judgment, and affects our heart. His composition always hastens to the most necessary point as its centre, and from that disseminates—to that leads back as rays all secondary ones. Group, form, and contrast are subordinate to the event, and common-place is ever excluded. The line of Raphael has been excelled in correctness, elegance, and energy; his colour far surpassed in tone, in truth, and harmony; his masses, in roundness, and his chiaro-scuro in effect; but, considered as instruments of pathos, they have never been equalled; and in composition, invention, expression, and the power of telling a story, he has never been approached.

FUSELI'S ERUDITION.

It pleased Fuseli, when in his fullest vein of conceit, to annoy certain of his companions with the display of his classic lore. He sometimes composed Greek verses in the emergency of the moment, and affected to forget the name of the author. He once repeated half a dozen sonorous and well-sounding lines to Porson, and said, "With all your learning, now you cannot tell me who wrote that." The Professor, "much renowned for Greek," confessed his ignorance, and said "I don't know him." "How the devil could you know him?" chuckled Fuseli—"I made them this moment." When thwarted in the Academy, and that was not seldom, his wrath aired itself in a polyglot. "It is a pleasant thing and advantageous," said the painter, on one of these occasions, "to be learned. I can speak Greek, Latin, French, English, German, Danish, Dutch, and Spanish, and so let my folly or my fury get vent through eight different avenues."

SALVATOR ROSA.—BY FUSELI.

Salvator had presumed to lift his hand against Michael Angelo, the throned god of Fuseli's idolatry, and here is his fierce resentment:

"The wildness of Salvator Rosa opposes a powerful contrast to the classic regularity of Poussin. Terrific and grand in his conceptions of inanimate nature, he was reduced to attempts at hiding by boldness of hand his inability of exhibiting her impassioned, or in the dignity of character: his line is vulgar; his magic visions, less founded on the principles of terror than on mythologic trash and caprice, are to the probable combinations of nature what the paroxysms of a fever are to the flights of a vigorous fancy. Though so much extolled, and so ambitiously imitated, his banditti are a medley made up of starveling models, shreds and bits of armour from his lumber-room brushed into notice by a daring pencil. Salvator was a satirist and a critic, but the rod which he had the insolence to lift against the nudities of Michael Angelo, and the anachronism of Raphael, would have been better employed in chastising his own misconceptions."

FUSELI AND BRITISH ARTISTS.

Fuseli, in his estimate of British art, treats its professors with scant justice, and this in not a few cases. To the majority he was unsparing of sarcastic and ironical commendation, and ludicrous comparison. One day, he called out, as the pictures were coming into the Academy for exhibition, "What pictures are come?" "Many—very many, sir," said the servant. "I know that, but whose are they?" "There are six landscapes, sir, by Mr. *Constable*." "Oh, don't name him, I know whom you mean. Bring me my great coat and umbrella, and I'll go and see them." This was his way of condemning their coldness.

When he edited Pilkington's *Dictionary of Painters*, in 1805, he introduced about 200 new artists as candidates for fame, but more in ridicule of their obscurity than in just estimate of their art. In some cases, his ill-treatment of other artists exposed him to ridicule. Thus, he affected not to know the Christian name of Gainsborough, though all the world knew it was Thomas; he was grossly unjust also to that elegant artist's merits; nay, such was his haughty bigotry that he classed the works of Hogarth among the daily vulgarities of common minds.

At a dinner-party, one of the company said: "Fuseli, there is a member of your Academy who has strange looks—and he chooses as strange subjects as you do." "Sir," exclaimed the Professor, "he paints nothing but thieves and murderers, and when he wants a model he looks in the glass."

During the delivery of one of Fuseli's lectures, wherein he calls landscape-painters the topographers of art, Beechey admonished Turner with his elbow of the severity of the sarcasm; presently, when Fuseli described the patrons of portrait-painting as men who would give a few guineas to have their own senseless heads painted, and then assume the air and use the language of patrons, Turner administered a similar hint to Beechey. When the lecture was over, Beechey walked up to Fuseli, and said, "How sharply you have been cutting up us poor labourers in portraiture!" "Not you, Sir William," exclaimed the Professor, "I only spoke of the fools who employ you!"

ALDERMAN BOYDELL.

This public-spirited man was a firm patron of Fuseli; and his influence on Painting and Engraving generally in this country can scarcely be overrated. It is said that "he contrived to employ every aspirant to distinction, in these arts, whose energies wanted encouragement." He was himself an artist, and his love of the profession he chose may be judged of by the fact that, at the age of twenty-one, he walked, from Stainton, in Shropshire, to London, against the wishes of his father, to put himself apprentice to an engraver. That by his own exertions he rose to fame and fortune is less his praise than that he very greatly assisted other artists in their rise to eminence; men, too, whom he helped to surpass himself in his own profession. The Shakspeare Gallery, though the greatest undertaking of Boydell, formed but a portion of his patronage of Art. This magnificent scheme was an additional means of employing the best painters of the British School in large and important works at a time when the Church refused to patronise Painting, and the titled and wealthy of the land, with the single exception of the King, encouraged portrait only. It did much also for Engraving; and among other admirable specimens of that Art, we owe to the Shakspeare Gallery Sharpe's transcendent work from West's *Lear*, a work showing that the power of a first-rate engraver, even of other men's designs, does not lie within the scope of mere talent; but that it is *genius*, and of a higher order than that displayed by many a painter, who looks upon engravers as artists much below him.

Boydell built, for the reception of his pictures, the rooms in Pall Mall, now belonging to the British Institution, and employed the greatest sculptor living, (Banks,) to decorate the front. It was his intention to bequeath the building and its contents to the nation. But the outbreak of the French Revolution, by stopping entirely the sale of his prints on the Continent, where it had been extensive, and the war that followed, diminishing the demand for them at home, his means were so crippled, that he was unable to fulfil his patriotic wish.—*Abridged from Leslie's Handbook for Young Painters.*

PRESENTATION OF A CUP TO FUSELI.

Before the Academy closed, in 1807, a little matter occurred quite characteristic of the English students. Two or three of the body who wished to ingratiate themselves with the Keeper, Fuseli, proposed to present him with a vase. A subscription was opened, and a committee, without either plan or principle, formed itself, of which Wilkie and Haydon were members. They were perfectly ignorant of such matters, and after a good deal of discussion a plan was laid before the students. It was received with shouts of laughter and derision! After a good deal of *altogethery* speaking and discussion, and when everything was going against the proposition, Haydon made a telling speech, enlarging greatly upon the estimable qualities of Keeper Fuseli; and finally proposing that the self-elected committee should be dissolved and another formed. This was seconded by Wilkie, and carried unanimously. Haydon, Wilkie, and Denman, (a pupil of Flaxman,) hired a room at the Garrick's Head, opposite Covent Garden Theatre, for their future meetings. Wilkie was voted to the chair; a Scotchman, a friend of his, was made secretary; and Haydon treasurer. They raised fifty guineas, at 10s. 6d. each; and Haydon, remembering that Coutts' were Fuseli's bankers, called, and asked Sir Edward Antrobus, if he would allow the money to be paid in on account of the committee, explaining the object they had in view. Sir Edward drily replied: "Why, sir, we don't usually open an account with so small a sum!" "Small!" thought Haydon, "why there's no end to it!" However, he promised to take care of the money, and did so. Wilkie, Flaxman, and Haydon, were now deputed to arrange with a silversmith, and Rundell and Bridge agreed to execute a vase for fifty guineas, which should be worthy of Fuseli's acceptance.

The Committee was composed of a great many students, who, while regulating the business, had many pleasant meetings, so that they hoped it would not be a rapid performance on the part of Rundell and Bridge. Wilkie, at that time, was a capital fellow: he had a little kit, on which he played Scotch airs with a gusto that a Scotchman only is capable of.

They got so fond of these committee-meetings, that Fuseli

grew fidgetty, and at last roared out : " Be Gode ye are like de Spaniards; all ceremony and noting done!" Haydon reported that the Keeper was getting sore, and so they agreed to settle at the next committee-meeting what the inscription should be. Among the students was a Scotch ornamental painter, called Callender, very like Wilkie in face and figure. Who he was nobody knew, but being an Edinburgh man— where they never snuff candles at a meeting without addressing the chair, and appointing a sub-committee to take the propriety of the act into consideration—he was thoroughly versed in all the duties of chairman, deputy, secretary, and vice. The students swore that he was Wilkie's brother—he was so like him.

They soon settled the inscription; the vase was sent home, and the day approached upon which it was to be presented. Wilkie, however, was obliged to go to Scotland, and Haydon was chosen to present the gift in his place. The day came : the night before, Haydon rehearsed to himself the speech—action and expression. He imagined he was in Fuseli's presence; he took up a Latin dictionary for the cup, and concluded his speech exactly as he placed the supposed cup upon the table before Fuseli. Haydon's account of his rehearsing the speech before a broken looking-glass—for the effect—is a characteristic instance of his complacency and conceit.

The committee met in Fuseli's middle chamber, and then repaired to his gallery, with Haydon at their head. Fuseli came out, bowed, and looked agitated. The vase was on the table in front : Haydon advanced to the table, and said : "Mr. Fuseli—sir," in such a tremendously loud and decided tone that they all started, but he quickly modulated his voice, and as he concluded, placed the vase before the Keeper. Fuseli made a very neat reply, and Flaxman a long speech, which bored everybody. They then all retired to a cold collation, drank Fuseli's health with three times three, and separated ; the committee privately inquiring of each other whether all the business was concluded, or rather, if no possible affair could be invented for another committee-supper. Flaxman said, as they came down to lunch, "The students hit upon the right man in young Haydon," and afterwards complimented him on his able speech. "Really," says Haydon, " I have often thought that this little affair, of which I was the head and front, *first sowed the seeds of enmity against me* in the minds of many of the Academicians."

Hoppner was in a fury, and on the first opportunity, gave Wilkie a tremendous *rowing*, called the students a set of impudent puppies, and declared that had he been in the Council, he would have turned them all into the streets! While they were discussing the thing in its early stages, the Council used to listen at the door, and say, "Now they are talking about it; shall we do anything?" Northcote was on the Council, and told this to Haydon.

Within a very short time, so jealous were the Council and the general meeting of this deserved honour to Fuseli, that they actually passed a law, forbidding the students ever again to exercise their judgment in such matters, as it belonged to the Academicians, and to the Academicians alone, to decide on the merits of their officers. As if, in such a case, the students, the persons really benefited by the Keeper, were not the best judges whether they were benefited or not! The malignant feeling that this simple mark of respect roused among Fuseli's brother Academicians excited every one's contempt.

However, Haydon (from whose *Autobiography* we abridge the above,) seems to rejoice in his martyrdom : he says— "They never forgave me, and I never respected them afterwards."

FUSELI AND LAWRENCE.

The fierceness of the Keeper was a revengeful overmatch for the bland President. Fuseli had sketched a picture of Prospero and Miranda from the *Tempest*, and was considering of what dimensions he should make the finished painting, when he was told that Lawrence had sent in for exhibition a picture on the same subject and with the same figures. His wrath knew no bounds. "This comes," he cried, "of my simplicity in showing my sketches—never mind—I'll teach the face-painter to meddle with my Prospero and Miranda." He had no canvas prepared—he took a finished picture, and over the old performance dashed in hastily, in one laborious day, a wondrous scene from the Tempest—hung it in the Exhibition right opposite that of Lawrence, and called it "a sketch for a large picture." Sir Thomas said little, but thought much—he never afterwards exhibited a poetic subject.

One evening, in company, when Sir Thomas Lawrence was discoursing on "the historic grandeur" of Sir Joshua, and contrasting him with Titian and with Raphael, Fuseli fired up: "Blastation! you will drive me mad—Reynolds and Raphael!—a dwarf and a giant!—why will you waste all your fine words!" He rose and left the room, muttering something about a tempest in a pint-pot. Lawrence followed, soothed him, and brought him back.

Yet, these two eminent men loved one another. They were often together; and Allan Cunningham heard Sir Thomas say, that he never had a dispute with Fuseli save once—and that was concerning their pictures of Satan. Indeed, the Keeper, both with tongue and pen, took pleasure in pointing out the excellencies of his friend, nor was he blind to his defects. "This young man," thus he wrote in one of his early criticisms, "would do well to look at nature again; his flesh is too glassy." Lawrence followed the advice. When he had risen into reputation and had money at command, he said, laying his hand upon one of Fuseli's sketches, "Make me a painting of this fine subject, and I will give you the price of one of my best paintings." "The fit is off me for this subject," said Fuseli; "I wish you would choose some other."

Sir Thomas Lawrence was at Putney Hill, and cheered the last moments of Fuseli, who seemed uneasy and restless when Lawrence was away from his side.

"SOMETHING NEW."

One day, Fuseli's attention was attracted by a serpent with its tail in its mouth, a common-place emblem of eternity, which was carved upon an exhibited monument. "It won't do, I tell you," said Fuseli to the sculptor, "you must have something new." The *something new* startled a man whose imagination was none of the brightest, and he said, "How shall I find something new?" "Oh, nothing so easy," said Fuseli, "I'll help you to it. When I went away to Rome I left two fat men cutting fat bacon in St. Martin's-lane; in ten years time I returned, and found the two fat men cutting fat bacon still: twenty years more have passed, and there the two fat fellows cut the fat flitches the same as ever. Carve them! if they look not like an image of eternity I wot not what does."

This anecdote is related by Cunningham: it is told with a slight error, which does not, however, affect the point of its absurdity. The two fat men were the brothers who, for many years, kept the ham and beef shop in St. Martin's *court;* where rounds of beef were often cooked for the royal table, and conveyed to Carlton House in the days of the Regency.

CONSTABLE AND FUSELI.

Fuseli, speaking of this excellent landscape-painter, said: "I like de landscapes of Constable: he is always picturesque, of a fine colour, and de lights always in de right places; but he makes me call for my great-coat and umbrella."

WORKS OF FUSELI.

As Mr. Allan Cunningham was a contemporary of Fuseli, and was intimate with the Keeper, his estimate of his genius and works is entitled to special notice: it is written with great judgment, and in a spirit of fairness to the merits of Fuseli.*

Cunningham says: "Out of the seventy exhibited paintings on which he reposed his hope of fame, not one can be called common-place—they are all poetical in their nature, and as poetically treated. Some twenty of these alarm, startle, and displease; twenty more may come within the limits of common comprehension; the third twenty are such as few men could produce, and deserve a place in the noblest collections; while the remaining ten are equal in conception to anything that genius has hitherto produced, and second only in their execution to the true and recognised masterpieces of art. It cannot be denied, however, that a certain air of extravagance and a desire to stretch and strain is visible in most of his works.

"His sketches amount to 800.

"Those who are only acquainted with Fuseli through his paintings know little of the extent of his genius; they should see him in his designs and drawings, to feel his powers and know him rightly. The variety of those productions is truly wonderful, and their poetic feeling and historic grandeur more wonderful still. It is surprising too how little of that extravagance of posture and action which offends in his large paintings is present here; they are for the most part uncommonly simple and serene performances."

Sir Thomas Lawrence possessed a large number of Fuseli's serious drawings.

* Lives of British Artists, vol. ii.

The vigorous, energetic, and startling productions of Michael Angelo were closely akin to the fancy of Fuseli; Cunningham has well described its meteor-like shining upon impassable places, and its lighting the darkness of that region which forms the border-land between sense and absurdity. "Fuseli rejoiced in the muscular glory of his great master; for he thought there was no dignity without action—no sublimity without exaggeration. He lived in a species of intoxication—affected the dress and mimicked the manners of Michael—assumed the historic shoe, and would have preferred the sandal. In drawing and in sketching he tried to imitate his master's dashing energy and extravagance of breadth, which induced Piranesi to exclaim, 'Fuseli—this is not designing, but building a man!' When time had mellowed his taste, and in his turn he had become an instructor, he continued to prefer that broad nervous freedom of hand, and held in derision all that was cautiously neat or timidly graceful. He would seize the chalks of his students, stamp with his tiny foot till they stared or smiled—cry 'See!' and delineate a man in half the time and with a broader stroke than a tailor uses in chalking out a garment. Yet coarse as such hasty outlines seemed to the inexperienced, in the view of those acquainted with design, they contained the elements of the truest art, and presented such materials for study as none but the hand of a master could dash off.

"He loved to dream along the road, (when he was at Rome,)—to follow the phantasies of an unbridled imagination —to pen sarcastic remarks—sketch colossal groups, and would call out ever and anon, when some strange thought struck him, 'Michael Angelo!'"

He used to vow that there was more genius in the *claw* of one of Michael Angelo's eagles than in all the *heads* with which the Academy was swarming. Indeed, Michael Angelo was the alpha and omega—the beginning and the end—of Fuseli's existence.

SIR THOMAS LAWRENCE, P.R.A.

BIRTH AND PARENTAGE OF LAWRENCE.

Thomas Lawrence was born in the parish of St. Philip and St. Jacob (within a few doors of the birthplace of Robert Southey, the poet laureate,) in the city of Bristol, on the 4th of May, 1769, and was christened on the 6th of the same month. He was the youngest of a family of sixteen children; and at the time of his birth, his parents kept the White Lion inn at Bristol, and next the Black Bear inn at Devizes. Their son Thomas was a very beautiful boy, and had been remarkable from infancy for his sprightly and winning manners. His father taught him to recite poetry; and when the child was only four or five years old, it was usual for him to be presented by his parent to visitors to the inn: at four years old, he could recite the story of Joseph and his Brethren; at five, Pope's "Nymphs of Solyma;" and at seven, Milton's Lycidas.

LAWRENCE'S FIRST PORTRAIT.

The boy had already shown considerable aptitude for sketching, though only in his sixth year, when, late one evening, Mr. (afterwards Lord) Kenyon and his wife arrived at the Bear inn at Devizes. Mr. Lawrence soon entered their sitting-room, and proposed to show them his wonderful child. "The boy," he said, "is only five years old, but he can take your likenesses, or repeat to you any speech in Milton's Pandæmonium;" when in rushed the child; and as Mrs. Kenyon used to relate, her vexation was suddenly changed into admiration. He was riding on a stick, when Mrs. Kenyon, as soon as she could get him to halt, asked him if he could take the likeness of that gentleman, pointing to her husband. "That I can," said little Lawrence, "and very like too." A high chair was placed at the table, pencils and paper were brought, and the infant artist soon produced a striking likeness.

Mr. Kenyon now coaxed the child, and asked him if he could take the likeness of the lady. "Yes, that I can," was the reply, "if she will turn her side to me, for her face is not straight." This remark produced a laugh—it was correct enough. He then drew a profile portrait of Mrs. Kenyon, which was recognised by a friend twenty-five years after: the drawing was about five inches broad, and delicately shaded.

A Derbyshire Baronet, struck with the genius of the lad, offered to send him to Rome at the expense of 1,000*l*., but his father replied that "his son's talents required no cultivation."

YOUNG LAWRENCE SENT TO SCHOOL.

At the age of six, Lawrence was sent to school at the Fort, near Bristol, where he had for his school-fellow the Earl of Shaftesbury, who, in writing to Lawrence many years after, respecting his portrait, reminded the painter of the circumstance. The boy does not appear to have received any instruction after the age of eight, (except some lessons in Latin and French grammar,) his father being his only instructor in English, especially in recitation.

LAWRENCE'S EARLY DRAWINGS.

At the age of five years, little Lawrence made some drawings of *eyes*, which attracted the admiration of Mr. Prince Hoare. In after life, Lawrence became of all artists the most celebrated for his excellent painting of the eye. Even Fuseli, who could rarely abstain from depreciating his works, would exclaim with enthusiasm: "But, by G—t, he paints eyes better than Titian!" At the age of seven, too, the prodigy became so celebrated as to be taken and engraved by Sherwin.

We have mentioned the portraits of Mr. and Mrs. Kenyon. The first book upon art which he read was Rogers's *Lives of Foreign Painters*, lent him by a clergyman of the neighbourhood, who also left him a small legacy.

But young Lawrence's father was averse to his reading upon the subject of Painting; and would only permit his son to see the collections of pictures, mostly by old masters, at the show-houses in this part of the country. In this manner, at the age of eight, he was taken to Corsham House, Wilts, where he strayed away from his friends, and was found in one of the rooms, before a picture by Rubens, when upon being taken away, he murmured, with a sigh, "Ah! I shall never be able to paint like that!" At Wilton, the seat of the Earl of Pembroke, there is one of Lawrence's early paintings, a head of the full life size.

At the age of ten, he attempted original compositions of the highest class. He now painted "Christ reproving Peter for his denial;" also "Reuben's application to his father, that Benjamin might accompany him and his brethren into Egypt;" and "Haman and Mordecai;" all which he finished with great rapidity. Daines Barrington attests this success; adding that in about seven minutes, the boy scarcely ever failed in drawing a strong likeness of any person present: "he is likewise an excellent reader of blank verse, and both understands and feels the striking passages of Milton and Shakspeare."

LAWRENCE'S RECITATIONS.

These readings became so celebrated as to attract to the Bear Inn, at Devizes, crowds of fashionable visitors from Bath. Here Garrick, Foote, Wilkes, Sheridan, Burke, Johnson, Churchill, and others, were to be found, resting for the night, when Mr. Lawrence never failed to exhibit his precocious son. Mr. Hugh Boyd, one of the supposed authors of *Junius*, invited father and son to his house in town, and the latter, in his tenth year, exhibited great talent with his pencil. Mr. and Mrs. Garrick were among the visitors to the Bear Inn, in their way to Bath, when the father used to address the great actor with, "Tommy, Sir, has learned one or two speeches since you were here;" which he used to deliver before Garrick and his wife, in a summer-house of the inn garden; and at this time, the future walk in life of the boy was poised between the pencil and the stage: fortunately he chose the former.

At one of the lad's recitations, Sir William Chambers was present; and a Colonel Hamrich gave the child half-a-guinea for the beautiful handwriting in his copy-book.

As a boy, he is described as remarkably handsome: he wore his collar thrown back, and his hair, which was beautiful, was so redundant, that its rich dark curls obscured his face when he stooped to draw.

Mr. John Bernard, in his piquant *Retrospections of the Stage*, describes Lawrence at this period—"as a reader, little Tom was but little Tom,—a very clever child at nine years of age, whilst, as a sketcher of likenesses, he disclosed the future powers of the President.

"There was something about little Lawrence, however, which excited the surprise of the most casual observer. He was a perfect man in miniature. His confidence and self-possession smacked of one-and-twenty. Lawrence frequently brought his boy to the green-room, and we would set him on a table, and make him recite Hamlet's directions to the Players. On one occasion, Henderson was present, and expressed much gratification. The little fellow, in return for our civilities and flatteries, was desirous to take our likenesses, the first time we came to Devizes, and Edwin and myself afforded him an opportunity soon after, on one of our non-play-day's excursions. After dinner, Lawrence proposed giving us a reading as usual, but Tom reminded him of our promise. We preferred a specimen of his talents, as being most novel. The young artist collected his materials very quickly, and essayed my visage the first. In about ten minutes he produced a faithful delineation in crayon, which for many years I kept as a curiosity. He next attempted Edwin's, who, startled at the boy's ability, resolved (in his usual way) to perplex him. (This he did by changing the form of his features,—raising his brows, compressing his lips, and widening his mouth.) Tom no sooner perceived the change than he started in supreme wonder, attributing it to a defect in his own vision. The first outline was accordingly abandoned, and a second commenced. Tom was now more particular, and watched him narrowly, but Edwin, feature by feature, and muscle by muscle, so completely ran, what might be called the gamut of his countenance (as the various compartments of its harmony,) that the boy drew and rubbed it out, till his hand fell by his side, and he stood silently looking in Edwin's face, to discover, if possible, its true expression. Edwin could not long maintain his composure at his scrutiny, and revealed the hoax with a burst of merriment and mimic thunder.

"Little Tom could not take up Shakspeare or Milton, and read at random. He had been instructed in particular speeches, and to these he referred. There was one in Milton

(Satan's Address to the Sun) he had long wished to learn, but his father, from an apprehension that his mind was yet unequal to the grasp, had passed it over."

YOUNG LAWRENCE IN BATH.

In 1779, Mr. Lawrence and his family left Devizes, and in their road to Weymouth, visited Oxford, where the young artist took the likenesses of several eminent persons; and the leading men of the University subscribed for his portrait, painted by Mr. Prince Hoare, of Bath, and engraved by Sherwin.

In 1782, the Lawrences visited Bath; and it became the fashion to sit to young Lawrence for his oval crayon likenesses, at one guinea and a half. His portraits of Mrs. Siddons and Admiral Barrington were now engraved. From the collection of the Hon. Mr. Hamilton, on Lansdown Hill, young Lawrence copied, in crayons, the *Transfiguration* of Raphael; the *Aurora* of Guido; and other celebrated pictures, for which copies Lawrence's father refused 300 guineas. He usually finished three or four crayon paintings in a week, and received three guineas for half-lengths,—at that time, and for Bath, a very extraordinary sum.

Here he opened a public exhibition of his works, his father performing the office of exhibitor.

LAWRENCE AND THE STAGE.

As young Lawrence grew up, his Shaksperean readings, and his frequent visits to the theatre, imbued him with a strong dramatic propensity. About his sixteenth year, he had serious intentions of making the stage his profession. Mr. Bernard heard him recite Jaffier (in *Venice Preserved*), but could not perceive any evidence of talent he could balance against that which he was acknowledged to possess in his artistic pursuits. Mr. Bernard then disclosed what had passed to Lawrence's father, who, relying much upon his son's efforts for support, grew alarmed, and besought Mr. Bernard to use all his influence in dissuading young Lawrence from his design. This it was suggested would be best effected by a surprise. Mr. Bernard then arranged that Lawrence should come to his house next morning, with some friends, and Mr. Palmer, the Manager of the Bath Theatre.

"By half-past twelve the next day, all the parties were

assembled: old Lawrence, and his friends, in the back parlour; young Lawrence, Mr. Palmer, and myself, in the front. The Manager was no sooner introduced, than, with great adroitness, he desired a specimen of young Lawrence's abilities, and took his seat at one end of the room. I proposed the opening scene between Priuli and Jaffier. We accordingly commenced, I, Priuli; he, Jaffier: he went on very perfectly till, in the well-known passage, 'To me you owe her,' he came to the lines

> 'I brought her, gave her to your despairing arms:
> Indeed you thank'd me, but——'

here he stammered, and became stationary. I held the book, but would not assist him; and he recommenced and stopped, reiterated and hemmed, till his father, who had heard him with growing impatience, pushed open the door, and said, 'You play Jaffier, Tom! hang me if they would suffer you to murder a conspirator.' Mr. Palmer, taking young Lawrence by the hand, assured him, in the most friendly manner, that he did not possess those advantages which would render the stage a safe undertaking. The address did not produce an instantaneous effect; it was obvious that the young artist was of a reverse opinion. A conversation ensued, in which I, abusing the life of an actor, and other friends representing the prospects of a painter, young Lawrence at length became convinced, but remarked, with a sigh, 'That if he had gone on the stage, he might have assisted his family much sooner than by his present employment.' My reader can appreciate the affection of this sentiment, but I am unable to describe its delivery, or the effect it took upon every person present." The filial attachment of Lawrence to his family was, from his earliest days, proverbial.

Young Lawrence went away, renouncing his intentions and retaining his friends; and Mr. Bernard congratulating himself upon having so successfully lent his aid to check an early propensity, which, if encouraged, must have led to a renouncement of the pencil.

LAWRENCE RECEIVES THE SOCIETY OF ARTS PRIZE.

In the Session of 1785, the Society of Arts, in the Adelphi, voted young Lawrence their Medal, and the reward of Five Guineas for the most successful copy from the old masters—a crayon drawing of the *Transfiguration of Raphael*, being a copy of the copy which Lawrence had already made. He received "the greater silver palette, gilt," by special vote of the Committee; and had not the Drawing been made two years before, it would have received the Society's first reward.

Lawrence was now anxious to remove to London, and to become a student of the Royal Academy, to which his father assented. On their way to the metropolis, in 1787, they halted at Salisbury, where the young artist executed several crayon portraits.

Next year, 1787, he first exhibited at the Royal Academy, when he sent seven pictures—an extraordinary number for a painter eighteen years of age. In the following year, he sent six portraits; in 1789, thirteen; and in 1790, twelve pictures.

LAWRENCE'S EARLIEST OIL-PAINTINGS.

It was not until 1786, and when Lawrence had passed his seventeenth year, that he made any attempt at oil-painting. In that year he painted a whole-length figure of *Christ bearing the Cross;* the canvas was eight feet high.

Young Lawrence next painted his own portrait—a head, or three-quarters' size. "In this he evidently aimed at the style of Rembrandt, in his middle life, when he had neglected his higher finish, and before he had availed himself of the broad fulness of the brush, with deep contrasts, and sudden transitions, and with great breadth of shadow. To his study of Rembrandt in this portrait, he added a few signs of his imitating Sir Joshua Reynolds himself." *

In a letter to his mother, young Lawrence thus speaks of the above portrait: "To any but my own family I certainly should not say this; but, excepting Sir Joshua, for the painting of the head, I would risk my reputation with any painter in London." In the same letter, he says: "I have had the pleasure of seeing the great Mr. Barry; he did not recollect my name, nor did I wish to make myself known."

LAWRENCE SETTLES IN LONDON—INTRODUCTION TO REYNOLDS.

Upon reaching the metropolis, Mr. Lawrence hired for his son a suite of handsome first-floor apartments at No. 4, Leicester-square, then, and for many years after, occupied by

---

* Life and Correspondence of Sir Thomas Lawrence. By E. D. Williams, vol. i. p. 81.

a confectioner. They soon, however, removed to No. 41, Jermyn-street. They next applied for an interview with Sir Joshua Reynolds, which was willingly granted; and the father and the young artist proceeded to Leicester-square. Young Lawrence took with him his oil portrait of himself, with which Sir Joshua was evidently much struck. Then turning to the boy, he said gravely: "Stop, young man, I must have some talk with you. Well, I suppose, now, you think this is very fine, and the colouring very natural—hey! hey!" He next began to point out the imperfections in the painting, which he then took out of the room: he soon returned, said a few kind words, and in conclusion, "It is clear you have been looking at the old masters; but my advice to you is, to study nature; apply your talents to nature." Reynolds then dismissed him with marked kindness, assuring him that he would be welcome whenever he chose to call.

On September 13, 1787, Lawrence was admitted a student at the Royal Academy, and soon left all his competitors in the antique school far behind.

About this time, Mr. Lawrence, with two legacies, left to his son and his daughter Anne, purchased a museum then exhibiting in the Strand; and to its stuffed birds and other natural curiosities, were added his son's paintings; but this speculation did not pay its expenses, and the curiosities were soon sold for a trifle.

Sir Martin Archer Shee, writing in 1789, describes Lawrence as a very genteel, handsome young man, but rather effeminate in his manner. "A new paper that puffs him here very much says he is not yet one-and-twenty; and I am told by some of the students who knew him in Bath, that he is three-and-twenty. When I lodged in Aungier-street, I remember poor Stokes showing me a picture of Lady Leeson, painted by him in Bath, and at that time he was looked upon as an artist of great merit there. He is wonderfully laborious in his manner of painting, and has the most uncommon patience and perseverance. His price is ten guineas a head, and I hear he intends raising it. There is no young artist in London bids so fair to arrive at excellence, and I have no doubt he will, if he be careful, soon make a fortune."

In the previous year he exhibited the portrait of the Princess Amelia: he pleased the Princess by his pencil, and by his manners; and he won the regard of the foreign domestics by well-timed and gentle flirtations with the spouse of one of the court musicians. These latter were in their nature so harmless, as to amuse the lady herself, and excite merriment in the King and Queen, who occasionally rallied the young painter upon his gallantry.

HISTORICAL PIECE FROM HOMER.

In 1788, whilst Lawrence was in lodgings in Jermyn-street, (opposite St. James's Church,) he painted for Mr. Richard Payne Knight his historical piece of *Homer reciting his poem to the Greeks*. The figure in the foreground of the young victor in the foot-race was a study from the living model, Jackson, the pugilist. His figure was large, but he had a distinct and marked indication of every individual muscle; and his joints were small, and knit in the manner which is inimitably copied in many of the statues and paintings of Michael Angelo. Lawrence was much struck with this subject, which he painted with great care and study.

LAWRENCE'S EARLY PORTRAITS.

In 1790, Lawrence painted the celebrated beauty and actress, Miss Farren, afterwards Countess of Derby. She is represented in a white *satin* cloak and a muff: the success of the picture excited much jealousy, which led Mr. Burke to say to the painter, "Never mind what little critics say, for painters' proprieties are always best."

In 1792, Lawrence painted two elaborate whole-length portraits of George III. and Queen Charlotte, which Lord Macartney took out as presents to the Emperor of China. He next painted a whole-length portrait of the King, for which he received the then large sum of 300 guineas.

LAWRENCE ELECTED A.R.A.

In November, 1791, at the express desire of His Majesty and the Queen, young Lawrence, after one defeat, was admitted an Associate of the Royal Academy, by the suspension of a law against the admission of an Associate under the age of twenty-four. His reception, however, was much opposed by several Academicians, notwithstanding his election was supported by Sir Joshua Reynolds. It was virulently attacked by Peter Pindar.

DEATH OF SIR JOSHUA REYNOLDS.

In the funeral procession of Reynolds, on March 3, 1792, were Lawrence and twelve other Associates, among whom were Bourgeois, Bonomi, Stothard, Smirke, and Shee.

Lawrence, now only in his twenty-third year, was unanimously elected Sir Joshua's successor as Painter to the Dilettanti Society, who rescinded their law, "that no person was admissible as a member who had not crossed the Alps."

"SERJEANT-PAINTER TO THE KING."

Next, the King appointed Lawrence to succeed Sir Joshua as his painter in ordinary; though at this period were living, in high repute, West, Fuseli, Barry, Opie, and Northcote.

The slight shown to Hogarth's talents by George II. was enough to procure him favour in the household of his grandson, George III., soon after whose accession Hogarth was appointed Serjeant-Painter to all his Majesty's works, which his enemies jeeringly interpreted as chief "panel-painter." The office was held by Sir James Thornhill in the reign of George I., who knighted him in 1720.

To Hogarth succeeded Allan Ramsay, and next Sir Joshua Reynolds, upon whose decease Mr. Lawrence succeeded as state-painter, as the office was now designated. It is hardly necessary to remind the reader that Sir Joshua was succeeded in the chair of the Royal Academy by Benjamin West, whose name stood high as a painter of history, and who, with the personal favour of King George III. enjoyed the nominal rank of historical painter to his Majesty, and a salary or allowance of 1,000*l.* per annum from the privy purse, in that capacity. The office of Serjeant-Painter, or painter in ordinary, was, however, the only recognised appointment in the royal household, connected with the arts.

LAWRENCE IN OLD BOND STREET.—ELECTED R.A.

With increase of honour, the painter grew more expensive in his dress and style of living: he took handsome apartments at No. 24, Old Bond-street, made his friend Farington his secretary, and allowed 20*l.* per week for domestic outlay. Yet, thus early he was indebted a large sum of money which

Mr. Angerstein had advanced him. "I began life wrongly," said Lawrence, in after years. "I spent more money than I earned, and involved myself in debt, for which I have been paying heavy interest." His usual price at this period for a full-length portrait, was one hundred guineas; for a half length fifty; and for the head size twenty-five. The success of Lawrence in portrait-painting led to his being attacked by unprincipled critics, as well as by envious artists. It was whispered that he could only copy, not create. This taunt stung him so sharply that he resolved to attempt history; and, while he was hesitating as to subjects, the Royal Academy, December 4, 1795, admitted him a member. This brought a gay crowd of sitters—he recollected that he was labouring on borrowed money—and he returned to portraiture. He was now living at No. 29, Old Bond-street.

To this year's Exhibition he sent the portrait of Cowper, the poet, with whom there grew up a correspondence and intimacy: the poet invited the painter to Weston; and his last words were, "When will you give me a drawing of the old oak?"

FAILURE OF A PORTRAIT.

Mr. Hayes, the surgeon, of Charlotte-street, Fitzroy-square, used to relate the following occurrence in Lawrence's *atelier* when he resided in Old Bond-street. It happened that he had painted the portrait of a Mr. Sheepshanks, a friend of Mr. Hayes, who, when the picture was finished, brought with him to the artist's room a friend from the town where Mr. Sheepshanks resided, and who was well acquainted with him. Now, the visitor was a rough old squire, a perfect Tony Lumpkin, rich, and master over all things in his neighbourhood except himself. Mr. Hayes introduced him among the portraits, and anticipated his instant recognition of the likeness of his country friend and neighbour, Mr. Sheepshanks.

The squire, however, gaped and gazed, without the slightest emotion; and at last, as if tired, and wishing to depart, he begged that the portrait of his friend might be shown to him at once.

At this, Mr. Hayes, who was somewhat peppery, fired up. "Zounds," cried the astonished surgeon, "that is it which you have been looking at these five minutes!"

"That he! hang me if it is a bit like un—no more like un than it's like our parson."

In vain did Hayes try to persuade the country gentleman that it was an admirable painting and a correct likeness. His friend as sturdily maintained that he "was not to be done arter that fashion—that the portrait wasn't a bit like un, and he wouldn't give a guinea for a score of such pictures."

With coarseness and stupidity on the one side, and anger on the other, a strange scene ensued:

> So high at last the contest rose,
> From words they next proceed to blows,
> When luckily came by a third.

This third was the astonished Mr. Lawrence, who had been below stairs, and knew nothing of the dispute and *fracas;* but hearing a scuffle in his painting-room, he ran up stairs, and to his surprise, saw the two infuriated combatants, and the portrait, the innocent cause of the battle, knocked off the easel upon the floor.

Having parted "the friends," Lawrence learnt the source of their quarrel. He bore the explanation with great equanimity, and reconciled the parties; nor would he suffer them to leave till they shook hands, embraced, and, probably, hated each other most cordially ever after.

THE TWO SATANS.

In 1794, there had been for some time much gossip in the studios about Lawrence's engagement upon a grand poetic work, which his private friends were admitted to see, during its progress. They fondly talked of the grandeur of the outlines, the magnificent colouring, and sublime sentiment of the picture till their eulogy knew no bounds. The secret of the subject, was, however, preserved intact till the Exhibition of 1797, when the Catalogue revealed: "170. *Satan calling his Legions.* T. Lawrence, R.A." This was high game for Anthony Pasquin, and at it he flew, and applied to the painter's rash attempt in this path of sublimity, Pope's stinging line

> "For fools rush in where angels fear to tread."

"The picture, (says Pasquin) is a *mélange* made up of the worst parts of the divine Buonarotti and the extravagant Goltzius. The figure of Satan is colossal and very ill-drawn: the body is so disproportioned to the extremities, that it appears all legs and arms, and might at a distance be mistaken for a sign of the spread eagle. The colouring has as little analogy to truth as the contour, for it is so ordered, that it conveys an idea of a mad German sugar-baker dancing naked in a conflagration of his own treacle; but the liberties taken with his infernal Majesty are so numerous, so various, and so insulting, that we are amazed that the ecclesiastical orders do not interfere in behalf of an old friend."

Such was the scurrilous stuff of the *Critical Guide* of 1797. But there was another who considered he had a greater right to be heard, and, obeying the epigraph,

"Awake, arise, or be for ever fallen,"

up rose Fuseli: he complained that Lawrence had stolen his Devil from him; and his criticism was, that the figure was the lubber fiend, and not the master fiend of Milton; in short, a fine piece of colour, and a failure. But Fuseli thought no one had the right or power to paint from our great poets but himself.

Lawrence, however, explained the *coincidence* to Allan Cunningham, who thus relates the story in his Life of Sir Thomas:

"Fuseli, sir," these were his words, "was the most satirical of human beings; he had also the greatest genius for art of any man I ever knew. His mind was so essentially poetic, that he was incapable of succeeding in any ordinary object. That figure of Satan, now before you, occasioned the only interruption which our friendship, of many years' standing, ever experienced. He was, you know, a great admirer of Milton, from whom he had many sketches. When he first saw my Satan, he was nettled, and said, 'You borrowed the idea from me.'—'In truth, I did take the idea from you,' I said; 'but it was from your person, not from your paintings. When we were together at Stackpole Court, in Pembrokeshire, you may remember how you stood on yon high rock which overlooks the bay of Bristol, and gazed down upon the sea, which rolls so magnificently below. You were in raptures; and while you were crying "Grand! Grand! Jesu Christ, how grand! how terrific," you put yourself in a wild posture; I thought on the devil looking into the abyss, and took a slight sketch of you at the moment: here it is. My Satan's posture now, was yours then.'"

Lawrence's success in the historic style fell short of his portraiture. Nevertheless. this picture fulfilled its object—to show his brethren in art that he was not a mere face-painter. "The Satan," he said, "answered my secret motives in attempting it: my success in portraits will no longer be thought accident or fortune; and if I have trod the second path with honour, it is because my limbs are strong. My claims are acknowledged by the circle of taste, and are undisputed by competitors and rivals."

DEATH OF LAWRENCE'S PARENTS.

In 1797, his father and mother were living with him in Greek-street;* and from his leaving Bath he had fulfilled towards them all the duties of an affectionate and liberal son.

In May of the above year, his mother expired in his house. He writes to Miss Lee: "I have mentioned other griefs in order to turn my thoughts from that pale Virtue, whose fading image I now contemplate with firmness. I kiss it, and not a tear falls on the cold cheek. You can have no notion of the grand severity it has assumed. I think, I cannot but persuade myself, since the fatal stroke, it seems as if the soul, at the moment of departure, darted its purest emanations into the features, as traces of its happier state. Have you seen death often? It cannot be a common effect.

* * * *

But half an hour since, I had the dear hand in mine, and the fingers seemed unwilling to part with me. Farewell!"

In the succeeding October he lost his father, who, for the improvement of his health, had removed to Rugby. Lawrence was engaged with a sitter in Piccadilly when a letter reached him, saying that his father was dying. He hurried into the country, but came too late. He writes to Miss Lee: "The cause of my silence is a terrible one,—my father's death. He died before I could reach him; but he died full of affection to us, of firm faith and fortitude, and without a groan."

Lawrence had written four months previously of his father: "to his children, whatever difference of character or disposition there may have been, his essentially worthy nature and general love for them make him too dear an object of regard, not to form the greatest portion of their solicitude. To be the entire happiness of his children is perhaps the lot of no parent."

* Lawrence had now removed to No. 57, Greek-street, Soho, where he let apartments to his young friend, Westall, who was then at work for Alderman Boydell.

PORTRAITS OF JOHN KEMBLE.

In 1798, Lawrence painted *Coriolanus at the Hearth of Aufidius*, a work uniting the imaginative with the reality of portrait; or, as the painter called it, "*a half-history portrait.*" He found the noble Roman in the looks and form of John Kemble: the figure and posture are fine, and the colouring admirable. But the portrait lacks the heroic spirit of the proud soldier.

Rolla, *Cato* and *Hamlet* followed the character portrait of *Coriolanus*. The Rolla is splendidly painted, but the figure of the chief is gigantic; the child was painted from one of Sheridan's offspring. The picture is very melodramatic; but the play of *Pizarro* ranks scarcely above fustian.

The *Cato*, in the painter's words, is "a generalised portrait of Kemble, or rather Cato meditating on the Phædo of Plato, for which I take Kemble as my model. The scene in the fourth act, where the body of the son is brought in, is nobly and powerfully affecting. Perhaps it will be the last picture I shall paint with Kemble for my subject, and I know it will be my best." The painter was in error twofold: it was not his last picture of Kemble, nor is it one of his finest works: Kemble's look is not "native and to the manner," but is too much acting.

Lawrence, however, retrieved his fame in this class of subject in the "*Hamlet* apostrophizing the skull," in the churchyard scene: it is a full-length, life size: it was painted in 1801, and was presented to the National Gallery, by William IV. in 1836. Cunningham justly describes it as a work of the highest kind,—sad, thoughtful, melancholy; with looks conversing with death and the grave; a perfect image of the great dramatist. This picture Lawrence himself placed above all his works, except the Satan; but it far surpasses the Satan in propriety of action, accuracy of expression, and grandeur of colouring. The light touches the face and bosom, and falls on the human skull on which he is musing. It is one of the noblest paintings of the modern school.

VERSES BY LAWRENCE.

Lawrence wrote verses at a very early age. The indulgence of this harmless *penchant* would, probably, have been left to oblivion, had not his future fame rendered of interest nearly every incident of his early life. How many of us write rhymes which do not survive our teens!

The verses with which the painter garnished his letters were "mostly in the despairing Thyrsis strain;" but they were cold and lacked passion. In a lighter style he was more successful, as in the following :—

"THOUGHTS ON BEING ALONE AFTER DINNER.

"How shall I, friend, employ my time,
 Alone, no book of prose or rhyme,
  Or pencil to amuse me;
 No pen or paper to be found,
 Nor friend to push the bottle round,
  Or for its stay abuse me?

"The servants come and find me here,
 And stare upon me like the deer
  On Selkirk in Fernandez;
 And, quite as tame, they wipe the chairs,
 And scrub, and hum their favourite airs,
  And ask what my command is.

"I wish one knew the way to change
 Customs so barbarous and strange,
  So savage and inhuman;
 I wish the sex were kinder grown,
 And when they find a man alone,
  Would treat him like a woman.

"Well, here's to her, who, far away,
 Cares not that I am grave or gay;
  So now no more I'll drink,
 But fold my arms and meditate,
 And clap my feet upon the grate,
  And on grave matters think.

"'Tis, let me see, full sixteen years,
 And wondrous short the time appears,
  Since, with inquiry warm,
 With beauty's novel power amazed,
 I follow'd, midst the crowd, and gazed
  On Siddons' beauteous form.

"Up Bath's fatiguing streets I ran,
 Just half pretending to be man,
  And fearful to intrude;
 Busied I looked on some employ,
 Or limp'd to see some other boy,
  Lest she should think me rude.

"The sun was bright, and on her face,
 As proud to show the stranger grace,
  Shone with its purest rays;
 And through the folds that veil'd her form,
 Motion display'd its happiest charm,
  To catch the admiring gaze.

> " The smiling lustre of her eyes,
>   That triumph'd in our wild surprise,
>   Well I remember still :
>   They spoke of joy to yield delight,
>   And plainly said, if I'm the sight,
>   Good people, take your fill.
>
> " And can it be that 'neath this roof,
>   Whilst I sit patiently aloof,
>   This watching form can be ?
>   Quick let me fly—avaunt my fears !
>   'Tis but a door and sixteen years
>   Divide this fair and me.
>
> " Alas ! that beauty should grow old
>   Alas ! that passion should be cold !
>   Alas ! that rhymes should fail !
>   That no due coffee-bell should ring,
>   *   *   *   *
>   To close my mournful tale.
>
> " Ye youths debarr'd your fair one's eye,
>   Ye that for love to memory fly,
>   Attend this moral rhyme,
>   List to the pensive lay it pours,
>   The Devil take your doors and hours,
>   Your carpenters and time."

The following lines are in a graver strain :—

> " Unjust one ! dost thou scorn the wand'ring wretch,
> Forc'd on the pavement her cold limbs to stretch ?
> From generous weakness first her errors flow'd,
> Some sacrifice the direful arm bestow'd ;
> The hardness of her sex her sorrow spurn'd,
> And but from want to wickedness she turn'd.
> And dost thou triumph no such crimes are thine,
> No stain in thee pollutes thy boasted line ?
> That lost one at the throne of God shall rise,
> And supplicate thy entrance to the skies ;
> Give to thy youthful vanity the blame,
> Take from the worst of crimes its hateful name,
> And ask of Heav'n in mercy to forget
> The mean ambition of the cold coquette."

LAWRENCE SUPPOSED IN LOVE.

One of Lawrence's early friends was Mrs. Siddons, the great actress. She had sat to him when he was young, in the character of Zara, and afterwards in that of Aspasia. She had two lovely daughters, to *both* of whom Lawrence, as the story has it, when they grew up, was very attentive in public, and overflowing with love in private. To one, however, he was warmer in his vows and protestations than to the other ;

and the favoured lady believed him sincere. "He had no sooner," says Cunningham, "gained her affections, than, without cold words, altered looks, or any dispute whatever, he turned from her to her sister, and had the audacity to make love and offer her marriage in the same breath. This opened the eyes of both; but it was too late for one: the perfidious lover was dismissed; but the young lady was so affected that she drooped and died."

Such was the story; but as Lawrence continued after on good terms with Mrs. Siddons and her family, his apologists generally silenced the public rumour and the private scandal; though this was not accomplished until after much mischief and suffering.

Mr. Cunningham was assured by one who knew both Lawrence and Mrs. Siddons well, that the young lady died much in the usual way—of disease and a doctor.

The tale of common rumour had, however, another phase; adding that as the anniversary of the death of Miss Siddons came round, Lawrence gave way to fits of melancholy; that he wore mourning for her sake, while he lived; and sealed his letters with black wax. This is untrue; at least we may infer it to be so.

The egregious public, in this case, seem to have followed the advice of the scandal-monger in one of Douglas Jerrold's piquant comedies,—"when you do not know anything, think the worst."

PORTRAIT OF CURRAN.

In 1800, Lawrence sent to the Exhibition a *portrait of Mr. Curran*, which was considered a failure. Shortly after, the painter dined casually with Mr. Curran, and saw him in all his glory of animation; when Lawrence could not help exclaiming to him, "I have not painted your portrait at all,—I never saw your proper character before. Come to-morrow, and give me another sitting." Mr. Curran accordingly gave the painter one sitting, in which he finished the most extraordinary likeness of the most extraordinary face within the memory of man: the fire of the eye is marvellous.

BUST OF MR. W. LOCK.

In 1801, Lawrence modeled with great success his friend, Mr. W. Lock, of Norbury Park. The clay was put together on a modeling board, and conveyed to Norbury, whither

Lawrence went on a visit, during which he took sittings of Mr. Lock, and produced an admirable bust in the antique style: the hair was singularly fine, in flowing tresses, and the character of the aged countenance studied with great accuracy. This was Lawrence's first and probably his last essay in modeling: several casts were made of the bust.

LAWRENCE AND THE PRINCESS OF WALES.

In 1802, the Princess and Princess Charlotte of Wales, then living at Montague House, Blackheath, sat to Lawrence for their portraits, which led to an intimacy between the Princess and the painter. This led to a scandalous report, attributing his frequent visits to improper motives; and to such a degree had this slanderous annoyance increased, that in 1806, when "the Delicate Investigation" into the conduct of the Princess was pending, Lawrence offered himself to the scrutiny of the Commissioners (Lords Grenville, Spencer, Erskine, and Ellenborough), who, though acquitting the Princess of criminality, were of opinion that her manners and conduct must be considered as unbecoming levity. As this charge alluded to the Princess' conduct towards Mr. Lawrence and another gentleman, upon this Lawrence ill-advisedly made an affidavit at Hatton Garden police-office, avowing that he slept several nights at Montague House in 1801, but that he never was left alone with her Royal Highness, but in the drawing-room; "and never with the door locked, bolted, or fastened" but that any person outside could open it.

The Painter's affidavit was transmitted to the King, with the defence of the Princess, explaining that Mr. Lawrence was, in 1800 or 1801, painting a large picture of her Royal Highness and her Daughter, at Montague House, and that, at his own request, he remained some few nights in the house, so as to begin painting early in the morning. A similar request for a like occasion had been made by Sir William Beechey, and Mr. Lawrence had occupied the same apartment. Lawrence did not dine with the Princess; but occasionally he read in the evening before her Royal Highness and her suite, passages from Shakspeare's plays; and sometimes he played at chess with the Princess.

One of the ladies mentioned by the Princess, in a private letter, alluded, in affectionate terms, to the great danger Mr.

Lawrence was in, of "losing his head." The painter's servant was examined; and shortly after, Lord Eldon, in conversation with Mr. Lawrence, said to him: "Sir, you are a very fortunate man indeed." "Why so, my Lord?" "Because you have the most faithful, clever, and prudent servant, who has served you cunningly at the hour of need."

LAWRENCE AND HARLOW.

George Henry Harlow, whom Lawrence characterised as "the most promising of all our painters," was born in London in 1787; showed early some talent for drawing; and when about sixteen, was placed with De Cort, the Flemish landscape-painter: he left him for Mr. Drummond, R.A., the portrait-painter, with whom he remained about twelve months, when he grew desirous of another instructor. By the recommendation of the beautiful Duchess of Devonshire, he was placed under the care of Lawrence, in Greek-street. He was to pay one hundred guineas yearly as a pupil; that is to say, "for permission to have access to Lawrence's house at nine o'clock in the morning, with leave to copy his pictures till four o'clock in the afternoon, but *to receive no instruction of any kind.*" At the expiration, however, of a year and a half, the master and the pupil quarrelled. Lawrence used to employ Harlow to deaden colour, and Harlow had so far a share in painting a much-admired dog in the picture of Mrs. Angerstein, which, at the Angersteins, he had the imprudence to claim as his own. This came, of course, to the ears of Lawrence, who, in consequence, said to the pupil: "As the animal you claim is among the best things I ever painted, of course you have no need of further instruction from me. You must leave my house immediately." It is allowed that Harlow entered more largely into the peculiar style and character of Lawrence's performances than any other of his pupils, so that to his short term in Lawrence's studio may be attributed much of Harlow's success in portrait-painting.

Harlow revenged Lawrence's resentment in an odd way. He made an excursion into the country, and took up his quarters at the Queen's Head, a small roadside inn, on the left hand, as you leave the town of Epsom for Ashtead. Here the young painter stayed some time; when, burning to annoy Lawrence, he painted for the landlord a sign-board, in a bold *caricatura* style, of the Queen's Head, and in one corner of the board he wrote, "T. L., Greek-street, Soho!" Lawrence, it is known, became apprised of such a liberty with his name and reputation; but the caricature signboard did service, and remained there for many years. We remember to have seen the sign as early as 1815: upon the obverse was painted a queenly portrait, (the face,) and upon the reverse, the back of the head and bust of the queen. Some twenty years after, missing this peculiar sign from its suspensory iron, (where a written board had been substituted,) we made inquiry at the inn as to the fate of Harlow's *Queen's Head*, but could not learn anything of its whereabouts.

Lawrence did not, however, remain long estranged from Harlow, for we find him assisting him in his greatest picture —the *Trial of Queen Katherine*.

Sir Thomas used to relate that great was the distress of Harlow, when painting this superb scene from Henry the Eighth, at the impossibility of getting John Kemble to sit for his likeness. The painting proceeded, and great John still refused. At last, Sir Thomas advised his pupil to go to the front row of the pit of the theatre, four or five times, and sketch the actor's countenance, from which he might be able to make out a likeness, and introduce it into the painting. This expedient was adopted, and not only an inimitable likeness was the result, but the clever artist caught the fine expression of the Cardinal at the point of his surprise, and anger, and self-possession, at the boldness of the Queen. Had Mr. Kemble sat for the portrait, his face would have been in repose, or at best but in a forced imitation of the remarkable expression excited in it by *playing the character* with the appropriate circumstances and accessories around him.

The painting of this remarkable picture, and the assistance which Fuseli rendered to the painter, is described at page 200. Harlow caught the characteristic excellence of his master, Lawrence, in painting eyes: his eyes of John Kemble, in the *Trial* Scene, are a fine specimen of his power.

There is, however, still further evidence that Lawrence was neither jealous of Harlow, nor bore him any resentment of his unjustifiable conduct. When Mr. Lewis, the engraver, brought to Russell-square a proof of Harlow's best work, (his portrait of Northcote,) Lawrence resolved to retouch it; observing, "It shall never be said that the finest work, from so great a man, went into the world without such assistance as I can give. Harlow had faults; but we must not remember the faults of one who so greatly improved himself in his art."

PORTRAIT OF THE PERSIAN AMBASSADOR.

During the short sojourn, in 1810, of the Persian ambassador, Mirza Abul Hassan Khan, in England, Sir Thomas Lawrence contrived, in the space of seventy-four days, to paint a beautiful portrait of his Excellency. Sir Thomas was so proud of it that on Sir Gore Ouseley's return to Persia, he made him promise never to let any one but himself clean or varnish it.

One morning, at Tehran, Mirza Shefi, prime minister of the King of Persia, called upon Sir Gore Ouseley, the British ambassador, so unexpectedly, that he had not time to remove the Persian ambassador's portrait from the sofa on which it had been placed, on being taken from its packing-case.

Sir Gore Ouseley received the minister at the drawing-room door, and was leading him to the sofa, when he unaccountably drew back. On looking behind to learn the cause of his hesitation, Sir Gore perceived the old minister's countenance inflamed with anger, which, before he could inquire the cause, burst forth. "I think," said the minister, "that when the representative of the King of England does me the honour of standing up to receive me, in due respect to him, you should not be seated." Then, turning to Sir Gore, he said: "Yes, it is your Excellency's kindness to that impertinent fellow that encourages such disrespect, but with your permission, I will soon teach him to know his distance." Shaking his cane at the picture, he poured forth a volley of abuse at poor Mirza Abul Hassan, and said, that if he had forgotten all proper respect to Sir Gore Ouseley, he must at least show it to the representative of his own sovereign. His rage was unbounded, and Sir Gore was obliged to bring him close to the picture before he was undeceived.

On approaching the painting, he passed his hand over the canvas, and with a look of unaffected surprise, exclaimed, "Why! it has a flat surface! Yet, at a little distance, I could have sworn by the Koran that it was a projecting substance—in truth, that it was Abul Hassan Khan himself." *

* Abridged from a Letter from Sir Gore Ouseley to Mr. Thomas Campbell; in the *Life of Lawrence.*

NAPOLEON THE FIRST.

Sir Thomas Lawrence, writing from Aix-la-Chapelle to Mrs. Wolfe, says: "Lord Liverpool gave me an account of the Commissioner's interview with Bonaparte, when his doom of St. Helena was announced. Throughout the whole, he preserved the most calm and dignified composure; once only being at all agitated, when, in speaking of the Regent, he said that posterity would be the judge of his conduct towards him. At that moment, a quivering in his upper lip, and his eyes filling, spoke an emotion that betrayed itself at no other time during the conference."

REMOVAL TO RUSSELL SQUARE.

Lawrence was now on the verge of middle life; he had built up a stately reputation in Art; and ranked at the head of his profession. He next removed from Greek-street to 65, Russell-square. Here he set up his easel, never to be removed by his own hand. His painting-room was filled with portraits in all stages of study or progress. Here might be seen the heads of sitters, awaiting their turn to be mounted upon shoulders; and here at one time might be seen, in this condition, the heads of Scott and Campbell, West and Fuseli, and scores of other distinguished persons. His house was a museum of choice specimens of painting, sculpture, architecture, and engraving; his pictures, drawings, and studies of the great masters of modern art, were arranged by his own hand, but the house exhibited no luxurious appearance beyond the treasures of art which his taste and fortune had enabled him to collect. Of the designs of Fuseli he had thousands, and loved to show them to his friends in the evening; every new drawing had its anecdote history; he was extremely fond of talking of Fuseli. His bust was placed in Lawrence's evening-room, beside those of Flaxman and Stothard; and statues of Michael Angelo and Raphael by Flaxman—these were the Penates of the painter's private room. Hoppner, his most formidable rival in portraiture, was now dead; and Lawrence largely increased his prices, yet without reducing the number of opulent sitters.

His principal expenses were on account of his art: his great ambition was to rear up a school of his own; and among other evidences of his enthusiasm was a plan for transforming his house into a series of studios and galleries, on which he consulted Smirke, the architect ; but the scheme was far too costly, and required time.

PORTRAITS OF THE EMPEROR OF RUSSIA, THE KING OF PRUSSIA, BLUCHER, AND PLATOFF.

In 1814, Lawrence took advantage of the presence of the Allies in Paris to visit that capital, and inspect the treasures of the Louvre. He was, however, soon recalled by the Prince Regent—to paint the Emperor of Russia, the King of Prussia, Prince Blucher, and the Hettman Platoff. They sat for their portraits in the mansion which then occupied the ground between Stable-yard and St. James's Park ; which is now the site of Stafford House, the mansion of the Duke of Sutherland.

The pictures painted in memory of the visits of the conquerors were exhibited next year, with a portrait of the Duke of Wellington bearing the Sword of State at St. Paul's, on the day of Thanksgiving for the Peace. The portraits of Blucher and Platoff are excellent.* The Prince Regent, it is said at the suggestion of the Emperor of Russia, conferred the honour of knighthood upon Mr. Lawrence ; the Regent assuring him of his esteem for a man whose genius had so greatly elevated the character of the country for the arts, in the estimation of Europe.

LAWRENCE AND CANOVA.

During Canova's visit to England, in 1816, he sat to Sir Thomas Lawrence for his portrait, with which he was much pleased ; and the great Sculptor, on his return to Rome, was principally instrumental in procuring the honorary distinctions of the Academy of St. Luke's for Lawrence and Flaxman.

About the same period, Sir Thomas painted, it is said, after death, the portrait of James Watt, the inventor of the present power of the steam-engine ; but the likeness never became so popular as Chantrey's bust of the great inventor.

* The Rev. Mr. Mitford has left this interesting record of Platoff's sitting at Sir Thomas's house in Russell-square : "We shall never forget the Cossacks mounted on their small white horses, with their long spears grounded, standing centinels at the door of the great painter, while he was taking the portrait of their General Platoff."—*Gentleman's Magazine*, Jan. 1818.

LAWRENCE AND MRS. WOLFE.

Among Sir Thomas's fair sitters was Mrs. Wolff, the wife of the Danish consul, but living apart from her husband; a young and beautiful woman, and of considerable taste in art and literature. The painter and the sitter became intimate: the one complained of the coldness of spinsters; and the other condoled with his entanglements in love. Of course, the lady's advice was pure and platonic. Lawrence called her in his correspondence Aspasia, and designed a picture of the building of the Parthenon, with Aspasia and Pericles directing the workers in ivory and gold in raising the temple. But he soon laid aside the sketch. His letters were garnished with strange and flighty speculations; but he also confided to the lady his troubles of actual life and the working-day world —how he had enemies abroad accusing him of "forming his squad," so that he might have everything his own way. He also revealed to Mrs. Wolff the vexations of his own studio. "I have," he says, "the cares of an overwhelming business, and all its dissatisfactions, together with the perplexing adjustment of those incumbrances that once so nearly ruined me. I am perpetually, too, mastered by my art; and am as much endowed by the picture I am painting, as if it had a personal existence, and obliged me to attend to it." Mrs. Wolff adored Lord Byron, and Lawrence, to gratify her, dashed off with his pen the head of the poet, but with somewhat too dark a shade. To conclude, there seems to have been much impassioned talk in the letters, of which the painter's love mostly consisted: but the lady retired into Wales, and so the story ends.

Mrs. Wolff, however, continued to correspond with Lawrence until her death, in the middle of the year 1829. He was deeply affected at her loss: he laid aside his pencil for nearly a month; and in sadness of spirit, he wrote: "I have lost a faithful and revered friend; one worthy, from genius, right principle, benevolence, and piety to be the companion of the best."

THE ELGIN MARBLES.

On the merits of these celebrated antiques, Lawrence, in 1816, gave the following evidence:

"I am well acquainted with the Elgin marbles: they are of the highest class of art; and to purchase them would be an essential benefit to the arts of this country. They would be of high importance in a line of art which I have very seldom practised; I mean, the historical: for, though I have seen the marbles in Paris, and know other figures of great name, the Elgin marbles present examples of a higher style of sculpture than any I have seen. I think they are beyond the Apollo. There is in them a union of fine composition and grandeur of form, with a *more true and natural expression of the effect of action upon the human frame*, than there is in the Apollo, or in any other of the most celebrated statues. I consider, on the whole, the Theseus as the most perfect piece of sculpture of a single figure that I have ever seen as *an imitation of nature:* but, as an imitation of character, I would not decide, unless I knew for what the figure was intended."

Sir Thomas appears to have been misunderstood or misrepresented at the time he gave these opinions, in which the majority of our artists agree—in pronouncing the Theseus to have been a closer imitation than the Apollo. Lawrence, except the President of the Royal Academy, was the only painter who was consulted upon the subject. The last of worldly affairs that engaged his attention was the able defence of Flaxman upon the Elgin marbles, by their mutual friend, Mr. Campbell. Whilst Lawrence's feelings were absorbed in this subject, he expired,—little reflecting that the defender of Flaxman would, in a few days, be called upon to perform the office of his biographer.

LAWRENCE AT CLAREMONT.

In 1817, Sir Thomas was commissioned to paint the portrait of the Princess Charlotte a second time, and he stayed at Claremont nine days. In letters to a friend he has described the habits of the royal pair, in an unostentatious and delightful picture of their domestic life.

"The Princess he describes wanting in elegance of deportment: her manner (he says) is exceedingly frank and simple, and if she does nothing gracefully, she does everything kindly. She both loves and respects Prince Leopold, who, from the report of the gentlemen of his household, is considerate, benevolent, and just, and of very amiable manners. In his behaviour to the Princess he is affectionate and attentive, rational, and discreet.

"Their mode of life is very regular: they breakfast together about eleven; at half-past twelve, she came in to sit to me, accompanied by Prince Leopold, who stayed great part of the time. About three she would leave the painting-room to take her airing round the grounds, in a low pony-phaeton, the Prince always walking by her side. At five she would come in and sit to me till seven; at six, or before it, he would go out with his gun to shoot hares, or rabbits, and return about seven; soon after which we went to dinner, the Prince and Princess appearing in the drawing-room just as it was served up. Soon after the dessert appeared, the Prince and Princess retired to the drawing-room, whence we soon heard the pianoforte, accompanying their voices. At his own time, Colonel Addenbroke, the chamberlain, proposed our going in.

"After coffee, they sat down to whist, the young couple being always partners, the others changing. (Owing to Sir Thomas's superiority at whist, he did not obey the command.) The Prince and Princess retire at 11 o'clock.

* * *

"I was at Claremont, on a call of inquiry, the Saturday before the Princess' death. Her last command to me was, that I should bring down the picture to give to Prince Leopold upon his birthday, the 16th of the next month.

"It was my wish that Prince Leopold should see the picture on his first entering the room to his breakfast, and accordingly, at 7 o'clock, I set off with it in a coach. I got to Claremont, uncovered it, and placed it in the room in good time. Before I took it there, I carried it in to Colonel Addenbroke, Baron Hardenbrock, and Dr. Short, who had been the Princess' tutor. Sir Robert Gardiner came in, and went out immediately. Dr. Short looked at it for some time in silence, but I saw his lips trembling, and his eyes filled to overflowing.

"I learnt that the Prince was very much overcome by the sight of the picture, and the train of recollections it brought with it. Colonel Addenbroke went in to the Prince, and returned shortly, saying, 'The Prince desires me to say who much he is obliged to you for this attention, and that he shall always remember it.' (Soon after Sir Thomas proceeded to the Prince.) As I passed through the hall Dr. Short came up to me, (he had evidently been and was crying,) and thanked me for having painted such a picture. 'No one is a better judge than I am, sir,' said he, and turned away.

"The Prince was looking exceedingly pale. He spoke at once about the picture, and of its value to him more than to all the world besides. From the beginning to the close of the interview, he was greatly affected. He checked the first burst of affection by adverting to the public loss, and that of the royal family. 'Two generations gone!—gone in a moment! I have felt for myself, but I have felt for the Prince Regent. My Charlotte is gone from this country—it has lost her. She was good, she was an admirable woman. None could know my Charlotte as I did know her. It was my happiness, my duty, to know her character, but it was my delight.'

"During a short pause, I spoke of the impression it had made on me. 'Yes, she had a clear, fine understanding, and very quick—she was candid, she was open, and not suspecting, but she saw characters at a glance, she read them so true. You saw her; you saw something of us—you saw us for *days*—and you saw our *year!* Oh! what happiness!'

"I tried to check this current of recollection, that was evidently overpowering him (as it was me), by a remark on a part of the picture, and then on its likeness to the youth of the old King. 'Ah! and my child was like her, for one so young (as if it had really lived in childhood). For one so young, it was surprisingly like.'

* * * *

"'My Charlotte! My dear Charlotte!' And now, looking at the picture, he said, 'Those beautiful hands, that at the last, when she was talking to others, were always looking out for mine!'

* * * * *

"'She was strong, and had courage, yet once she seemed to fear. You remember, she was affected when you told her that you could not paint my picture just at that time; but she was much more affected when we were alone—and I told her I should sit when we went to Marlborough House after her confinement. "Then," she said, "if you are to sit when you go to town and after my confinement—then I may never see that picture." My Charlotte felt she never should.'"

PORTRAITS OF THE ALLIED SOVEREIGNS.

After Napoleon had been consigned to St. Helena, the sovereigns met in congress at Aix-la-Chapelle, and this was deemed by the Prince Regent of England a fit opportunity for commemorating the crowning glory of the War by a collection of portraits of the principal personages engaged in it. The Regent accordingly dispatched his painter to the imperial and royal head-quarters: he was to be allowed one thousand a year for contingent expenses, and the portraits were to be painted at the usual price. From Aix-la-Chapelle, Lawrence was to proceed to Vienna, and thence to Rome, to complete the commission. Our Government caused to be constructed in this country three immense portable rooms of wood, which were shipped with all Sir Thomas's canvass and *matériel*—the rooms to be erected in the grounds of our ambassador at Aix. Sir Thomas, however, arrived there before the packages; when the Magistrates of the city granted him the use of part of the large gallery of the Hôtel de Ville, which was immediately fitted up as a painting-room, "and," says Sir Thomas, "it is certainly the best I ever had." Sir Thomas, in his letters, minutely describes the several sittings—the courts and assemblies, and public entertainments: he tells us how the Emperor of Russia chose to be painted in the close green hussar uniform which he had worn at the battle of Leipsic; how the features of the Emperor of Austria are anything but good, though the expression is that of a paternal monarch, who "has a face, when speaking, of benevolence," and how the painter was happy enough to catch that expression; how the King of Prussia is taller than either, has good features, and is of a sincere and generous nature; and how the head of the Archduke Charles is that of a fine, eager, soldier-like, undismayed man. The sovereigns of Austria and Prussia each gave the painter a superb diamond ring, and all kinds of courtly commendations were showered upon him.

From Aix-la-Chapelle, Lawrence went to Vienna, to paint Schwartzenburg, and other imperial generals. Count Capo d'Istrias was the best portrait he painted there. From Vienna he went to Rome, where he painted most magnificently Pope Pius VII. and Cardinal Gonsalvi. "His Holiness (says Lawrence,) has a fine countenance, stoops a little; with a firm and sweet-toned voice, and as I believe, is within a year or two of eighty; and through all the storms of the past he retains the jet black of his hair. Cardinal Gonsalvi, the Pitt of Rome, is one of the finest subjects for a picture that I ever had—a countenance of powerful intellect, and symmetry; his manners but too gracious; the expression of every wish was pressed upon me, and the utterance of every complaint."

These two portraits are by far the finest which Lawrence painted during his long journey. He arrived in England in March, 1820.

We shall presently tell more of his stay in Rome. With respect to his commission, the gallery at Windsor, we may state that of these princes and rulers of the earth he now painted Francis, Emperor of Austria, Louis XVIII. and Charles X. successively kings of France, the Archduke Charles, Prince Metternich, General Tchernicheff, General Ouvaroff, Baron Hardenberg, Count Nesselrode, Baron Gentz, Earl Bathurst, the Earl of Liverpool, Robert Marquis of Londonderry, the Duke of Cambridge, and Mr. Canning. The whole collection of the *European* portraits which he painted amounted in number to twenty-four.

This collection of pictures is now in the *Waterloo Hall*, at Windsor Castle. "Among a great number of portraits," says Dr. Waagen, "all cannot be equal in merit. I was particularly pleased with those of the Pope, Cardinal Gonsalvi, and the Emperor of Austria. Besides the graceful and unaffected design, the clear and brilliant colouring, which are peculiar to Lawrence, these are distinguished by greater truth of character, and a more animated expression than is generally met with in his pictures." The praise here given to Sir Thomas Lawrence is just, but it is not complete: he possessed the happy talent of idealizing his forms, without departing from nature, or destroying the likeness. He evidently profited by the sound advice given him by Sir Joshua Reynolds, "not so to imitate the old masters as to give a richness of hue rather than the ordinary hues of nature, but to paint what he saw;" but at the same time, "not to fall into the vulgar error of making things too like themselves."

Thus was formed the magnificent collection of historical portraits in the Waterloo Hall, by George the Fourth, the most munificent patron of art in England since Charles the First; the magnificence of the commemoration is, however, but in just proportion to the importance of the event which it seeks to perpetuate by this noble triumph of pictorial art.

ON TURNER, BY LAWRENCE.

Sir Thomas Lawrence, writing to Mr. Farington, from Rome, in 1819, says:

"Turner should come to Rome. His genius would here be supplied with materials, and entirely congenial with it.

It is one proof of his influence on my mind, that, enchanted as I certainly am, whenever I go out, with the beauty of the hues, and the forms of the buildings—with the grandeur of some, and variety of the picturesque in the masses of the ordinary buildings of the city—I am perpetually reminded of his pencil, and feel the sincerest regret that his powers should not be excited to their utmost force. He has an elegance, and often a greatness of invention, that wants a scene like this for its free expansion; while the subtle harmony of this atmosphere, that wraps everything in its own milky sweetness—for it is colourless, compared with the skies of France and England, and more like the small Claude of Mr. Angerstein's and Lord Egremont's, though the latter has a slight tendency—has it not?—to heaviness;—this blending, I say, of earth and heaven, can only be rendered, according to my belief, by the beauty of his tones. I must already have written the substance of this to you, as I have to Lyrons; but my dwelling on the subject arises from no affectation or assumed feeling. It is a fact, that the country and scenes around me do thus impress themselves on me, and that Turner is always associated with them; Claude, though frequently, not so often; and Gaspar Poussin still less."

(It will be seen that before the close of the year, Turner visited Rome.)

LAWRENCE PAINTING IN ROME.

About three weeks after Sir Thomas had left Rome, there appeared in the *Collector*, dated July 20, 1820, the following tribute to his genius and popularity:

"We have recently seen here quite a constellation of English talent. Lawrence, Turner, Jackson, Chantrey, and Moore—to say nothing of a milky-way of secondary geniuses. The first named (Lawrence) has made a sensation beyond description. You will see a proof of the likelihood of this in the works he has taken over with him; but you cannot figure to yourself the effect here of the contrast they presented to the cold, insipid, weak things of the present school of Rome. To the Italians he seemed to introduce a new art, and he gave them all plenty of opportunity to see not only his works, but his manner of working, by leaving them freely open to inspection in all their different stages. With great liberality, and an utter absence of quackery and affectation, he admitted the public, without distinction or exception, between each sitting, into the room where his pictures were. He was regarded as a superior being, and a wonder indeed he was here. His elegant manners made him so many friends, and these and his talents procured him so many distinctions, that he could scarcely prevail on himself to quit the place. Lawrence has declared that Rome supplies the test of the painter and the poet. It has, I believe, inspired him with high resolves, which I hope his return to London will not dissipate. His portraits of sovereigns, &c., you will see; but one small work which he has left here exceeds, in the estimation of everybody, all that he has done beside, without exception. It is the head of Canova, which he did in London, entirely repainted; and it may now be cited as the most poetical, elegant, enthusiastic delineation of acute genius, without flattery, that has ever been executed. Its animation is beyond all praise. '*Per Baccho, che uomo e questo!*' I heard Canova cry out when it was mentioned. And then, the effect of the whole exceeds even the Emperor's. Crimson velvet, and damask, and gold, and precious marble, and fur, are the materials which he has worked up to astonishing brilliancy, without violating good taste, or the truth of nature. This painting is a present to his Holiness, and a noble one it is."

SIR THOMAS LAWRENCE ELECTED PRESIDENT OF THE ROYAL ACADEMY.

Shortly before the return of Lawrence, in 1820, Benjamin West, the venerable President of the Royal Academy, died full of honours; and to the first intimation which he received of this event, it was added that he was to be elected in his place. Sir Thomas replied: "There are others better qualified to be present. I shall, however, discharge the duties as well and wisely as I can. I shall be true to the Academy; and in my intentions just and impartial." He was chosen unanimously, and the King, in giving his sanction to the choice of the Academicians, added a superb gold chain and medal of himself, inscribed thus: "From His Majesty George IV. to the President of the Royal Academy."

When Sir Thomas took the presidential chair among his brethren, it was generally acknowledged that for reputation in art, gentlemanly accomplishments, and acquaintance with the requirements of the station, a better choice could not have been made. Even Fuseli, who was rarely satisfied with anything, growled his approbation in these words: "Well! Well! since *they must* have a face-painter to reign over them, let them take Lawrence: he can, at least, paint eyes!"

RECOVERY OF A MICHAEL ANGELO.

About the year 1810, Mr. Ottley accidentally picked up an old drawing that had belonged to Sir Joshua Reynolds, who had written under it the name of Donatello, in indication of his attributing it to the pencil of that artist. Mr. Ottley, however, was intimately acquainted with the style and works of Michael Angelo, and he wrote under the drawing in pencil "*a presso Michael Angelo.*" Being at Paris in 1820, Mr. Ottley, by chance, saw in a shop the original drawing, and immediately purchased it. The subject was an old sorceress, or prophetess, one of the finest productions of Michael Angelo. On his return to England, Mr. Ottley presented it to Sir Thomas Lawrence, who, in reply, wrote: "The Beauty is arrived! The copy is tolerably accurate; but it is just in what it differs that the superior grandeur of the original consists."

Donatello died in 1366, about 140 years before Michael Angelo was born. The mistake was curious in such a man as Sir Joshua: but Lawrence's letter conveys an odd idea of a "tolerably accurate" copy: *i.e.* a copy of a grand master, that differs only in the points of grandeur.

LAWRENCE'S JUSTICE TO REYNOLDS.

Sir Thomas Lawrence had a great contempt for impertinent pretensions, and he rarely lost an opportunity of exposing them.

In 1821, when Lucien Bonaparte's pictures were offered for sale in Pall Mall, a common friend of Sir Thomas, and of Mr. Robson, the artist, requested that they would view the pictures together, and point out such as they would recommend him to purchase. They accordingly went one morning, and found there, among other visitors, a Scotch gentleman, who was very loud in his abuse of those portraits by Sir Joshua Reynolds, the property of Mr. Piozzi, which had then been recently submitted to sale.

Sir Thomas heard this evidently with some impatience.

At length he went up to the opinionated person, and in an apparently cool manner, said, "Sir, allow me to tell you that those pictures which you have abused, no man now alive in Europe can produce—they are excellent. I say this to you in kindness, that you may not again commit yourself in a public room by such unfounded opinions." After a pause, he added, "My name is Lawrence." This silenced the gentleman, who was not long in making his retreat from the room.

LORD BYRON AND LAWRENCE.

When Sir Thomas was at the full height of professional reputation, he met Lord Byron, who rated the painter as a talker very highly. In his Diary, Jan. 5, 1821, he records: "The same evening I met Lawrence, the painter, and heard one of Lord Grey's daughters play on the harp so modestly and ingeniously that she looked music. I would rather have had my talk with Lawrence, who talked delightfully, and heard the girl, than have had all the fame of Moore and me put together. The only pleasure of fame is, that it paves the way to pleasure; and the more intellectual, the better for the pleasure, and us too."

SIR WALTER SCOTT AND SIR THOMAS LAWRENCE.

Lawrence knew how to be silent when the occasion called for deferential respect. This is a valuable accomplishment for success in life, since deference is the most elegant species of flattery. Allan Cunningham relates that (about this time, 1821,) he dined with Lawrence and Sir Walter Scott at the table of the venerable Dr. Hughes. He said little, and seemed chiefly anxious to hear the great poet, who certainly spoke in a way to charm every ear. The painter objected, in a most gentle way, to persons criticising works of art who were not themselves artists. "Nay," said the poet; "consider, art professes but to be a better sort of nature; and, as such, appeals to the taste of the world; surely, therefore, a wise man of the world may judge its worth, and feel its sentiment, though he cannot produce it. He may not know how it is produced; yet I see not but that he may animate its beauty." Sir Thomas smiled, and said, "Certainly." The conversation took another turn.

SKETCH-BOOK OF LEONARDO DA VINCI.

Sir Thomas Lawrence, from his celebrity and position, had many opportunities of purchasing rare works of art for his collection. In 1821, he missed a rare treasure of this description. One day, a servant-maid from Winchester brought to his house in Russell-square an old vellum sketch-book, that had belonged to Leonardo da Vinci: his title to it was written in choice Italian on the outside, whilst in the inside was written the donation of it by its English possessor, in the hand and spelling of a century ago. There was no trickery in it, no deception; the old vellum leaves were in many cases decayed, and the twelve drawings in it were done with the silver point; the last being three skulls, originally by the same hand, but subsequently traced over with a black-lead pencil, strengthening and spoiling them. The person who brought the book stated that five guineas had been offered for it in the country; Sir Thomas proffered seven guineas, but was told that a lady patroness must be consulted before the offer could be accepted. He was vexed at losing a cheap bargain, but awaited the answer from the country: it came, and was favourable. But, lo! in the interval, the book was shown to another artist, and by him sent to Mr. Knight, who offered 24l. for it! Sir Thomas could not, for shame, bid 25l., after his first valuation of 7l.; and so the vellum sketch-book of Leonardo da Vinci became the property of Mr. Knight. The reader will perhaps say—"What could have made Sir Thomas so blind as to part with it?" Nothing, but his doubt of its *being* Leonardo's: that, probably, it was by some old Florentine artist—and not by Leonardo. In such cases, Sir Thomas usually consulted his friend, Mr. Ottley, who was at the time absent at Boulogne; and he concludes the letter narrating the transaction with this piece of banter: "To the loss of the said sketch-book by the uxorious impatience of the said W. Y. Ottley, Esq.—fifty pounds:—and so ends, till the payment of the said fifty pounds, this puzzling, irritating transaction."

HONOURS TO SIR T. LAWRENCE.

In addition to the honour of knighthood by the Prince Regent, and admission to the Academy of St. Luke in Rome, he became, in 1817, a member of the American Academy of the Fine Arts. This honour Sir Thomas repaid by painting a full-length portrait of their countryman, Benjamin West; and West, in return, said of Sir Thomas—" He is not a mere portrait-painter: he has invention, taste, rich colouring, and a power of execution truly wonderful." The Academy of Florence, having heard that Lawrence had painted one of his finest portraits as a present to the American Society, instantly elected him a member of the first class: but Sir Thomas, suspecting the motive of their kindness, sent nothing. The Academy of Venice added their election in 1823; that of Bologna followed: and Turin in 1826. He was, moreover, elected a member of the Imperial Academy at Vienna, and got the diploma of the Danish Academy, through the personal interposition of King Christian-Frederick. Finally, he was made a chevalier of the Legion of Honour, in France, in 1825; the King of England giving him permission to wear the cross of the order.

PRESENTS TO LAWRENCE.

Throughout his brilliant career, Lawrence received many honorary and friendly presents from foreign princes: of these gifts the following list was furnished by his sister.

"By the King of France, (Charles the Tenth,) in the autumn of 1825, he was presented with the Legion of Honour, (the medal or jewel of which is in my son John's possession); a magnificent French clock, nearly two feet high; two superb green and gold china jars; and a dessert set of Sèvres porcelain which Sir Thomas left to the Royal Academy.

"By the Emperor of Russia, a superb diamond ring, of great value.

"By the King of Prussia, a ring, with his Majesty's initials, F. R., in diamonds.

"He likewise received presents from the foreign ministers assembled at Aix-la-Chapelle, where he painted all of them: from the Archduchess Charles and Princess Metternich at Vienna; from the Pope, a ring, and the Colosseum in mosaic, with his Holiness' arms over the centre of the frame; from the Cardinal Gonsalvi, besides other presents, a gold watch, chain, and seals of intaglios, and many beautiful bonbonniereboxes of valuable stones set in gold, gold snuff-boxes, &c.; a fine gold snuff-box, from Lord Whitworth, many years before.

"From the Dauphin, in 1825, a breakfast-set of porcelain, and a tea-tray painted with the court of Louis XIV.

"By Canova, at Rome, some magnificent casts, valuable engravings, &c."

CAST OF THE EMPEROR NAPOLEON'S HEAD.

While at Paris, in 1825, Sir Thomas Lawrence visited Dr. Antommarchi, to inspect the cast he had taken of the Emperor Napoleon's head and face after his death. Sir Thomas examined it with great interest, and expatiated upon it for more than an hour. He expressed his admiration of the perfect beauty of the outline, and regularity of features; and pronounced that no portrait of him had equalled this model. In no instance has any cast, statue, or portrait of the Emperor Napoleon represented him with a ruffled brow, or with lines indicative of disturbed passions.—*Williams's Life of Lawrence.*

LAWRENCE AND THE FREEDOM OF BRISTOL.

The author of the Life of Sir Thomas Lawrence describes the commencement of the year 1829, as "the most blissful period of his life. His chief source of enjoyment, the solace of his solitary hours, and that which shed an enviable influence over his exertions—the happiness and prosperity of his relations—were ample, and in every respect, satisfactory and unalloyed."

In the spring he received from his native Bristol the freedom of the city, procured for him, as he states in his acknowledgment, by Mr. Acraman and his friends. This tribute to Lawrence came very late, seeing the honours and gifts which had long before been heaped upon him from almost every part of the civilized world; and it certainly did not deserve the courteous letter in which Lawrence acknowledged it. This homage of his birthplace was, probably, the last public honour which the great Painter received.

LAWRENCE'S LAST YEAR.

The Exhibition of the Academy this year (1829) contained eight fine portraits by Lawrence, of almost undiminished excellence. They were portraits of the Duke of Clarence, Miss Macdonald, the Duchess of Richmond, Lord Durham, Robert Southey, the Marchioness of Salisbury, and Mrs. Lock, sen. This was the last public exhibition of Lawrence's paintings during his life. He was now most active in his correspondence. Early in the year appeared the engraving of his portrait of the King, which the painter describes as " universally popular, and the most faithful portrait of his Majesty that has yet been given to his subjects." He sends a first finished proof to Mr. Peel, with a letter saying : "The frame is that in which I presented the engraving for his Majesty's inspection. It will give me the greatest pleasure to see, in the collection of the *second patron* of my pencil, this portrait of the *first*." He also sends a proof to his loved sister.

Next month he addressed a letter to Mr. Peel on the Roman Catholic question, with congratulations on the success of the Emancipation Bill; and he next exerted himself in the Oxford University election in favour of Mr. Peel by his efforts to neutralise the votes of two of his family, and to secure in Mr. Peel's favour the vote of another.

Amidst this activity the painter was, however, much pressed to finish in time his whole-length portraits of the Duke of Clarence and the Duchess of Richmond in time for the Exhibition. He writes to his sister: "The pressure of business on me has been very great, and the lassitude proportioned to it. My labours have fortunately succeeded, and perhaps, my two whole-lengths of the Duchess of Richmond and the Marchioness of Salisbury, *are the best that I have painted;* and the former the most popular and beautiful. I may rationally be proud of succeeding this year, since it is indisputably the best exhibition we have had; and it is universally considered so.

"Many thanks for your remembering my birthday. It is not attended to as it ought to have been ; but at least, professional fame is mine; the hope of my youth, and pursuit of my life are comparatively achieved ; and the love of my family still continued to me."

His letters to Mr. Peel are now frequent: in one he requests the loan of the Speaker's mace for a day ; in another an admittance for an American friend to Mr. Peel's picture-gallery ; then requests a frank ; and we find this odd postscript, which shows how kindly Lawrence used his influence :

"I have a petitioner—an honest watchman of our Square for four years ; *with all certificates of good conduct ;* but alas ! five feet *six*. It is not possible to have him included in the new Police !"

This year he evinced his friendly and impartial feelings

towards the two rival Societies of Arts established at Birmingham. But, he felt that he was overworked: writing to Mr. Angerstein in November, he says: "For me, to use your dear father's expression, I shall live and die in harness." However, there came a slight relief, as the next anecdote will narrate.

MISS FANNY KEMBLE.

In the autumn of 1829, this highly gifted lady made her theatrical *début;* and Sir Thomas Lawrence, in a letter to Mr. Angerstein, dated Nov. 22, 1829, thus gives his genuine and private opinions of her success.

"We have little stirring in town, one novelty excepted, which enlivens the evenings of this otherwise dull period. Your respect and regard for Mrs. Siddons and Mr. Kemble, will make you glad to know that the genius and sense of both are recalled to us by the really fine acting of Miss Fanny Kemble, the daughter of their brother Charles. She is not quite nineteen, yet has so satisfied the judgment of the warmest patrons and ablest critics of the stage, that, in its worst season, she has drawn full houses (and continues to draw them) for upwards of twenty-two nights, three nights in each week, without intermission, to one of Shakspeare's finest, but certainly most hackneyed plays, *Romeo and Juliet,* and the boxes are already taken to Wednesday se'ennight.

"Her face is not regularly handsome, but she has a fine and flexible brow, with eyes and hair like Mrs. Siddons in her finest time. In stature she is rather short, but with such admirable carriage and invariable grace of action, that on the stage she appears fully of woman's height. Her voice is at once sweet and powerful; and blest with a clear 'Kemble' understanding, (for it is peculiar to her family,) she has likewise fine literary talent, having written a tragedy of great interest, besides lighter pieces of admirable verse. Her manner in private is characterised by ease, and that modest gravity which I believe must belong to high tragic genius, and which, in Mrs. Siddons, was strictly natural to her, though, from being peculiar in the general gaiety of society, it was often thought assumed.

"I have for many years given up the theatre, (not going above once or twice in the year,) but this fine genius has drawn me often to it, and each time to witness improvement and new beauties. If she is not taken from the stage, there is probability that she may remain on it a fine actress for twenty years, and thus have supported the ascendancy of one family in the highest department of the Drama for upwards of seventy years!"

Such of our readers as remember the appearance of Miss Fanny Kemble, and the success with which her genius upheld the falling fortunes of Covent Garden Theatre, will also recollect that immediately after her *début*, there appeared a charming lithograph portrait of the lady, by Mr. Lane, from a drawing by Sir Thomas Lawrence. Of this exquisite work many thousand impressions were disposed of by the print-sellers within an incredibly short space of time.

Lawrence touched no drawing after this beautiful lithograph. In its progress he took exceeding interest. Mr. Lane worked at the sketch for several days, at Sir Thomas's house, under his own eye: he frequently added touches, and was delighted with the process. On the day after Christmas Day, 1829, he writes to his sister, regretting that he has not received the impression of this drawing in time to send to her: this was but twelve days before his death. The portrait affords a specimen of the touch of the master-hand upon a material hitherto strange to him: had he lived, he would soon have executed a drawing on stone, entirely of his own production.

LAWRENCE'S DECLINING HEALTH.

The gaiety of the painter began to fail in the year 1828; and in a letter to Mrs. Macdonald, we find him excusing himself for retiring early from a ball, from his practising "the down-hill slope;" "where gentlemen of a certain age have but to fold their arms, and cross their feet, and they go down so comfortably, that the dance is finished before they desire it."

In a similar vein we see him on the last day of the year 1829, when we find him declining an invitation from Mrs. Macdonald on account of the annual dinner at the Academy. "To own the truth," he writes, "as some of us are like the President, bald and grey-headed, we sometimes break up before the hour that proclaims it; but then the knowledge of the scarcity of worth makes us careful of our health, and afraid of listening to syren strains, that might lure it from us. This old-fashioned winter may possibly usher in our gone-by spring and summer; and in the former Miss Macdonald shall find me gay as Mr. Greenwood himself (a gentleman known to her father), and ready to obey her summons at a moment's call."

Thus, he sported upon his age and worth, and the care of his health. He presided at the Academy dinner, the last time of his appearing in public.

This month (December), Lawrence's toils were incessant, and he felt them severely. Some of his friends asserted that they saw no difference in his appearance; but his biographer maintains that he witnessed symptoms of organic disease, at least of an exhausted temperament. His complexion became unhealthy, and drowsiness frequent. He had no suspicion of any disease; and all he complained of was the incessant toils of his profession, and that he was exhausted by his exertions. How often does this forebode the break-up of an active life—although the selfish world has little sympathy with such sufferings!

His anxiety for his sister's recovery from a long and painful disease was now very great. The Academy annual election and distribution of the gold medals took place on Dec. 10, and he was thenceforth detained in town. However, he writes to his sister, Dec. 17: "I am grieved to the soul, that urgent circumstances keep me at this time from the comfort of seeing you; but in the *next* month I will certainly break away from all engagements to be with you." And on the day after Christmas Day, he writes: "On the 6th I have sacredly pledged myself to be with you."

"I am chained to the oar, but painting was never less inviting to me—business never more oppressive to me than at this moment."

Mr. Williams, his biographer, relates that a friend at whose house Sir Thomas dined on Dec. 24, remarked that he was unusually communicative; and in conversation, said that from the *regularity* of his living, and the care which he took of his health, he thought he might attain old age. He spoke with candour of his pecuniary circumstances, mentioned his age, and requested to be informed what annual sum he must pay if he insured his life for 3,000*l*. This information was given; and it was his intention to have insured his life on the *Friday*, but he died on the *Thursday* previously.

On the above day, Lawrence seemed in good health, although his countenance was more pallid than usual. He remained till twelve o'clock: the conversation ran chiefly on the fine arts, and he sometimes recurred to the memory of a common friend, Fuseli.

The only complaint Lawrence made was, that his eyes and forehead became heated of an evening, and he requested cold water and a towel to bathe them; but this he was in the habit of doing.

On Dec. 31, Miss Croft called in Russell-square, and found Sir Thomas apparently as well as usual. On New Year's Day, this lady called to wish him years of continued happiness: he was engaged with a sitter (Lord Seaforth). Soon after four, he called on Miss Croft, in Devonshire-street: she was hardly glad to see him walking out so late, but he said he was carefully wrapped up, and added: "If I catch cold, don't you take the blame of it, for I have been standing in the street this morning before the Athenæum." He said he was going to have Mr. Mulready to dine with him; and Mrs. Ottley, and her children, to pass the evening with him. This day, Lawrence had been retouching the portrait of Mr. Canning, acknowledged by many persons to be the best portrait Sir Thomas ever painted.

Next day, (Jan. 2,) he complained to Miss Croft of having most of the preceding night acute pains in the stomach, which had commenced round his jaws and throat. He added, that for thirty years he had not passed such a night, or breakfasted at the late hour of eleven; but, "instead of murmuring, (said he,) I ought to bless God for such a season of uninterrupted health." Dr. Holland was then sent for, as Lawrence had engaged to dine with Mr. Peel that day, about which he was very anxious. He added, pointing to Mr. Canning's portrait on the easel: "There seems a fatality attending that picture, for the first time I sent it home, in June last, I was prevented dining with Mr. Peel, by a deeper calamity, which you shared with me." He expressed great pleasure in a visit from Mr. Peel the preceding day, and represented him as much pleased with the picture, and saying that he felt dissatisfied when Sir Thomas's pencil was not employed in some way for him; he added that Mr. Peel had expressed an earnest wish that he should paint his own portrait for him.

Miss Croft found Sir Thomas more cheerful, and taking his coffee as usual, about two o'clock. Dr. Holland had called, considered it to be an attack of the stomach, had written for him, and had given him leave to go to Mr. Peel's, on condition of his being careful as to what he should eat and drink. He accordingly went. Washington Irving sat opposite to him at Mr. Peel's, and relates that Sir Thomas "seemed uneasy and restless; his eyes were wandering; he was as pale as marble; the stamp of death seemed on him. He told me he felt ill; but he wished to bear himself up in the presence of one whom he so much esteemed as his entertainer. He went away early." On his return home he complained only of fatigue; he slept comfortably, and had so far recovered by Tuesday, that he painted nearly an hour on the King's portrait,* and went out in his carriage, to a committee meeting at the Athenæum club-house.

DEATH OF SIR THOMAS LAWRENCE.

During the night of Wednesday, the 6th of January, Sir Thomas experienced a violent relapse. Dr. Holland found him in a very alarming state, with scarcely any pulse at the wrist till after he had lost sixteen ounces of blood. The Doctor did not leave him till Thursday morning, the 7th. Miss Croft then found Sir Thomas, for the first time, in a sick chamber; but he assured her that he was greatly relieved, and desired her not to be alarmed at the change in his looks. He was now considered out of danger, except by his physician. Sir Henry Halford came with Dr. Holland in the afternoon: Sir Henry approved of all that had been done, and merely ordered a more active cathartic. In the evening, Lawrence sent for Mr. Keightley, who came with Miss Croft. They found him altogether relieved; and he took some tea and toast. He then said to Mr. Keightley, "Read that to me"—an article by Campbell, the poet, on the genius of Flaxman. As Mr. Keightley began to read, Sir Thomas's countenance changed; he put his hand to Miss Croft's, pressed hers in an agitated way, and desired them to leave the room, and send his servant John to him. In about ten minutes the servant cried imploringly for help. On Keightley running up, he found Sir Thomas had slipped from his seat down on the floor. His last words were,—"John, my good fellow, this is dying." "Oh! no, sir," replied the servant, "it is only fainting." He expired without a groan, Jan 7, 1830.

Mr. Etty has left a touching account of the Painter's death. "The year 1830," (says Etty's biographer, Mr. Gilchrist,)

* This is a fine full-length portrait of George IV.: Sir Thomas was painting one of the orders on the breast. The picture was never finished: it is in the coffee-room of the Athenæum club-house.

opened with a fresh sorrow: the sudden death, in mature life and faculty, of his old Master, Sir Thomas Lawrence. There are men whose external character draws after them a personal *following*, independently of their intrinsic gifts, often dispro portionately. The successful Portrait Painter, the more than successor—as far as fashionableness went—of Reynolds, was one of these. His varied accomplishments, polished *savoir- vivre*, his suavity, and seeming openness, covering real self- command and refined worldly wisdom, as his plausible talents disguised an essentially common-place mind,—had their irresistible influence: winning him the personal affection and even homage of most with whom he came in contact, above all, of simple, enthusiastic natures like Etty, inducing unreserved adherence to the popular estimate of his supre- macy." Etty preserved to the last a proud and affectionate remembrance of his old Master, and spoke of him as "a man who, for splendour and brilliancy of talent, for benevolence and gentleness of heart, for elegance and suavity of manners, for nobleness and beauty of person, has left no parallel."

He felt, vehemently, the abrupt close of Lawrence's success- ful life. "It seems almost a dream, a hideous dream, (he writes to his friend Bodley, Jan. 27,) to think that he, the pride and boast of our country, and of his brethren, whose beautiful smile, delightful manner, cheerful conversation, cast a sunshine around, when, a few nights before, he sat among us at dinner, with health on his cheek, happy and cheerful as he could apparently be; to think that on that very night week, at the same hour, he should droop his head in death!

"The night my dear friend and honoured Master died, I heard Mr. Shee say he was poorly."—"I thought of going to Russell-square that night, after the School was over. I went. I knocked three times; but as I had not knocked *loud*, got no answer. I then rang: a little boy came. I asked if it was true Sir Thomas had been unwell. He *had* been some days. I asked if he kept his bed. 'Not exactly: he kept his bed-room, and sat by the fire.'—I told him to take my com- pliments, and I wished much to know how he was. 'I can't go into the room, sir; his doctor is with him; but he is a great deal better to-day.' . . . Gracious and merciful God! he was dying about that very moment:—about nine o'clock, in a small bed-room, in the upper part of the house.

"A gentleman—his executor—and Miss Croft, had been sitting with him in his bed-room, reading and conversing. So well did he feel, that he said cheerfully, when tea was brought, 'I'll officiate—I'll make tea to-night;' and did so. Afterwards, he requested them to withdraw for a few moments; and feeling faint, asked if there was a fan in the house. The servant got one; and tried to refresh his languor by fanning him—he found himself going; and said, "I am dying." Casting his eyes upwards, he fell back; and left this world for ever...."

A post-mortem examination of the body was made by Mr. Green: his death was reported to have been traced to an extensive ossification of the aorta and vessels of the heart; but this was found, upon closer examination, to have been very slight. The real cause was probably extreme loss of blood, by the orifices made by the leeches, and the bandages on the arm, not being properly secured; when such loss of blood proved fatal to a system previously enfeebled by illness and depletion.

FUNERAL OF SIR THOMAS LAWRENCE.

As soon as the first impressions of surprise and grief had subsided, the Council of the Royal Academy officially signified to the executor that every mark of respect should be paid to the remains of their illustrious President. Accordingly, arrangements were made for interring the body in St. Paul's Cathedral, and for conveying it thither with public honours.

The portion of the south crypt of the Cathedral in which our great artists have been interred has been termed "Painters' Corner;" and the last of the Royal Academicians deposited here was Mr. George Dawe, in the previous year 1829.* Sir Thomas Lawrence was present at the funeral of his brother Academician, and after the service when he descended into the crypt, he was observed to look wistfully about him, as if contemplating the place as that to which he himself would some day be borne; and when the service was concluded, it was remarked that he stopped to look at the inscription on the stone which covers the body of his predecessor, West. Three months had not elapsed from that period, when his presumed anticipation was realized; and he was the next to whom the vault was opened.

* Mr. Dawe, R.A. spent much of his artistic life in Russia, where he painted, it is said, about 400 portraits of the chiefs and leaders of the Russian army. He made much money by this means, but did not live long to enjoy it; for he died six weeks after his return to England in 1829.

On Jan. 20, the body was placed in an oak coffin, covered with lead, which was inclosed in an outer coffin, covered with black velvet; the handles and head and foot plates, and nails, were of silver.

The remains were removed in a hearse on Wednesday evening from the mansion in Russell-square to Somerset House, and were followed by four members of the family, and the executor, attended by an old and faithful servant. At the Royal Academy, the body was received by the Council and officers, and placed in the Model-room, which was hung with black cloth, and lighted with wax in silver sconces. At the head of the coffin was placed a large hatchment of the armorial bearings of the deceased; and the pall over the coffin bore escutcheons of his arms wrought in silk. The members of the Council and the family having retired, the body lay in state all night; the old servant of the President watching through the night the remains of his beloved master.

On Thursday morning, the body lay in state in this room: the academicians, associates, and students, were in attendance, and none but the private friends of the deceased were admitted. The family then assembled in the Library, and the mourners and members of the Academy met in the great Exhibition-room.

The Earl of Aberdeen, Earl Gower, Sir Robert Peel, Lord Dover, Sir George Murray, the Right Honourable J. W. Croker, Mr. Hart Davis, and Earl Clanwilliam, were pall-bearers. The carriages of the Lord Mayor and Sheriffs went before the hearse; the whole members of the Royal Academy accompanied it; 164 noblemen and gentlemen followed in 64 carriages. On the lid of the coffin was inscribed,—" Sir Thomas Lawrence, Knt., LL.D., F. R. S., President of the Royal Academy of Arts in London, and Knight of the Royal French Order of the Legion of Honour, died 7th January, 1830, in the sixty-first year of his age."

The body having reached the choir was placed on trestles, the chief mourner being seated at the head of the coffin, attended by the old servant of the deceased. The venerable Dr. Hughes read the Lesson; the proper portions of the Service were chaunted by the choir, and the fine anthems were sung. The body was then removed into the crypt, and placed under the centre of the dome; the mourners, clergy, and choir forming a large circle around the perforated brass plate in the floor of the nave, when the remainder of the Service was read by the Bishop of Llandaff, who was also Dean of St. Paul's.

The ceremony being concluded, the mourners retired. The executor, and some of the family of the deceased, went down into the crypt, and saw the body deposited in the grave, at the head of the late President West, not far from the remains of Sir Joshua Reynolds—under an arch, on the wall of which, over the grave, is a bust of Mr. Barry, R.A.

Etty, who followed, says : "Since the days of Nelson, there has not been so marked a funeral. The only fine day we have had for a long time was *that* day. When the melancholy pageant had entered the great western door and was half-way up the body of the church, the solemn sound of the organ and the anthem swelled on the ear, and vibrated to every heart. It was deeply touching. * * * The organ echoed through the aisles. The sinking sun shed his parting beams through the west window; and we left him alone,—Hail, and farewell!"

WILL OF SIR THOMAS LAWRENCE.

The Will is dated July 28, 1828, and directs that Sir Thomas's collection of Drawings by the Old Masters, estimated at 20,000*l.*, should be offered at that sum to various persons : this was done, and the several parties declining the purchase, the collection was otherwise disposed of. Next were to be offered in similar manner, two volumes of Drawings by Fra Bartolomeo, at 800*l.*; the series of original Cartoons of the Last Supper, by Leonardo da Vinci, at 1,000*l.* ; the picture, by Rembrandt, of the Wife of Potiphar accusing Joseph, at 500*l.* ; two small pictures by Raphael, (the *Entombment* and *Charity*,) at 1,000*l.* ; but the several offers being declined, the drawings and pictures, and a collection of architectural casts, were mostly sold by auction.

The superb service of Sèvres porcelain, presented to Sir Thomas by Charles the Tenth, was bequeathed to the Royal Academy of Arts, to be used on the birthday of the King; at the annual dinner on the opening of the Exhibition, and on other public occasions, "in remembrance of the honour conferred by a foreign Prince on the President of the Royal Academy of Great Britain."

The Will then directs that all other works of art in his

possession, whether pictures, drawings, engravings, casts, marbles, bronzes, or models, and books, plate, linen, china, and other effects, should be sold. The produce of such of Sir Thomas's collections of works of art as were sold by auction, was 15,445$l.$ 17$s.$ 6$d.$; and the Testator's estate was about equal to the demands upon it.

LAWRENCE'S HOUSE.

Haydon, on May 25, 1832, visited the house of Sir Thomas Lawrence, in Russell-square. He records, in his Journal: "Nothing could be more melancholy or desolate. I knocked and was shown in. The passages were dusty—the paper torn—the parlours dark—the painting-room, where so much beauty had once glittered, forlorn, and the whole appearance desolate and wretched—the very plate on the door green with mildew.

"I went into the parlour, which used to be instinct with life. 'Poor Sir Thomas!—always in trouble,' said the woman who had the care of the house. 'Always something to worrit him.' I saw his bedroom, small, only a little bed; the mark of it was against the wall. Close to his bedroom was an immense room, (where was carried on all his manufactory of draperies, &c.) divided, yet open over the partitions. It must have been five or six small rooms turned into one large workshop. Here his assistants worked. His painting-room was a large back drawing-room: his show-room a large front one. He occupied a parlour and a bedroom; all the rest of the house was turned to business. Any one would think that people of fashion would visit from remembrance the house where they had spent so many happy hours. Not they,—they shun a disagreeable sensation. They have no feeling, no poetry. It is shocking. It is dirty."

CHARACTERISTICS, RETROSPECTIVE OPINIONS, AND PERSONAL TRAITS.

LAWRENCE AND REYNOLDS COMPARED.

Sir Thomas Lawrence's likenesses were celebrated as the most successful of his time; yet no likenesses exalted so much, or refined more upon the originals. He wished to seize the expression, rather than copy the features. His attainment of likenesses was most laborious : one distinguished person, who favoured him with forty sittings for a head alone, declared he was the slowest painter he ever sat to, and he had sat to many.

Sir Joshua Reynolds seems to have created and idealized the individual person as well as the groups when under his pencil, showing a boldness and diversity of arrangement unexampled in the history of portraiture. Lawrence, compared to Reynolds, was confined and limited far more than his powers could have justified, admitting but small deviation in the placing of the heads—small variety of pictorial composition. The features were painted nearly in all his heads, in the same light and in the same position; but they derived from this a perfection of execution not to be surpassed. In the drawing and touching of the human eye, he gave a lustre and life which Rubens and Vandyck have equalled but not excelled. The question, however, will be how far this deviation from actual appearances may be allowed; for it will be said, can anything be a better representation of a man than the transcript of himself, or can it be a better likeness by being unlike to man ?*

Burnet has well compared the two painters. "The Reynolds' exhibition was richness itself, and glowing with deep-toned brightness, so much so, that the best portraits by Titian or Rembrandt might have been interposed on the walls without gaining the least ascendancy: the gallery during the Lawrence exhibition, on the contrary, looked cold, and many

* Life of Sir David Wilkie.

of the pictures chalky; even the surface, though pure white in the draperies, had become a slate-colour, from the absence of a rich vehicle to preserve the white lead from the action of the atmosphere."

HOWARD'S CHARACTER OF LAWRENCE.

Mr. Howard, the Secretary of the Royal Academy, has left this interesting sketch of Lawrence's talents :—

"In the first part of his career, he was inclined to carry his taste for the colouring of the old masters a little too far, and the pursuit of tone, *chiaro-scuro*, and breadth, led him into a style rather artificial, and approaching to manner; but he gradually got the better of this error, and, by incessant study and application, became at once artful and more natural. Indefatigable, and never satisfied with his productions, like Pope, he laboured hard to gain a reputation, and then laboured hard to maintain it. On one occasion, he is known to have painted thirty-eight hours together, without reposing or taking any sustenance but coffee. It is remarkable that in the latter part of his life, when his great practice might have been expected to make him more rapid in the completion of his work, the increased pains he took, arising no doubt from his improved perceptions, acquired for him the character of slowness,—for him who had painted that admirable picture of Hamlet in so short a time as one week!

* * * * *

"He was a finished draughtsman, had a perfect knowledge of the human figure in its various classes, an exquisite feeling of the beautiful, the grand, and the pathetic, with a rich and luxuriant taste in landscape and background — in short, seemed deficient in no one requisite. He possessed, too, an enthusiastic love for the higher qualities of the art, as was evinced by his admiration of Michael Angelo and Raphael, of Fuseli, Flaxman, and Stothard, which, in a country where there was any demand for historical painting, would have inevitably have led him to the first rank of excellence. The few examples he has left of his talents in this way help to prove it; if we ought not rather to say, that many of his portraits, such as his Kembles, Mrs. Siddons, young Lambton, &c. belong equally to this class of art.

* * * * *

"His great technical excellence seems to have been drawing,

which is, undoubtedly, the true formation of painting. Reynolds is a remarkable and almost solitary instance of what *chiaro-scuro* and ingenuity may do to conceal the want of it; but it enabled Lawrence to make out his heads with a surprising minuteness and accuracy of detail, such as perhaps were never before combined with so much breadth and delicacy.

* * * * *

Proofs of these high qualities are to be found, more or less, in almost all his works, beginning with the lovely portrait of Miss Farren down to Lady Londonderry and the Duchess of Richmond. Those of His Majesty George the Fourth, the Pope, Cardinal Gonsalvi, the Emperor of Austria, Duke of Wellington, Duke of Bedford, Sir W. Grant, young Lambton, the children of Mr. Calmady, &c. are among the finest the art ever produced.

* * * * *

His talents were by no means confined to painting. A nobleman of acknowledged taste, (the late Marquis of Abercorn,) said of him, "He knows only one language, but *that* he knows better than any other man." When young, he displayed great taste in singing, and so much dramatic power, that Sheridan declared him to be the best amateur actor in the kingdom."*

LAWRENCE AND ETTY.

In early life, Etty tells us that he placed himself under Lawrence. Though he painted in the house of Sir Thomas, he received little or no instruction from him. "Still," says Leslie, "the contemplation and copying the works of that eminent man could not but in some degree affect his style; indeed, the Art of Lawrence had so much of fascination in it as to maintain a widely-spread influence over the rising talent of the day, and gradually to undermine till it almost entirely superseded the taste imparted by Reynolds and Gainsborough to higher portraiture.

* Of two plays acted at the seat of Lord Abercorn, in which Lawrence performed along with the Hamiltons and Lindsays, he used to give an account, Fuseli said, in the style of a stage manager. It will be enough to say, that he acted the part of Lord Rakeland, in "The Wedding Day," and of Grainger, in "Who's the Dupe?" before the Prince of Wales, the Duke of Devonshire, the Marquis of Abercorn, and Sheridan; was applauded; and imagined he gained rather than lost in the esteem of the great by this exhibition.

"If Etty acquired a tinge of something in the house of Lawrence which he might better have been without, it is greatly to his praise that he came from it a colourist destined to rank with the very best that have lived; for the school of the great portrait-painter was certainly not one of colour. But I believe his first impressions of harmony were derived more from Fuseli, who, even if his pictures did not prove his sensibility to the refinements of colour, had sufficiently shown it in his lectures, and in no sentence more than that in which he tells us he had always 'courted colour as a despairing lover courts a disdainful mistress,'—a mistress much less disdainful than he imagined."—*Leslie's Handbook*, p. 305.

CAUSE OF LAWRENCE'S EMBARRASSMENT.

It is a remarkable fact, that Lawrence, whose popularity ought to have made him rich, was actually embarrassed in his circumstances throughout life. Was his money spent in profligate dissipation? No: it is quite clear, as far as a negative can be proved, that he was neither a gambler nor viciously extravagant. That a part of his pecuniary difficulties arose from his generosity as to his relatives must be inferred from his own statements, but not to the degree to be considered the principal, still less, the sole cause, of his embarrassed affairs. If he had been a twentieth part as circumspect in money management as in conversation, and half as cautious to avoid innocent extravagance, he would have been, in spite of his generosity to his family, a rich man. But he was utterly heedless of accounts: he kept his books so imperfectly, as to have omitted a debt of 500 guineas due to him from one of the noblest families in the kingdom; and it is probable that he omitted other sitters, who were not so punctilious as that family in volunteering the payment of the unclaimed debt to the executor. He was munificent in his kindness to his brother artists, and was prodigal to all who applied for his charity; and a vast deal more of his time than was commonly supposed, was spent in gratuitous drawings or paintings, of which he made presents to his friends.—*Letter from Mr. T. Campbell; in the Preface to the Life of Lawrence.*

Sir Thomas Lawrence, (says Leslie,) was, perhaps, hindered from rising to the highest rank as a colourist by his early and first practice of making portraits in colourless chalk only. His wish to please the sitter made him yield, more than his

English predecessor had done, to the foolish desire of most people to be painted with a smile.

Of indefatigable industry, Lawrence's habit of undertaking too many pictures at the same time was a serious drawback, in many cases, to their excellence. He began the portraits of children which he did not finish till they were grown up; and of gentlemen and ladies while their hair was of its first colour, but which remained incomplete in his rooms till the originals were grey. The most beautiful of his female heads, and beautiful it is, is the one he painted of Lady Elizabeth Leveson Gower (afterwards Marchioness of Westminster). This was begun and finished off-hand; and so was the best male head he ever painted, his first portrait of Mr. West, not the whole-length in the National Gallery, in which he has much exaggerated the stature of the original. He took especial delight in painting the venerable and amiable President, who offered a remarkable instance of the increase of beauty in old age, and of whom this portrait is a work of great excellence.

It is said, that when money was in his pocket, he dealt it freely among all applicants,—whether mendicant artists, or importunate creditors; and that some of the former found, when they opened his sealed envelope, that, instead of the five pounds which they had solicited, they had obtained fifty. To supply this daily drain upon his income, he was driven to become importunate in money matters himself. Having received one moiety of the price for a portrait, he was frequently obliged to apply for the other before the work was done; and his correspondence with Sir Robert Peel, the greatest patron, under a prince, the painter ever had, is chiefly remarkable for the neat way in which he plays the politician about payment, and solicits the price before the completion of the picture.

Haydon relates, in his coarsest manner, of Lawrence, that in 1825, he addressed the Duke of Wellington at the Royal Academy dinner, and appealed to him for aid to build an academy. The Duke rubbed his face with his hand.

"Here was Lawrence owing the Duke 2,000*l.* nearly, which he had advanced him for a large picture of all his general officers in Spain, and which he had never touched, to the Duke's great anger—here was Lawrence addressing the Duke, both he and the Duke feeling conscious of their private relations, and Lawrence the merest tool of the Academicians, who had set him on. It is pitiable! I never saw any man who had so subdued a look as Lawrence, as if he was worried out of his senses."

PORTRAITS OF SIR THOMAS LAWRENCE.

In Mr. Williams's *Life of Lawrence,* are engraved three portraits by himself, one, when a boy of sixteen, his first attempt in oil; another from a crayon drawing; and the third, in oil. The latter is the picture he was occasionally persuaded to show to his friends, from its concealment beneath his sideboard.

In the collection of the Marquis of Abercorn, at Chesterfield House, South Audley-street, is an unfinished portrait of Sir Thomas Lawrence, by himself.

Sir Thomas once told Mr. West, " the only portrait he ever sat for, was for the character of a soldier in Trumbell's painting of the Siege of Gibraltar."

A person once went to him with an original portrait, by Sir Joshua Reynolds, of Mrs. Piozzi, and which Sir Thomas readily purchased. The bargain concluded, the vendor said "Sir Thomas, I have something in my pocket that will surprise you—it is a portrait of yourself." Sir Thomas, indeed, seemed surprised, and begged to see it, when the stranger took from his pocket a frontispiece from the *Percy Anecdotes.* Lawrence burst out laughing, and saying it was something like, got rid of the person.

In stature, Sir Thomas Lawrence was five feet nine inches high, with handsome limbs, and a body finely proportioned. His appearance was extremely graceful and gentlemanlike. When young, he was an accomplished fencer and dancer. His countenance was open and noble; and his eyes were large and lustrous, and very expressive, insomuch that a lady of taste once said that their light was never tamed down by the gentler emotions, nor the polished suavities of conversation, into harmony with the mild character of his face; the light seemed to kindle still, and he could not put it out. His personal friend, Mr. Baily, the sculptor, was allowed to take a cast of Sir Thomas's fine features after death. His head was finely shaped, and bald: he bore a striking resemblance to Mr. Canning, though his face was not of so elevated an expression or character

THE PAINTER'S DAY AND PRACTICE.

Cunningham thus describes Sir Thomas's diligence:—He rose early, and he worked late; for though no one excelled more in rapid sketches, he had a true enthusiasm for his art, and would not dismiss hastily any thing for which he was to be paid as a picture. He detained his sitters often for three hours at a time; had generally eight or nine of these sittings; and all the while studied their looks anxiously, and seemed to do nothing without care and consideration. His constant practice was to begin by making a drawing of the head full size on canvass; carefully tracing in dimensions and expression. This took up one day; on the next he began to paint; touching in the brows, the nose, the eyes, and the mouth, and finally the bounding line in succession. Lawrence sometimes, nay often, laid aside the first drawing of a head, and painted on a copy. This was from his fear of losing the benefit of first impressions, which in such cases are often invaluable. It may be added, that he stood all the while, and was seldom so absorbed in his undertaking, that he did not converse with his sitter, and feel either seriousness or humour, whilst giving thought to the brow, or beauty to the cheek. He adhered to the old rule of receiving half payment at the beginning of a portrait.

The distinguished person who favoured him with *forty sittings* for his head alone, was Sir Walter Scott. The picture was painted for George the Fourth, and Lawrence was anxious to make the portrait the best of any painted from so celebrated a character.

At other times, however, he was as dexterous as any artist. He once told Burnet that he painted the portrait of Curran in *one day:* he came in the morning, remained to dinner, and left at dusk; or, as Lawrence expressed it, quoting his favourite author,

"From morn till noon,
From noon to dewy eve."

The following were his progressive prices:

	Three-quarters. Guineas.	Half-length. Guineas.	Whole length. Guineas.
1802	30	60	120
	35	70	140
1806	50	100	200
1808	80	160	320
1810	100	200	400

The following were his latest prices:

For a head-size, or three-quarters, the great painter received 210*l.* ; for a kit-kat, 315*l.* ; for a half-length, 420*l.* ; for a bishop, half-length, 525*l.* ; and for a full-length, 630*l.* ; for an extra full length, 735*l.*

Lord Gower paid Lawrence fifteen hundred guineas for his admirable portrait of his lady and child ; and six hundred guineas was the sum paid by Lord Durham for his portrait of Master Lambton.

PAINTING EYES.

One of the critics of this day described the eyes of certain portraits by Lawrence as " starting from their spheres." This remark is curious, for scarcely can ancient or modern art produce a better painter of eyes than Sir Thomas Lawrence. Sir Joshua Reynolds laid it down as a fixed principle that, to create the beautiful, the eyes ought always to be in mezzotint. Sir Thomas Lawrence, though always aiming at the beautiful, never pursued this rule ; for his eyes had scarcely any tint at all, or were tinted above the mezzo. In his painting-room in Russell-square, the light was high ; but in that at 57, Greek-street, it was higher than artists usually paint from, for it was introduced from the second story by the removal of the floor.

He is ever insisting upon the importance of *eyes* in pictures. Writing to a young artist, he says: " The eyes of the boy are two dark blots, and ill-formed. Let this carelessness be soon impossible to you. Be at the pains often to draw that feature: I can quote high authority for it ; I have a sheet of eyes, drawn by Michael Angelo, for some young painter, like yourself, whose genius had excited the friendly effort."

Lawrence excelled in painting fine mouths and dark eyes ; and he took great pleasure in painting an ear, the intricate and elegant drawing of which, he said, required mastery to imitate.

It was once the lot of Sir Thomas to converse with a thorough wrong-head, who maintained that " Mr. Lawrence, the painter, had been a regular pupil of Sir Joshua Reynolds." At last, somewhat irritated, he replied, " Sir, I am the identical Mr. Lawrence you allude to ; and the only instruction I ever received from Sir Joshua was a kind offer to correct my drawings, if I brought them to him."

LAWRENCE'S PORTRAITS.

That there is much truth in the following criticism by Haydon is admitted more than it was some thirty years since, when it was written.

"Lawrence's flesh has certainly no blood. He sacrifices all for the head; and what an absence of purity of tint, in comparison with Vandyke or Reynolds! His excellence is expression, but it is conscious expression; whereas the expression of Reynolds, Vandyke, Titian, Tintoretto, and Raphael is unconscious nature.

"Lawrence is not a great man: indeed posterity will think so. Lady Lyndhurst's hands are really a disgrace in drawing, colour, and everything. He affects to be careless in subordinate parts, but it is not the carelessness of conscious power; it is the carelessness of intention.

"Since he went to Italy, his general hue is greatly improved, but his flesh is as detestably opaque as ever.

"Lawrence is dead!—to portrait-painting a great loss. Certainly, there is no man left who thinks it worth while, if he were able, to devote his powers to the elevation of commonplace faces.

"He was suited to the age, and the age to him. He flattered its vanities, pampered its weaknesses, and met its meretricious taste.

"His men were all gentlemen, with an air of fashion, and the dandyism of high life; his women were delicate, but not modest—beautiful, but not natural. They appear to look that they may be looked at, and to languish for the sake of sympathy. They have not that air of virtue and breeding which ever sat upon the women of Reynolds.

"Reynolds's women seem as unconscious of their beauty, as innocent in thought and pure in expression—as if they had shrunk from being painted. They are beings to be met with reverence, and approached with timidity. To Lawrence's women, on the contrary, you seem to march up like a dandy, and offer your services, with a cock of your hat, and a 'd——e, will that do?' Whatever characteristics of the lovely sex Lawrence perpetuated, modesty was certainly one he entirely missed.

"Twenty years ago, his pictures (as Fuseli used to say,) were like the scrapings of a tin-shop, full of little sparkling bits of light which destroyed all repose. His latter pictures are by far his best. His great excellence was neither colour, drawing, composition, light and shade, nor perspective, for he was hardly ever above mediocrity in any of these,—but expression, both in figure and feature. Perhaps, no man that ever lived contrived to catch the fleeting beauties of a face to the exact point, though a little affected, better than Lawrence. The head of Miss Croker is the finest example in the world. He did not keep his sitters unanimated or lifeless, but by interesting their feelings, he brought out the expression which was excited by the pleasure they felt.

"As a man Sir Thomas Lawrence was amiable, kind, generous, and forgiving. His manner was elegant, but not high-bred. He had too much of the air of always submitting. He had smiled so often and so long, that at last his smile had the appearance of being set in enamel."

CORONATION PORTRAITS.

Immediately after the coronation of George IV. the King sent for Sir Thomas Lawrence, and directed him to paint a full-length portrait of him in his coronation robes, seated in St. Edward's chair, with his regalia, as he appeared at the altar in Westminster Abbey. It will surprise the public to learn, that the numerous full-length portraits of his Majesty, in his Garter robes, were paid for only at the rate of 300 guineas each,—less than one-half of Sir Thomas's regular price.*—*Life of Lawrence, by Williams.*

Leslie tells us that Sir Thomas Lawrence made a sketch of George the Fourth in the armour of the Black Prince; but had the good sense not to carry the matter further than a sketch.

THE LAWRENCE DRAWINGS.

When Sir Thomas Lawrence's collection of Drawings was offered for sale to the Government, Sir Charles Eastlake, as might have been expected, was eager in urging their purchase. "When the drawings were in Mr. Keightley's hands," says Sir Charles, "I requested permission to take some of them to Lord Brougham, then Lord Chancellor. Lord Lansdowne and Talleyrand were present: the drawings were

* We have been informed that for copies of regal portraits subsequently painted—half-lengths, for presents—the price has been twenty guineas!

examined by them, and I remember Talleyrand saying: 'If you do not buy these things, you are barbarians.' And barbarians we proved; but the real barbarians in the Lawrence case were Lord Grey and Sir Martin Archer Shee."

This celebrated collection became the property of Mr. S. Woodburn, at whose death it was dispersed by auction. The drawings were purchased by Mr. Woodburn from the representatives of Sir Thomas Lawrence, and among the works enumerated in the catalogue were some precious ones of Michael Angelo and Raphael, several of the former having been procured direct from the Buonarotti family, and many of them engraved by Ottley. In this rare collection were also some splendid specimens of Correggio, Rubens, and Rembrandt, and other great masters, as well as the celebrated portrait of the Duke of Reichstadt, by Sir Thomas Lawrence.

LAWRENCE'S ENGRAVED PORTRAITS.

The painter considerably increased his income by lending his portraits to be engraved, and he knew well how to bargain with a print-publisher: indeed, he is said to have been hard to deal with. He considered that as the painter he retained a right in the picture after he had been paid for it, as well as to choose the engraver and direct the work. If this view was not supported by law, it was by practice, or the painter considered himself shabbily treated.

Lawrence's pencil generally elicited the finest specimens of engraving that ever did honour to English talent. The painting of the Calmady children was engraved in line by Mr. Doo; and the sketch was exquisitely given by Mr. Lewis, in the perfection of the power, delicacy, and truth of his engravings of the beautiful plain and tinted drawings of Lawrence.

When the engraving of the Calmady sketch was brought to him, he exclaimed that it was the most beautiful he had ever seen, and asked Mr. Lewis if he would dispose of the plate. A sum was named, and Lawrence immediately paid twenty guineas more than was asked. Mr. Lewis observed to him that the world thought he flattered in his likenesses. "I have never pleased myself as to nature, but only as to likeness," said Lawrence; "there, you see (pointing to the Calmady sketch,) what a falling off we make from nature."

When Sir Thomas first sent for Mr. Lewis, he politely said,

"You are, I believe, the artist that engraved Michael Angelo's Last Judgment for Mr. Ottley, and you are able to do anything for me. I am extremely anxious to have a portrait of a friend, Sir Charles Stewart (Lord Londonderry,) engraved." Mr. Lewis replied that he had never engraved a portrait, and was diffident of his powers on such a finished drawing. Lawrence, immediately shaking him by the hand, rejoined, "I am most happy to confide it to you;" and he insisted upon its performance.

Lawrence was above all vanity or selfishness; for he used to say to Mr. Lewis, "You must not any longer engrave from my drawings; you must engrave the drawings of Michael Angelo, Raphael, and of Claude and Rembrandt, at the Museum. The Museum intends to appoint you engraver, and I long to possess your copies of the Claudes." But Sir Thomas (says Williams) forgot that our Government bestows no patronage upon the arts; and to their shame be it said, that at this time, the votes to the British Museum were very much reduced in amount, owing to the heavy expenses of the sovereign!

No man could be more friendly, liberal, and generous to his engraver, than Sir Thomas. He greatly evinced these feelings to his favourite lithographic artist, Mr. Lane. Sir Thomas, though imbued with a rational piety, seems to have respected Sir Joshua Reynolds's remark, that the man who made Sunday an idle day, would never make a great painter. Mr. Lane found him one Sunday morning touching a proof of one of his engravings. After a few observations upon not being at church, Lawrence begged him to alter, on the stone, the touches he had just added to the proof. Mr. Lane excused himself by observing, that he had pledged himself to his dying father, never to work on a Sunday. Sir Thomas smiled, but he respected the sacred character of the promise, and concluded the interview with feeling and delicacy. It is, however, well known that some years before his death, Lawrence felt scruples about working on the Sunday, which, in his earlier years he had practised without concern: he then became almost constant in his attendance at church.

Sir Thomas was careful not to hurry his engravers. It was feared that all posthumous prints would evince the want of careful and repeated touches which he gave to every plate during his life-time: but this was not the case. The plates of Lady Georgiana Ellis, and of young Lambton, were engraved after the death of Lawrence. Some time previously, one day, when he was shown his fine drawing of this boy, he was much affected, and observed, "How very little I have improved since that."

KINDNESS AND GENEROSITY TO ARTISTS.

Among Lawrence's amiable traits was his rejoicing at the success of the clever and the enthusiastic. He writes these lines of fair encouragement dated March, 1829, to a young artist whom he had requested to draw a view of Rome :—
"I need not tell you how sincerely I rejoice in your success: hitherto you have 'won your spurs by your own valour,' however much the kindness of friendship may have cheered you in the contest. The painting of your figures last year convinced me of your increasing ability in the study of the human figure ; and, unless you attempt the higher dramatic or epic style of composition, you already walk in perfect safety, and need fear no pit-fall in your path. I am anxious to see the picture you are now sending, of which I heard, last night, a very favourable opinion from Mr. Turner. There is a gentleman here who is desirous of having two small pictures of you, about the size of the Boy and Girl, at your own price and subject. He is not in the circles of fashion, but known to almost all our artists by his liberal patronage and gentlemanly conduct. His name is Vernon. Let me know that you undertake them for him. There are many competitors for your little picture of 'The Youthful Italian Lovers ;' but having your own authority for considering it to be Mr. Bailey's, I retained it for him. Beautiful as your drawing of the same subject was, I preferred the picture. I am well acquainted with the talents and intelligence of Mr. Havell ; if you now go to complete those sketches which were but slightly traced with him, and add to them the colour and effects of nature, your tour with a man of such known taste and knowledge of composition, whether beautiful or grand, will have been all gain, and the benefit lasting. I shall not fail to give your remembrances to Callcott, who will be much gratified with the report of your success. You are fortunate in having still the society of Mr. Eastlake ; an advantage that cannot be too highly appreciated."

Cunningham has preserved this interesting record of Sir Thomas Lawrence's liberality.

"I may say with safety," writes a now well-known painter,

"that Sir Thomas Lawrence was one of the best friends I ever had. I found him at all times most ready and liberal in his advice and visits; and when the oppressive number of his engagements would not allow him to go out of the house, he would always see the humblest student at home. I had the pleasure of making him a great number of drawings in water colours—always sketches done on the spot; and I know he frequently conferred this honour upon me, more to assist and encourage my exertions than from any wish to possess the drawings themselves: and for all I did for him in this way he paid me at the moment, and always handsomely; generally more than any one else who encouraged me. He never lost an opportunity of recommending my drawings and paintings among his distinguished friends; and I am even now feeling the effects of this generosity."

A painter, of considerable merit, but without patronage, left at the house in Russell-square three of his pictures for Sir Thomas's inspection. He called one evening to learn the President's opinion, and to take away the pictures: he sent up his name, when Lawrence followed the servant down stairs, and put a folded paper into the hand of the artist, saying: "I had left this should you have called whilst I was from home. I much admire your productions, and wish you every success." The painter had only patience to get to the first lamp, when, unfolding the paper, he found within it a 30$l.$ bank-note, which saved him from despair.

We are gratified in the Memoirs of Mr. Uwins, R.A. with this frank testimony to Lawrence's sincerity and service to his brother artists: it occurs in a letter to the writer's brother, Mr. David Uwins:

"You must not suppose the President, though so very polite, is on that account insincere. It will always be recorded to his glory, that he has ever shown himself the kind friend and protector of aspiring talent. I have received from him much kind instruction and advice, and with many it does not stop there: his connexion and even his purse have been ready to back his counsels. There are many who owe their reputation to his fostering aid, and others who without him could never have been able to make their first step in life with courage and stability. His manner is most courtier-like, but his purpose is firm, and his opinion sincere. Poor West used to overwhelm young men with flattery, and often spoil them; Lawrence befriends them without spoiling them. He puts them firm on their legs, but never lifts them into stilts. This is the voice not only of my own experience, but the experience of hundreds, and my conscience would never allow me to pass in silence any opportunity of defending him from the censure which his extreme politeness often brings upon him."

LAWRENCE'S SENSITIVENESS.

In 1823, while John Thurtell lay in prison, committed for trial for the murder of Mr. Weare, Sir Thomas Lawrence expressed a wish to be allowed, without observation, to take a glance at Thurtell, as he took his exercise in the prison-yard. This request was not only refused, but misrepresented as an application to take a cast of the prisoner's face, and this cruel misstatement found its way into the newspapers. Sir Thomas read this gross impeachment of his humanity with much pain one morning, when he had to wait upon George the Fourth at the palace to take a sitting for the celebrated "sofa portrait." The Painter was so affected, and depressed in spirits that he could hardly proceed with his work. The King observed his distress, inquired the cause, and upon its being explained, expressed his sympathy with Lawrence's susceptibility.

But this sensitiveness conduced to the perfection of his art. "That fineness of feeling," said one of his most gifted friends, "which made him so sensible to the slights and caresses of the world, probably gave him in his art a delicacy of thought and of touch scarce ever surpassed: making him alike sensible to the utmost refinements of nature in his own labours, as well as powerfully alive to any deficiency in them, in the works of others. This, however, which made so much of the charm of his art, with which he could seize, and give an interest to the scarcely visible irregularities of beauty, and touch the feathers, or the silver tissue, with a lightness which seemed to suspend them in the air itself, was in him, as it always must be with genius, accompanied by a strength where strength was wanted, which gave to all that was fine and delicate its true value. When once asked what he was doing, he said, 'All uncertainty—taking refuge in difficulties.'"

His forgiveness of slight or injury has been shown in many instances: in his conduct to Harlow, this was strikingly evident. His goodnature was exhaustless. He had not the power to say nay, either for his purse or his pencil. A lady, who had been liberal in her invectives against him, requested him to make some change in the portrait of her mother after her death. A friend, on reading the request, said, "Why should you waste your time on her; she who heaps many a scandal on you with witty and persevering malice?" He replied, with a smile,—"Oh, never mind: I know she does as you say: but nobody else can do what she wants, and I must do it for her;" and he did.

ON THE GENIUS OF FLAXMAN, BY LAWRENCE.

In Sir Thomas's Address to the Royal Academy, upon delivering the Medals to the successful candidates, on December 11, 1826, he thus descanted upon our greatest sculptor.

"Mr. Flaxman's genius, in the strictest sense of the word, was original and inventive. His purity of taste led him, in early life, to the study of the noblest relics of antiquity; and a mind, though not then of *classical education*, of classic basis, urged him to the perusal of the best translations of the Greek philosophers and poets; till it became deeply imbued with those simple and grand sentiments, which distinguish the productions of that favoured people. When engaged in these mingling studies, the patronage of a lady of high rank,* whose taste will now be remembered with her own goodness, gave birth to that series of compositions from Homer and the Greek tragedians, which continues to be the admiration of Europe. These, perhaps, from their accuracy in costume, and even from the felicitous union between their characters and subjects, to minds unaccustomed to prompt discrimination, may have conveyed the idea of too close an imitation of Grecian art. Undoubtedly, the *elements* of his style were founded on it; but only on its noblest principles: on its deeper intellectual power, and not on the mere surface of its skill. He was more the sculptor of sentiment than of form; and while the philosopher, the statesman, and the hero, were treated by him with appropriate dignity, not even in Raphael have the gentler feelings and sorrows of human nature been traced with more touching pathos, than in the various designs and models of this estimable man. The rest of Europe know only the productions of his genius when it bent to the grandeur

* The late Dowager Countess Spenser.

of the antique; but these, which form its highest efforts, had their origin in nature only; and in the sensibility and virtues of his mind. Like the greatest of modern painters, he delighted to trace from the actions of familiar life, the lines of sentiment and passion; and from the populous haunts and momentary peacefulness of poverty and want, to form his inimitable groups of childhood, and maternal tenderness, with those nobler compositions from holy writ—as beneficent in their motive, as they were novel in design—which open new sources of invention from its simplest texts, and inculcate the duties of our faith.

"In piety, the minds of Michael Angelo and Flaxman were congenial. I dare not assert their equality in art—the group of 'Michael and the Fallen Angel' is a near approach to the greatness of the former; and, sanctified as his memory is by time and glory, it gained no trivial homage in the admiration of the English sculptor; whose Shield of Achilles—that divine work! unequalled in its combination of beauty, variety, and grandeur—*his* genius could not have surpassed.

"But I trespass too long on the various business of this evening. To be wholly silent on an event so affecting to us all, was quite impossible.*

"I know the great and comprehensive talents that are around me; I know the strength remaining to the Academy: but with long experience of the candour which accompanies it, I feel that I may safely appeal to this assembly, for their acknowledgment with mine, that the loss of Mr. Flaxman is not merely a loss of power, but a loss of dignity to the Institution—deep and irreparable loss to art—to his country and to Europe!—not to posterity—to whom his works, as they are to us, will be inestimable treasures; but who, knowing how short and limited the span that Providence has assigned to the efforts of the longest life, and the finest intellect; and learning that his genius, though its career was peaceful, had inadequate reward,—will feel it to be their happier destiny, to *admire*, and not to *mourn* him—to be thankful that he had *existed*, and, not like us, to be depressed that he is gone, to revere and follow him as their master, and not, as is our misfortune, to lament him as their friend!

"He died in his own small circle of affection;—enduring

* Mr. Flaxman died on the 7th of December, 1826, aged 72; and on the 15th Sir Thomas Lawrence attended his funeral to the churchyard of St. Giles's-in-the Fields.

pain—but full of meekness, gratitude, and faith! recalling to the mind, in the pious confidence of his death, past characters of goodness; with the well-remembered homage of his friend—

> 'And ne'er was to the bowers of bliss convey'd,
> A *purer* spirit, or more *welcome* shade.'"

PORTRAITS OF THE DUKE OF WELLINGTON, BY LAWRENCE.

England's greatest hero is best known by the portraits painted of him by Sir Thomas Lawrence; of whose laborious painstaking the Duke seems, however, to have been occasionally impatient.

The Duke of Wellington once said Lawrence was a man of no mind. Set the thing before him, and he could do it; but he had no invention. Wellington stood for Lawrence three hours with his hands across. After he had done, he stepped down, and said, "Pshaw! that is not like my sword." "Please your Grace, I'll do it next time." "Do it now." "I must go to the Princess Augusta's." "Oh, no! you must put my sword right. It is really bad." This was done.

Yet Wellington was not always so impatient, but would take a lesson. Upon one occasion, when about to sit to another painter, he said, "I know—Lawrence told me how to sit."

There are four portraits of the Duke by Sir Thomas Lawrence, of each of which numerous repetitions exist.

The first in order of date is that representing the Duke with the Sword of State, painted for the Prince Regent, for the Waterloo Gallery at Windsor, and exhibited at the Royal Academy in 1815. This picture was engraved in line by Bromley, with the following inscription:—"The Duke of Wellington, as he appeared on the Day of Thanksgiving at St. Paul's, for the ratification of that Peace, the attainment of which his valour, genius, and wisdom had so essentially promoted; distinguished by the insignia of those honours with which a grateful country and applauding Europe had invested him, and bearing, by command, the Sword of England." This is a very dazzling picture, ambitious in style, with a very broad light from above and behind—where, also, is a view of St. Paul's. It is, however, by no means the most pleasing of Lawrence's portraits of the Duke.

The next is the portrait of the Duke, "in the Dress that he wore, and on the Horse that he rode, at the Battle of Waterloo," painted for Earl Bathurst, and exhibited in 1818. This is a very spirited moving picture: the Duke mounted on his charger, "Copenhagen," waving his hat, and giving the word for the Guards to make that eventful and resistless charge which decided the fortune of the day of Waterloo. Of this picture, Wilkie, who saw it before it went to the Exhibition, writes to Sir George Beaumont, 19th January, 1818 :—
"Sir Thomas Lawrence has almost completed his equestrian portrait of the Duke of Wellington. This I have seen, and think it a happy effort. He is dressed in a plain blue coat, and a large cloak of the same colour over it. It is the dress he wore at Waterloo; and, not being a regimental dress, has a very uncommon, though inherently military look about it. It is one of those images of the Duke that is likely to supplant every other; and I should not be surprised if it were to become as common throughout the country as Sir Joshua's Marquis of Granby. It is rather a dark picture, and I could wish that it had something of a quality which has almost gone out of fashion in the present day—I mean *tone* in the colouring."

The third portrait, painted by Lawrence, is that done for Mr. Arbuthnot, in 1816. It is a half-length, representing the Duke in a military cloak, with the right hand thrown across to the left shoulder. This has been repeatedly engraved; in mezzotint, by Cousins and by Jackson; in line, by Dean Taylor and by Charles Smith; and in smaller sizes, in mezzotint, by M'Innes, Burgess, and others.

This was always the favourite portrait with the Duke; and we think not without reason; for the expression is very pleasing, combining manliness with delicacy and refinement of sentiment. It may be mentioned that the great Commander, though never betraying a particle of personal vanity in the little sense, was proud of the estimation in which he was held both by the public and a numerous circle whom he honoured with his friendship; and a very usual mode of marking his esteem was the presentation of a print of himself, generally the Arbuthnot one, with his autograph affixed, and in a plain little maplewood frame. This, for instance, was his usual *souvenir* to the hundreds of brides whom he had "given away," and, probably, the most gratifying testimonial he could bestow. Only a few days before his death, he gave one of these modest keepsakes to an individual of illustrious rank.

It happened that, in September, 1852, the Duke and Duchess of Mecklenburg-Strelitz, on their return from England to the Continent, paid a visit to the Duke at Walmer, when, in the course of conversation, the Duchess asked "the Duke" which of the many portraits existing of him he considered the best. The latter immediately pointed to the little maple frame hanging from the wall, in which was a print of the "Arbuthnot picture," and announced his preference for it. Upon the Duchess remarking that she would send to London for a copy, "the Duke," with his usual gallantry, declared she need not do so; and, taking the print down from the nail whereon it hung, begged her to accept it, which she did. No sooner had his visitors left the room, however, than the Duke took thought of the blank space which he had made on his wall, and also the absence of his portrait from the line of Lord Wardens, Pitt, and others, which he had arranged thereon, and, with his usual love of order, promptly set about refilling it. The very next morning a note reached Messrs. Graves and Co., in the Duke's hand—"F. M.'s compts.," &c. —requesting that they would, with as little delay as possible, procure for him a copy of the Arbuthnot portrait, framed in maplewood, and forward it to Apsley House, whence it would be transmitted to Walmer. No time was lost in putting into execution his Grace's order, and a message was sent to the steward at Apsley House, announcing that the print, framed, would be ready for delivery on the following day. In the meantime, four days only after the first note, came another from the Duke, dated "7th Sept. 1852," in which he referred to the order already given, and "begged to know if it had been received, and what progress had been made in the execution thereof?" The print, framed, as ordered, crossed this second note on the road, and was hung up by the Duke in the place of the former one, one little week before he died.

Last in order is a whole-length of the Duke in a military cloak, standing on the field of Waterloo, and holding his reconnoitering telescope; an admirable likeness, and soldier-like figure. This picture was painted in 1818, for Sir Robert Peel, who, both on account of the veneration in which he held the original, and also his value for it as a painting, so jealously prized it, that for many years he was not to be induced to let it go out of his possession for the purpose of being engraved. It was, however, eventually engraved, in 1848, in mezzotint, by Cousins; and how it came to be so is so creditable to all parties, that we record the circumstances. It will be recollected that, in 1847, Sir Robert Peel gave a day *conversazione* to men of arts and letters at his house, in Privy Gardens. Mr. Colnaghi, the print-publisher, on that occasion, lent his services to the ex-Premier in arranging the various prints and works of art in the rooms, lending, indeed, several for the purpose. A few days afterwards, Sir Robert Peel called to thank him, and asked what he was in his debt. Mr. Colnaghi replied that he was very happy to have been of service in the matter, but could not think of making any charge. Sir Robert appreciated the delicacy with which this was said, but, thanking the worthy publisher, begged to know if there was no way in which he could make some return for his kindness. Mr. Colnaghi then took courage, again broached the subject of the Duke's portrait; and, after a brief hesitation, Sir Robert consented, only requiring to know for how long he would have to part with the picture. "One twelvemonth," was the reply. "I consent," rejoined the Statesman; "but recollect, that whether the engraving is finished or not, I must have the portrait back one twelvemonth from the day you receive it." Mr. Colnaghi promised, and kept his word. The picture was punctually returned to Drayton Manor on the day twelvemonth; but the engraving not being then quite finished, Mr. Cousins was obliged to go down after it, to put the finishing touches. This was not very long before the untimely death of England's illustrious statesman, and art's considerate patron.

From Lawrence's hand we have also a life-size head of the Duke, in crayons (a vehicle which this artist commanded with the happiest delicacy and precision), drawn in 1815; and engraved in chalk by F. C. Lewis. There appears to have been two plates of this sketch—one square, the other surrounded by an oval line. The latter has the following quotation from Napier's "Peninsular War":—

Iron hardihood of body; a quick and sure vision; a grasping mind; untiring power of thought, and the habit of minute and laborious investigation and arrangement: all these qualities he possessed; and with them, that most rare faculty of coming to prompt and sure conclusions on sudden emergencies. Steadily holding on his own course, he proved himself a sufficient man, whether to uphold or conquer kingdoms. How many battles he fought—victorious in all.

If we mistake not, one of the first who had the honour of painting the Duke, after the death of Sir Thomas Lawrence, was Wilkie; to whose style the Duke was always very partial, and who, we believe, was the only artist that ever received a "commission" from him; namely, in the case of the *Chelsea Pensioners.**

WORKS OF SIR THOMAS LAWRENCE IN LONDON, ETC.

These few notes of the location of some of Sir Thomas's finest portraits in the metropolis may be interesting to his admirers, as they are mostly accessible, with proper means.

At Mr. Murray's, 50, Albemarle-street, the portrait of *the poet Moore*, painted for the late John Murray.

At St. Bartholomew's Hospital, West Smithfield, in the Court-room, a fine portrait of *Mr. Abernethy*.

In the Dulwich Gallery is a portrait of *Mr. W. Linley*.

At Chesterfield House, May Fair, Lawrence's unfinished portrait of himself.

At Stafford House, St. James's: Portraits of *Earl Clanwilliam;* the *Marchioness of Westminster;* and *Lady Gower and Child.*

At the Athenæum Club-house, Pall Mall, of *George IV.*, a fine, full-length, unfinished portrait, the last work of Lawrence: he was painting one of the orders on the breast a few hours before he died.

At the Garrick Club-house, King-street, Covent Garden, a drawing of *Mrs. Siddons.*

At Merchant Tailors' Hall, Threadneedle-street, a full length portrait of the *Duke of York*, second son of George III.

At Sir Robert Peel's, Privy Gardens, Whitehall, fifteen pictures, all painted for the late Sir Robert Peel, next to George IV. the great patron of Lawrence: *Lady Peel*, in a hat, companion to the *Chapeau de Paille; Miss Peel*, with a dog; *Duke of Wellington*, full-length, in his military cloak, and holding a telescope; *Lord Chancellor Eldon*, seated, *Lord Stowell*, seated; the *Earl of Liverpool*, full-length; *Mr. Canning*, full-length, speaking in the House of Commons; *Lord Aberdeen*, three-quarters, standing.

Burlington House, Piccadilly: In the Royal Society's meeting-room, portrait of *Sir Humphry Davy, Bart.*

* These characteristic details, from the pen of an able art-critic of the day, appeared in the *Illustrated London News* shortly after the death of the Duke of Wellington, in 1852.

Royal Academy, Trafalgar Square: Diploma picture, *a Rustic Girl.*

Soanean Museum, Lincoln's Inn Fields: in the dining-room, a portrait of *Sir John Soane,* the architect.

In the National Gallery, (British School,) are portraits of *Mr. Angerstein; a Lady; John Philip Kemble, as Hamlet; Benjamin West,* P.R.A.; *Mrs. Siddons;* the *Dowager Countess of Darnley; John Fawcett,* comedian; and *Sir John Soane,* R.A.

CELEBRATED PORTRAITS.

In 1810, the Exhibition of the Royal Academy contained four capital pictures, by Lawrence. The first portrait—*Viscount Castlereagh*—was an admirable likeness and well painted, but was violently abused by Mr. Peter Finnerty, in the *Morning Chronicle.* He had, by his strong political writings, drawn upon himself the vengeance of the Irish government, of which Lord Castlereagh was then Secretary, and whom he hated as the origin of the Union, and as the advocate of English or Anglo-Irish politics in Ireland. Lord Castlereagh's amenity of disposition never forsook him, and whenever he met Finnerty in the streets, he bowed to him with suavity, and inquired after his health. Peter's ire was not, however, to be in the least quenched by this gentle bearing; and in reviewing the Royal Academy Exhibition of this year, he so attacked the portrait of Lord Castlereagh, that poor Mr. Lawrence, who read the abusive critique in the *Morning Chronicle* next day, was altogether disgusted, and was for many days unable to resume his placidity of disposition. He complained bitterly to Mr. Perry, his friend, whose inexhaustible good nature made him really regret the mischief, and led him to do all he could to pacify the artist; but there seemed to be a fatality attending the subject. In 1814, another portrait of Lord Castlereagh was exhibited at the Academy by Lawrence: here was an opportunity of making the *amende honorable* for the former injury. The subject had, however, escaped Perry's recollection, and the identical Finnerty was again sent to review the Exhibition. Peter, true to his political animosities, pounced again upon the Secretary's portrait, and here is his account of it: The " Portrait of Lord Castlereagh, by Lawrence, is not a likeness. It has a smug, smart, upstart, haberdasher look, of which there is nothing in Lord Castlereagh. The air of the whole figure is direct and forward;

there is nothing, as there ought to be, characteristically circuitous, involved, and parenthetical in it. Besides, the features are cast in quite a different mould. As a bust, Lord Castlereagh's is one of the finest we have ever seen : it would do for one of the Roman emperors, bating the expression." The reader may imagine the distress of the sensitive Lawrence upon reading this second outrageous tirade ; though the portrait, it must be confessed, conveyed no idea of the figure and carriage, and very little of the face, of Lord Castlereagh.

The second Portrait upon our list (exhibited in 1810,) was that of *Mr. Canning*, the first of that statesman Lawrence had taken ; "and (says Mr. Williams,) contrary to the almost invariable character of the artist's works, Mr. Canning's fine face and form were the only ones, which his pencil did not, in this instance, or in any other, improve. He generally made the face more wrinkled and haggard than it was, nor did he impart to it its really fine animation and intellectual expression. The portrait, a three-quarters, is both the most pleasing, and the most accurate, of any of those taken by Lawrence. There must have been some extraordinary difficulty in catching the expression of this great man's countenance, for no artist succeeded in the attempt, whilst Sir Thomas Lawrence was remarkably correct in comparison with others."

One of Sir Thomas's latest works was another portrait of Mr. Canning: indeed, it was almost the last portrait to which the painter gave the finishing touch. On the Saturday morning preceding the Thursday on which he died, he wrote to a friend and patron : " I have the pleasure to tell you that Lord Seaford thinks it much the best portrait of Mr. Canning that I painted. It is, I think, acknowledged to be so by the casual visitors to my rooms ; but the authority of so near a personal friend is still more gratifying than the general impression."

The portrait of *Lord Melville* was the third in the exhibition of 1810. Lawrence used to relate a strange disclosure which his Lordship made to him during one of the sittings for this picture. Parts of the metropolis were at this time agitated by a demagogue who had been active in the Reform and Revolutionary Societies of 1793, and who continued to this hour his patriotism, at "so much per speech." "You know not," said Lord Melville to Lawrence, "the sources of those sentiments towards the English public (taking the expression in its lowest sense), with which men in office are so often reproached. That man, who is now an idol of the populace, and for whom they are disturbing the peace of London, and endangering their own safety, was long in my pay at three guineas a-week, when I was Secretary of State, and he was one of the secretaries of the Reform Society. Every week he used to bring me the correspondence, minutes, and private books of the Society, and acquaint me with all the open and concealed members, and with the whole arcana of what was going on; and when I was fully satisfied that he had told me everything, and with veracity, I used to pay him his weekly bribe of three guineas." This confession to Lawrence, on the part of Lord Melville, must have argued extreme candour, or extreme insensibility to the nature of the transaction. " His Lordship," Mr. Williams adds, "must be exonerated from the subsequent practice which prevailed, of not using information thus obtained, at a time when moderate punishment would check the disaffected, but of allowing the informer to stimulate to crime, or at least of renewing the information, until the criminals were deemed fit for the executioner!"

But we willingly pass to a pleasanter reminiscence of 1810 —the fourth picture—*A group of Portraits, consisting of Mrs. Wall, and her brother, T. Baring, Esq., and the sons of the late Lady Baring.*

In a letter to Miss Lee, Lawrence describes this picture as " a work embracing many difficulties in the art. A group of five portraits comprising a single domestic scene, from its design approaches more to historical character than is usually seen in pictures of this kind; yet I think, with a great deal of nature in it, the colouring and effect are carried farther and on higher principles than in any other I have painted, and this with more general harmony and freedom from my defects. It has less manner and more style."

DEATH OF MR. LOCK, AND MR. HOPPNER, R.A.

This year, (1810,) Lawrence had the misfortune to lose his intimate friend, Mr. W. Lock, of Norbury Park, Surrey, a zealous protector of the arts, and an enlightened amateur. Mr. Lock, early in life, made a choice collection of pictures, models, and fine works of sculpture. He was the associate or patron of Reynolds, Barry, Hoppner, and Cipriani; of Wilson, Barrett and Sandby; and West and Fuseli. He was a man of excellent taste and judgment, and his scholarship procured him a public testimony from Dr. Johnson. In the mansion of his beautiful seat, Norbury Park, one of the most picturesque estates in the country, he left a memorial of his taste in a magnificent saloon, the walls of which were painted according to Mr. Lock's plan, by Barrett, Cipriani, Gilpin, and Pastorini; these embellishments being intended as a seeming continuation of the views through the saloon windows—the vale included by Box-hill, and the hills of Norbury and Dorking. Mr. Lock was a fine example of the English gentleman, and we are familiar with his name and family through Madame D'Arblay's interesting *Diary*. At Norbury, they were beloved, and almost venerated. Mr. Lock died at the age of seventy-eight. Lawrence attended his funeral, which was conducted in the simplest manner, exactly as that of his mother had been—a walking funeral, and the coffin borne by his labourers, to the fine Anglo-Norman church at Mickleham.

In the same year died Hoppner, the formidable rival of Lawrence, who called several times upon him during his last illness in the spirit of friendship and sympathy; but Hoppner unfeelingly denounced these visits as merely the gratification of a rival's joy at his approaching dissolution! Assuredly no such feeling ever actuated Lawrence, whose kindness to Mr. Owen, and to all his friends, in sickness, was excessive. In a letter, Lawrence writes: "The death of Hoppner leaves me, it is true, without a rival, and this has been acknowledged to me by the ablest of my present competitors; but I already find one small misfortune attending it, viz., that I have no sharer in the watchful jealousy, I will not say hatred, that follows the situation." In a previous letter, he had written with this fine feeling: "You will be sorry to hear it, my most powerful competitor, he whom only (to my friends) I have acknowledged as my rival, is, I fear, sinking to the grave—I mean, of course, Hoppner. He was always afflicted with bilious and liver complaints, (and to these must be greatly attributed the irritation of his mind,) and now they have ended in a confirmed dropsy. But though I think he cannot recover, I do not wish that his last illness should be so reported by me. You will believe that I can sincerely feel the loss of a brother artist, from whose works I have often gained instruction, and who has gone by my side in the race these eighteen years."

CONSTABLE AND SIR THOMAS LAWRENCE.

Constable called, according to custom, after he had been chosen Academician, to pay his respects to the President, Sir Thomas Lawrence, who did not conceal from his visitor that he considered him peculiarly fortunate in being chosen an Academician at a time when there were historical painters of great merit on the list of candidates. So kind-hearted a man as Lawrence could have no intention to give Constable pain; but their tastes ran in directions so widely different, and the President, who attached great importance to subject, and considered high art to be inseparable from historical art, had never been led to pay sufficient attention to Constable's pictures to become impressed with their real merit; and there can be no doubt but that he thought the painter of, what he considered, the humblest class of landscape, was as much surprised at the honour just conferred on him, as he was himself. Constable was well aware that the opinions of Sir Thomas were the fashionable ones; he felt the pain thus unconsciously inflicted, and his reply intimated that he looked upon his election as an act of justice rather than favour.

Shortly after this interview, at the opening of the year 1830, Constable wrote to Leslie as follows: "January, 1830. My dear Leslie,—I send the 'Churchyard,' which my friends in Portman-place are welcome to use for any purpose but to go into it. * * The motto on the dial is, '*Ut umbra, sic vita.*'" This note was singularly followed by his next: "January 8th. My dear Leslie,—I have just received the distressing intelligence of the death of poor Sir Thomas Lawrence. This sad event took place last night, in consequence of internal inflammation. I could not help sending to you; the Council is called in consequence."

Constable, though always on friendly terms, had never been very intimate with Sir Thomas Lawrence; but he felt, in common with every artist in the kingdom, the magnitude of the loss of so eminent a painter, cut off with such apparent suddenness; at a time, too, when he was pursuing his art with all the energy of youth, though in his sixty-first year; and when, indeed, so far from betraying any diminution of power, he seemed to be improving on himself. This (says the writer) I think was acknowledged by all who had an opportunity of seeing the scarcely finished but very fine portrait of the Earl of Aberdeen, in the Exhibition at the Academy that followed the death of the President.

When the painting materials of Sir Thomas were sold, Constable purchased a palette which had belonged to Sir Joshua Reynolds, and had been given by him to Sir George Beaumont, who gave it to Lawrence. He presented this interesting relic to the Academy, with its history inscribed on a silver plate inlaid on it.—Selected from *Memoirs of the Life of John Constable, Esq., R.A., composed chiefly from his Letters*, by C. R. Leslie, R.A. 1845.

"MR. CALMADY'S CHILDREN."

This group of two lovely infants, in its history, exhibits Sir Thomas Lawrence in a most amiable point of view.

It appears that Mr. Lewis, the engraver, had often suggested to Mrs. Calmady, that her two children, Emily and Laura, would make excellent subjects for a painting; and he assured her that if Sir Thomas Lawrence were to see the children, he would be glad to paint them on any terms. But the question of terms was one of great difficulty with the parents.

In July, 1823, Sir Thomas saw the two girls. The terms, upon his card, on his mantelpiece, descended from 600 guineas to 150, which was the price of the smallest head size. Having two in one frame increased the price by two-thirds, and thus the regular charge for the portraits would have been 250 guineas.

Sir Thomas, captivated by the loveliness of the children, and sympathising with the feelings of the mother, asked only 200 guineas. "I suppose," says Mrs. Calmady, "I must still have looked despairingly, for he immediately added, without my saying a word, 'Well, we must say 150 pounds, for merely the two little heads in a circle, and some sky—and finish it at once.'"

Sir Thomas commenced his task the next morning at half-past nine; and never did artist proceed with more increasing zeal and pleasure.

Upon the mother expressing her delight at the chalk drawing, as soon as the two heads were sketched in, he replied that "he would devote that day to doing a little more to it, and would beg her acceptance of it, as he would begin another."

The public, in one sense, must be glad at this liberality; for a more beautiful sketch was scarcely ever made: it even gave promise of a more exquisite work than that which Lawrence afterwards completed. Both the faces were full, and that of the child now in profile was more lovely than the side-face; and both were more soft and delicate than in the finished picture.

During the progress of the painting, Sir Thomas kept saying that "it would be the best piece of the kind he had ever painted;" and not only would he detain the children many hours, with their father and mother, keeping them in good humour by reading stories to them, or otherwise amusing them, but he often kept them to dinner, that he might get another sitting that day. Sir Thomas was once seen with one child on his knee, feeding it with mashed potatoes and mutton chop, whilst he was coaxing and caressing the other fed by the servant. Whenever he kept the children for the day, he always fed them himself, and played with them; and when the meal and sport were over, they were again placed in the chair, and the business of the portrait proceeded.

At one sitting he was interrupted by the arrival of a packet from the King of Denmark, which he opened and read to Mr. and Mrs. Calmady. It contained his election to the rank of Honorary Member of the Royal Academy of Denmark, signed by the King. After reading the compliments paid to him by his Majesty, Sir Thomas smiled, and said: "The fact is, they have heard I am painting this picture."

At one sitting, after Sir Thomas had the shoe of little Emily Calmady often taken off, and had attempted to catch her playful attitudes and expressions, he could not help exclaiming: "How disheartening it is, when we have nature before us, to see how far—with our best efforts and all our study—how very far short we fall of her."

One day having fed the children with their dinner, as they sat on his knees, he drew to the table to take his luncheon; but when he rose, to his surprise, he found that the child had got hold of his palette and paints, and with her hands had daubed her face in a ludicrous manner; and when Mrs. Calmady entered the room, she found Sir Thomas and his servant busily washing the child's face and hands.

These anecdotes and traits are trifling, but they show Sir Thomas's kindly nature. Sir Joshua Reynolds's delight at the gambols of children was equally in accordance with his amiable manners and kind heart; and to this we owe his exquisite paintings of infants and children, some of which may survive his best historical or fancy pictures.

At length, Sir Thomas finished the painting of the Calmady children, when he declared: "This is my best picture. I have no hesitation in saying so—my best picture of the kind, quite—one of the few I should wish hereafter to be known by."

This picture was sent to the Royal Lodge, Windsor Park, for the inspection of the King, who had heard of it from the Duchess of Gloucester. The engraving of it had a very large sale; and so much did that of the chalk drawing please Sir Thomas that he insisted upon the engraver, Mr. Lewis, taking eighty instead of sixty guineas for his production.

It has been stated that "Sir Thomas Lawrence lost large sums of money, by trying to bring young engravers into notice, and to get them employed." About the time of engraving these two children, there was a young engraver, to whom Sir Thomas gave a drawing to execute. When he brought the plate, Lawrence, in paying him his demand, observed, "it is of no use to me." The poor engraver, from these words being spoken "in so kind a manner," had no idea that he alluded to the worthless plate, but thought he referred to the money; and he observed that it was very odd, though it was very polite, in Sir Thomas saying when he paid him the money, "that it was of no use to him."

PORTRAIT OF THE HON. C. W. LAMBTON.

This beautiful picture was exhibited at the Royal Academy in 1828, and the admiration which it then excited was extended by the mezzotinto print from it, which became extremely popular. A smart critic of the time described it as one of the most exquisite representations of interesting childhood that he had ever beheld. The simple action and sweet expression of infantile nature which we see in this portrait, were never excelled by Sir Joshua Reynolds, in his happiest moments. The boy is seated amid some rocky scenery, enjoying, apparently, a waking dream of childhood, and, for the moment, unconscious of external objects. His attitude is simple and natural—just as a child might throw himself down on a green bank, after being fatigued with sport,

x

when the flow of his animal spirits subsides, without being exhausted. His dress being of crimson velvet, is, of course, very rich; yet it never attracts the attention for an instant from that soft look of innocence, and those engaging eyes, which reflect the loveliest light of a pure and happy mind. It is, indeed, one of those works that make the painter forgotten in the reality of the creation which he has produced. The colouring is warm and chaste; the execution is marked with equal feeling and accuracy.

Allan Cunningham, however, gives a very different account of the work. "It is a magnificent piece of colour; but there is a total absence of all simplicity. He has seated the boy on a rock, his legs and arms extended for the purpose of covering space, and his look fixed above, with all the upturned intensity of a Newton."

The young gentleman upon whom the painter had bestowed so much of his art, was the eldest son of J. G. Lambton, afterwards Earl of Durham, by his second wife, daughter of Charles, Earl Grey, and was born in January, 1818. He was seven years of age when Sir Thomas Lawrence painted the above portrait: he died in 1831, the year after that in which the painter laid down his pencil for ever.

It is hardly possible to look upon this interesting picture of innocent childhood, of imitative art and beautiful nature, without feeling one's heart more than "idly stirr'd" at the brief existence of this graceful scion of a noble house. The reader may lament that

> Rough winds do shake the darling buds of May,
> And summer's lease hath all too short a date.

But it is better to take refuge in the home philosophy of our great metaphysical poet:

> Thus fares it still in our decay;
> And yet the wiser mind
> Mourns less for what Time takes away
> Than what he leaves behind.

PORTRAIT OF THE HON. MRS. HOPE.

This truly splendid portrait of the amiable wife of the author of *Anastasius* was one of the bright stars of the Academy Exhibition of 1826. Sir Thomas Lawrence's judgment is evinced by choosing a picturesque costume and national character, to which the lady's face was adapted; and the colouring, with every minor adjunct, combines to produce an unity of expression. Mrs. Hope's features and complexion were of the Grecian cast, prominent and aquiline, though delicate, with a fine oval contour; and a lively, intellectual air, heightened by a clear dark complexion. Sir Thomas has represented the lady as an oriental Fatima, in a turban superbly embroidered with gold, and a dress of rich, glowing red, ornamented with splendid jewels. The hands are small and delicate, and free from that dark colour with which the painter so often tinged the hands of his sitters.

Time has brought the whole colour of this beautiful picture to an excellent tone: it is glowing, rich, and gorgeous, without being meretricious, or in the least over-painted. By giving the name of an individual to a painting, it is taken from the highest branch of art, and considered only as a portrait; but this work may be enjoyed as the emanation of a rich and fertile fancy—a picture of great art, and in the school of imagination.—(*Williams's Life of Lawrence*, vol. ii.)

This picture is the gem of the family portraits at the Deepdene, in Surrey. Here also is a portrait of Thomas Hope, Esq., in a Turkish dress, a full-length, painted by Sir William Beechey. Sir Thomas Lawrence also painted Master Charles Hope (who died young), as the Infant Bacchus: an excellent mezzotint has been executed from this picture by Cousens. Here likewise are portraits of Lady Decies, (the mother of the Hon. Mrs. Hope,) and her infant daughter, painted by Sir Joshua Reynolds.

COWPER AND LAWRENCE.

The following is one of the poet's graceful letters of renewed invitation to the painter to visit him in the country:

"DEAR SIR,

"As often as I have comforted myself with the hope of seeing you again soon, I have felt a sensible drawback upon that comfort, from the fear of a disappointment, which, considering your profession and your just pre-eminence in it, appeared to me extremely probable.

"Your letter, most welcome otherwise, gave me this most unwelcome information the moment I saw your name at the bottom of it. We all feel our loss, and much as I suppose you are beloved by my friend Rose, who has pretty acute discernment, I will venture to say he is not more mortified than myself. You do me justice, if you believe that my invitation did not consist of words merely: in truth, it was animated by a very sincere wish that it might prove acceptable to you: and once more give the same assurance, that, at any time when you shall find it possible to allow yourself some relaxation in the country, if you will enjoy it here, you will confer a real favour on one whom you have already taught to set a high value on your company and friendship. I am too old to be very hasty in forming new connexions; but, short as our acquaintance has been, to you I have the courage to say, that my heart and my door will always be gladly open to you.

* * * * * *

"Mrs. Unwin sends her compliments, and sincerely joins me in the wish that you will never hereafter consider us strangers, or give us reason to think you one.

"I remain, dear sir, affectionately yours,
"WILLIAM COWPER.

"Weston, Oct. 13, 1793.

"When will you come and give me a drawing of the old oak?

"To Thomas Lawrence, Esq.
Old Bond-street, London."

LAWRENCE'S PORTRAIT OF WILBERFORCE.

There are few of the portraits of Lawrence in which the accomplished President was more happy in hitting off the character of his subject—his inner man, as well as his outward mien and manner—than in that of Wilberforce, the respected champion of Slave Trade abolition. There is here none of the grandiose "make up" of his princes and ministers —none of the haberdashery display which we find in some of his lords and ladies of fashion; nothing but the homely, honest features of an accomplished and benevolent gentleman as he sat in his easy-chair conversing on matters of, to him, engrossing interest with some familiar friend. This fine portrait, dated 1828-9, was left unfinished by the artist, only the face, the collar of the coat, cravat, &c. being completed— the rest of the figure being loosely sketched in. But it is, perhaps, on that very account all the more interesting to the connoisseur and student, every touch being unquestionably that of the great master of modern portraiture. This picture was presented to the National Portrait Gallery by the executors of Sir Robert Harry Inglis, Bart. in 1857.

J. M. W. TURNER, R.A.

BIRTH-PLACE OF TURNER.

SOME ninety years ago, when Covent Garden was a fashionable part of the town, it was famed for its *perruquiers*, or hair-dressers, and dealers in articles of dress and personal ornament, and the streets were crowded with carriages at shopping hours. Tavistock-street and Henrietta-street appear to have been especially noted for *perruquiers*, who have scarcely disappeared altogether. Some thirty years since, we remember two of these court hair-dressers, one in each of the above streets, where, during the operation of hair-cutting, might be heard some gossip of the fashionable celebrity of the locality. A minor street shared this distinction, in addition to other fame : this was Maiden-lane, extending from Southampton-street to Bedford-street. There is evidence of this celebrity in the sign of the *White Peruke*, in Maiden-lane, at which lodged Voltaire, who was in England three years.

As you proceed through Maiden-lane, near its west end, on the right hand, opposite the Cyder Cellars, (opened about 1730,) is a small paved place, with an arched entrance, named Hand-court ; and here, at the corner of the court, in the house No. 26, lived William Turner, who "dressed wigs, shaved beards, and in the days of queues, top-knots, and hair-powder, waited on the gentlemen of *the Garden* at their own houses, and made money by his trade, then a more flourishing profession than that of a hair-dresser of the present day." Here, in the spring of 1775, in the chamber over the shop, was born the barber's son, Joseph Mallord (supposed to have been originally Mallard) William Turner, "the most prolific, the most varied, and the greatest landscape-painter of the English school." Neither his mother's name, nor the day of his birth is known ; but his baptism is recorded in the register of St. Paul, Covent Garden, on the 14th of May, in the same year in which he was born.*

---

* With regard to the home of Turner's childhood, Mr. Alaric Watts states, on the authority of Mr. Duroveray, that it may have been even lowlier than was at first represented ; since that gentleman believed that it was the cellar under the hairdresser's shop in Maiden-lane which "was

When, or in what way, the young Turner first evinced a love for art, no one has told us. His first drawing is said to have been a lion, copied from an emblazoned coat of arms, in the house of one of his father's customers. He went thither with another object—to take a lesson in hair-dressing from the practice of his father whom he accompanied; but the boy's attention was more occupied by the coat of arms on the table, than with the old man's skill with the comb and curling-tongs. The rich colours in the arms attracted the lad's attention; but his imitation got no further than the lion. The father was not displeased at this effort in an opposite direction to hair-dressing, for which he was intended: when asked, as he often was, "Well, Turner, what is William to be?" he would reply, with a look of delight, "William is going to be a painter." He was, accordingly, provided with water-colours and brushes, and the father was proud to show his customers the boy's coloured drawings. He soon evinced skill beyond these boyish exercises, and was employed to colour prints by John Raphael Smith, the crayon-painter and mezzotinto engraver, who lived in Maiden-lane, and next in King-street, Covent Garden. Another of Smith's *colourers* at this period was Thomas Girtin, the founder of our English school of water-colour art. Girtin, (according to Bryan,) was the same age as Turner, and from him it was that Turner acquired his love for landscape-painting. Meanwhile, his father did not attempt to make him a scholar, and the great painter never advanced far beyond the rudiments of an ordinary English education.

At this period, too, he had excellent practice in the art he had chosen, by putting skies and foregrounds into the designs and elevations of Porden,* the architect. The skill which he thus acquired was of use to him in after life; "when, (says Mr. P. Cunningham,) tempted by large sums, he threw a thunder-cloud, or a summer-sky, a rainbow, or some novel effect in nature, over the careful but unartistic representations of places made by architects and amateurs for the purposes of the engraver."

inhabited by the family, and that drawings of a similar character (to an early one after Paul Sandby) were hung round its entrance, ticketed at prices varying from one shilling to three."

* Porden was an architect of some note in his day: he built the Royal Stables, with the noble dome, at Brighton, for the Prince Regent. The daughter of Mr. Porden was the first wife of Sir John Franklin, the Arctic navigator.

TURNER ADMITTED A STUDENT OF THE ROYAL ACADEMY.

When only twelve years old, (in 1787, supposing his baptismal year was the year of his birth,) Turner exhibited at the Royal Academy, (under the name of W. Turner,) two drawings, *Dover Castle*, and *Wanstead House*. In 1789, in his fourteenth year, he was admitted a student of the Academy. It is, however, hardly probable that he received much direct instruction in the Academy schools, or that he followed their prescribed course. If he studied in the Antique, or later in the Life School, he certainly never acquired mastery over the human form, and no instruction was given the student in landscape-drawing or painting. Still, it is not likely that a young enthusiast, as he certainly was, would attend the schools and form acquaintance with professors and students without acquiring from them much technical information, even if he received no systematic instruction.

He sent to the next year's exhibition, in Somerset House, his next exhibited work, *A View of the Archbishop's Palace at Lambeth*, a water-colour drawing, which was hung in the room set apart for "sculptures and drawings."

Having thus felt his way to Somerset House, he sent to the next year's exhibition two views—*The Palace at Eltham*, and *Swakeley House, near Uxbridge*. He had now walked beyond Maiden-lane and the banks of the Thames at Lambeth, to a day's excursion in Kent and Middlesex; and he soon sought more distant subjects for his pencil. These he found in *Malmesbury Abbey*; in *The Avon near St. Vincent's Rocks*; in *St. Anselm's Chapel, Canterbury Cathedral*; in *The Forest of Malvern*; in *Tintern Abbey*; in *The Second Fall of the Monach, in Cardiganshire*; and in cathedrals, castles, and other picturesque subjects.

His love for strange effects showed itself very early: he was fond of throwing a remarkable sunshine over a crumbling tower or boiling torrent. In 1792, he painted *The Pantheon in Oxford-street*, after the fire in January of that year; and in the following year, *A Rising Squall over St. Vincent's Rocks at Bristol*, which was recognised as a work of great promise.

Turner was essentially a self-made painter. It is said, in a brief notice of him published in 1805,—when, though only in his thirtieth year, he was already considered as the first of living landscape-painters,—"Turner may be considered as a striking instance of how much may be gained by industry, if accompanied with perseverance, even without the assistance of a master. The way he acquired his professional powers was by borrowing, when he could, a drawing or picture to copy ; or by making a sketch of any one in the exhibition early in the morning, and finishing it up at home. By such practices, and by a patient perseverance, he has overcome all the difficulties of the art."—(*Dayes's Professional Sketches of Modern Artists.*) This passage was written by one eminent in his day as an instructor of young landscape-painters, and the teacher and friend of Girtin, Turner's earliest artistic associate ; and it coincides with what other authorities, both written and traditionary, have always related of his career.

TURNER'S FIRST PATRONS.

Turner used to say his best academy was "the fields and Dr. Monro's parlour." The doctor, who was a warm-hearted patron of young artists, had an excellent collection of water-colour drawings and engravings at his house in the Adelphi, and he not only gave his two *protégés*, Turner and Girtin, free access to his treasures, with permission to copy them, but directed their studies, and encouraged them to make sketches of the scenery round London, which he readily purchased at prices satisfactory to the modest students. Nor was Turner unmindful of Monro's kindness. "There," said he, in a conversation with David Roberts, "there," pointing towards Harrow, "Girtin and I often walked to Bushey and back, to make drawings for good Dr. Monro, at half-a-crown apiece,—and the money for our supper, when we got home."

Monro, it is said, was attracted to Turner's works by the rare merit of certain drawings exposed in a shop in Maiden-lane. This was, probably, Raphael Smith's shop.

In their sketching rambles, Turner and Girtin were constant companions, and they formed for themselves a style of water-colour painting very different from that of any of their predecessors,—unless it be Cozens, a man of some genius, and a friend of Dr. Monro, from whose drawings and conversations much was probably learned by the two young painters. As Girtin was the more regularly educated artist, it is not unlikely that he was, to some extent, Turner's tutor : certain it is that their drawings were very similar in style—the chief difference being that Turner made out his details more carefully; and some have fancied that had Girtin lived, he would have been as great a painter as his friend. He gave way, however, to intemperance, and died Nov. 1802, in his 27th year; John Cozens died three years previously, in a madhouse, under Dr. Monro's care; and Dayes died in 1804, by his own hands. The end of these three early companions of Turner was very remarkable. Turner, with more self-control and perseverance than either of them, laboured steadily on, and rose in good time to the undisputed supremacy of his branch of art.

Mr. Cunningham mentions as Turner's early patrons, Mr. Tomkison, the pianoforte-maker, who lived in Soho; and the Rev. Mr. Crowle, whose illustrated copy of Pennant's *London* is one of the treasures of the British Museum.

It may be as well to add that John Cozens was the son of Alexander Cozens, a Russian by birth. He followed a mode of composing his landscapes, which Turner imitated on many occasions. His process was to dash out, in dark brown or bistre, and on several pieces of paper, large blots and loose flourishes of effects, such as may or may not be seen in nature. From these he would select certain forms and combinations, which led at times to very grand ideas; although it is said that his selections were too often sombre and heavy, like nature viewed through a dark-coloured lens. His son, John Cozens, was an abler artist. He was patronised by Beckford, and his drawings are eagerly sought for by collectors in the present day. His style is said, by Edwards, to have "served as a foundation to the manner since adopted by Turner and Girtin, both of whom copied many of his drawings."

Turner, (says Ruskin,) began with water-colours; a mode of painting which he practised at later periods of his life with wonderful power. He acknowledged great obligations to Cozens, and still more to Girtin, but had inferior power to either. Had Turner died as young as Girtin, his name would only have survived as that of a second-rate painter. His genius was of later development, and first appeared in those grand, classic, and marine subjects which he painted in the early part of the century. The sea-pieces were his own; the others were made up from various sources in Art, and though noble works, yet are not generally those on which his fame will ultimately rest. His *Snowstorm in the Alps*, however, *with Hannibal and his Army*, would alone justify the highest praises of his friends; and his *Ulysses*, painted at a much later period, is a poem of matchless splendour and beauty.

Turner continued his topographical drawings, as alike pleasurable and profitable; and for this purpose he made fresh excursions in the English counties. His pictures of 1795 show him to have been in the previous year to Oxford, Peterborough, Lincoln, Shrewsbury, and Wrexham; the Exhibition of 1796—that he had been to Ely, Llandaff, and the Isle of Wight; and the Exhibition of 1798, that he had strayed among the abbeys of Yorkshire, the castles of Northumberland, and the fells and lakes of Cumberland.

As early as 1796, he began to paint sea-shore scenes—the Exhibition of this year having his *Fishermen at Sea;* that of 1797, *Fishermen coming on Shore at Sunset, previous to a Gale;* and 1798, *Fishermen Becalmed, previous to a Storm—Twilight*—pictures, which Mr. Cunningham tells us, competent judges state to possess many of the qualities which are recognised in the best works of Turner's best time.

TURNER'S EARLY STYLE.

Cozens is likewise considered by Burnet to have paved the way for both Girtin and Turner, in striking out a broad effect of light and shade. The early pictures of Turner possess their breadth, but are destitute of the brilliant power of light and colour afterwards pervading his works, and ultimately carried to the greatest extreme in his last pictures. Breadth of light seems to have been latterly his chief aim, supported by the contrast of hot and cold colour: two of his unfinished pictures in the lecture at the Academy exemplified this principle; they were divided into large masses of blue where the water or sky was to come, and the other portions laid out in broad orange-yellow, falling into delicate brown where the trees and landscapes were to be placed. This preparation, while it secured the greatest breadth, would have shone through the other colours when finished; giving the luminous quality observable in his pictures. In many instances, his works sent for exhibition to the British Institution had little more than this brilliant foundation, which was worked into detail and completed in the *varnishing days*, Turner being the first in the morning, and the last to leave; his certainty in the command over his colour, and the dexterity in his handling, seemed to create, in a few hours, "an unsubstantial pageant" into a finished landscape. These *ad captandum* effects, however, are not what his fame will depend on for perpetuity: his finest pictures are the production of great study in their composition, careful and repeated painting in the detail, and a natural arrangement of the colour and breadth of the chiaroscuro.—*Burnet; Turner and his Works.*

TURNER ELECTED R.A.

For some ten or twelve years Turner painted in water-colours, with the exception of two or three fancy subjects, such as the *Battle of the Nile*, 1799, and the *Fifth Plague of Egypt*, 1800. Already it was felt that in his pictures were brilliancy of execution and close observation of nature which placed his works high above those of his contemporaries. This opinion received confirmation by his election, in 1799, as an Associate of the Royal Academy; and in 1802, he became an Academician.

His diploma picture, presented to the Academy on his election, and still preserved by that body, is a view of *Dolbadern Castle, North Wales*, thought by some a favourable example of his art at this period.

TURNER VISITS THE CONTINENT.

In the year in which Turner was elected an Academician, he made his first visit to the Continent. He now launched boldly into oil-painting on canvasses of large size. He had previously visited Scotland, and the Exhibition of 1802 showed as his contributions, the *Falls of the Clyde; Kileburn Castle; Edinburgh, from the Water of Leith; Ben Lomond* mountains; *the Traveller;* besides, *Jason;* the *Tenth Plague of Egypt; Fishermen upon a Lee-shore in squally Weather,* and *Ships bearing up for Anchorage.*

In his Continental visit, he found his first subject on landing—*Calais Pier, with French Poissards preparing for Sea; an English Packet arriving.* From Calais he went to witness the *Vintage of Mâcon*, of which he painted a large and fine picture for Lord Yarborough. He then pushed on into Savoy and Piedmont, and returned with his portfolio full of sketches for future pictures, of which the chief were *Bonneville, with Mont Blanc; Château de St. Michael, Bonneville, and Fall of the Rhine at Schaffhausen,* one and all leading attractions at the Academy Exhibitions from 1803 to 1806.

His favourite master was now Richard Wilson. In the

Vintage of Mâçon, he endeavoured to combine the qualities of Claude and Gaspar Poussin; in others he sought to combine all the English qualities of Gainsborough's art with the characteristics of Claude. Some of his sea-pieces were in Loutherbourg's manner, but with the freshness and poetry of Gainsborough's works of this class.

"THE GODDESS OF DISCORD IN THE GARDEN OF THE HESPERIDES."

> " All amidst the gardens fair
> Of Hesperus, and his daughters three,
> That sing about the golden tree;
> Along the crisped shades and bowers,
> Revels the spruce and jocund spring;
> The graces and the rosy-bosom'd hours,
> Thither all their bounties bring."
>
> <div align="right">Milton's <i>Comus</i>.</div>

This magnificent picture, which has been bequeathed by the painter to the nation, was painted in 1806, and is in his early manner. It does not remind one of Wilson, but of a compound of Salvator's Calabrian rocks, and Dughet's Vales of Romagna. This picture is full of grand invention: we are sensible of a feeling of sublimity in its beetling cliffs and thunder-cloud; while below we have the placid vale, with its chequered lights and umbrageous recesses. The figures, too, are excellent—far beyond the usual Turner. In his later pictures, real men and women are as if wraiths of Children of the Mist; but here the Immortals are given with all the beauty and grace of the tangible flesh and blood of those delicious southern regions which furnished models for the chisel of a Phidias, and the pencil of a Nicholas Poussin. In none of the pictures of Turner is the story told with more distinctness. The daring feat of the Dragon is successful: we do not deride, but curiously examine the monster guardian of the fruit, who was destined in the sequel to be destroyed by Hercules; and we admit one of the most difficult feats of painting has been accomplished. This work stands at the threshold of Turner's so-called classical style; up to this time he had almost exclusively painted home scenery. No longer tied down by the effort to surmount technicality, he now ventures a bolder flight to the airy regions of fancy. This grand work will be found *engraved for the first time* in the *Illustrated London News* for Jan. 31, 1857; whence the above details are abridged.

THE LIBER STUDIORUM.

An important circumstance in the earlier career of Turner was his publication of the *Liber Studiorum*, which was commenced in 1808. This now famous work was undertaken in rivalry of the book of sketches known as the *Liber Veritatis* of Claude, in the possession of the Duke of Devonshire, of which a series of fac-simile aqua-tinta engravings were made by Earlom and others. Turner's series, engraved in a similar style, some of them by Turner himself, embraced examples of all the principal forms of landscape composition, and displayed a fertility of resource and an intimate observation of nature, such as the publications of no previous landscape-painter had approached. The work was long extremely rare, and when brought to sale commanded a very high price.

Among the earliest scenes of this great work occur the magnificent Mont St. Gothard and Little Devil's Bridge. Now, it is remarkable that after Turner's acquaintance with this scenery, so congenial in almost all respects with the energy of his mind, the proportion of English to foreign subjects should in the rest of the work be more than two to one, and that those English subjects should be—many of them—of a kind peculiarly simple, and of every-day occurrence; such as the Pembury Mill, the Farm-yard composition with the White Horse, that with the Cocks and Pigs, Hedging and Ditching, Watercress Gatherers (scene at Twickenham), and the beautiful and solemn rustic subject called a Water-mill; and that the architectural subjects, instead of being taken, as might have been expected of an artist so fond of treating effects of extended space, from some of the enormous Continental masses, are almost exclusively British: Rivaulx, Holy Island, Dumblain, Dunstanborough, Chepstow, St. Katherine's, Greenwich Hospital, an English Parish Church, a Saxon ruin, and an exquisite reminiscence of the English lowland castle in the pastoral with the brook, wooden bridge, and wild duck; with the greys of Vandevelde. The sea in the Great Yarmouth should be noticed for its expression of water in violent agitation, seen in enormous extent from a great elevation. There is almost every form of sea in it,—rolling waves dashing on the pier—successive breakers rolling to the shore—a vast horizon of multitudinous waves—and winding canals of calm water along the sands, bringing fragments of bright sky down into their yellow waste. There is hardly one of the views of the *Southern Coast* which does not give some new condition or circumstance of sea.

"ULYSSES DERIDING POLYPHEMUS."

This is one of Turner's grandest triumphs, and was painted in 1829. The subject is taken from that immortal voyage which is the Patriarch of all Romaunt. A narrowly-understood Christianity leads us to look down with contempt on the mythology of the Greeks. Not so the sympathetic imagination of a more Catholic Christianity, which can, without effort, look upward to the religious sentiment and religious forms of the Greeks from the lower plane of darker ages, cruder intelligence, and the more ungraceful mythology of Baal and Osiris. Ruddy sky, such as we never saw in any other picture, is graduated with fan-like expression through floating clouds of gold in one part of the picture, which harmoniously contrasts with cool, grey-tinted masses of supernatural shadow at the other extremity. A magnificence of invention and conception strikes at once upon the spectator. Great as the execution is, we feel that form and colour have limits which do not express but rather shackle the soul of the poet-painter. This picture is more than Claude in execution, and almost more than Milton in that power which lies in a vague impression of preternatural sublimity.*

TURNER AN AFFECTIONATE SON.

Turner was always attentive and affectionate to his father; and as soon as he expressed a wish to leave Maiden-lane, and retire from business, he was received by his son into his own house. The father died in Queen Anne-street in 1829, at the age of 84, and was buried in the church of St. Paul, Covent Garden, where his grave is marked by a very simple tablet erected by his son.

The father's habits of getting and saving were as eager as Turner's own. It is said that the old man took shillings from visitors for showing his son's pictures; but this is peremptorily denied by Mr. Alaric Watts.

Turner's father was born at Southampton, Devonshire, which place he left at an early age, to settle in Maiden-lane.

A son of Stothard, living at the time of Turner's death, perfectly remembers his father relating to him that, in early

---

* Illustrated London News, Jan. 31, 1857.

life, he went one day to Turner, the hair-dresser's shop in Maiden-lane to get his hair cut, when the barber remarked to him in conversation, "My son is going to be a painter."

THE OLD TEMERAIRE TOWED INTO HER LAST BERTH.

Turner invested this subject, exhibited in 1839, with all the interest it was capable of receiving. The *Fighting Téméraire*, as the sailors used to designate her, was well known to veterans of the war with France: she was taken from the French at the battle of the Nile, and after a warrior's career, finished it gloriously at the battle of Trafalgar, leading the van under Collingwood, and breaking the line of the combined fleets. She was always, therefore, a crack ship with our British tars, and the subject, no doubt, of many a long yarn; when she left Plymouth on her last cruise for Greenwich, she was saluted with several hearty cheers by the officers and men in the dockyards. She was towed round to her last destination off Deptford, as the hospital-ship for the seamen of all nations. Turner has, therefore, treated her, in the evening of her days, with a glorious sunset. Haydon, in his picture of *Bonaparte musing at St. Helena*, and his *Wellington on the field of Waterloo*, had availed himself of the same association of ideas; but it was reserved for Turner to spread a halo over the last days of a British man-of-war.—*Burnet; Turner and his Works.*

"THE SLAVE-SHIP."

This was the chief Academy picture of the Exhibition of 1840; when nothing could exceed the critical violence with which it was attacked. "But," says Mr. Ruskin, "I think, the noblest sea that Turner has ever painted, and if so, the noblest, certainly, ever painted by man, is that of the Slave-ship. It is a sunset on the Adriatic, after prolonged storm; but the storm is partially lulled, and the torn and streaming rain clouds are moving in scarlet lines to lose themselves in the hollow of the night. The whole surface of sea included in the picture is divided into two ridges of enormous swell, not high, nor local, but a low, broad heaving of the whole ocean, like the lifting of its bosom by deep-drawn breath after the torture of the storm. Between these two ridges, the fire of the sunset falls along the trough of the sea, dyeing it with an awful but glorious light, the intense and lurid splendour of which burns like gold, and bathes like blood. Along this fiery path and valley, the tossing waves by which the swell of the sea is restlessly divided, lift themselves in dark, indefinite, fantastic forms, each casting a faint and ghastly shadow behind it along the illumined foam. They do not rise everywhere, but three or four together in wild groups, fitfully and furiously, as the under strength of the swell compels or permits them; leaving between them treacherous spaces of level and whirling water, now lighted with green and lamp-like fire, now flashing back the gold of the declining sun, now fearfully dyed from above with the indistinguishable images of the burning clouds, which fall upon them in flakes of crimson and scarlet, and give to the reckless waves the added motion of their own fiery flying. Purple and blue, the lurid shadows of the hollow breakers are cast upon the mist of the night, which gathers cold and low, advancing like the shadow of death upon the guilty* ship as it labours amidst the lightning of the sea, its thin masts written upon the sky in lines of blood, girded with condemnation in that fearful hue which signs the sky with horror, and mixes its foaming flood with the sunlight,—and, cast far along the desolate heave of the sepulchral waves, incarnadines the multitudinous sea.

"I believe, if I were reduced to rest Turner's immortality upon any single work, I should choose this. Its daring conception—ideal in the highest sense of the word—is based on the purest truth, and wrought out with the concentrated knowledge of a life; its colour is absolutely perfect, not one false or morbid hue in any part or line, and so modulated that every square inch of canvass is a perfect composition; its drawing as accurate as fearless; the ship buoyant, bending, and full of motion; its tones as true as they are wonderful;† and the whole picture dedicated to the most sublime of subjects and impressions—(completing thus the perfect system of all truth, which we have shown to be formed by Turner's

---

* She is a slaver, throwing her slaves overboard. The near sea is encumbered with corpses.

† There is a piece of tone of the same kind, equal in one part, but not so united, with the rest of the picture, in the storm scene illustrative of *the Antiquary*, (also by Turner)—a sunset light on polished sea. The sea in the Lowestoffe is a piece of the cutting motion of shallow water, under storm, altogether in grey, which should be especially contrasted, as a piece of colour, to all of which we have nothing foreign to oppose but three slight, ill-considered and unsatisfactory subjects, from Basle, Lauffenbourg, and Thun.

works)—the power, majesty, and deathfulness of the open, deep, illimitable sea."—*Modern Painters*, vol. i.

FAILURE OF TURNER'S VERY RECENT WORKS.

Mr. Ruskin, in his able work just quoted, has strictly limited the perfection of Turner's Works to the time of their first appearing on the walls of the Royal Academy. "No *picture* of Turner's (he adds,) is seen in perfection a month after it is painted. The *Walhalla* cracked before it had been eight days in the Academy rooms; the vermilions frequently lost lustre before the exhibition was over; and when all the colours began to get hard a year or two after they were painted, a painful deadness and opacity came over them, the white especially becoming lifeless, and many of the warmer passages settling into a hard valueless brown, even if the paint remained perfectly firm, which was far from being always the case. I believe that in some measure these results are unavoidable; the colours being so peculiarly blended and mingled in Turner's present manner as almost to necessitate their irregular drying; but that they are not necessary to the extent in which they sometimes take place, is proved by the comparative safety of some of even the more brilliant works. Thus, the *Old Téméraire* is nearly safe in colour, and quite firm; while the *Juliet and her Nurse* is now the ghost of what it was; the *Slaver* shows no cracks, though it is chilled in some of the darker passages, while the *Walhalla* and several of the recent *Venices* cracked in the Royal Academy. It is true that the damage makes no further progress after the first year or two, and that even in its altered state the picture is always valuable, and records its intention; but it is bitterly to be regretted that so great a painter should not leave a single work by which in succeeding ages he might be estimated. The fact of his using means so imperfect, together with that of his utter neglect of the pictures in his own gallery, are a phenomenon in the human mind which appears to me utterly inexplicable; and both are without excuse. Fortunately, the drawings appear subject to no such deterioration. Many of them now are almost destroyed, but this has been, I think, always through ill treatment, or has been the case only with very early works. I have myself known no instance of a drawing properly protected, and not rashly exposed to light, suffering the slightest change. The great foes of Turner, as of all other great colourists especially, are the picture cleaner and the mounter."

DECLINE OF TURNER'S HEALTH.

Turner was not an exhibitor at the Royal Academy Exhibition of 1851, and was missed from its walls by all classes of connoisseurs. He was present, however, at the private view; where it seemed to Mr. Cunningham, and to others to whom he observed the circumstance, that he was breaking up fast—in short, that he would hardly live the year out. And so it proved.

DEATH OF TURNER.

In December, the Painter was taken very ill. A physician was sent for who knew his disease, and Turner watched with eagerness the eye of his friend, soliciting at the same time to know the worst. The worst was communicated to him. "Go down stairs," was the reply, "take a glass of sherry, and then look at me again." This was done, and led to the same result.

He had for a considerable time lodged at a river-side cottage at Chelsea, leaving his house in Queen Anne-street shut up. This cottage is situate upon the bank of the Thames beyond Chelsea old church, upon the road to Cremorne Gardens. His fondness for Thames scenery he evinced throughout his life. One of his earliest drawings was Lambeth Palace; he lived some time at Hammersmith, by the Thames-side; and subsequently at Twickenham.* This "ruling passion" showed itself in his last days at Chelsea, where, during his last illness, he was wheeled in a chair to the window that he might look on the calm December sunshine which shed its golden hues upon the river and its craft.

This river-side abode has little in itself to recommend it to the lover of the picturesque: it is a plain-fronted house, with trellis-work and greenery about the door and windows, and a sort of prospect-gallery upon its roof. Here the great Painter had long enjoyed the prospect up the river, and watched those beautiful atmospheric changes which Turner could so ably transfer to canvas. The old Dutch-like character of Chelsea

---

* Mr. Alaric Watts tells us, that Turner is "still very well recollected at Twickenham, by more than one septuagenarian neighbour, as a parsimonious recluse, fond of fishing, who was named Blackbirdy by the boys, from his chasing them away from the blackbirds' nests, which were plentiful in his garden."

in the opposite direction may possibly have interested the painter, to whom a river-bank is generally a poetic locality.

Here he had long lived *incog*. He loved retirement, and with the peculiar dislike to having his address known, had, with his immense wealth, the feelings of the poorest bankrupt. He was unmarried, and left his house-keeper in Queen Anne-street; so that he himself engaged the apartments— in the following manner. He liked the Chelsea lodgings, asked the price, found them cheap, and that was quite as much to his liking. But the landlady wanted a reference. "I will buy your house outright, my good woman," was the reply, somewhat angrily. Then an agreement was wanted, met by an exhibition of bank-notes and sovereigns, and an offer to pay in advance, an offer which was quite satisfactory. The painter's difficulties were not, however, yet over. The landlady wanted her lodger's name, "in case any gentleman should call." This was a worse dilemma. "Name, name," he muttered to himself in his usual gruff manner. "What is *your* name?" "My name is Mrs. Booth," was the reply. "Then I am Mr. Booth;" and as Admiral Booth he was known in the neighbourhood, his sailor-like appearance favouring this belief. In this retreat from the busy world, however, age and disease were too much for him, and he died on the 19th of December, 1851, in his seventy-sixth year.

FUNERAL OF TURNER.

There was a clause in Mr. Turner's will, requesting that he should be buried in St. Paul's Cathedral, near Sir Joshua Reynolds; and this request was complied with.

His remains were interred, with some state, on the 30th of December, in St. Paul's Cathedral. Many of the Royal Academicians, painters, and sculptors, and private friends, paid the last tribute of respect to the great painter, following the hearse, and a procession of mourning-coaches and private carriages. Among those who attended the ceremonial were Mr. Harper, chief mourner, and the executors.

Sir Charles Eastlake, Mr. Mulready, Mr. Chalon, Mr. Cooper, Mr. Baily, Mr. Leslie, Mr. Pickersgill, Mr. Stanfield, Mr. Maclise, Mr. Witherington, Mr. Roberts, Mr. Barry, Mr. Knight, Mr. Landseer, Mr. Webster, Mr. Herbert, Mr. Cope, Mr. Westmacott, Mr. Grant, Mr. Hart, Mr. Creswick, Mr. Redgrave, Mr. Cockerell, Mr. Copley Fielding, Mr. Haghe, Mr. Munro, Dr. Mayo, Colonel Thwaites, Mr. Windus, the

Rev. Mr. Kingsley, Mr. Stokes, Mr. Marsh, Dr. Price, Mr. Bartlett, Mr. Drake, Mr. Round, &c. Mr. Turner's housekeeper was also among the mourners, with Mrs. F. Danby. The funeral service was read by the Dean Milman, Archdeacon Hale, and the Rev. Mr. Champneys.

The coffin was deposited in the south crypt of the Cathedral, next the remains of Sir Joshua Reynolds. And thus were laid in the "Painters' Corner" the remains of our greatest landscape painter.

WILL OF MR. TURNER.

Whatever may have been related of Turner's coarseness and love of money—and this doubtless with much false colour and exaggeration—it is certain that he had hoarded money for no selfish purpose. For many years he had refused to sell some of his best pictures, and when any such, painted and sold in earlier years, were offered for sale, he, if possible, purchased them; and his house was filled from basement to attic with these accumulated art-treasures.

On his death, it was found that he had by his will bequeathed to the nation all the Pictures and Drawings thus collected in his residence, No. 47, Queen Anne-street West, on condition that a suitable gallery was erected for them within ten years. His funded property, some 60,000*l*. he bequeathed to found an Asylum at Twickenham for decayed artists. Unfortunately, the will was unskilfully drawn, and a suit in Chancery ensued. In accordance, however, with a compromise between the parties in litigation, it was decided by an order of the Court of Chancery, dated March 19, 1856, that all pictures, drawings, sketches, finished or unfinished, by the hand of Turner, should belong to the Nation; and that all engravings and some other property should belong to the next of kin, who disputed the will.* The finished pictures thus acquired for the National Gallery, amount to about 100 in number.

The Turner Pictures and Drawings, after being temporarily exhibited to the public at Marlborough House, have been removed to South Kensington, where the bequest (103 Pictures and 97 frames of Drawings,) will be exhibited until

---

* Turner's sole surviving relatives were five first cousins, of whom Mr. Thomas Price Turner, a professor of music in the city of Exeter, was one.

accommodation is provided in the main building of the National Gallery, in accordance with the intentions of the Testator.

His executors were his friends, Mr. Hardwick, R.A.; Mr. Jones, R.A.; Mr. Munro, of Hamilton-place; Mr. Ruskin; Mr. Charles Turner, the engraver; and Mr. Griffiths, of Norwood. To each executor he left 19*l*. 19*s*. 6*d*. legacy-duty being payable on sums amounting to 20*l*. and more.

The oil paintings include many of Turner's finest works, as well as examples of his pencil from the very outset to the termination of his career. The finished drawings, which number several hundreds, and the sketches, which amount to some thousands, have been or are being arranged, cleaned, and mounted with rare skill and patience, by Mr. Ruskin, who volunteered his services to the Government. Among those exhibited are many admirable Drawings in colour; and numerous sepia drawings made for the *Liber Studiorum*, the *Rivers*, &c., some of which are of exquisite beauty and brilliancy of effect, probably unequalled among drawings of that character.

The Nation also possesses in the collections presented by Mr. Vernon and Mr. Sheepshanks, several other choice examples of Turner's pencil.

Mr. Leslie records this excellent trait of Turner—that he never heard him disparage any living painter, or any living man. Now, vanity generally leads its possessor to depreciate others; hence, we may conclude, Turner was not a vain man. But Turner may, probably, have felt acutely the ignorance and impertinence with which some critics were accustomed to fasten upon his pictures, year by year, in the exhibition; and much of this abuse was levelled at some of Turner's best pictures. However, the painter lived to see these miserable attempts at writing down fail, when the public, having become more educated in art, began to *understand* Turner's pictures; had the abuse continued, the country might have missed Turner's splendid bequest of his paintings, which, in that case would have been dispersed, instead of forming as they now do the sun or splendid centre of our National Collection.

CHARACTERISTICS, RETROSPECTIVE OPINIONS, AND PERSONAL TRAITS.

TURNER'S PRE-EMINENCE PREDICTED.

The late Thomas Greene, of Ipswich, author of *Extracts from the Diary of a Lover of Literature*, was a devoted admirer of the fine arts, and possessed a sound and cultivated judgment. In this *Diary* we find the following evidence of his early appreciation of Turner's genius.

"June 2, 1797. Visited the Royal Exhibition. Particularly struck with a sea-view by Turner: fishing-vessels coming in, with a heavy swell, in apprehension of a tempest gathering in the distance, and casting, as it advances, a night of shade, while a parting glow is spread with fine effect upon the shore. The whole composition bold in design, and masterly in execution. I am entirely unacquainted with the artist; but *if he proceeds as he has begun, he cannot fail to become the first in his department.*"

"June 3, 1799. Visited the Royal Exhibition, and was again struck and delighted with Turner's landscapes; particularly with fishermen in an evening, a calm before a storm, which all Nature attests is silently preparing, and seems in death-like stillness to await; and Caernarvon Castle, the sun setting in gorgeous splendour behind its shadowy towers. The latter in water-colours, to which he has given a depth and force of tone, which I had never before conceived attainable with such untoward implements. Turner's views are not mere ordinary transcripts of Nature—he always throws some peculiar and striking *character* into the scene he represents."

These extracts read like passages from *Modern Painters*, and exhibit a remarkable appreciation of the genius of a young and almost unknown artist, (Turner was then twenty-five) and a striking belief in its continuous development, which time has confirmed. Some seventeen years later, a distinguished painter gave similar presage.

Leslie, who went to see Turner's pictures, at Somerset House, in 1816, notes: "Turner is my great favourite of all the painters here. He combines the highest poetical imagination with an exquisite feeling for all the truth and individuality of nature; and he has shown that the *ideal*, as it is called, is not the improving of Nature, but the selecting and combining objects that are most in harmony and character with each other."

In the first year of his Associateship, he exhibited *The Fifth Plague of Egypt;* in the second year, *The Army of the Medes destroyed in the Desert by a Whirlwind;* and in the third year, *The Tenth Plague of Egypt*. These Scriptural subjects were not among the Painter's greatest successes; and his admirers willingly turned from them to *Dutch Boats in a Gale;* his *Pembroke Castle*—a *thunderstorm approaching ;* his *Fishermen on Lee-shore in squally weather;* and his view of *Ben Lomond*, with its wild Ossianic effect.

TURNER'S THREE PERIODS.

Turner's career comprehends, independently of his imitations of Claude, *three distinct styles.* He made three visits to Italy in 1819, 1829, and 1840, and after each his style underwent a remarkable change; although the usual division, and it is the most convenient one, does not exactly correspond with these visits.

The *first period* reaches to about Turner's 27th year, when he was elected into the Academy, and during which he was chiefly noticeable as a water-colour painter diligently occupied in drawing from Nature, and at the same time forming for himself a style, by carefully studying (and imitating) the methods of his English predecessors, Wilson, Loutherbourg, and in a less degree, Gainsborough : "his early drawings," says Mr. Wornum, "are conspicuous for their careful completion, subdued colour, and effective light and shade ; his earliest oil pictures resemble those of Wilson in style."

In the *second period*, Turner's middle life, ranging from 1802 to 1830, he is seen at first a follower of Claude, and in a less degree, of Gaspar Poussin, but rapidly disencumbering himself from the trammels of every kind of pupillage to great names, and striking out a style of Landscape-painting entirely original, and wholly unrivalled for brilliancy of colouring and effect. The majority of his greatest works belong to that time, from his *Calais Pier*, 1803, to the *Ulysses deriding Polyphemus*, 1829.

In the *third period*, dated from Turner's second visit to Rome, in 1830, during the last twenty years of his life, light, with all its prismatic varieties, seems to have chiefly engrossed his attention ; or rather, everything else was sacrificed in the effort to attain the utmost splendour of light and colour—to make, in the strange language of his own MS. "Fallacies of Hope:"

> The sun
> Exhale earth's humid bubbles, and emulous of light,
> Reflect her forms each in prismatic guise.

Yet, some of Turner's finest works belong to this period,—as his *Childe Harold's Pilgrimage*, exhibited in 1832, and the *Téméraire*, exhibited in 1839.

Yet, during the whole of these periods, like every great artist, Turner's conceptions were always advancing and expanding, and in each period were painted pictures that would seem justly to belong to another. Judges of art pronounce widely different opinions as to the period at which he painted best. It is quite certain that up to some ten or twelve years of his death, his knowledge of the phenomena of Nature and of the resources of art continued to grow and expand, even when his hand failed to express faithfully his intentions, or his impatience prevented him setting them forth with due elaboration. Mr. Ruskin has thus nobly expressed the above views :

"There has been marked and constant progress in his mind; he has not, like some few artists, been without childhood; his course of study has been as evidently as it has been swiftly progressive ; and in different stages of the struggle, sometimes one order of truth, sometimes another, has been aimed at or omitted. But from the beginning to the present height of his career, he has never sacrificed a greater truth to a less. As he advanced, the previous knowledge or attainment was absorbed in what succeeded, or abandoned only if incompatible, and never abandoned without a gain ; and his present works present the sum and perfection of his accumulated knowledge, delivered with the impatience and passion of one who feels too much, and has too little time to say it in, to pause for expression, or ponder over his syllables." Mr. Ruskin thus eloquently sketches the former rank and progress of Turner ; the standing of his present works : and a powerful proof that their mystery is the consequence of their fulness. "There is in them the obscurity, but the truth, of prophecy; the instinctive and burning language, which would express less, if it uttered more, which is indistinct only by its fulness, and dark with its abundant meaning. He feels now, with long-trained vividness and keenness of sense, too bitterly the impotence of the hand, and the vainness of the colour to catch one shadow or one image of the glory which God has revealed to him. He has dwelt and communed with Nature all the days of his life; he knows her now too well, he cannot palter over the material littlenesses of her outward form; he must give her soul, or he has done nothing, and he cannot do this with the flax, the earth, and the oil. 'I cannot gather the beams out of the east, or I would make *them* tell you what I have seen; but read this, and interpret this, and let us remember together. I cannot gather the gloom out of the night-sky, or I would make that teach you what I have seen; but read this, interpret this, and let us feel together. And if you have not that within you which I can summon to my aid, if you have not the sun in your spirit, and the passion in your heart, which my words may awaken, though they be indistinct and swift, leave me; for I will give you no patient mockery, no laborious insult of that glorious Nature, whose I am, and whom I serve. Let other servants imitate the voice and the gesture of their master, while they forget his message. Hear that message from me; but remember, that the teaching of Divine truth must still be a mystery.'"

Any one who studies Turner's works chronologically, which he may readily do by Mr. Wornum's admirable arrangement of them in the South Kensington Museum—and at the same time, has diligently studied Nature—may satisfy himself as to the accuracy of this estimate of the great painter's works.

WHO WERE TURNER'S PATRONS?

By many, and perhaps by the best judges, Turner will be placed in that class

> Whose genius is such
> That we never can praise it or blame it too much.

The artists, with scarcely one exception, had, from the beginning of his career, done him justice. But he passed through life little noticed by the aristocracy, and *never by Royalty*. Callcott, and other painters, immeasurably below him, were knighted; and whether Turner desired such a distinction or not, it is probable that he was hurt by its not having been offered to him. Probably, also, he expected to fill the chair of the Academy, on the death of Sir Martin Shee; but greatly as his genius would have adorned it, on almost every other account, he was incapable of occupying it with credit to himself or the institution; for he was a confused speaker, and wayward and peculiar in many of his opinions, and expected a degree of deference on account of his age and high standing as a painter, which the members could not invariably pay him, consistently with the interests of the Academy and of the Art.

His few patrons among the aristocracy were Lord Egremont; Lord Yarborough, for whom he painted one of his largest and grandest pictures; and the Marquis of Stafford, for whom he painted another, as fine. Mr. Rogers, with less means of patronage, was always his great admirer; and has associated his name with that of Turner in one of the most beautifully illustrated volumes that has ever appeared.

TURNER'S INDUSTRY.

Nothing but a constant observation of Nature, and a contemplation of the best coloured pictures, can ever lead to excellence. Turner was a great example of this: his industry was indefatigable, and his study uninterrupted. His physical and bodily powers were calculated for this fatigue, and his love for pre-eminence in his profession made it an enjoyment. His memory was most retentive; and the sketches and trials he made—and he must have made many,—served as beacons to guide him with certainty in his career. Wilkie and Etty were contemporary examples of the same untiring progress; and it may be remarked that all the three were men of the same opinion with regard to the situation of hot and cold colours. Wilkie, in his Journal, speaking of the great picture of Correggio, says,—"And here I observe that *hot shadows* prevail, not cold, as some of us would have it. This he has to a fault, making parts of his figures look like red chalk drawings; but the sunny and dazzling effect of the whole may be attributed to this artifice." In a letter to Phillips, he says, no one knew the value of this treatment better than Turner.—*Turner and his Works.*

TURNER'S LANDSCAPE ART.

It may be generally stated, (says Mr. Ruskin,) that Turner is the only painter, so far as I know, who has ever drawn the sky, (not the clear sky, which belonged exclusively to the religious schools, but the various forms and phenomena of the cloudy heavens,) all previous artists having only represented it typically or partially; but he absolutely and universally: he is the only painter who has ever drawn a mountain or a stone; no other man having ever learned their organization, or possessed himself of their spirit, except in part, or obscurely. He is the only painter who ever drew the stem of a tree, Titian having come the nearest before him, and excelling him in the muscular development of the larger trunks, (though sometimes losing the woody strength in a serpent-like flaccidity,) but missing the grace and character of the ramifications. He is the only painter who has ever painted the surface of calm, or the force of agitated water; who has represented the effects of space on distant objects, or who has rendered the abstract beauty of natural colour. These assertions I make deliberately, after careful weighing and consideration, in no spirit of dispute, or momentary zeal; but from strong and convinced feeling, and with the consciousness of being able to prove them.—*Modern Painters*, vol. i.

STUDYING NATURE.

It is often said, study Nature; but Nature does not compose: her beautiful arrangements are accidental combinations, and none but an educated eye can discover why they are so. Nature ought to form, and does form the materials for a fine picture; but to select, and reject, to adapt the individual parts to the production of a perfect whole, is the work of the artist, and this it is that stamps the emanations of genius. Much of this knowledge must be acquired by the artist himself. Turner was not a solitary being, because his rambles were unaccompanied by others; he was holding discourse with the beautiful imagery of Nature, and inquiring the cause of such beautiful effects.

Turner's sketches from Nature were generally slight pencil outlines, but he had an eye capable of perceiving her beautiful imagery, and a memory to retain it. Mr. Woodburn told Mr. Burnet an example of this power in Turner. Driving down to his house at Hendon, a beautiful sunset burst forth: Turner asked to have the carriage stopped: this was done, and he remained a long time in silent contemplation. Some weeks afterwards, when Mr. Woodburn called on him in Queen Anne-street, he saw this identical sky in his Gallery, and wished to have a landscape added to it; Turner refused the commission—he would not part with it. Wilkie used to call these studies "his stock in trade."

TURNER'S "COLOUR"—A HINT FROM ADDISON.

To convey any adequate idea of the beauty of Turner's colour, either by words or imperfect sketches, is difficult; but it is possible to point out wherein it consists; and could we divest the public mind of that proneness to investigate the faults of any one in preference to the beauties of their works, we might succeed to a certain extent; time and the accumulation of approval alone can accomplish this. Colour is the great ornament and decoration of Nature's works. Addison, in one of his papers in the *Spectator*, observes, what a poor show her works would present were they of one uniform colour. His words are: "things would make but a poor appearance to the eye if we saw them only in their proper figures and motions; and what reason can we assign for their exciting in us so many of those ideas which are different from anything that exists in the objects themselves, for such are light and colours, were it not to add supernumerary ornaments to the universe, and make it more agreeable to the imagination? We are everywhere entertained with pleasing shows and apparitions; we discover imaginary glories in the heavens and in the earth; and we see some of this visionary beauty poured out upon the whole creation.

"But what a rough unsightly view of Nature should we be entertained with did all her colouring disappear, and the several distinctions of light and shade vanish."

No one has been more alive to this doctrine than our artist, whose works teem with incontrovertible examples; yet, when his pictures are reduced to mere black and white, by means of engravings, they appear to lose less of their beauty than her own productions; this, of course, arises from the elegance of the composition of form, and the scientific combinations of light and shade. This, among many other proofs, shows that Turner's arrangement of colour is based upon the foundation of chiaroscuro. In her most accidental, and apparently unpromising materials, for a work of art, Nature always has some redeeming points that assert her superiority over the laboured compositions of fireside inventions; but these must be seen and appreciated by the artist, and no one could perceive and aggrandise these beauties in a clearer or greater degree than Turner.—*Burnet: Turner and his Works.*

PORTRAITS OF TURNER.

Mr. Leslie regrets that "Turner never would sit for a portrait excepting when he was a young man, and then only for a profile by Dance. This is, therefore, the only satisfactory likeness of him extant." But there is a portrait of Turner in the collection at South Kensington: it was painted by himself, about 1802; bust, life-size, and in evening dress.

In the year 1800, he sat for a series of small-sized portraits of members of the Royal Academy. He always had an impression that any knowledge of his burly form and uncouth farmer-looking appearance would affect the poetry of his works. He considered that it would throw a doubt upon their genuineness. "No one," he said, "would believe, upon seeing my likeness, that I painted those pictures." One or two portraits were, however, taken of him surreptitiously. Mr. Smith, of the British Museum, obtained a sketch of him. A very fair full-length sketch of Turner was published May 10th, 1845, in the *Illustrated London News.* The best and only finished portrait of him is, however, one of half-size, in oil, by J. Linnell. It was the result of a plot, which may now be revealed without offence to the honoured victim. The Rev. Mr. Daniell, a gentleman who was extremely intimate with Turner, prevailed upon his eccentric friend occasionally to dine with him. Linnell, without exciting any suspicion of his object, was always one of the party, and by sketching on his thumb-nail, and, unobserved, on scraps of paper, he at length succeeded in transferring the portly bust and sparkling eye of the great artist to his canvas. The picture was finished, and passed in due time, at the price of two hundred guineas, into the possession of Mr. Birch, a gentleman residing near Birmingham. Turner never knew it. Posterity may now come to be acquainted with the likeness of his mortality, without prejudice to the immortality of his works.

Soon after Turner's death, there appeared in the shop-windows a sketch by Count d'Orsay, taken at an evening party, at Mr. Bicknell's, of Clapham, which Mr. Leslie considers "most execrable."

Mr. Peter Cunningham describes Turner as "short, stout, and bandy-legged, with a red, pimply face, imperious and covetous eyes, and a tongue which expressed his sentiments with a murmuring reluctance. Sir William Allan was accustomed to describe him as a Dutch skipper. His hands were very small, and owing to the long cuffs to his coats, only his fingers were seen. His look was anything but that of a man of genius."

But a second glance would find far more in his face than belongs to any ordinary mind. There was a peculiar keenness of expression in his eye, which denoted constant habits of observation. His voice was deep and musical, but he was a confused and tedious speaker. He was very joyous at table, and was very apt at repartee. He was a social man in his nature; and Mr. Leslie considers the recluse manner in which he lived to have arisen from his strong wish to have his time entirely at his command. We are inclined to agree with the writer; had it not been for his "recluse manner," Turner would, most probably, have proved a very inferior artist. The world are strangely inconsiderate, not to say dishonest, as regards the time of artists and professional persons generally: being fitted to shine in society, their "valuable time" is too often filched away by a description of persons who are the first to throw up their hands and eyes at the failings of a man of genius!

TURNER ON VARNISHING DAYS.

"Turner, (says Mr. Leslie,) was very amusing on varnishing, or rather, the painting, days at the Academy. Singular as were his habits, for nobody knew where or how he lived, his nature was social, and at our lunch on those anniversaries, he was the life of the table. The Academy has relinquished, very justly, a privilege for its members which it could not extend to all exhibitors. But I believe, had the varnishing days been abolished while Turner lived, it would almost have broken his heart. When such a measure was hinted to him, he said, 'Then you will do away with the only social meetings we have, the only occasions on which we all come together in an easy unrestrained manner. When we have no varnishing days, we shall not know one another.'"

In another page we have told how Turner availed himself of the *varnishing days* at the British Institution, where he was the first in the morning, and the last to leave; and where he completed many a fine landscape upon a brilliant foundation.

It was upon a varnishing day at the Royal Academy, that, some sixteen years since, a clever artist* who was present, sketched Mr. Turner, as he stood before one of his pictures. At this time, there was no accessible portrait known of the great painter, and his whole-length being required for a series of portraits, to appear in the *Illustrated London News*, it was thus secured surreptitiously, and engraved in No. 158 of that journal: here he is—a portly figure, his handkerchief half out of his pocket; and to conceal where the sketch was obtained, he holds in his hand a sketch-book.

Mr. Leslie relates a capital story of Turner eclipsing a brother artist on a varnishing day. In 1839, when Constable exhibited his *Opening of Waterloo Bridge*, it was placed in one of the small rooms at Somerset House, next to a sea-piece, by Turner—a grey picture, beautiful and true, but with no positive colour in any part of it. Constable's *Waterloo* seemed as if painted with liquid gold and silver, and Turner came several times into the room while he was heightening with vermilion and lake the decorations and flags of the city barges. Turner stood behind him, looking from the *Waterloo* to his own picture, and at last brought his palette from the Great Room, where he was touching another picture, and putting a round daub of red lead, somewhat bigger than a shilling, on his grey sea, went away without saying a word. The intensity of the red lead, made more vivid by the coolness of his picture, caused even the vermilion and lake of Constable to look weak. "I came into the room," (says Mr. Leslie,) "just as Turner left it." "He has been here," said Constable, "and fired a gun." On the opposite wall was a picture, by Jones, of *Shadrach, Meschach, and Abednego in the Furnace*. "A coal," said Cooper, "has bounced across the room from Jones's picture, and set fire to Turner's sea." Turner did not come again into the room for a day and a half: and then, in the last moments that were allowed for painting, he glazed the scarlet seal he had put on his picture, and shaped it into a buoy.

* Charles Martin, son of John Martin.

The gossip of varnishing days is very amusing.

One cold day, Chantrey stopped before a picture by Turner, and seizing the artist's arm, placed his hands before a blaze of yellow, in an attitude of obtaining warmth, and said, with a look of delight, "Turner, this is the only comfortable place in the room. Is it true, as I have heard, that you have a commission to paint a picture for the Sun Fire Office?"

In 1827, when Turner exhibited his *Rembrandt's Daughter*, in a red robe, the portrait of a member of one of the Universities was hung by its side, with a college-gown, that was still redder. Upon finding this out on varnishing day, Turner was observed to be very busy adding red lead and vermilion to his picture. "What are you doing there, Turner?" asked one of the hangers. "Why, you have checkmated me," was the reply, pointing to the University gown, "and I must now checkmate you."

It was often remarked that Turner had never been known to give a dinner. But, when dining one day at Blackwall, the bill, a heavy one, being handed to Chantrey, (who headed the table,) he threw it to Turner, by way of joke, and *Turner paid it*, and would not allow the company to pay their share.

Mr. Leslie, who relates this anecdote, adds: "I know also that Turner refused large offers for the *Téméraire*, because he intended to leave it to the nation."

TURNER'S SEA-PIECES.

Turner executed no subjects with greater care or more spirit than his Sea-pieces, especially when the tempest-tossed waves threaten "to swallow navigation up;" nothing can exceed the appearance of turbulent motion with which he imbues them; their forms can only be caught sight of ere they hurry into confusion, and become lost. However well Backhuysen or Vandervelde may have painted storms at sea, Turner's representations are more like Nature than either, even to the loose unsteady handling of his flowing pencil; everything in his pictures seems to be under the influence of the most boisterous hurricane—such as we see represented in his painting of the *Wreck of the Minotaur*, in Lord Yarborough's collection: while others are contented with loss of a few sails or spars carefully painted, Turner gives us the entire canvas blown from the masts, mingling in one mass with the foamy surge below, that seems rising up to engulph the whole in one great chaos; the boats approaching the wreck are driven in all directions, while the agitated waters heave up and down in wild confusion. Admiral Bowles, when looking at the above picture in the British Institution, said : " No ship or boat could live in such a sea ;" that was what Turner meant to express and convey to us—the fearless, death-defying courage of English sailors.

While we are upon this subject, we must not overlook the truth of character and bluff forms of Turner's fishermen and English sailors: they are transcripts of the men they represent, and though others might draw them with greater correctness in the detail, yet in the general appearance they are portraits. The complete unity of his figures with the scene shows the advantage that the whole work derives from their being painted by the same hand. Turner used to delight to go to sea in rough weather, with smugglers or fishermen, whose trade is with storms.—*Burnet; Turner and his Works.*

TURNER'S VERSES.

The great Painter was ambitious to become a poet: he is even said to have left a long manuscript "poem," from which he selected several subjects for his pictures, and epigraphs for the Catalogue. The MS. has not, however, been found among the painter's papers. Its title was "the Fallacies of Hope"— and its rhyme and reason are so faulty as to form the best illustration of the "poem" itself: it was, indeed, a fallacy to suppose Turner a poet, save in his pencil.

Specimens of the curious *Fallacies of Hope* may be seen in old Exhibition Catalogues, or more readily in Mr. Wornum's Catalogue of the British School, now at South Kensington. It may be amusing to quote a few passages. The first we find appended to the *Snow-storm, Hannibal and his Army crossing the Alps:*

> "Craft, treachery, and fraud,—Salassian force
> Hung on the fainting rear; then plunder seized
> The victor and the captive,—Saguntum's spoil
> Alike became their prey; still the chief advanc'd.
> Looked on the sun with hope; low, broad and wan.

---

* There seems long to have been a fashion for painters to accompany the titles of their pictures with rhymes, or quotations from accredited poets. We all remember the rhymes beneath Hogarth's subjects in his prints: they were written for the painter by various hands. The fashion was continued in Exhibition catalogues.

> While the fierce archer of the downward year,
> Stains Italy's blanched barrier with storms.
> In vain each pass, ensanguined deep with dead,
> Or rocky fragments, wide destruction roll'd."
> *Fallacies of Hope.*

The next extract accompanies *The Battle of Fort Rock, Val. d'Aouste, Piedmont,* 1796:

> "The snow-capt mountain and huge tower of ice,
> Thrust forth their dreary barriers in vain:"

Sir David Wilkie died on board the *Oriental* Steamer off Gibraltar, on his return from his visit to the East, June 1, 1841: the coffin was lowered that night into the sea. Turner painted this melancholy scene, and exhibited the picture in 1842, as—*Peace. Burial at Sea of the Body of Sir David Wilkie:* with this couplet in rhyme:

> "The midnight torch gleamed o'er the steamer's side,
> And merit's corse was yielded to the tide."

The next passage is so odd as to make one regret its association with so sublime a scene as the great Flood. He exhibited this picture in 1843, as *Shade and Darkness.—The evening of the Deluge:*

> "The moon put forth her sign of woe unheeded,
> And the last token came; the giant framework floated;
> The scared birds forsook their nightly shelter, screaming,
> And the beasts waded to the ark."

This work had its companion—pictorial and poetical,—as —*Light and Colour.—The morning after the Deluge:*

> "The ark stood firm on Ararat; the returning sun
> Exhaled earth's humid bubbles, and emulous of light,
> Reflected her lost forms, each in prismatic guise."

In the same year Turner exhibited, *The Opening of the Walhalla,* 1842, *Honour to King Ludwig the First of Bavaria*—

> "But peace returns—the morning ray
> Beams on the Walhalla, reared to science and the arts,
> And men renowned, of German fatherland."

Next, in the same Exhibition was a scene at Venice, which city has had a tolerably extensive poetic commemoration; but Turner preferred his own:—*The "Sun of Venice," going to Sea:*

> "Fair shines the morn and soft the zephyr blows,
> Venetia's Fisher spreads his painted canvas gay,
> Nor heeds the Demon who in grim repose
> Expects his evening prey."

Nor was the painter satisfied with Shakspeare's line,

"Frisk it, frisk it, by the moonlight beam,"

to accompany his *Queen Mab's Grotto*, exhibited in 1846; but he gilded refined gold by adding:

"Thy orgies, Mab, are manifold."

Still more unromantic and commonplace is the couplet which he has appended to *Æneas relating his Story to Dido*:

"Fallacious hope beneath the moon's pale crescent shone,
Dido listened to Troy being lost and won."

These lines assort ill with the magnificence of the subject.

"Onwards the van progressive forc'd its way,
Propell'd; as the wild Reuss, by native glaciers fed,
Rolls on impetuous, with ev'ry check gains force,
By the constraint uprais'd; till to its gathering powers
All yielding, down the pass wide devastation pours
Her own destructive course, the rapine stalk'd
Triumphant; and plundering hordes exulting strew'd,
Fair Italy, thy plains with woe."

The next passage illustrates the fine picture of *Caligula's Palace and Bridge,—Bay of Baia*, exhibited in 1831:

"What now remains of all the mighty bridge
Which made the Lucerne lake an inner pool,
Caligula, but massy fragments left
As monuments of doubt and ruined hopes
Yet gleaming in the morning's ray, that tell
How Baia's shore was loved in times gone by."

In the same year, Turner exhibited his *Vision of Medea*, and to aid his illustration of the old classic poet, called in his own hobbling muse:

"Or Medea, who in the full tide of witchery
Had lured the dragon, gained her Jason's love,
Had fill'd the spell-bound bowl with Æson's life,
Yet dash'd it to the ground, and raised the poisonous snake
High in the jaundiced sky to writhe its murderous coil,
Infuriate in the wreck of hope withdrew,
And in the fired palace her twin offspring threw."

Sometimes, his application of his rhymes bordered upon burlesque, as in his odd *mélange* with Campbell's words for *The Fighting Téméraire:*

"The flag which braved the battle and the breeze,
No longer owns her."

This is fine bathos. And the next—appended to *War— The Exile and the Rock Limpet*, is of the same mintage:

"Ah! thy tent-formed shell is like
A soldier's nightly bivouac, alone

> Amidst a sea of blood ———
> ———but you can join your comrades."

Sometimes, he painted satire, as in *the Garreteer's Petition*—a poet at work in his attic, consuming the midnight oil: on his wall are pasted a plan of Parnassus, and a table of Fasts. In the Catalogue is this epigraph :

> "Aid me, ye powers! O bid my thoughts to roll
> In quick succession, animate my soul;
> Descend, my Muse, and every thought refine
> And finish well my long, my *long-sought* line."

In the two next, he is not content with Ring's translation of Virgil, but prefers his own prefix:

Mercury sent to admonish Æneas :—

> "Beneath the morning mist
> Mercury waited to tell him of his neglected fleet."
> *Fallacies of Hope.*

> "The Lord of heaven and earth, almighty Jove
> Sends me with awful warnings from above.
> What are your motives for this long delay?
> Why thus in Libya pass your life away?—*Ring's Æneid.*

The Departure of the Trojan Fleet :—

> "He then commanded all the Trojan host
> To launch the fleet now scattered on the coast.
> The pitchy keel now glides along the flood.
> * * *
> At once the seas with sails are cover'd o'er,
> And not a Trojan left upon the shore."—*Ring's Æneid.*

> "The orient moon shone on the departing fleet,
> Nemesis invoked, the priest held the poisoned cup."
> *Fallacies of Hope.*

The *Visit to the Tomb*, exhibited in the same year with the above (1850), has this single line :

> "The sun went down in wrath at such deceit."

Turner thought much of his *Fallacies of Hope*, perhaps as much as his admirers thought of his pictures; but the Painter's conceit exposed him to a cutting joke. He refused to sell his picture of *Carthage*, adding, "I shall be buried in my *Carthage.*" "But they will dig you up, and get your picture for nothing," was the insidious reply; "if you really want to be buried and rest in one of your own works, be buried in your own MS. *Fallacies of Hope*, and no one will dig you up." Poetry, or rather rhyming, is liable to as many hard rubs as Painting.

"TALKING DOWN."

Hogarth was talked down, and Penny, a now forgotten painter, talked up by no less a critic than Barry. Wilson and Gainsborough were talked down; while Smith of Chichester, and Barrett were talked up. Stothard, Flaxman, and Constable suffered, when living, the same kind of depreciation, while lesser artists were praised and patronised; and Turner, when in the meridian of his glory, was ridiculed without mercy by the fashionable leaders of taste. (*Leslie's Handbook*, p. 256.)

The fashionable Sir George Beaumont, a painter as well as a patron of art, strongly avowed his heresy of Turner, whom he ridiculed, and endeavoured to talk down; and Fuseli was coarsely abused, and his exaggerated designs ridiculously attributed to his disturbed dreams: he is said to have supped on raw pork-chops, that he might dream his picture of *the Nightmare!*—but, unfortunately for the story, Fuseli always went to bed supperless. He was known among his brother artists by the name of "Painter in ordinary to the Devil:" he smiled when some one mischievously told him of this, and replied, "Ay, he has sat to me many times."

Sir George Beaumont held that in every landscape there should be at least one brown tree; and that every picture should have a first, second, and third light. "I see," he said, looking at a picture by Constable, "your first and your second lights, but I can't make out which is your third." Constable told this to Turner, who said, "You should have asked him how many lights Rubens introduced."

TURNER AND WILKIE.

After his visit to the Continent, Turner again chose his subjects from English scenery and character, all of which he invested with the poetry of his art. In the same year, (1807,) he somewhat oddly painted and exhibited *The Sun rising through Vapour, Fishermen cleaning and selling Fish;* and *a Country Blacksmith disputing upon the price of Iron, and the price charged to the Butcher for Shoeing his Pony;* two pictures, which, (says Cunningham,) *killed* every picture within the range of their effects. Oddly enough, a modest picture thus injured by being hung between the two fires was *The Blind Fiddler*, then the second exhibited picture of a lad raw from Scotland, contriving to exist, without getting into debt, on eighteen shillings a week. On the varnishing day, Turner, it is said, reddened his sun, and blew the bellows of his art upon the blacksmith's forge, "to put the Scotchman's nose out of joint who had gained so much reputation by his *Village Politicians.*"

This story is told, without naming Turner, in Allan Cunningham's *Life of Wilkie,* and was condemned as an untruth by the reviewer of the *Life* in the *Quarterly Review.* But there is no doubt of the truth of the story; and that Wilkie remembered the circumstance with some acerbity—though he never resented it openly—Mr. Peter Cunningham undertakes to say. When *the Forge* was sold at Lord de Tabley's sale, Wilkie was in Italy; and Collins, the painter, in describing the sale to him, in a MS. letter before the writer, adds: "and there was your *old enemy—the Forge.*"

TURNER AND CHANTREY.

Many a lively gossip passed between these two friends. Turner had expressed an eccentric intention to be buried in his picture of *Carthage;* and said to Chantrey, "I have appointed you one of my executors; will you promise to see me rolled up in it?" "Yes," said Chantrey, "and I promise you also that as soon as you are buried, I will see you taken up, and unrolled." Mr. Leslie tells us, this story was so generally believed, that when Turner died, and Dean Milman heard he was going to be buried in St. Paul's, he said, "I will not read the service over him if he be wrapped up in that picture."

"THE SCOTTISH TURNER."

Turner was very chary of his opinions on art; but on the occasion we are about to relate, he said more than was expected. He was taken to see the pictures of Thomson, of Duddingstone, called by his countrymen, in the fondness of their admiration, "the Scottish Turner." The friend who took him was anxious to hear what the original Turner thought of his Scottish representative. Thomson, too, was equally eager. Turner examined with attention, mumbled some sounds of apparent approbation, and began and ended by asking—"Where do you get your frames, Mr. Thomson."

ARTISTIC PREDICTION.

In the year 1820, Constable, the painter, wrote thus: "The art will go out: there will be no genuine painting in England in thirty years." And it is remarkable, that within a few months of the date thus specified, Turner should have died, almost literally fulfilling, as some of his admirers may think, Constable's prophecy. Turner died December 19, 1851.

TURNER'S EARLY VIEWS OF LAMBETH PALACE.

This water-colour drawing, the second exhibited by Turner at the Royal Academy, (see page 311) was, in 1853, in the possession of a lady residing in Bristol, to whose father the drawing was given by the artist after the Exhibition season, and it had never been in other hands. It seems that Turner, when young, was a frequent visitor at the above gentleman's house; and on one occasion he lent Turner a horse, to go on a sketching tour through South Wales.

The same lady had also a small portrait of Turner, done by *himself*, when visiting her family about the year 1791 or 1792. She had likewise three or four other early drawings by Turner, among which was a view of Stoke Bishop, near Bristol, the seat of Sir Henry Lippincott, Bart., which the artist made as a companion to the Lambeth Palace view. Mr. Walter, the Marine Painter, of Bristol, observes: "As early indications of so great an artist, these drawings are very curious and interesting; but no person that knows anything of the state of water-colour painting at that period, and previous to the era when Turner, Girtin, and others, began to shine out in the new and glorious style, that has since brought water-colour works to their present style of splendour, excellence and value,—will look for anything approaching the perfection of our days."

CHANGES OF RESIDENCE.

As Turner rose in fame, he thought it advisable to remove from "over his father's shop," and shifted to apartments of his own in Hand-court. Immediately after his election as an Associate of the Academy, he removed to the house No. 75, Norton-street, Portland-road, where he stayed three years. Thence he removed to No. 64, Harley-street, then a more fashionable and expensive locality than now.

Nor was this all the change. In former times, he had been content to exhibit as "W. Turner;" but with his new affix of letters (A. R. A.) after his name, he had recourse to other initials before his name. From and after his elevation into the Academy, he is "J. M. W. Turner," in Court Guides, and Exhibition Catalogues.

In 1808, when Turner was living in Harley-street, he had country quarters in the Upper Mall at Hammersmith. Four years later, he removed from Harley-street to No. 47, Queen Ann-street West; and 1814, he left the Mall at Hammersmith for what he at first called "Solus Lodge, Twickenham," but soon dropped for Sandycombe Lodge, a kind of cit's country-box, with pleasant peeps over the Thames. When at Hammersmith, he had Loutherbourg for his neighbour. He is said to have left Twickenham about 1828.

SECRET OF HIS ADDRESS.

Turner had some odd motives for concealing his new abode, whenever he changed it; and his ingenuity in baffling the curiosity of his friends was marvellous—almost equal to that of Dr. Paul Heffernan. Offers were made to walk home with him from the Athenæum Club, for a chit-chat about Academy matters. No: he had got an engagement, and must keep it. Some of the younger sort attempted to follow him, but he managed to steal away from them, to tire them out, or pop into cheap omnibuses, or round dark corners. If he suspected that he was followed, he would set off for a tavern haunt; but as soon as this got to be known, he left it, and the landlord lost his customer. Once his hiding-place was nearly discovered. Turner had dined with some friends at Greenwich, had drunk freely, and, on reaching town, was thought to be not sufficiently collected to call a cab. The party, as had been plotted, dropped off, and there was left with Turner only one friend, who placed him in a cab: thinking to catch the bemused painter unawares, he shut the cab-door, and said, "Where shall he drive to?" Turner was not, however, to be caught, and collectedly replied, "Along Piccadilly, and I will tell him where."—*Turner and his Works.*

TURNER AND THE CRITIC.

One of the critics termed his *Snow-storm—Steam-boat off a Harbour's mouth, making Signals,* " a mass of soapsuds and whitewash;" to which Turner adroitly replied, " I wish they had been in it."

QUID PRO QUO.

Once, at a dinner, where several artists, amateurs, and literary men were convened, a poet, by way of being facetious, proposed as a toast the health of the *painters and glaziers* of Great Britain. The toast was drunk, and Turner, after returning thanks for it, proposed the health of the British *paper-stainers*.

PICTURES FROM THOMSON AND MILTON.

In Turner's early life, his favourite poet was Thomson, and he has taken from his *Seasons* four effects in four of his pictures, while he was yet in the infancy of his reputation. Round Dunstamborough Castle, on the coast of Northumberland, he has shown an effect of sunrise after a squally night, such as he imagined was in the poet's eye, when

> The briny deep,
> Seen from some pointed promontory's top,
> Far to the blue horizon's utmost verge,
> Restless, reflects a floating gleam.

On Norham Castle, on the Tweed, he threw an effect of a summer's morning:

> But yonder comes the powerful King of Day,
> Rejoicing in the East—the lessening cloud,
> The kindling azure, and the mountain's brow
> Illumed with fluid gold, his near approach
> Betoken glad.

On one occasion he had recourse to Milton, summoning to his canvas:

> Ye Mists and Exhalations! that now rise
> From hill or streaming lake, dusky or grey,
> Till the sun paint your fleecy skirts with gold,
> In honour to the World's great Author rise.

And what his genius could embody in the way of exhalation he has given us as an effect of morning among the Coniston Falls, in Cumberland. He was thus early alive to the varieties of Nature, and copied her, when he chose, with a master's hand.—*P. Cunningham; Turner and his Works.*

TURNER'S ACCURACY.

Nearly thirty years ago, an antiquarian writer bore testimony to the accuracy of architecture of the backgrounds of Turner's pictures, at the same time that he acknowledged the beauty of the great Painter's colour: the former point having been often disputed. This testimony occurs in the opening of a paper on *Historical Propriety in Painting*, in Brayley's *Graphic Illustrator*, 1834; and is as follows:

"The *greatest master of colour* amongst the painters of the present day is at the same time the most remarkable for propriety in his architectural backgrounds: these *frequently exhibit designs that may be studied with advantage by the architect:* and in expressing my admiration of Turner, I wish to avoid the appearance of advocating that servile imitation which an antiquary is supposed to require."

The writer who has taken the trouble to disinter the above, and send it to *Notes and Queries*, 2nd Series, No. 36, adds: " The king of colourists here gets his due, and nothing more; he did not often get *that* twenty years ago. It is different now."

TURNER'S ORIGINALITY.

In what does this consist? Let us hear John Burnet in reply. "Since the revival of painting, handed down to us by a succession of eminent artists, it would be strange if there could be anything original in treatment, or, indeed, of any other principle; but in Turner's works we find the practice of former painters given under the greatest variety of circumstances, and he has always the skill of concealing the means by which his works are produced, rendering what has been taken from his predecessors his own. The varieties in Nature are endless, but those of art are merely like the letters of the alphabet, altered by transposition; nevertheless, to read a picture is as difficult as to read a book printed in an untaught language: this it is that makes the ignorant scout the idea of rules in art, or the imbecile attempt to paint without them; those only can produce something original in painting, who have been taught the orthography and grammar of the art. Reynolds, Gainsborough, Richard Wilson, and others, were not understood in their own time, though now so highly valued; the works of Turner must pass through the same ordeal. The engravings from his finest pictures have been unproductive, though executed by some of the best artists, and at present only called into notice since his death. His paintings, being a gift to the nation, will have an advantage over others of the English school, and may become sooner understood."—*Turner and his Works.*

TURNER'S COMPOSITION.

The mode Turner took to improve his talent for this branch of the art seems to have been to select a picture of Vandervelde's, such as the Earl of Ellesmere's, or one of Claude's, like Lord Egremont's, and paint companions to them of the same character; this was a severe trial, but having a point to start from, and examining these works, he more easily imitated their beauties, and eschewed their defects. Judging of the composition of Turner from his earliest drawings, we are led to believe it was of slow growth, nor does he seem to have fixed the principles in his mind which afterwards shone through all his works; there are few in the possession of all artists, but when once known and felt, are capable of endless changes.

UNDERSTANDING TURNER.

Burnet has well said that "Art is highly conventional; and the more ideal and poetical it is rendered, the more difficult it becomes for the public to comprehend it. This is one cause why the works of Turner convey a greater pleasure to the artist than the casual observer; and the higher the gratification becomes, the more they are studied and contemplated. The tutored eye sees fresh beauties spring up into notice, strictly in accordance with the effects in nature, but unperceived by him until rendered visible in Turner's works. This is the great charm of his pictures—they gain upon you; some forms are clear, others are only suggestive of what the imagination embodies.

* * * * * * *

"What we find in the historical works of Correggio, Titian, and Paul Veronese, we find adopted in the landscapes of Turner. The delicacy of his tints, and the dreamy character and indistinctness of many of the forms, add to the poetical look of the pictures. His colours appear also of a very refined quality, and never convey a vulgar or common look. This arises not only from the situation he places them in, but in mixing several tints together; and is very observable when one of his pictures is placed in contact with one by another artist. The effect is very evident in the lighter pictures of Rubens, and in those of Teniers. The general public do not yet appreciate the beauty of his compositions. People want something more definite and topographical in the character; in fact, more easy to be comprehended."

MR. RUSKIN'S CRITICISM ON TURNER'S WORKS.

To the ignorance and incompetence of the Art-critics of a few years since in appreciating the genius of Turner, we owe the production of Mr. Ruskin's *Modern Painters*. He tells us, in the Preface to the First Edition, that this work "originated in indignation at the shallow and false criticisms of the periodicals of the day on the works of the great living artist to whom it principally relates. It was intended to be a short pamphlet, reprobating the matter and style of those critiques, and pointing out their perilous tendency as guides of public feeling." From this small beginning the work has grown to five large 8vo volumes.

In the Preface to Vol. I., second edition, Mr. Ruskin says: "For many a year we have heard nothing with respect to the works of Turner, but accusations of their want of *truth*. To every observation on their power, sublimity, or beauty, there has been but one reply: They are not like Nature. I therefore took my opponents on their own ground, and demonstrated by the thorough investigation of actual facts, that Turner *is* like Nature, and paints more of Nature than any man who ever lived. I expected this proposition (the foundation of all my future efforts) would have been disputed with desperate struggles, and that I should have to fight my way to my position inch by inch. Not at all. My opponents yield me the field at once."

THE TRUTH OF TURNER.

Mr. Ruskin devotes a chapter of his great work, above named, to the positive rank of Turner as a Painter of Nature, having previously shown the extent of his knowledge, and the truth of his practice, by the deliberate examination of the characteristics of the four great elements of landscape—sky, earth, water, and vegetation. Our author then proceeds to show the exceeding refinement of the truth of Turner,—to the last line, and shadow of a line. "Such indeed is the case with every touch of this consummate artist; the essential excellence—all that constitutes the real and exceeding value of his works—is beyond and above expression: it is a truth inherent in every line, and breathing in every line, too delicate and exquisite to admit of any kind of proof, nor to be ascertained, except by the highest of tests—the keen feeling attained by extended knowledge and long study. Two lines are laid on canvas—one is right, and another wrong. There is no difference between them appreciable by the compasses—none appreciable by the ordinary eye—none which can be pointed out if it is not seen. One person feels it—another does not; but the feeling or sight of the one can by no words be communicated to the other: it would be unjust if it could, for that feeling and sight have been the reward of years of labour. And there is, indeed, nothing in Turner—not one dot nor line—whose meaning can be understood without knowledge; because he never aims at sensual impressions, but at the deep final truth, which only meditation can discover, and only experience recognise. There is nothing done or omitted by him which does not imply such a comparison of ends, such a rejection of the least worthy, (as far as they are incompatible with the rest,) such careful selection and arrangement of all that can be united, as can only be enjoyed by minds capable of going through the same process, and discovering the reasons for the choice.

"And, as there is nothing in his works which can be enjoyed without knowledge, so there is nothing in them which knowledge will not enable us to enjoy. There is no test of our acquaintance with Nature so absolute and unfailing as the degree of admiration we feel for Turner's painting. Precisely as we are shallow in our knowledge, vulgar in our feeling, and contracted in our views of principles, will the works of this artist be stumbling-blocks or foolishness to us; precisely in the degree in which we are familiar with Nature, constant in observation of her, and enlarged in our understanding of her, will they expand before our eyes into glory and beauty. In every new insight which we obtain into the works of God, in every new idea which we receive from His creation, we shall find ourselves possessed of an interpretation and guide to something in Turner's works which we had not before understood. We may range over Europe, from shore to shore; and from every rock that we tread upon, every sky that passes over our heads, every local form of vegetation or of soil, we shall receive fresh illustration of his principles, fresh confirmation of his facts. We shall feel, wherever we may go, that he has been there before us—whatever we see, that he has seen and seized before us: and we shall at last cease the investigation, with a well-grounded trust, that whatever we have been unable to account for, and what we still dislike in his works, has reason for it, and foundation like the rest; and that even where he has failed or erred, there is a beauty in the failure which none are able to equal, and a dignity in the error which none are worthy to reprove."

Mr. Ruskin then eloquently illustrates Turner's adherence to nature, in his great picture of the *Pools of Solomon* :—

"Now this is Nature! It is the exhaustless living energy with which the universe is filled; and what will you set beside it in the works of other men? Show me a single picture in the whole compass of ancient art, in which I can pass from cloud to cloud, from region to region, and from first to second and third heaven, as I can here, and you may talk of Turner's want of truth. Turn to the *Pools of Solomon*, and walk through the passages of mist as they melt on the one hand into those stormy fragments of fiery cloud, or, on the other, into the cold solitary shadows that compass the sweeping hill; and when you find an inch without air or transparency, and a hair's breadth without changefulness and thought; and when you can count the torn waves of tossing radiance that gush from the sun, as you can count the fixed, white, insipidities of Claude; or when you can measure the modulation and depth of that hollow mist, as you can the flourishes of the brush upon the canvas of Salvator—talk of Turner's want of truth!"

CLAUDE AND TURNER COMPARED.

The *Sun rising in a Mist*, and the *Dido building Carthage*, were bequeathed by Turner to the National Gallery, on condition that they should be hung between two Claudes, now placed by their side. The *Sunrise* was exhibited at the Royal Academy in 1807, and was exchanged with Sir John F. Leicester, for the *Shipwreck*, and was repurchased by Turner, at the De Tabley sale in 1827.

The principal object in the foreground of the *Carthage* is a group of children sailing toy-boats. The exquisite choice of this incident, as expressive of the ruling passion, which was to be the source of future greatness, in preference to the tumult of busy stone-masons or arming soldiers, is quite as appreciable when it is told as when it is seen—it has nothing to do with the technicalities of painting; a scratch of the pen would have conveyed the idea and spoken to the intellect as much as the realizations of colour. Such a thought as this is far above all art; it is epic poetry of the highest order. Claude, in subjects of the same kind, commonly introduces people carrying red trunks with iron locks about, and dwells, with infantine delight, on the lustre of the leather and the ornaments of the iron. The intellect can have no occupation here; we must look to the imitation or to nothing. Consequently, Turner rises above Claude in the very first instant of the conception of his picture, and acquires an intellectual superiority which no power of the draughtsman or the artist, (supposing that such existed in his antagonist,) could ever wrest from him.

"Were we disposed to look for blunders in Turner," says Leslie, "we might notice that palpable one in the *Dido Building Carthage*, of a shadow from a beam of wood projecting from the brick wall on the extreme left of the spectator, in a direction which can only come from a sun much higher than that in the picture."

It is unfortunate for Turner that his *Dido Building Carthage* is placed in the National Gallery beside Claude's *Embarkation of the Queen of Sheba;* for Mr. Ruskin's notice of the two pictures of Carthage is among the few instances in which he admits a fault in Turner. "The foreground," he says, "of the *Building of Carthage*, and the greater part of the architecture of the *Fall of Carthage*, are equally heavy and evidently faint, if we compare them with genuine passages of Claude's sunshine." Upon this Mr. Leslie remarks: "For my part, when I look at the *Building of Carthage*, I feel as if I were in a theatre, decorated with the most splendid drop-scenes; but when I stand before Claude's *Embarkation*, I am in the open air, enjoying the sea-breeze, and listening to the plash of the waves on the beach. Yet this does not convince me that Claude was a greater master than Turner, because it is a comparison of one of the most artificial pictures of the English painter with one of the most natural works of the Frenchman; and I only make the comparison to show that Claude is not to be deposed, to place on his throne one who wants it not, because he has raised himself to a throne, unoccupied before, and from which his sway is extended over a wider dominion, though, for that very reason, with less absolute power in every corner of it. Claude could not paint a storm; Turner's sea-storms are the finest ever painted; and though Claude is best seen in tranquil sunshine, yet there are many beautiful and brilliant mid-day appearances of perfect stillness, that were never seen on canvas, till Turner gave them with a power precluding all imitation."

TURNER'S YORKSHIRE DRAWINGS.

Mr. Ruskin considers the influence of the scenery of Yorkshire to be traced most definitely throughout Turner's works; and of all his drawings, those of the Yorkshire series to have the most heart in them, the most affectionate, simple, unwearied, serious finishing of truth. These drawings have unfortunately changed hands frequently, and have been abused and ill-treated by picture-dealers and cleaners; the greater number of them are now mere wrecks. In them may be traced the peculiar love of the painter for the rounded forms of hills. "It is, I believe," says Mr. Ruskin, "to the broad-wooded steeps and swells of the Yorkshire downs that we in part owe the singular massiveness that prevails in Turner's mountain-drawing, and gives it one of its chief elements of grandeur. Let the reader open the *Liber Studiorum,* and compare the painter's enjoyment of the lines in the Ben Arthur, with his comparative uncomfortableness among those of the aiguilles about the Mer de Glace.

"The Yorkshire drawings indicate one of the culminating points of Turner's career. In these he attained the highest degree of finish and quantity of form united with expression of atmosphere, and light without colour. His early drawings are singularly instructive in this definiteness and simplicity of aim. No complicated or brilliant colour is ever thought of in them; they are little more than exquisite studies in light and shade, very green blues being used for the shadows, and golden browns for the lights. The difficulty and treachery of colour being thus avoided, the artist was able to bend his whole mind upon the drawing, and thus to attain such decision, delicacy, and completeness, as have never in any wise been equalled, and as might serve him for a secure foundation in all future experiments. Of the quantity and precision of his details, the drawings made for Hakewill's *Italy* are singular examples. The most perfect gem in execution is a little bit on the Rhine, with reeds in the foreground, in the collection of G. B. Windus, Esq. of Tottenham; but the Yorkshire drawings seem to be on the whole the most noble representatives of his art at this period."

TURNER'S TREES.

The many admirers of Turner are angry with Mr. Leslie for saying that he (Turner) was a poor hand at painting a tree. "With the exception of here and there a willow, and, in his Italian views, the frequent pine and cypress, I look in vain," says Mr. Leslie, "for a specific discrimination in his trees; or in the vegetation of his foregrounds, in which there is little that is English. I cannot remember an oak, an elm, an ash, or a beech in any picture by him; nor do I remember anything much like the beauty of an English hedge. Neither has he expressed the deep verdure of his own country; hence he is the most unfaithful among great painters to the essential and most beautiful characteristics of English midland scenery."

Turner kept most profoundly the mystery of his art: he never allowed any brother artist to see him at work. When he was painting for Lord Egremont at Petworth, he worked with the door of the room locked. Only Lord Egremont, his patron, was admitted, and this by a pre-arranged knock at the room-door. Chantrey, when also at Petworth, by a cunning trick, obtained access. By a bribe, he ascertained from one of the servants of the house the peculiar knock, which Lord Egremont was accustomed to give at Turner's door. Thus prepared, he imitated Lord Egremont's step and cough, and imitated the very knock of the patron. The door was at once opened, and in walked Chantrey! Turner was annoyed, but was soon won over,—but only by the recollection that Chantrey, though once a painter, was now living by sculpture.

THE FIRST OF TURNER'S PICTURES SENT TO AMERICA.

Mr. James Lenox, of New York, wishing to possess one of Turner's pictures, (which he knew only from engravings,) wrote to Mr. Leslie to that effect. Mr. Leslie replied that Turner's rooms being full of unsold pictures, doubtless, he would part with one. Mr. Lenox then consented to give 500*l.*, and left the choice to Mr. Leslie. He called on Turner, and asked if he would let a picture go to America. "No: they won't come up to the scratch." This referred to another American friend having offered him a low price for the *Téméraire*. Mr. Leslie named 500*l.*, which a friend would give for anything Turner would part with. His countenance brightened, and he said at once, "He may have that, or that, or that,"—pointing to three not small pictures. Mr. Leslie chose a sunset view of Staffa: it was in an old frame, but Turner had a new frame made for it. When it reached New

York, and Mr. Lenox had hastily glanced at it, he wrote to Mr. Leslie, expressing his great disappointment. He almost fancied the picture had sustained some damage on the voyage,—it appeared to him so indistinct throughout. Still, he did not doubt its being very fine, and he hoped to see its merits on further acquaintance; but the above was his then impression.

A night or two after Mr. Leslie received Mr. Lenox's letter, he met Turner at the Academy, and he asked if he had heard from Mr. Lenox, to which Mr. Leslie was obliged to say yes.

"Well, and how does he like the picture?"

"He thinks it indistinct."

"You should tell him," he replied, "that indistinctness is my fault."

In the meantime, Mr. Leslie had answered Mr. Lenox's letter, pointing out the merits of the picture, and saying, "If, on a second view, it gains in your estimation, it will assuredly gain more and more every time you look at it." Mr. Lenox, in reply, said, "You have exactly described what has taken place. I now admire the picture greatly, and I have brought one or two of my friends to see it as I do, but it will never be a favourite with the multitude. I can now write to Mr. Turner, and tell him how conscientiously I am delighted with it." *

NUMBER OF PICTURES BY TURNER, AND PRICES.

From the time of Turner's becoming a Royal Academician, to his death, a period of nearly forty-nine years, he was absent on four occasions only from the Exhibition walls. These were 1805, 1821, 1824, and 1851.

The number of his exhibited works is 252; to these we must add some dozen pictures sent to the British Institution, and some forty more never publicly exhibited. This would bring his oil pictures to some 300; while to these we must add, perhaps, 1,000 finished drawings, of which 500 at least are of his best period.

Turner's prices for his pictures between 1803 and 1815—certainly his best period—were far from large. They ranged from 150 to 200 guineas, and at such prices he obtained a

* Autobiographical Recollections of the late C. R. Leslie, R.A. edited by Tom Taylor, Esq. 2 vols. 1860.

ready market. In 1810, Lord Yarborough gave him 300 guineas for *The Wreck,*—a large price for a landscape by a living artist. This same *Wreck,* at Christie's (says Cunningham), would sell for 2,000*l.*

In June, 1855, the *Burning of the Houses of Parliament,* exhibited that year, was sold for 810 guineas ; and *The State Barges conveying the Pictures of Gian Bellini to the Church of the Redeemer,* exhibited in 1841, brought the large sum of 1,360 guineas.

In May, 1854, three of Turner's fine pictures, from the collection of Mr. Wadmore, were sold by Christie for nearly four times the price he had paid for them. First was *Cologne —the Arrival of a Packet-boat—Evening,* a picture of the year 1826, which was knocked down, amidst murmurs of delight, at 2,000 guineas. Then came the *Harbour of Dieppe,* a picture of the year 1825, sold to the same purchaser for 1,850 guineas. Then came a small unexhibited picture, painted, it is said, in 1809, and known to collectors as *The Guard-ship of the Nore,* which was knocked down for 1,530 guineas. Turner is said to have received 250*l.* for the *Guard-ship,* and the same sum for the *Cologne* and *Dieppe* respectively. Mr. Wadmore, in 1828, gave 1,500*l.* for the three pictures, which in 1854 were sold for 5,640*l.*

Some of Turner's pictures have been known to crack before the Exhibition was closed in which they first appeared : he often used water-colours over oil, and then again oil-colours over water.

TURNER'S BARGAINING.

Mr. Cunningham tells a good story or two of Turner's skill in bargain-making. When arranging with Hurst and Robinson for a new work in numbers, the price of each drawing was settled, not without deliberation, at twenty-five *pounds*. He went away, expressing full satisfaction. He came speedily back, thrust his head in at the door, and cried, " Guineas ?" " Guineas, be it," said the publishers. In a few minutes, a hasty step was heard, and Turner put in his whole person, saying, " My expenses ?" " Oh, certainly, sir," was the answer. But this was not all : a few minutes after, he was for a third time at the door, breathless and eager, with his whole body in the room, for he expected resistance to his new demand— " and twenty proofs ?" No resistance was made, and the drawings were set about with an ungrumbling reluctance.

When George Cooke, the engraver, related this story to Allan Cunningham, (from whom it was received by his son Peter,) he added : " I am told that Turner's father, who was a barber, having been paid a penny for a shave, followed his customer down Maiden-lane, to demand a halfpenny for soap."

Mr. P. Cunningham relates another story. Turner had painted a picture for the famous Jack Fuller, and was asked by Fuller to breakfast with him next morning, to bring the picture with him, and was told that the cheque for the picture would then be ready. To this Turner consented. He took the picture in a hackney-coach, breakfasted, received the cheque, thanked the purchaser, and left. He was not gone above five minutes, when a knock was heard at the door; the painter was back—" I must see Mr. Fuller." He was shown in. "Oh! I'd forgotten ; there is three shillings for the hackney-coach." The sum was paid. Fuller, who was laughing all the while, loved to relate this story to his friends.

TURNER'S BOOK-PLATES.

These were more successful speculations for the print-sellers than the larger engravings from his works. Large sums were cleared by his *Southern Coast, Seine and Loire Tours,* and *Provincial Antiquities.* His Illustrations for Sir Walter Scott's Poetry and Prose realised large sums : indeed, those for the *Waverley Novels,* though timidly undertaken by the publishers, were immensely profitable. His drawings for Murray's seventeen volume edition of Byron are admirable ; but those for Rogers's Poems take precedence of all others. His drawings for Sir Egerton Brydges's edition of Milton were not altogether successful.

Mr. Cunningham states his prices for such drawings at from 20 to 25 guineas. In some cases, Turner lent the drawings to publishers, with the right to engrave. More which he sold outright brought large prices; as the Scott drawings, sixty-four at 12 guineas each, to Mr. Windus. His Richmondshire drawings, for which he received 20 guineas each from the publishers, have since been sold at from 80 to 100 guineas each.

HIS PRESENT RANK AS A LANDSCAPE-PAINTER.

The merits of our great Painter, though infinitely better understood than at any former period, are still denied, and with some firmness—which may probably have arisen from the indiscriminate eulogy which has of late years been heaped upon him. Between the two extremes it will be well to read the calm judgment of a German writer, whose authority is admitted, and whose opinion is the result of repeated examination of his works.

Dr. Waagen says: "In point of fact, no landscape-painter has yet appeared with such versatility of talent. His historical landscapes exhibit the most exquisite feeling for beauty of lines and effect of lighting: at the same time, he has the power of making them express the most varied moods of Nature—a lofty grandeur, a deep and gloomy melancholy, a sunny cheerfulness and peace, or an uproar of all the elements. Buildings he also treats with peculiar felicity; while the sea, in its most varied aspects, is equally subservient to his magic brush. His views of certain cities and localities inspire the spectator with poetic feelings, such as no other painter ever excited in the same degree, and which is principally attributable to the exceeding picturesqueness of the point of view chosen, and to the beauty of the lighting. Finally, he treats the most common little subjects, such as a group of trees, a meadow, a shaded stream, with such art as to impart to them the most picturesque charm. I should, therefore, not hesitate to recognise Turner as the greatest landscape-painter of all times but for his deficiency in one indispensable element in every work of art, namely, a sound technical basis."

ACCURACY IN SHIPPING.

Among the earliest sketches from Nature which Turner appears to have made, in pencil and Indian ink, when a boy of twelve or fourteen, it is very singular how large a proportion consists of careful studies of stranded boats. After some fifteen years of conscientious labour, with the single view of acquiring knowledge of the ends and powers of art, Mr. Ruskin tells us that he has come to the conclusion—that of all our modern school of landscape-painters, next to Turner, and before the rise of the Pre-Raphaelites, the man whose works are on the whole most valuable, and show the highest intellect, is Samuel Prout. It is very notable that also in Prout's early studies, shipping studies took not merely a prominent but a principal place.

The reason of this is very evident: both Turner and Prout had in them an untaught, inherent perception of what was good and pictorial. Prout afterwards left his first love ; but Turner retained the early affection to the close of his life, and the last oil picture he painted, before his noble hand forgot its cunning, was the *Wreck and Buoy.* The last thoroughly perfect picture he ever painted, was the *Old Téméraire.*

The studies which he was able to make from Nature in his early years, are chiefly of fishing-boats, barges, and other marine still life ; and his better acquaintance with this kind of shipping than with the larger kind is very marked in the *Liber Studiorum,* in which there are five careful studies of fishing-boats under various circumstances ; viz., Calais Harbour, Sir John Mildmay's picture, Flint Castle, Marine Dabblers, and the Calm ; while of other shipping there are only two subjects, both exceedingly unsatisfactory.

Turner, however, deemed it necessary to his reputation at that period, that he should paint pictures in the style of Vandervelde ; and in order to render the resemblance more complete, he appears to have made careful drawings of the different parts of old Dutch shipping. Mr. Ruskin found a large number of such drawings among the contents of the Painter's neglected portfolios at his death ; some were clearly not by his own hand, others appeared to be transcripts by him from prints or earlier drawings ; the quantity altogether was very great, and the evidence of his prolonged attention to the subject more distinct than with respect to any other element of landscape. Of plants, rocks, or architecture, there were very few careful pieces of anatomical study ; but several drawers were entirely filled with these memoranda of shipping.

In executing the series of drawings for the *Southern Coast,* Turner appears to have gained many ideas about shipping, which, once received, he laid up by him in use for after years ; and it is believed that in the watch over the Cornish and Devonshire coasts, which the making of those drawings involved, he received all his noblest ideas about sea and ships.

Mr. Ruskin is certain that Turner never drew anything that could be *seen,* without having seen it. That is to say, though he would draw Jerusalem from some one else's sketch, it would be, nevertheless, entirely from his own experience of ruined walls ; and though he would draw ancient shipping, (for an imitation of Vandervelde, or a vignette to the voyage of Columbus) from such data as he could get about things which he could see no more with his own eyes,—yet, when, of his own free will, in the subject of Ilfracombe, he, in the year

1818, introduces a shipwreck, Mr. Ruskin is perfectly certain that, before the year 1818, he had *seen* a shipwreck, and moreover one of that horrible kind,—a ship dashed to pieces in deep water, at the foot of an inaccessible cliff. Having once seen this, the image of it could not be effaced from his mind. It taught him two great facts, that he never afterwards forgot; namely, that both ships and sea were things that broke to pieces. *He never afterwards painted a ship quite in fair order.* There is invariably a feeling about his vessels of strange awe and danger : the sails are in some way loosening, or flapping as if in fear ; the swing of the hull, majestic as it may be, seems more at the mercy of the sea than in triumph over it ; the ship never looks gay, never proud, only warlike and enduring. The motto he chose in the Catalogue of the Academy, for the most cheerful marine piece he ever painted,— *the Sun of Venice going to Sea*,—marked the uppermost feeling in his mind :

> "Nor heeds the Demon that in grim repose
> Expects his evening prey."

Mr. Ruskin noticed the subject of his last marine picture, *the Wreck Buoy*, and is well persuaded that from the year 1818, when first he saw a ship rent asunder, he never beheld one at sea, without, in his mind's eye, at the same instant, seeing her skeleton.

But he had seen more than the death of the ship. He had seen the sea feed her white flames on the souls of men ; and heard what a storm-gust sounded like, that had taken up with it, in its swirl of a moment, the last breaths of a ship's crew. He never forgot either the sight or the sound. Among the last plates prepared by his own hand for the *Liber Studiorum*, (all of them, as was likely from his advanced knowledge, finer than any previous pieces of the series, and most of them unfortunately never published, being retained beside him for some last touch—for ever delayed,) perhaps the most important is one of the body of a drowned sailor, dashed against a vertical rock in the jaws of one merciless, immeasurable wave. He repeated the same idea, though more fully expressed, later in life, in a small drawing of Grandville, on the coast of France. The sailor clinging to the boat in the marvellous drawing of Dunbar is another reminiscence of the same kind. He hardly ever painted a steep, rocky coast without some fragment of a devoured ship, grinding in the blanched teeth of the surges,—just enough left to be a token of utter destruction.

In conclusion, Mr. Ruskin says: "I am aware of no painting, from the beginning of his (Turner's) life till its close, containing *modern* shipping as its principal subject, in which he did not put forth his full strength, and pour out his knowledge of detail with a joy which renders those works as a series, among the most valuable he ever produced."—*From the Illustrative Text to Turner's Harbours of England*, 1856.

TURNER AND LORD DE TABLEY.

Mr. Jerdan, in his *Autobiography*, relates the following :— Turner, of whom Lord de Tabley had been a most liberal patron, spent a day or two at Tabley when I was there. In the drawing-room stood a landscape on an easel, on which his lordship was at work, as the fancy mood struck him. Of course, when assembled for the tedious half hour before dinner, we all gave our opinions on its progress, its beauties, and its defects. I stuck a blue wafer on, to show where I thought a bit of bright colour, or a light, would be advantageous; and Turner took the brush and gave a touch here and there, to mark some improvements. He returned to town, and, can it be credited, the next morning at breakfast, a letter from him was delivered to his lordship, containing a regular bill of charges for "instructions in painting." His lordship tossed it across the table indignantly to me, and asked if I could have imagined such a thing; and as indignantly, against my remonstrances, immediately sent a cheque for the sum demanded by the "drawing-master."

This was a deplorable instance of Turner's eccentricity, and not to be excused on any imaginable ground. Yet sometimes he was lavish in the midst of his general penuriousness. On a continental trip, Mr. Thomas Hunt, the well-known writer on Tudor architecture, accidentally encountered him on a continental excursion. Turner took a fancy to so excellent a boon companion, invited him to travel with him, and treated him in a princely style, without costing him a shilling through the whole of their tour.

PICTURES BY TURNER IN THE ART-TREASURES EXHIBITION AT MANCHESTER, 1857.

Above twenty specimens of Turner's pictures, exhibiting pretty fairly his several manners, formed one of the most interesting contributions to the Manchester saloons; but, of course, this great artist is to be thoroughly understood nowhere except in his own Collection, bequeathed to the nation. His first picture at Manchester was an example of his worst style —*Pluto carrying away Proserpine*. The next was a specimen of his very best manner—*Cologne: the Arrival of a Packet-boat*, belonging to Mr. Naylor, by whom it was purchased in 1854 for two thousand guineas. The golden glow of the setting sun, the charming composition of the whole subject, and the bustle of the debarkation contrasted with the repose of the evening scene, form a whole not easily forgotten. The opposite effect of a sunrise was equally well shown in Mr. Wells's *Mouth of the Thames, with Men of War;* and Lord Yarborough's *Vintage at Macon*, exhibited in 1803, was another delicious feast of colour, in the early manner of the artist. Nor is *Dolbadarn Castle*—Turner's diploma picture on admission into the Royal Academy—a whit inferior. *Saltash* is a glorified vision of that picturesque town, bathed in a liquid amber light, such as one dreams of, but seldom—perhaps never—sees in this climate. We pass over some less remarkable specimens to come to *Barnes Terrace*, a beautiful evening view of that quiet and familiar Thames scene. With this may be compared *Walton Bridge*, also on the Thames; and one powerful *Coast Scene* may likewise be noticed.

The *Van Tromp*—in the later manner of Turner—is beyond the comprehension of ordinary mortals. It would puzzle any one to say which is sky, and which sea, of the splashes of crude paint that are crowded on the canvas. There is more intelligible feeling in the *Meeting of the Waters*, but the colour is somewhat dark and indistinguishable. We recur to his earlier manner in *Tabley Lake and Tower;* but the picture is a strange idealization of a tame Cheshire mere—with a staring, modern mansion on its bank—into a kind of rough inland sea, bustling with varied and abounding shipping. The next picture bearing Turner's name — the *Sun rising through Vapour*—is full of poetry and magic. The sea and the shipping are such as Vandervelde never conceived, much less executed. And the *Falls of Schaffhausen* is a work of painted poetry, masterly and impressive in the highest degree. The last work of our greatest English painter which we shall touch upon is one of his most celebrated—Lord Yarborough's *Wreck of the Minotaur*. No artist has ever imagined anything more awful than the sweep of the surf on the iron-bound coast. The colour unfortunately has somewhat failed, and the light seems scarcely strong enough in the place where the picture is hung. Lord Yarborough has caused this picture, and also his other great Turner, *The Vintage at Macon*, to be engraved at his own cost in aid of the Artists' Benevolent Institution. It is a matter for great congratulation that the noblest landscape-painter that England has produced should have been so well represented at Manchester.—*Saturday Review*, July, 1857.

APPRECIATION OF STOTHARD.

Turner exhibited a picture in 1828, *Boccaccio relating the Tale of the Bird-cage*, in imitation of Stothard, for whose works he had the profoundest admiration. "I only wish," said Turner to one of the Academy Professors, "he thought as much of my works as I think of his. I consider him the Giotto of the English school."

PAINTINGS OF FIRES.

Turner was always on the alert for any remarkable effects. In 1792, when he was eighteen years of age, the Pantheon in Oxford-street was burnt down. It happened to be a hard frost at the time, and huge icicles were seen the next morning depending from different parts of the ruins. The young artist quickly repaired to the spot, and his picture, *The Pantheon on the Morning after the Fire*, exhibited at the Royal Academy in the following May, witnessed the force with which the scene was impressed upon him. In like manner, the *Burning of the Houses of Parliament* forty years afterwards was an event that could not escape the pencil of Turner. He repaired to the spot to make sketches of the fire at different points, and produced two pictures, one for the Academy, and another for the British Institution. Here was a glowing subject for his palette. Lord Hill, on looking close to the latter picture, exclaimed, "What's this? Call this painting? Nothing but dabs!" But upon retiring and catching its magical effects, he added, "Painting! God bless me, so it is!" The picture of *Hail, Rain, and Speed*, with its wonderful interpretation of a night railway train, produced at a still later period of Turner's life, was another instance in which the great artist's attention had been caught by the hissing and puffing, and glowing fire of the locomotive.

TURNER'S RECREATIONS.

The great Painter was very fond of fishing, and would angle together for hours. This was Turner's chief source of relaxation. On the occasion of a professional visit to Petworth, it was remarked to Lord Egremont, "Turner is going to leave without having done anything; instead of painting, he does nothing but fish!" To the surprise of his patron he produced, as he was on the point of leaving, two or three wonderful pictures, painted with the utmost reserve during early morning before the family were up.

His conversation was sprightly, but desultory and disjointed. Like his works, it was eminently sketchy. He would converse in this manner for half an hour, and then be amused at finding his companion in doubt of what he had been talking about. He either never knew, or never would tell, his birthday. One who was a fellow-student with him at the Academy, and his companion from boyhood, once said to him, "William, your birthday can't be far off? when is it? I want to drink a glass of wine to my old friend." "Ah!" growled Turner, "never mind that; leave your old friend alone." He was never married, and had no relations, excepting two or three cousins, to whom, probably, it never occurred to ascertain the day of his birth.

He wrote few letters, and these were, like his conversation, abrupt, and referred little to art. The following, accepting an invitation to dine with his valued friend and patron, Mr. Windus, of Tottenham, on the occasion of his birthday, is characteristic: "My dear Sir,—*Yes*, with very great pleasure. I will be with you on the *B. D.* Many of them to yourself and Mrs. Windus; and, with the compliments of the season, believe me, yours faithfully, J. M. W. TURNER."

PROFESSOR OF PERSPECTIVE.

In some of his earlier works, before he had gained the honours of the Academy, we find Turner making use of the architectural knowledge acquired, along with Girtin, in working for Porden. This led to his being selected, in 1808, for the Academic Professor of Perspective; and his drawings consisted chiefly of abbeys, churches, castles, palaces, and gentlemen's seats, with an occasional subject of a more imaginative kind, such as *Morning—a study at Milbank*, a small picture of much beauty and transparency, and of deep tone.

Turner's disjointed and diffuse manner of conversation rendered him, however, little qualified for the lecture-room; and although he retained the office of Professor of Perspective until 1837, he did not lecture more than two or three years out of the thirty, which caused occasional dissatisfaction. Wilkie jokingly dubbed the Professor, R.A., P.P.

TURNER'S BRILLIANCY.

It is not easy to estimate the loss of Turner's works from the walls of the Academy, where for so many years they had exercised an influence upon the pictures, not only of the landscape-painter, but of all that were hung in contact with them. Brilliancy was at all times a remarkable characteristic of Turner's colouring. When, at the annual Academy dinner, the gas was turned on, as is customary on the Sovereign's health being drunk, his pictures shone like so many suns upon the walls. While other meritorious works looked flat in comparison, there was an effulgence in Turner's, that seemed to grow upon the observer, making the contrast more apparent. "They seem to represent so many holes cut in the wall," said a veteran connoisseur, at one of these art-festivals, "through which you see Nature." This observation was probably suggested, however, by one made some years before by Northcote. Turner's pictures were always the terror of exhibitors, from showing whatever were the defects in colour of those placed near to them. Northcote had a dark picture in the Exhibition, and was very angry with the arrangers for putting a bright one of Turner's immediately below it. "You might as well have opened a window under my picture," said the painter. The compliment was as handsome as it was unintentional.

VIEWS IN ENGLAND AND WALES.

Mr. Alaric Watts, in his very interesting memoir prefixed to Bohn's edition of the *Liber Fluviorum*, relates the following particulars concerning the disposition of his *England and Wales*. "This fine work," says Mr. Watts, "was to have consisted of thirty parts or more, but stopped short at the twenty-fourth, for want of sufficient encouragement. Having been undertaken on joint account between the engraver, Mr. Charles Heath, and his publishers, it became desirable, on the abrupt termination of the work in 1838, to sell off the stock and copper-plates, and balance the accounts. The whole property was offered to the publisher of the present volume (Mr. Bohn) for 3,000*l.*, and he offered within 200*l.* of the amount; which being declined, it was placed in the hands of Messrs. Southgate and Co. for sale by auction. After extensive advertising, the day and hour of sale had arrived, when, just at the moment the auctioneer was about to mount his rostrum, Mr. Turner stepped in, and bought it privately, at the reserved price of three thousand pounds, much to the vexation of many who had come prepared to buy portions of it. Immediately after the purchase, Mr. Turner walked up to Mr. Bohn, with whom he was very well acquainted, and said to him, 'So, Sir, you were going to buy my England and Wales, to sell cheap I suppose;—make umbrella prints of them, eh?—but I have taken care of that. No more of my plates shall be worn to shadows.' Upon Mr. Bohn's replying, that his object was the printed stock (which was very large) rather than the copper-plates, he said, 'O! very well, I don't want the stock, I only want to keep the coppers out of your clutches. So, if you like to buy the stock, come and breakfast with me to-morrow, and we will see if we can deal.' At nine the next morning Mr. Bohn presented himself, according to appointment, and after a few minutes Mr. Turner made his appearance, and forgetting all about the breakfast, said, 'Well, sir, what have you to say?' 'I come to treat with you for the stock of your *England and Wales*,' was the reply.—'Well! what will you give?'—Mr. Bohn told him, 'that in the course of the negotiation, the coppers and copyright had been estimated by the proprietors at 500*l.*, and therefore he would deduct that sum, and the balance, 2,500*l.*, should be handed to him immediately.'—'Pooh! I must have 3,000*l.*, and keep my coppers; else good morning to you.' As this was not very likely after having refused both stock and coppers at 3,000*l.*, 'Good morning,' was the reply; and so they parted. The stock, or the greater portion of it, is still lying in Queen-Anne Street, of course not improved by keeping, and having, in the course of the fourteen years which have since elapsed, swallowed up another 3,000*l.*, reckoning compound interest at five per cent. per annum."

TURNER BIDDING FOR HIS OWN PICTURES.

Turner never allowed a picture from his pencil to be sold by public auction, without sending some person to bid for it; and his wishes on this subject were so generally known, that auctioneers made a point of calling his attention to the catalogue, whenever they had any of his pictures for sale. If time pressed, and he was unable to attend in person, he would sometimes, but rarely, intrust his commission to the auctioneer; his ordinary practice was to send some agent, with written instructions, to bid in his behalf, and he was not always very fastidious in his selection. At the sale of the pictures of Mr. Green, the well-known amateur, of Blackheath, two pictures by Turner were among the most attractive lots, though neither important in size nor of his best time. In those days, their market value might have been about eighty guineas each. They would, however, have been knocked down for considerably less, but for the impetus given to the biddings by one of Turner's agents, whose personal appearance did not warrant the belief that he was in search of pictures of a very high order. He was, in fact, a clean, ruddy-cheeked, butcher's boy, in the usual costume of his vocation, and had made several advances, in five guinea strides, before anything belonging to him, excepting his voice, had attracted Mr. Christie's notice. No sooner, however, did the veteran auctioneer discover what kind of customer he had to deal with, than he beckoned him forward, with a view, no doubt, of reproving him for his impertinence. The boy, however, nothing daunted, put a small piece of greasy paper into his hand; a credential, in fact, from the painter himself. The auctioneer smiled, and the biddings proceeded.

There must, however, be in circulation, or in collections, many a work by Turner, which was less nicely cared for and watched over.

"The father of the late hall-porter of Mr. Walter Fawkes, of Farnley Hall, Yorkshire, who kept the village ale-house, received from him a drawing of great value in liquidation of a trifling score of some four or five pounds. The manner in which this transaction was discovered is curious enough. On retiring from Mr. Fawkes's service to replace his father as host of the village house of entertainment, the man was desirous of purchasing the old hall-chair, in which he had been accustomed to sit for so many years; and having been allowed to appraise it himself at four pounds, offered, instead of hard cash, a capital drawing by Turner, which had been given to his father in acquittance of his bill. One of his best sea-pieces is said to have been transferred to a Margate boatman under nearly similar circumstances."

"VAN TROMP'S BARGE."

The freshest and most life-like piece of daylight that Turner had yet produced, was *Admiral Van Tromp's Barge at the entrance of the Texel;* and in the year after, a somewhat eccentric picture, entitled *Watteau, a study by Fresnoy's rules*, which caused a great deal of merriment among the artist's detractors. This little picture was, perhaps, the extremest type of the *white school* that Turner ever painted, and was intended to show artistically that white in its purity can be used either to make an object retire or to bring it near. The point was illustrated by presenting a distant white building through an open window in contact, so to speak, with an equally white object in the room. As an experiment, it was a happy idea. In other respects, the picture was meant as a laugh at the public. This ridicule was, however, held in check by the exhibition at the same time of more than one picture in the manner of *Van Tromp's Barge*. In the following year, Turner exhibited *Van Tromp returning after the Battle off the Dogger Bank*, with his sails in tatters, the whole wildly and picturesquely treated; and with it appeared two works commencing that brilliant series of Venetian views in which he afterwards, at frequent intervals, seemed to revel. Affording, as they did, so much of what his art at that time demanded in bright skies, in glancing waters, and vari-coloured architecture, no wonder that he loved them; but in the facilities they afforded for introducing those infinite varieties of brilliant tints in which he gloried, if only to show his mastery over the world of atmospheric effects, we believe he was led in some measure into a looseness of drawing in detail, which has been felt by his warmest admirers, in his later examples of this class.

TURNER AND HIS EULOGISTS.

One element in Turner's success was his indifference to praise. Though proud of his works, he was not a vain man. His reputation never suffered from the disappointments arising out of a premature desire for fame. He was not pleased with Mr. Ruskin's superlative eulogies. Had the author of *Modern Painters* written with less violent enthusiasm, his opinions would have had more weight. "He knows a great deal more about my pictures than I do," said Turner; "he puts things into my head, and points out meanings in them that I never intended." It was not easy to draw his attention to the admiration of his own pictures. A well-known collector, with whom the artist had long been intimate, once invited him to be present at the opening of a new gallery, in which the principal pictures were from his pencil. To the disappointment of the connoisseur, Turner scarcely noticed them, but kept his eye fixed upon the ceiling. It was panelled and neatly grained in oak. "What are you looking at so intently?" said the host. "At those boards," was the reply; "the fellow that did that must have known how to paint." And nothing would induce him to turn to the magnificent pictures that sparkled on the walls. He never talked about his own pictures, but would occasionally give hints to other artists; and when these were adopted, they were always certain improvements. We never heard of his saying anything, however, that would give pain, and he felt keenly the ignorant criticisms and ridicule with which his own pictures were often treated.

TURNER'S WATER-COLOUR DRAWINGS.—SECRET OF HIS SUCCESS.

Turner's water-colour drawings did more for extending his reputation than his oil pictures, for contemporary with these his style in oil began to change. He indulged more freely in the use of primitive tints, and consummate as was the skill with which he used them, exciting the admiration of many to the highest pitch of enthusiasm, they were yet as *caviare* to the multitude. There can be no doubt that a still greater elaboration of the same principle, founded as it is in Nature, might have refined them into a neutrality of effect that would have been pleasing to the ordinary beholder, while they retained for the artist and connoisseur all that has made his name so great among them as a colourist. Mr. Thackeray, upon a certain occasion, made light of Turner's style in the columns of *Punch*, by drawing some obscure outline, signifying nothing, as an example of the master. Shortly afterwards he was introduced to the gallery of a well-known connoisseur, especially rich in his pictures, both oil and water-colour. "Astounding!" said the author of *Vanity Fair;* "I will never abuse Turner again."

The great secret of Turner's fame was his constant recourse to Nature, and his wonderful activity and power of memory, coupled with great natural genius, and indifference to praise. His religious study of Nature was such, that he would walk through portions of England, twenty to twenty-five miles a day, with his little modicum of baggage at the end of a stick, sketching rapidly on his way all good pieces of composition, and marking effects with a power that daguerreotyped them in his mind with unerring truth at the happiest moment. There were few moving phenomena in clouds or shadows which he did not fix indelibly in his memory, though he might not call them into requisition for years afterwards.

Turner's faculty of observation was prodigious, and his mind was always intent upon the work of his profession. He could not walk London streets without seeing effects of light and shade and composition, whether in the smoke issuing from a chimney-pot, or in the shadows upon a brick-wall, without storing them in his memory for use at any time when needed. Frequently on looking at another artist's landscape, all the details of the scene would rise to his recollection, and he would good-humouredly criticise any exaggeration for effect. "Now those trees," he would say, "are not in that corner—they are there." He saw beauties in things and groups of things, that nobody else could see,—and painted pictures of them. He frequently started off to the Continent, nobody knew when and nobody knew where, until the result of his labours came forth to illustrate some costly book—now to France, now to Venice, and not unfrequently painted his views in oil on the spot. His pencil was always in requisition. An intimate friend, while travelling in the Jura, came to an inn where Turner had only just before entered his name in the visiting book. Anxious to be sure of his identity and to be in pursuit of him, he inquired of the host what sort of man his last visitor was. "A rough clumsy man," was the reply; "and you may know him by his always having a pencil in his hand." Nature was his inspiration in the fullest sense of the word.

Few were intimate with him, and few even knew him. Once, upon being told that an eminent publisher had boasted of having obtained admission to his studio, "How could you be such a fool as to believe it?" replied Turner, in his usual abrupt manner. And his reserve in this respect was responded to by a most faithful servant who had lived forty-two years with him, to the day of his death.—*Abridged from the Literary Gazette,* 1852.

APPENDIX.

HOGARTH'S SOUTHWARK FAIR.
(Page 18.)

IT has been erroneously stated that the picture of *Southwark Fair* was destroyed by fire; whereas, it is in the possession of the Duke of Newcastle. It differs considerably in effect of light and dark from the print, and we see more distinctly in it what Hogarth intended as the principal points. His was a genius that delighted to touch, and knew how to touch, the master-chords of human nature; and in the foreground groups of this picture, the admiration of beauty by man, and of valour by woman, are the things on which the chief lights are thrown.—*Leslie's Handbook*, p. 124.

HOGARTH PAINTING "CHILDREN."

There is a charming picture by Hogarth at Holland House, in which children are the principal personages. It represents the private performance of a play at the house of Mr. Conduitt, the Master of the Mint, before the Duke of Cumberland and a few other people of fashion. Three girls and a boy are on the stage, and seem to be very seriously doing their best; but the attitude and expression of one little girl, on a front seat among the audience, is matchless. She is so entirely absorbed in the performance, that she sits bolt upright, and will sit, we are sure, immovably, to the end of the play, enjoying it, as a child only can, and much the more because the actors are children. The picture is beautifully coloured, and is one of those early works painted from nature, the execution of which prepared the way to Hogarth's greater efforts. — *Leslie's Handbook*, p. 131.

SIR JOSHUA'S FATHER.
(Page 96.)

The Rev. Mr. Reynolds had, like a few old divines of his time, a turn for astrology. Mr. Cotton, in his **volume** published in 1860, relates :—

"That old Mr. Reynolds was an astrologist, and used to cast nativities, I have been told by a lady staying at Ivybridge, whose mother had a servant that once lived with Mr. and Mrs. Reynolds, at Plympton, and she told her the following singular circumstance. When the birth of one of his children was about to take place, Mr. Reynolds diligently employed himself in taking its horoscope. Being informed of the exact time of the birth, he exclaimed: 'How unfortunate! for there is a most malign conjunction of the planets, which threatens danger to the child at a certain period of its life.' The greatest care was consequently taken of the infant on the day on which some evil was expected to happen. Mr. Reynolds mounted his horse, to allay the disturbance of his mind, and rode away some distance from home. As soon as he returned, he looked up to the room in which the child was supposed to be, and was overjoyed to see him at the window. At this moment the little boy over-reached himself, and falling from some height to the ground below, was killed. The fears and predictions of Mr. Reynolds were thus fulfilled in a most extraordinary manner."

REYNOLDS'S STUDIES IN ITALY.
(Pages 102—103.)

In January, 1859, Mr. Cotton published several Extracts from Reynolds's Italian Journals and Sketch-books, lately purchased by the Trustees of the British Museum. These passages supply, in some measure, the distinct record of Reynolds's method of study whilst in Italy. The Extracts from his note-books, published by Northcote, served in a measure to explain his practice during his long stay in Rome; but of his studies in Venice—and, as has always been said, it was upon the system of the great Venetian painters his own theory of colour was based—the only account was that furnished in his Notes to Mason's Translation of Du Fresnoy. When Mr. Ruskin was consulted as to the expediency of publishing these Italian memoranda, he replied, "Publish them by all means."

The notes before us commence with an account of the "Copies of Pictures I made at Rome," the earliest date being the 16th of April, 1750. As we know, he soon emancipated himself from "the drudgery of copying, ... at best a delusive kind of industry," as he long after told the Academy students; but the copies we here, at the opening of the book, find him making were such as could not but be of service to him in his own line of art, while the note shows at once his industry and the rapidity with which he already painted : " In the Corsini Palace, April 16. 1. 'Study of an Old Man's Head, reading,' by Rubens. 2. April 17 to 19, 'A portrait of Philip II., King of Spain,' by Titian. 3. April 20, ' Rembrandt's Portrait of Himself.' 4. April 21 to 23, 'St. Martin on Horseback,'" and so on.

By a note made in the following August, we see that Reynolds had by this time adopted his theory of generalisation. Studying in the Vatican, he thus notes :

"Raphael, in many books on painting, is praised to the skies for being natural, and because silks and velvets are so naturally painted (by him) that they would deceive any man. This is so far from being true, that they are further from it than the draperies of any other painter; nor ought they to be so natural as to deceive one, except in portraits, as in that of Leo X. at Florence, where the drapery is natural to the last degree, but in none of his history pictures. Those pretenders to painting think the whole art lies in making things natural. If that were the case, how many Raphaels has not Holland produced ? What I would endeavour to settle is the point to which the painter is to direct his attention, to give him an idea of what art is by the example of the Great Masters; for young painters, as well as connoisseurs, are sometimes puzzled in seeing a picture, in which there is nothing of what we call natural, preferred to another where there are satins, silks, jugs, &c., which deceive the sight."

What his ultimate views were on this point are most fully stated in his Third Discourse ; but Mr. Cotton has published a paragraph from some papers in the possession of Mr. R. Palmer, in which he has thus expressed his opinion still more forcibly.

"The object of all imitation is Nature. But art does not approximate perfection, in proportion as it approaches to deception, so as to mistake the imitation for the reality. Supposing this to be the state of any art, the pleasure of comparison, which Plato says is the cause of our pleasure in painting, ceases. It is, then, the thing itself. The art, therefore, of imitation in painting consists in the genius and judgment of the artist in selecting what are dominant and striking features, which may be sufficient to impress the idea of the original object strongly on the spectator. He feels that consummate pleasure which proceeds from the skill and address of the artist, who, with the appearance of so little labour, has expressed so much. This is the *buon maniera*."

He notes his impressions of all sorts of pictures and works of art, especially the Titians, and never forgetting to record when in a picture he meets with "angels and women wonderfully genteel ;" or a " Virgin—a fine figure.'

APPENDIX. 373

Reynolds arrived in Venice on his twenty-ninth birthday, and remained there little over three weeks. But during his stay at Rome he had devoted a large proportion of his time to the study of the Venetian pictures in that city; and the frequent comparison of them with similar pictures at Windsor and elsewhere may be taken as a proof that even before he went to Italy he had carefully studied the great Venetian masters wherever opportunities were afforded him. He made no attempt to copy whilst in Venice, contenting himself with making broad sketches of the light and shadow, and written memoranda of the colour of the principal paintings. The works of Titian, Paolo Veronese, and Tintoretto, were those to which his time was chiefly given. His note to Du Fresnoy contains this account of the plan he pursued. Speaking of the management of light and shade, he says:

"Titian, Paul Veronese, and Tintoretto were among the first painters who reduced to a system what was before practised without any fixed principle, and consequently neglected occasionally.... When I was at Venice, the method I took to avail myself of their principles was this: when I observed an extraordinary effect of light and shade in any picture, I took a leaf out of my pocket-book, and darkened every part of it in the same gradation of light and shade as the picture, leaving the white paper untouched to represent the light, and this without any attention to the subject, or to the drawing of the figures."

From pencil memoranda in the very pocket-books in which these *chiaro-scuro* studies were made, Mr. Cotton copied his notes. These books were inherited by the Marchioness of Thomond, at the sale of whose effects they were bought by Mr. J. L. Gwatkin. After Mr. Cotton was allowed to copy these notes, these books were purchased by the Trustees of the British Museum for 150 guineas, and added to the treasures of the Print-room.

The following "General Rule," is a specimen of the way in which Reynolds tried to generalise, for his own future guidance, from what he had been examining. It follows his notes on the *St. Agnes* of Tintoretto:

"A figure of figures on a light ground, the lower part dark, having lights here and there. The ground dark.
"When the second mass of light is too great, interpose some dark figure, to divide it in two.
"A white drapery edged and striped, or flowered with blue, as the bride in the *Marriage of Cana*, or the *Venus in the Colonna*, on a mellow oily ground.
"Zucchareili (*sic*) says Paolo and Tintoretto painted on a Gess ground. He does not think that Titian did. I am firmly of opinion they all did

"A portrait—putting on a morning gown—the figure relieved on one side only.

"Dark figures on a light ground, not relieved quite round."

To sum up, it may be gathered, from the new materials now collected, that of all Reynolds saw in Italy the great Venetian colourists, Titian, Paul Veronese, and Tintoretto, made the greatest impression on his mind. At Rome he gave the palm to Michael Angelo over Raphael, in respect of design; but he imitated in his own practice the school of Venice. Mr. Cotton remarks, with great probability, that Reynolds followed implicitly on his tour the guidance of Richardson, whose *Account of Pictures in Italy* was the popular handbook of the time. Thus, though he travelled from Rome to Florence by the eastern route, he takes no notice whatever of Assisi and its priceless treasures of early art; and at Perugia he observes nothing but one picture by the great master of the place, and two by Baroccio. At Florence he thinks John of Bologna the equal of Michael Angelo in sculpture. In his general remarks on the Florentine collections he says:

"We must arrive at what is unknown by what is known. Whoever seeks a shorter method only deceives himself; and, whilst he flatters himself that he is in possession of the art, is embracing a cloud, and produces only monsters and chimeras. In Raphael there is nothing of the affectation of painting—neither dark nor light—no indications of affected contrasts—no affected masses of light and shadow. He is the medium—Annibal Caracci too wild; ditto Michael Angelo; Domenichino too tame; Guido too effeminate."

At Venice the notes are chiefly technical. It is curious that his remarks at the time on the famous *Peter Martyr* of Titian scarcely bear out his subsequent warnings, in his Eleventh Discourse, against the minutely accurate drawing of the beech-tree in that picture which has been so much admired by Turner and Mr. Ruskin. Burnet does not hesitate to impute to Reynolds's own example of hasty and conventional execution that want of finish and natural truth in later English art from which præ-Raphaelitism is the reaction.

Mason's remarks on Sir Joshua's technical processes, which are included in Mr. Cotton's volume, are highly valuable, though merely fragmentary. This writer attributes to the free use of *lake*, against which Northcote is known to have warned Reynolds, that premature fading which even in his time was notorious.—*Abridged from the Saturday Review*, 1859.

SIR JOSHUA'S HOUSE IN LEICESTER SQUARE.
(Page 105.)

Nothing remains of the time of Reynolds in the rear of his house, No. 47, in Leicester-square. His studio had been removed before the re-arrangement of the theatre by Mr. Godwin, for the Western Literary Institution. Still, the sale-room of Messrs. Puttick and Simpson occupies the site of the great painter's studio; his wine-cellar serves as the *strong-room* of the auctioneers; and there remain also, nearly in their original condition, the paved hall and stone staircase by which Sir Joshua's distinguished visitors passed to the drawing-rooms.

THE PLYMPTON CORPORATION AND REYNOLDS'S PORTRAIT. (P. 114.)

Mr. Cotton, in his work (1860), labours hard to save the honour of Plympton, but he cannot get over the fact, that the new Corporation turned out Sir Joshua, and ultimately sold him. This is what Mr. Cotton says of the portrait :—

"It was sent to London to be valued by Messrs. Woodburn, and was then offered, first to Lord Mount-Edgcumbe, Recorder of Plympton; secondly, to his son, Lord Valletort; and thirdly, by Sir William Elford, to Sir Robert Peel. They all refused it. The Corporation then wished that the National Gallery should have it, and it was accordingly sent to the Trustees, together with its history. Reference was made by the Trustees to a well-known and accomplished painter, then President of the Royal Academy, who decided that the picture was a copy. His words were: 'It is a mere sketch, and certainly not an original.' This was sufficient to determine the Trustees of the National Gallery also to reject the picture, and it was consequently sent to Messrs. Christie's auction-rooms for sale. Mr. Eastlake kindly attended to vouch for its authenticity; but Messrs. Woodburn's valuation being the reserved price, and the Trustees of the National Gallery having pronounced against it, the picture was not sold. Eventually it was sent back into Devonshire, and was there purchased by Mr. Nicholas Condy, of Plymouth, a clever marine artist, for Lord Egremont, of Silverton Park, near Exeter," for 150*l*., Messrs. Woodburn's valuation.

REYNOLDS AND ERSKINE.—JAMES BOSWELL.

In Sir Joshua Reynolds's *Notes and Observations*, published by Mr. Cotton, in 1859, we find a characteristic letter from Lord Erskine to Reynolds, dated Jan. 26, 1783, thanking him for a copy of his Eleventh Discourse on Painting, which he declares, "conveys instruction equally important to the profession of all other arts: so close is the analogy between all the operations of genius, that it is the best dissertation upon the art of public eloquence that ever was or ever will be written!" This is the Discourse in which Reynolds seeks to prove that genius, in any pursuit, "consists principally in the comprehension of a whole."

Another letter, from the Bishop of London, acknowledges the receipt of Reynolds's last Discourse, but suggests "an amendment for the next edition . . . where you called Michael Angelo *a truly divine* man, which we ecclesiastics do not hold to be very good theology."

Another letter is from James Boswell, asking Reynolds to paint his portrait for Auchinleck, "the price to be paid out of the first fees which I receive as a barrister in Westminster Hall! Or if that fund should fail, it shall be paid at any rate five years hence, by myself or my representatives." This proposal is dated June 7, 1785. Sir Joshua has written under it: "I agree to the condition;" but Reynolds's account-book, to the close of 1789, contains no entry of payment by James Boswell.

REYNOLDS'S PORTRAIT OF MRS. HARTLEY.

In 1773, among the portraits exhibited by Sir Joshua, was "A Nymph with a Young Bacchus" (Mrs. Hartley, the actress), which Malone says was bought by the Earl of Carysfort: it is now the property of I. Bentley, Esq., of Portland-place. A repetition of the picture was sold at the Marchioness of Thomond's sale, in 1821, to Colonel F. G. Howard, for two hundred and ninety guineas. The following account of the death of Mrs. Hartley was kindly communicated to Mr. Cotton by Mr. Bentley. "She was going out to America, when the vessel in which she sailed was wrecked near the coast and her body washed on shore. It was found with the same child clinging to her, as represented in Reynolds's picture. Mr. Bentley's portrait of Mrs. Hartley is one of the most beautiful

Sir Joshua ever painted. It is remarkable for its richness of colour, its depth and clearness of tone, and exquisite beauty of the female countenance. None of the engravings do it justice. The face is far more lovely in the original. It is, moreover, in excellent condition: the colouring appears as perfect as when it was painted, which, unfortunately, can be said of so few of Reynolds's works. The breadth of light and shade in this picture is a near approach to Rembrandt; and we know how much Reynolds admired the wonderful *chiar-oscuro* of this great master. Mr. Bentley told me that, when he purchased this picture at Lord Carysfort's sale, a gentleman in the room came up and congratulated him on the acquisition of so fine a work of art, and strongly recommended him never to trust it in the hands of any picture-cleaner in the country. That gentleman was Sir Thomas Lawrence."— *Cotton*, 1860.

Sir Joshua, (says Haydon) always delights and improves me. Lawrence looks by his side like a miniature-painter in large, and West like a skilful sign-painter. Sir Joshua had the true feeling. Mr. Ottley, who remembered him, said, the first time he saw Sir Joshua he showed him a picture of the *Continence of Scipio*. Ottley said, it put him in mind of Parmigiano. Sir Joshua seemed angry, for it was stolen from that painter.

SIR JOSHUA'S PRICES.
(Page 144.)

In 1760, Reynolds obtained twenty guineas for each of his heads. Some of those heads have since sold for 500 guineas. "1766. This year's pocket-book contains a memorandum of the prices Mr. Reynolds then charged for his portraits:— Whole-length, 150*l*.; half-length, 70*l*.; kit-cat, 50*l*.; head, 30*l*." In the very year in which Reynolds received 500 guineas for his *Cardinal Beaufort*, his portrait of *Nelly O'Brien* was sold at a public auction for 10*l*. 10*s*.! Lord Carysfort, the first purchaser of *The Strawberry Girl*, paid 50 guineas for his bargain; Lord Hertford, its last purchaser, was only too happy to hand over a cheque for 2,100 guineas for the same portrait. The only instance we know of a depreciation in value of a picture by Reynolds is that of *Garrick between Tragedy and Comedy*. Lord Halifax bought it originally for 300 guineas; and after his death it was sold to Mr. Angerstein for 250.

SIR JOSHUA'S FISHMONGER.
(Page 148.)

In Coventry-street, Piccadilly, was, till 1859, a famous fish-shop of which Mr. P. Cunningham relates: It was kept, in Sir Joshua Reynolds's time, by a Mr. Robertson—in more recent days by Mr. Turner. Now, Sir Joshua was a great dinner-giver, and, being a Plympton or Plymouth man, was fond of fish. This fishshop, now disappeared, was the shop which supplied fish for Sir Joshua—feeding Dr. Johnson, Burke, Gibbon, and Boswell. But Sir Joshua was mean with tradesmen, and he had customers, or sitters. Then, he knew fish, and Miss Reynolds, his sister, could drive a bargain. A walk from Leicester-square to Coventry-street was a favourite morning's clearing of the palate with Sir Joshua. He was constantly at Robertson's, chose his fish, reversed their position on the leaden slope that invited customers, and then sent Miss Reynolds to settle about prices. "Miss Reynolds," said old Robertson—and a gentlemanly old fellow he was—"never chose; Sir Joshua never paid. Both were good at bargains."

REYNOLDS'S PORTRAIT OF MISS BOWLS.

Leslie relates, in his pleasing manner, the painting of this portrait. "His fondness of children is recorded on all his canvasses in which they appear. A matchless picture of Miss Bowls, a beautiful laughing child, caressing a dog, was sold a few years ago at an auction, and cheaply, at 1,000 guineas. The father and mother of the little girl intended she should sit to Romney, who, at one time, more than divided the town with Reynolds. Sir George Beaumont, however, advised them to employ Sir Joshua. 'But his pictures fade.' 'No matter, take the chance; even a faded picture by Reynolds will be the finest thing you can have. Ask him to dine with you, and let him become acquainted with her.' The advice was taken; the little girl was placed beside Sir Joshua at the table, where he amused her so much with tricks and stories, that she thought him the most charming man in the world, and the next day was delighted to be taken to his house, where she sat down with a face full of glee, the expression of which he caught at once, and never lost; and the affair turned out very happily, for the picture did not fade, and has, till now, escaped alike the inflictions of time, or of the ignorant among cleaners."—*Handbook for Young Painters*, p. 302.

EXHIBITION OF THE WORKS OF SIR JOSHUA REYNOLDS.

In the summer of 1813, the Directors of the British Institution exhibited at their rooms the most splendid collection of pictures that were ever seen together, as the production of one man; and the reputation of Reynolds, high as it was, was raised by this assemblage of his works. Mr. Constable, R.A., was present at the Dinner given by the Directors on this memorable occasion, and has thus described the proceedings of the day :—

"The company arrived at an early hour in the Gallery, from which there was a covered way to Willis's Rooms. On the arrival of the Prince Regent, the Marquis of Stafford and the Governors of the Institution hastened to conduct him upstairs. His manner was agreeable, and he shook hands with many of the company. Dinner was announced at seven, the Marquis of Stafford (the President) in the chair; behind which, on a considerable elevation, was placed a statue of Sir Joshua Reynolds, by Flaxman. The Earl of Aberdeen made an excellent speech: he said that 'although the style of Sir Joshua Reynolds might differ in appearance from the style of those specimens of art, which are considered the nearest to perfection in the ancient Greek sculpture, and the productions of the great school of Italy; yet his works were to be ranked with them, their aim being essentially the same—*the attainment of nature with simplicity and truth.*' The Regent left the table about ten, and returned to the Gallery, which was now crowded with ladies.

"Among them (says Mr. Constable) I saw Mrs. Siddons, whose picture is there as the *Tragic Muse*. Lord Byron was pointed out to me: his poetry is of the most melancholy kind, but he has great ability. Now, let me beg of you to see these charming works frequently, and form in your own mind the idea of what painting should be from them. It is certainly the finest feeling of art that ever existed."—*Leslie's Memoir of Constable*, 1845.

TURNER'S BOYHOOD.

Mr. Ruskin, in his fifth and concluding volume of *Modern Painters*, has exquisitely drawn a parallel of the boyhood of Giorgione and Turner, eloquently contrasting their birth-places and early fortunes. Of Turner's boyhood he says:

Near the south-west corner of Covent Garden, a square brick pit or well is formed by a close-set block of houses, to the back windows of which it admits a few rays of light. Access to the bottom of it is obtained out of Maiden-lane, through a low archway and an iron gate; and if you stand long enough under the archway to accustom your eyes to the darkness, you may see on the left hand a narrow door, which formerly gave quiet access to a respectable barber's shop, of which the front window, looking into Maiden-lane, is still extant, filled, in this year (1860), with a row of bottles, connected, in some defunct manner, with a brewer's business. A more fashionable neighbourhood, it is said, eighty years ago than now—never, certainly, a cheerful one—wherein a boy being born on St. George's Day, 1775, began soon after to take interest in the world of Covent Garden, and put to service such spectacles of life as it afforded.

No knights to be seen there, nor, I imagine, many beautiful ladies; their costume at least disadvantageous, depending much on incumbency of hat and feather, and short waists; the majesty of men founded similarly on shoe-buckles and wigs;—impressive enough when Reynolds will do his best for it, but not suggestive of much ideal delight to a boy.

"Bello ovile dov' io dormii agnello;" of things beautiful besides men and women, dusty sunbeams up or down the street on summer mornings; deep-furrowed cabbage-leaves at the green-grocer's; magnificence of oranges in the wheelbarrows round the corner; and Thames's shore within three minutes' race.

None of these things very glorious: the best, however, that England, it seems, was then able to provide for a boy of gift; who, such as they are, loves them—never, indeed, forgets them. The short wants modify to the last his visions of Greek ideal. His fore-grounds had always a succulent cluster or two of green-grocery at the corners. Enchanted oranges gleam in Covent Gardens of the Hesperides; and great ships go to pieces in order to scatter chests of them on the waves. That mist of early sunbeams in the London dawn crosses, many and many a time, the clearness of Italian air; and by Thames' shore, with its stranded barges and glidings of red sail, dearer to us than Lucerne lake or Venetian lagoon,—by Thames' shore we will die.

With such circumstances round him in youth, let us note what necessary effects followed upon the boy. I assume him to have Giorgione's sensibility (and more than Giorgione's, if that be possible) to colour and form. I tell you farther, and this fact you may receive trustfully, that his sensibility to human affection and distress was no less keen than even his sense for natural beauty—heart-sight deep as eye-sight.

Consequently, he attaches himself with the faithfullest child-love to everything that bears an image of the place he was born in. No matter how ugly it is,—has it anything about it like Maiden-lane or like Thames shore? If so, it shall be painted for their sake. Hence, to the very close of life, Turner could endure uglinesses which no one else of the same sensibility would have borne with for an instant. Dead brick walls, blank square windows, old clothes, market-womanly types of humanity —anything fishy or muddy like Billingsgate or Hungerford Market had great attractions for him; black barges, patched sails, and every possible condition of fog.

You will find these tolerations and affections guiding or sustaining him till the last hour of his life; the notablest of all such endurances being that of dirt. No Venetian ever draws anything foul; but Turner devoted picture after picture to the illustration of effects of dinginess, smoke, soot, dust, and dusty texture; old sides of boots, weedy roadside vegetation, dung-hills, straw-yards, and all the soilings and stains of every common labour.

And more than this, he not only could endure but enjoyed and looked for *litter*, like Covent Garden wreck after the market. His pictures are often full of it, from side to side; their fore-grounds differ from all others in the natural way the things have of lying about in them. Even his richest vegetation, in ideal work, is confused; and he delights in shingle, *débris*, and heaps of fallen stones. The last words he ever spoke to me about a picture were in gentle exultation about his St. Gothard: "That *litter* of stones which I endeavoured to represent."

The second great result of this Covent Garden training was, understanding of and regard for the poor, whom the Venetians, we saw, despised; whom, contrarily, Turner loved, and more than loved—understood. He got no romantic sight of them, but an infallible one, as he prowled about the end of his lane, watching night effects in the wintry streets; nor sight of the poor alone, but of the poor in direct relations with the rich. He knew, in good and evil, what both classes thought of, and how they dealt with, each other.

Reynolds and Gainsborough, bred in country villages, learned there the country boy's reverential theory of "the squire," and kept it. They painted the squire and the squire's lady as centres of the movements of the universe, to the end of their lives. But Turner perceived the younger squire in other aspects about his lane, occurring prominently in its night scenery, as a dark figure, or one of two, against the moonlight. He saw also the working of city commerce, from endless warehouse, towering over Thames, to the back shop in the lane, with its stale herrings—highly interesting these last; one of his father's best friends, whom he often afterwards visited affectionately at Bristol, being a fishmonger and glue-boiler; which gives us a friendly turn of mind towards herring-fishing, whaling, Calais poissardes, and many other of our choicest subjects in after life; all this being connected with that mysterious forest below London Bridge on one side;—and, on the other, with those masses of human power and national wealth which weigh upon us, at Covent Garden here, with strange compression, and crush us into narrow Hand-court.

"That mysterious forest below London Bridge"—better for the boy than wood of pine or grove of myrtle. How he must have tormented the watermen, beseeching them to let him crouch anywhere in the bows, quiet as a log, so only that he might get floated down there among the ships, and round and round the ships, and with the ships, and by the ships, and under the ships, staring and clambering;—these the only quite beautiful things he can see in all the world, except the sky; but these, when the sun is on their sails, filling or falling, endlessly disordered by sway of tide and stress of anchorage, beautiful unspeakably; which ships also are inhabited by glorious creatures—red-faced sailors, with pipes, appearing over the gunwales, true knights, over their castle parapets—the most angelic beings in the whole compass of London world. And Trafalgar happening long before we can draw ships, we, nevertheless, coax all current stories out of the wounded sailors, do our best at present to show Nelson's funeral streaming up the Thames, and vow that Trafalgar shall have its tribute of memory some day. Which, accordingly, is accomplished—once, with all our might, for its death; twice, with all our might, for its victory; thrice, in pensive farewell to the old Téméraire, and, with it, to that order of things.

Now, this fond companying with sailors must have divided his time, it appears to me, pretty equally between Covent Garden and Wapping (allowing for incidental excursions to Chelsea on one side, and Greenwich on the other), which time he would spend pleasantly, but not magnificently, being limited in pocket-money, and leading a kind of "Poor Jack" life on the river.

* * * * *

Schooled thus in manners, literature, and general moral principles, at Chelsea and Wapping, we have finally to inquire the most important point of all—the aspect of religion, namely, in the neighbourhood of Covent Garden. I say the aspect, for that was all the lad could judge by. Disposed, for the most part, to learn chiefly by his own eyes, in this special matter he finds there is really no other way of learning. His father taught him "to lay one penny upon another." Of mother's teaching we hear of none; of parish pastoral teaching, the reader may guess how much.

* * * * *

Under these influences pass away the first reflective hours of life, with such conclusion as they can reach. In consequence of a fit of illness, he was taken—I cannot ascertain in what year—to live with an aunt at Brentford; and here, I believe, received some schooling, which he seems to have snatched vigorously; getting knowledge, at least by translation, of the more picturesque classical authors, which he turned presently to use, as we shall see. Hence also, walks about Putney and Twickenham in the summer time acquainted him with the look of English meadow-ground in its restricted states of paddock and park; and with some round-headed appearances of trees, and stately entrances to houses of mark: the avenue at Bushy, and the iron gates and carved pillars of Hampton, impressing him apparently with great awe and admiration; so that in after life his little country house is—of all places in the world—at Twickenham! Of swans and reedy shores he now learns the soft motion and the green mystery, in a way not to be forgotten.

INDEX.

Analysis of Beauty, Hogarth's, 57.

Bartholomew's St., Hospital Staircase painted by Hogarth, 36.

Chelsea china painted by Thornhill, 22.
Churchill, Hogarth's Quarrel with, 67—70.
Corkscrew and Priest, 23.
Dawe, Mr., R. A., 272.

FUSELI, HENRY:
Anecdotes, miscellaneous, 210—212; Armstrong, Dr., 182; Art-studies, 182, 197; Attainments, 186; Barry, on the Milton Gallery, 193; Birth, 179; Boydell, Alderman, 221; British Artists, 220; British Institution, the, 195; Canova, 196; Character as an Artist, 212; Character by Lavater, 216; Company, ill-assorted, 188; Constable and Fuseli, 227; Coutts, Mr., his liberality, 194; Cowper's *Homer*, 184; Cunningham, Allan, on Fuseli's Works, 226; Cup presented to Fuseli, 222; David, the painter, 186; Day, Fuseli's, 198; Death of, at Putney Hill, 201; Elgin Marbles, 202; England, Fuseli comes to, 181; Entomology, love of, 180; Erudition, 219; Funeral, in St. Paul's, 202; Godwin, Mrs., 188; Godwin, William, 188; Harlow's conceit, 199; Harlow's *Trial of Queen Katherine*, 200; Haydon's sketch of Fuseli, 204; Herons in Raphael's Cartoon, 216; Johnson, Dr., 189; *Keeper* Fuseli, 197; Lawrence, Sir Thomas, 209—224; *Lazar House*, the, 193—195; Leslie's account of Fuseli's Pictures, 214; London Smoke,

FUSELI, HENRY:
197; London, Fuseli in, 184; Michael Angelo, on, 217; Milton Gallery, the, 181; *Nightmare*, the, 189; Nollekens, 211; Ottley, Mr., on Fuseli's Art, 212; Painting "the Devil," 198; Parentage of Fuseli, 179; Picture, first, 182; Picture-hanging, 206; Picture, last, 201; Poetic Tributes, 214; Portraits of Fuseli, 199; Raphael, on, 217; Religious Feelings, 208; Richardson's Novels, 185; Rome, visit to, 182; Salvator Rosa, 219; Sensibility of, 207; Shakspeare Gallery, the, 190; Sketches, first, 179; Slight resented, 196; "Something New," 225; Voltaire caricatured, 181; West, Benjamin, 186; Wit and Humour of Fuseli, 209; Wollstonecroft, Mrs., 186.

GAINSBOROUGH, THOMAS:
Birth-place, 156; *Blue Boy*, the, 166; Character, by Reynolds, 172; *Chatterton*, portrait, 174; *Cottage Door* and *Cottage Girl*, 168; Criticism, severe, 166; Death, at Schomberg House, 169; Detective Portraits, 158; Drawings and Sketches, 175; Frescoes, reputed, 164; *Garrick*, portraits, 159; Generosity, 169; *Girl and Pigs*, 167; Grave in Kew churchyard, 170—171; Gravelot and Houbraken, 161; Humphry's sun-dial, 157; Landscapes, 176; Lee and Gainsborough's landscapes, parallel, 177; London, Gainsborough first comes to, 157; Marriage, 158; Modelling, 163; Musical talent, 159; "Painter's Eye," the, 160; Pall Mall, settles in, 163; Pa-

384 INDEX.

GAINSBOROUGH, THOMAS:
rentage, 156; Portraits, 173; Reynolds, Sir Joshua, 165; Schomberg House, Pall Mall, 164; Sea-pieces, 176; *Shepherd's Boy*, 168; Siddons, Mrs., her nose, 167; sitter, handsome, 162; Sketches, first, 157; Thicknesse, Philip, 160, 161; Wiltshere, the carrier, 162; *Woodman*, 167.

Garrick and Hogarth, 43.

George II. and Hogarth, 49.

Hardham's 37 snuff, 144.

Henley, Orator, 22.

HOGARTH, WILLIAM:
Analysis of Beauty, 57; Anatomical Draughtsman, 31; *Apprentices, the City*, 53; Bartholomew's St., Hospital Staircase painted, 30; *Beggars' Opera*, 32; Birthplace, 1; Bowles, the Printseller, 16; *Calais Gate and Roast Beef of Old England*, 54; Canning, Elizabeth, 21; Caricature on, 59, 83; Chiswick, House at, 74; Coffee-room Scene, 25; Collections of Hogarth's Works, 77; Conceit, Hogarth's, 81; Copyright in Prints, 85; *Coram, Captain*, portrait, 46; *Credulity, Superstition, and Fanaticism*, 66; Death of Hogarth, in Leicester-square, 71; Early Education, 3; *Election Pictures, the*, 59; Ellis Gamble, 3; *Enraged Musician and Distressed Poet*, 38; Family, 2; *Fielding, the Novelist*, 65; *Finis, or the Tail-piece*, 70; Foundling Hospital Benefactions, 42—48; *Four Times of the Day*, 33; Garrick, 43; Genius of Hogarth, 89; George II., 49; *Goldsmith's Hostess*, 89; *Harlot's Progress*, 25; Hayman, the Painter, 4; Highgate incident, 4; Historical Value of Hogarth's Works, 91; Hoadley, Bishop and Dr., 84; House in Leicester-square, 15; Hudibras Prints, 11; *Industry and Idleness*, 52; Joe Miller's Ticket, 6; Johnson, Dr., 51;

HOGARTH, WILLIAM:
Journey into Kent, 19 · Kent the Architect, and Pope the Poet, 17; *Lady's Last Stake*, 58; "Little Hogarth," 4; Lovat, Lord, 51, 94; Malcolm, Sarah, and Blandy, Miss, 20, 21; *March to Finchley*, 47, 48; *Marriage à la Mode*, 39; *Marriage à la Mode* and the *Clandestine Marriage*, 43; *Marriage, Happy*, 44; Married to Jane Thornhill, 14; Maul-stick, 77; Misaubin, Dr., 27; Miser and Sir Isaac Sheard, 87; *Modern Midnight Conversation*, 23; Morris, the Upholsterer, 13; Nollekens, describes, 4; *Oratorio*, 87; Page, Sir Francis, 80; Painted by Himself, 83; Painting, first, 16; Palette, 86; *Paul before Felix*, 56; Parentage, 2; Plate, engraved, 5; Plate, first, 8; Shopcard, 9; Poetical Tributes to, 82; Portraits, Early, 78; Print, unique, 5; Prints, prices of, 93; Quarrel with Wilkes and Churchill, 67; *Rake's Progress*, 30; *Rosamond's Pond*, 37; Sale of Pictures, 79; Sale of *Marriage à la Mode* pictures, 42; Satire commenced, 9; Satirizes the Stage, 10; *Sigismunda*, 61; Silver-plate Engraver, 3; *Southwark Fair*, 19; *Strolling Actresses*, 31; Thornhill, Sir James, dies, 22; Tomb in Chiswick Churchyard, 73; Wall-paintings in Fenchurch-street, 87; Walpole, Horace, interview with, 63; *Wanstead Assembly*, 16; Widow Hogarth, 75, 76; Wilkes, John, 64; Vauxhall Gardens embellished, 35 —37.

"Hogarthian," pictures, 60.

Hudibras illustrated by Hogarth, 11.

Joe Miller's Benefit Ticket, by Hogarth, 6.

Johnson, Dr., and Hogarth, 51.

Kent, the architect, burlesqued by Hogarth, 17.

King, Tom, in Covent Garden, 34.

INDEX.

LAWRENCE, SIR THOMAS:
Academy dinner, 268; Allied Sovereigns, portraits of, 255; Associate elected, 236; Bath, the Lawrences in, 232; Bernard's Recollections, 231; Birthplace, 228; Bristol, freedom of, 264; Byron, Lord, 261; *Calmady's Children*, portraits of, 303; *Canning*, Mr. portrait of, 299; *Canova*, portrait of, 251; *Castlereagh, Lord*, portrait, 298; Character, by Howard, 277; Claremont, painting at, 253; Constable, Mr., R.A., 302; Coronation portraits, 285; *Cowper*, the poet, portrait of, 307; *Curran*, portrait of, 245; Croft, Miss, 269; Death of, 270; Drawings, collection of, 286; Drawings, early, 229; Elgin Marbles, the, 252; Embarrassment, cause of, 279; Etty, Lawrence's pupil, 278; Etty's account of Lawrence's death, 270-271; Flaxman, on his genius, 291; Funeral of, in St. Paul's, 272; Fuseli's Satan, 240; *Gonsalvi, Cardinal*, portrait of, 256; Harlow, his pupil, 247; Health declining, 267; Honours and presents, 262, 263; Hoppner, death of, 301; *Homer*, piece from, 236; House in Russell-square, 275; Illness, Lawrence's last, 269; *Kemble, Fanny*, portrait of, 266; *Kemble, John*, portraits, 242, 248; Kindness and generosity to artists, 288; *Lambton*, Hon. C. W., portrait of, 304; Last year, Lawrence's, 264; Leonardo da Vinci, sketch-book of, 262; Likenesses, Lawrence's, 282; *Lock, William*, bust of, 245; Lock, William, death of, 300; London, Lawrence settled in, 234; Love, supposed in, 245; *Melville, Lord*, portrait, 299; Michael Angelo, discovery of one, 260; *Napoleon I.*, 250; cast of, 264; Oil-paintings, earliest, 234; Painter's day and practice, 282; Painting Eyes, 283; Parents, death of, 241; Parentage, 228; Peel,

LAWRENCE, SIR THOMAS:
Mr.—Lawrence's patron, 265; *Persian Ambassador*, portrait of, 249; Person of Lawrence, 281; Portraits, early, 236; Portrait, failure of, 238; Portrait, first, 228; Portraits, celebrated, 283, 298; Portraits, engraved, 286; Portraits of, 281; President of the Royal Academy, 259; Prices for Portraits, 282; Princess Charlotte and Prince Leopold, 254; Princess of Wales, 246; Recitations, young Lawrence's, 230; Reynolds, Sir Joshua, 234; Reynolds, Lawrence compared with, 276; Reynolds, death of, 237; Reynolds, justice to, 260; Rome, painting in, 258; Royal Academician, elected, 237; Russell-square, Lawrence's removal to, 250; Satans, the Two, 239; School, Lawrence's, 229; Scott, Sir Walter, 261; Sensitiveness of Lawrence, 290; Serjeant-painter to the King, 237; Shee, Martin Archer, 235; Sign-painting, Harlow's, 247; Society of Arts Prize, 233; Somerset House, Lawrence's remains at, 273; Stage, Lawrence's predilection for, 232; Turner, J. M. W., Lawrence on, 257; Verses, &c., by Lawrence, 242; Uwins, Mr., R.A., on Lawrence's sincerity, 289; *Wall and Baring* portraits, 300; Waterloo Hall, portraits in, 257; *Watt, James*, portrait of, 251; *Wellington, Duke of*, portraits of, 293; *Wilberforce*, portrait of, 308; Will of, 274; Wolff, Mrs., 252; Works in London, 297.

Lincoln's inn, Hogarth's picture at, 57.
Lovat, Lord, portraits of, 50.

Pope burlesqued by Hogarth, 18.
Pope described by Reynolds, 101.

"Rape of the Lock" print, by Hogarth, 7.

C C

REYNOLDS, SIR JOSHUA:
Astley, John, 102; Baptism of Reynolds, 97; Barry, the Painter, 117; Birth-place of Reynolds, 95; *Bute, Lord,* portrait, 143; Carriage, paintings on, 122; Character in Portraits, 107; *Club, the Literary,* 110; Colours, experimental, 149; Copies and Originals, 107; Deafness, Reynolds's, 148; Death of Reynolds, in Leicester-square, 133; Dinners in Leicester-square, 147; *Discourses,* authorship of, 126; Epitaph, by Goldsmith, 116; Father of Reynolds, 95; Funeral in St. Paul's, 135; Gandy, of Exeter, 98; *Garrick,* portraits of, 106; *George III. and Queen Charlotte,* portraits of, 119; *Gibbon and Goldsmith,* portraits, 120; Goldsmith rebukes Reynolds, 116; Haydon and Wilkie's visit to Plympton, 96; *Heathfield, Lord,* portrait, 127; Hogarth referred to, 145; *Holland, Lord,* portrait of, 119; Hone's satiric picture, 117; Hudson, Reynolds's master, 100, 140; Humphrey, Ozias, liberality to, 146; Inchiquin, Lady, 105; *Infant Hercules,* 124; Italy, visits to, 102; Johnson, Dr., friendship of, 108; *Johnson, Dr.,* portraits of, 109; *Keppel, Admiral,* portraits, 120; Kindness to a schoolboy, 130; *Kitty Fisher,* 105; *Jesuits' Perspective,* 140; Landscapes, Reynolds's, 152; Lawrence's noble tribute, 153; Leicester-square, house in, 104; Lesson, first, in Art, 140; London, first abode in, 104; Malone, Mr., 126—his Account of Sir Joshua's Death, 133; Mayor of Plympton, 113; Models, 146; *Muscipula,* 121; *Nativity,* the, at Oxford, 118; Oxford window, designs for, 118; Painter-Stainers' Company, 123; Painting for posterity, 151; Palette, 137; Parsimony, 149; Pet Bird, 130; Plympton, 95; Pope, the poet, 101; Por-

REYNOLDS, SIR JOSHUA:
trait, first painted, 99; Portraits, early, 142; Prices and Sitters, 143; Prints from Reynolds's pictures, 153; *Ralph's Exhibition,* 131; Rembrandt, studies from, 150; *Robin Goodfellow, or Puck,* 128; Rogers's Sale, 139; Romney, the painter, 107; Royal Academy Dinner, the first, 112; Royal Academy, Origin of, 111; Royal Academy, retirement from, 129; Sales of Pictures, 138; Sales of Portraits, 137; School, at Plympton, 97; *Siddons, Mrs.,* 121; Sight, Reynolds's, declining, 131; sitter, last surviving, 151; Snuff, Sir Joshua's, 144; Somerset House, Royal Academy at, 112; *Sterne's* portrait, 106; *Strawberry Girl,* 114; Sundays, painting on, 110; Thomond, Lady, 105; Thronechair, and Barry, 136; *Thurlow, Lord,* portrait of, 108; *Tragic Muse,* 121; Villa at Richmond, 152; *Ugolino, Count,* 115; *Waldegrave, Ladies,* portraits, 120; Walpole, Horace, criticisms by, 123; Will of Sir Joshua, 135.
Richardson's Printing-office, 51.

Sigismunda, by Hogarth, 61.

Thornhill, Sir James, 14, 22.
TURNER, J. M. W:
Accuracy of, 345; Accuracy in Shipping, 357; Address, Secret of, 344; Affectionate son, 318; America, first picture sent to, 353; Artistic Prediction, 342; Bargaining, anecdotes of, 355; Bequests to the Nation, 325; Bidding for his own Pictures, 365; Birth-place, 309; Book-plates, Turner's, 356; Brilliancy, his, 364; Chantrey and the *Carthage* picture, 342; Chelsea Lodging, 323; Claude and Turner compared, 350; Colour—a hint from Addison, 332; Composition, 346; Continental Tour, 315; CoventGarden ninety years since, 309; Cozens, 313;

INDEX.

TURNER, J. M. W.:
Critic, wish for, 344; Dayes's account, 312; Tabley, Lord, Lesson to, 360; Death of, 322; *Dido building Carthage*, 351; Drawing, Turner's first, 310; Drawing, first exhibited, 311; *England and Wales* Views, 364; Eulogists of Turner, 367; *Fallacies of Hope*, 337—340; Fires, paintings of, 362; Funeral of, in St. Paul's, 323; Girtin and Cozens, 312, 313; *Goddess of Discord in the Hesperides Garden*, 316; Health declining, 322; Industry of, 330; *Lambeth Palace*, view of, 311, 343; Landscape Art, 331; Landscape painter, Turner's present rank as, 356; Leslie on Turner's works in 1816, 327; *Liber Studiorum*, the, 317, Manchester Art Treasures Exhibition, Turner's Pictures at, 360, 361; Munro, Dr. 312; Observation, powers of, 369; *Old Téméraire, the*, 319; Originality of, Turner, 346; Patrons, first, 312; Patrons, who were, 329; Pictures, number of, and Prices, 354; Pictures from Thomson and Milton, 345; *Pools of Solomon*, the, 350; Portraits of Turner, 333; Pre-eminence predicted, 326; Professor of Perspective, 363; Quid pro quo, 344; Recent works, Turner's, failure of, 321; Recreations of, 363; Residence, change of, 343; Royal Academician, elected, 315; Ruskin's Criticisms, 347; Turner's Shipping, 358, 359; "Scottish Turner," 342; Sea-pieces, Turner's, 336; *Slave-ship*, described by Ruskin, the, 319; Stothard, 362; Student of the Royal Academy, Turner, 311;

TURNER, J. M. W.:
Studying Nature, 331; Style, early, 314; Talking down, 341; Three Periods of Turner, 327—329; Trait, amiable, 325; Topographical Drawings, 312; Truth of, Turner, Ruskin on, 348; *Van Tromp's Barge*, 367; Varnishing-days, 334; Verses by, Turner, 337; *Ulysses deriding Polyphemus*, 319; Understanding, Turner, 347; Water-colour Drawings by, 368; Wilkie and Turner, 341; Will of Turner, 324; *Wreck of the Minotaur*, 336; Yorkshire Drawings, 352.

Vauxhall Gardens, embellished by Hogarth and Hayman, 35.

Waagen, Dr., on Hogarth's *Marriage à la Mode*, 41.
Walpole, Horace, and Hogarth, 63.
Walpole, Horace, and Sir J. Reynolds, 123.
Wilkes, Hogarth's Quarrel with, 67—70.
Willett Collection of Hogarth's Works, 41.

APPENDIX.

HOGARTH:
Painting children, 370; *Southwark Fair*, 370.
REYNOLDS, SIR JOSHUA:
Erskine and Boswell, 376; Exhibition of Works, 379; Father, 370; Fishmonger, 378; House in Leicester-square, 375; Plympton Corporation and Portrait, 375; Portrait of Mr. Hartley, 376; Portrait of Miss Bowls, 378; Prices, 377; Studies in Italy, 371.
TURNER's Boyhood, 380.

Uniform with the present Volume, 6s. cloth,

ANECDOTE BIOGRAPHY;

WILLIAM PITT, EARL OF CHATHAM,
EDMUND BURKE.

With fine Portraits on Steel of LORD CHATHAM and EDMUND BURKE;
and several other Engravings.

www.ingramcontent.com/pod-product-compliance
Lightning Source LLC
Chambersburg PA
CBHW051743300426
44115CB00007B/681